Second Edition

Broadcasting and the Public

Second Edition

Broadcasting and the Public

Harrison B. Summers   Robert E. Summers   John H. Pennybacker

The Ohio   Central   Louisiana
State University (emer.)   Michigan University   State University

Wadsworth Publishing Company, Inc.

Belmont, California

Communications Editor: **Rebecca Hayden**

Production Editor: **Larry Olsen**

Designer: **Joe diChiarro**

Copy Editor: **Ellen Seacat**

Cartoonist: **Sidney Harris**

Printed in the United States of America

1 2 3 4 5 6 7 8 9 10—82 81 80 79 78

Cover photos courtesy Public Broadcasting Service; Sidney Harris; KDEA Stereo Radio, Inc.; WWL, New Orleans; Rede Globo, Rio de Janeiro

Library of Congress Cataloging in Publication Data

Summers, Harrison Boyd
    Broadcasting and the public.

    First ed. (1966) by R. F. Summers and H. B. Summers.
    Bibliography
    Includes index.
    1. Mass media—United States.   2. Radio broadcast-
ing—United States.   3. Television broadcasting—United
States.   I. Summers, Robert Edward, 1918–   Broadcasting and the public.   II. Pennybacker, John H., joint
author.   III. Title.
P92.U5S9   384.54   77-15466
ISBN 0-534-00532-2

Preface

When media of mass entertainment claim the attention of millions of Americans for several hours each day, that situation should arouse the interest of all intelligent citizens. What kinds of programs do radio and television provide for the listening public? What basic values does broadcasting offer, and what are its shortcomings? In particular, can the *product* of broadcasting be improved, and if so, how?

These are important questions to those who listen to broadcast programs and to all who are interested in the possibility of raising the standards of radio and television service. Those who attempt to find answers to these questions need, first of all, an understanding of the system of broadcasting we have in the United States. They must be aware of how that system works and of the many complex factors affecting the kinds of programs offered. To provide such an understanding of American broadcasting—both as a social force and as a form of business enterprise—is the purpose of this book. Major topics include the characteristics of the system itself, the directions in which broadcasting has developed over the years, the regulation of broadcasting, the organization and operation of stations and networks, and the effects of economic considerations on those operations and on the selection of programs to be put on the air.

The second edition of this book reflects the increased tempo of regulatory activity that has been evident over the past decade. All of the forces in our society that contribute to the regulation of broadcasting—as well as the public which is to be served by broadcasting—seem ever more aware of the power and influence of electronic media. Their interest has been translated, in recent years, into a close inspection of virtually every facet of broadcasting. As a result, we have devoted more attention to the overall question of regulation in this edition than in the first.

We have also attempted to include some of the major criticisms of the services provided by radio and television, as well as some of the replies made by defenders of the industry. These contrasting opinions, combined with the available factual material about the broadcasting industry, should permit the reader to form his or her own opinions in controversial areas—or, at least, to start thinking critically.

We want to express our continued appreciation to all who contributed to the preparation of the first edition, which remains the base of this edition. In addition, we wish to thank Joseph R. Dominick and Millard C. Pearce of the University of Georgia, and the editors of the *Journal of Communication*, for permission to draw extensively from their studies of network television programming patterns. Thanks are also due Philip von Ladau of Marketron, Inc., and the editors of the *Broadcast Financial Journal* for permission to use his practical advice on the utilization of program ratings.

Our gratitude also goes to Burrell Hansen, Utah State University; Frank Kahn, Herbert Lehman University; Ernie Kreiling, University of Southern California; Roderick Rightmire, Ohio University; Christopher Sterling, Temple University; and Judith Wallace, University of Miami, who were kind enough to read early drafts of the manuscript and whose suggestions and criticisms have been extremely helpful. In addition, many friends and colleagues contributed suggestions and information during the preparation of this edition. They are too numerous to mention, but special thanks should be given Dick Block, Lorimar Productions, and Lawrence Lichty, University of Wisconsin, Madison.

H. B. S.
R. E. S.
J. H. P.

Contents

LIST OF TABLES

1

The Importance
of Broadcasting

No other forms of communication have affected the lives of so many people in so many countries in so few years as have the electronic media of radio and television broadcasting. At almost any hour of the day, from early morning to late at night, men, women, and children in millions of homes throughout the world are listening to radio or watching television. Almost every country, no matter how poor or backward, provides a broadcasting service for its people. Even in those nations where the majority of people are illiterate, there is almost always radio broadcasting and in all but a few countries some form of television as well.

Television, in particular, has become the status symbol of the third-world nations; it is felt to be proof of modernization and of their ability to join other nations of the world community on an equal basis. Some observers have facetiously noted that the first thing a new nation institutes upon achieving its independence is the appointment of ambassadors to the United States and the United Nations—then it provides a television service. All of the oil-rich Arab sheikdoms of the Persian Gulf have modern, up-to-date television systems. So does the tiny island of Mauritius in the middle of the Indian Ocean. Where terrain or national poverty proves too limiting for television, there is always radio. The transistor radio set is endemic throughout the world. Radios blare from thatch-roofed huts in remote villages in Asia, Africa, and South America, where none of the usual amenities of modern civilization such as running water, electricity, newspapers, or highways can be found.

Nowhere does broadcasting have a greater hold on its audiences, however, than in the United States, where, by the late 1970s, more than 71 million homes were equipped to receive television. In each of those homes, on the average, the set was in use for about 7 hours each day. During the same period, U.S. citizens also listened to radio—each for an average of about 2½ hours a day.

Estimates of the television viewing time an individual in the United States accumulates over a lifetime give impressive testimony to the impact of the medium. It is said, for example, that the average male viewer will, between his second and sixty-fifth birthday, watch television for a total of more than 3,000 *days*—roughly nine full years. Almost 15 percent of his lifetime will be spent before the television screen. Indeed, adults spend more waking hours watching television than with any other waking activity aside from working.

Some estimate that the average child will watch television for 3,000 to 5,000 hours before entering elementary school. By the time this student graduates from high school, he or she will have spent approximately 10,800 hours in school and 15,000 hours watching

Figure 1–1 The funeral procession for President John F. Kennedy and the first walk on the moon by Astronaut Edwin E. Aldrin illustrate how, in times of tragedy and moments of great national accomplishment, the nation joins together to watch significant events on television. (Courtesy United Press International)

"We limit him to an hour a day. He's up to March 29, 1987."

television. Others maintain that by age fourteen, this same child will have watched 350,000 commercials and seen 18,000 persons killed, with many such homicides shown as dramatized murders.

EFFECTS OF BROADCASTING

The long-range effects of radio and television upon listeners and viewers are sometimes difficult to ascertain. Critics of broadcasting abound, charging that broadcasting has been responsible for debasement of popular tastes in music and drama, for too much standardization of pop culture, for too much sloganry and theatrics in politics, for too much capsulization of news, for the rising crime rate, for lowering of moral standards, for increased violence in the streets, and for a decline in respect for law and order. Television is even offered as the reason why "Johnnie can't read" and why American students have scored progressively lower on college entrance examinations. Television and radio are not responsible for all the ills of American society; but it does seem reasonable to assume that media as pervasive as television and radio broadcasting would have significant effect on the behavior, tastes, opinions, attitudes, and values of the American people. In this chapter we will describe some of those effects—on the individual, on other forms of entertainment, on sports, on politics—and examine the relationship between media and the listener.

Effects on the Individual

The American people devote a substantial amount of time to television and radio listening[1]—significantly more than they devote to other sources of information and other forms of entertainment. According to various readership studies, by the 1970s, American adults spent an average of not more than 5 or 6 hours a week reading books, magazines, and newspapers; many did not regularly read any newspaper. Apart from school assignments, children do less reading than adults. Attendance at motion picture theaters indicated that by the 1970s Americans averaged less than an hour each week watching motion pictures in theaters and drive-ins. Another 2 hours per week would probably more than cover average time devoted to church activities, public lectures, concerts, and stage performances. An additional hour or so per week would take care of the average American's attendance at spectator sports events as well as the time devoted to actual participation in outdoor sports. By the mid-1970s, the average American spent much less time on all of these activities combined than he spent watching television and listening to the radio.

A 10-year study conducted in an Eastern city during the era of television's most rapid growth (from 1948) confirms the extent to which the introduction of television influenced the habits and interests of those who had access to the new medium.[2] Men and women in homes with television reported that after they had purchased television sets they went much less often to motion pictures; spent less time attending lodge meetings, club meetings, and social gatherings; and did less visiting with friends and neighbors. In addition, nearly half of the new owners of television sets stated that they devoted less time to reading books and magazines than they did before they had access to television programs. These changes in behavior patterns continued throughout the entire period covered by the study.

If television and radio listening occupy so many hours of the average American's day, we can infer that these media have tremendous power to mold individual opinions and tastes. For example,

---

[1]Throughout this book, the term *listener* will refer to any individual giving attention either to radio or to television programs. Those who watch television also listen; in fact, attention studies indicate that very frequently television "viewers" do not watch the picture tube continuously, although they do hear and give some degree of continuing attention to the sound portion of the program.

[2]*The First Decade of Television in Videotown, 1948–1957* (New York: Cunningham & Walsh, 1957).

there can be little doubt that American political attitudes toward the war in Vietnam were greatly influenced by a decade of television news coverage. Television coverage of military operations, as well as reports on peace groups, student activists, and protesters, certainly helped to turn public opinion against the war. In the area of entertainment, television has also had great impact. Consider the effect of the simultaneous airing of a single entertainment program to an entire nation. The Broadway musical *Oklahoma!* for example, in 6 years on the stage in New York, was seen by possibly 3 million people, and another 10 million people may have seen the screen version. In one night on television, about 35 million people were tuned in for one performance, according to the A. C. Nielsen Company. *Oklahoma!* is considered a landmark in American musical theatre and it changed the nature of the musicals that followed it, but its full impact was not realized by the American public until it was seen on television, almost 20 years after opening on Broadway.

Effects on Other Forms of Entertainment

Easy accessibility of home entertainment by means of radio and television has had striking effects on other forms of entertainment in the United States. The rise in the popularity of radio in the 1920s and early 1930s helped bring about the disappearance of vaudeville, the theatrical stock company, and the traveling tent theatre. The combined impact of radio, television, and motion pictures contributed to the decline of the Broadway stage. In the heyday of the Broadway stage—the 1926 and 1927 seasons—more than 260 new productions opened on Broadway; in the 5-year period between 1968 and 1973, the average number of new offerings each year had dropped to 58, of which only 25 were new plays, the remainder being musicals or revivals. Of course, the economic effects of the Great Depression, which began in 1929, and the dislocations brought on by World War II contributed greatly to the decline of Broadway. However, the new media of entertainment that could reach every corner of the United States surely helped to reduce the importance of the New York stage as the center of popular entertainment.

The motion picture industry was similarly affected by television. Most experts agree that television competition was a major factor in a drastic drop in motion picture attendance. In the period 1946 to 1948, at the start of the television era, paid admissions at motion picture theaters averaged 90 million to 100 million per week, and box-office receipts hit an all-time high. For the next quarter-century, box-office receipts and the number of paying customers declined sharply, bottoming out in 1971 when industry spokesmen estimated that average attendance had dropped to 15 million to 20 million per week. With smaller audiences, there was a corresponding decline in the number of theaters, and between 1950 and 1960 many small neighborhood movie houses and many first-run downtown theaters in major cities were forced to close.[3]

Whereas movie audiences used to consist primarily of family trade, today's moviegoer tends to be a teenager or a young adult. Admissions figures released by the Motion Picture Association of America (MPAA) indicated that by the 1970s about half of adult moviegoers were 16 to 24 years old and that three fourths of all admissions were accounted for by persons less than 40 years old.

In the 1930s, Hollywood was dominated by a small number of major studios, which had most of the important stars under contract and which produced about 350 new feature films each year. These were distributed nationally, intended for general, family audiences; there were few, if any, "adult" movies. Since 1960, however, the major studios have declined in importance, producing only about 150 new feature-length films each year, and independent producers supply much of the film product seen on the nation's screens today. The types of movies, too, are much different from the film products of the 1930s; in the period between 1968 and 1975, only 19 percent of some 3,300 movies rated by the MPAA were deemed suitable for family viewing. Of 422 rated by MPAA in 1975, more than 50 percent were in restricted audience categories, rated either R or X. Obviously, the movie habit of yesteryear has been replaced by the television habit in American homes.

Effects on Sports

Spectator sports have also felt the impact of television. In the early television years, broadcasts of athletic contests constituted a large part of each station's program schedule. Baseball, boxing, and wrestling suffered heavily from overexposure. Small local boxing clubs proved unable to compete with the lure of the big-time championship bouts carried on television and were unable to find enough paying customers to watch matches between young, relatively inexperienced, unknown fighters. Such local clubs—once a major source of boxing talent—have all but disappeared as a conse-

---

[3]By 1976 there were only about 14,300 movie houses in the United States and a third of these were drive-in theaters. The big movie "palaces" of the 1930s seem definitely a thing of the past.

quence. In addition, the television emphasis upon national championship bouts soon made it difficult to find qualified contenders of championship caliber and boxing nearly disappeared from television networks. In baseball, equally devastating effects occurred. Although major league teams agreed to protect each other by restricting television coverage of home games in cities with major league teams, the spread of weekend coverage of major league games in minor league areas severely reduced attendance. As a result, many minor leagues simply went out of business and the extensive "farm systems" once maintained by major league teams shrank significantly.

The fears of professional sports promoters that television might put them all out of business proved inaccurate. Most experts now agree that broadcasting of football, basketball, and more recently, ice hockey games has actually stimulated interest in these sports and promoted substantial increases in attendance at both intercollegiate and professional contests. Partly attributable to television, too, has been the rapid growth in the number of new professional football, basketball, and hockey clubs in cities in all parts of the country, which never before had shown any significant interest in professional sports. Most of these new clubs rely on the sale of television rights for a substantial part of their income and depend upon broadcast publicity to help develop a loyal following of sports fans. Interest in many minor sports has been heightened by television exposure—bowling, golf, tennis, and sports-car and stock-car racing, among others.

Effects on Newspapers and Magazines

Broadcasting has had its influence on the form and content of newspapers and mass-circulation magazines. Beginning in the 1930s, radio's greater speed in bringing information about important events to the public forced American newspapers to make substantial changes in the materials provided for their readers. The practice of issuing "extra" editions to report fast-breaking stories has been largely abandoned, and newspapers have sought other ways to meet broadcasting competition. Increasing use of pictures, detailed treatment of major stories, more syndicated columns, and feature material such as advice columns and comic strips have all been used to compensate for the time delay in printed media. Magazines, too, have been forced to modify their content. Short stories, which were the mainstay of pre-World War II mass-circulation magazines, could not compete with dramatic fiction presented on radio and television; the popular magazines that survived reduced their use of fiction in favor of more feature articles and human-interest materials. The major mass-circulation magazines, for the most part, have disappeared—*Collier's* died in 1957, *The Saturday Evening Post* in 1969, *Life* and *Look* in 1972. Since World War II, there has been a tremendous increase in the number of special-interest publications. Significantly, the magazine with the largest circulation of all is *TV Guide,* which ranks considerably ahead of the second-place *Reader's Digest* in total circulation. Two out of three Americans today credit television as their most important source of news, so the role of newspapers and magazines in this regard has necessarily changed.

Equally great has been the economic impact of radio and television on the print media. Newspapers and magazines depend for much of their revenue on the sale of advertising; income from subscriptions and newsstand sales rarely represents more than half the total income. Competition of broadcast networks and stations for the advertiser's dollar grows more intense each year. In 1940, radio's revenues from advertising amounted to only a little more than $150 million; by the mid-1970s, national and local advertisers were spending more than $6 billion a year for radio and television time. Much of that increase in advertising expenditures in broadcasting represents money that might otherwise have been spent for newspaper and magazine advertising. At least partly as a result of this competition from radio and television, many newspapers are operating on an extremely narrow profit margin, and the number of metropolitan daily newspapers is decreasing.[4]

Effects on Politics

Broadcasting has had an influence on many other elements in our national life. Radio's ability to reach and to influence millions of people was evidenced in striking fashion in the "fireside chats" presented by President Franklin D. Roosevelt, which made it possible for him to calm the fears of a nation beset by bank failures, unemployment, and economic disaster. Presidents since Roosevelt have used radio and television to explain their philosophies of government to the American people, and to win popular support for

---

[4]In the period between 1961 and 1974, the total number of daily newspapers increased from 1,755 to 1,768—a net increase of only 13. The number of cities with two or more competing dailies, however, declined from 61 to 37 in the same period. See *Changing Public Attitudes toward Television and Other Mass Media* (New York: Television Information Office, May 1977).

measures presented to Congress. Broadcasting has become a major factor in national political campaigns—candidates can reach far more voters through a single appearance on a national television network than through all other agencies of communication combined. As a result, campaigns for national candidates in recent years have been conducted largely over television and radio, from the first announcements of candidates for party nomination until the night before the election in November. Even the national nominating conventions are now planned by party organizations to take advantage of the special opportunities created by broadcasting, with important proceedings such as keynote speeches, nomination of candidates, and actual balloting scheduled at hours when the largest numbers of radio and television listeners are available. Many political experts believe that the personalities of rival candidates, as they are brought to voters by television, are at least as important as the campaign issues in determining the winners of national elections.

BROADCASTING AND THE LISTENER

Radio and television not only affect many of the elements in our everyday life, but they also exert a direct influence on the individual listener and on listeners collectively. This influence must be considerable, if only because of the number of individuals reached and the amount of time during which they are exposed to radio or television. Radio sets are to be found in about 98 percent of all American homes and in at least 95 percent of the automobiles on our highways; in 1974, an estimated 97 percent of all homes had television receiving sets—a considerably larger proportion of homes than had bathtubs or telephones or than received daily newspapers. As noted in earlier pages, the individual men, women, and children living in those homes spend an average of at least 45 to 50 hours each week listening to radio or television. To a much greater extent than any other agency of mass communication, broadcasting has an opportunity to influence the American public.

Furthermore, the listener to broadcast programs is usually *willing* to be influenced by what he hears or sees. Most of his listening is done in his home; since he listens largely for entertainment, he is relaxed; his mental guards are down, and he listens more or less uncritically. The ideas offered in the programs he hears are conveyed by the voices of people—the listener is already familiar with the voices and personalities of many of those people and he tends to regard them at least as acquaintances, if not as personal friends. In addition, the listener has a high degree of confidence in the reliability of the broadcasting media—of television in particular. This has been shown repeatedly in studies of listener attitudes. In one such study, conducted in 1976 by Roper Research Associates, men and women throughout the country were asked, "If you got conflicting reports of the same news story from radio, television, the magazines, and the newspapers, which of the four versions would you be most inclined to believe?" Of those reached by the Roper interviewers, 51 percent would believe television in preference to any of the other sources; 22 percent would accept the newspaper version; and 9 percent would believe the account printed in a magazine.[5] Radio, over shadowed by television in recent years, still was considered most believable by 7 percent of the respondents; the remaining 11 percent expressed no preference. This willingness to accept the ideas presented in television programs offers striking evidence of the extent to which broadcasting can influence listeners.

LISTENER EVALUATIONS OF BROADCASTING

What *kinds* of influences do radio and television exert on their listeners? This is a most important question, but one about which opinions differ widely. Some critics of broadcasting believe that radio and television programs leave much to be desired and that operators of networks and stations have failed to make effective use of broadcasting's tremendous potential as a force to raise the cultural standards of the American public. Most listeners, on the other hand, seem to be fairly well satisfied with the service that radio and television provide. In the 1976 Roper study already referred to, when men and women were asked their opinions concerning television's performance, 70 percent of the respondents believed that television stations were doing either an "excellent" or a "good" job, as compared with 59 percent who gave a similar rating to newspapers and only 41 percent who had an equally good opinion of the activities of local governmental agencies. The public's general approval of broadcasting is indicated even more strikingly by the fact that television and radio sets are in use in the average home for a combined total of more than 8 hours a day. Of course, even the most enthusiastic listener to radio or television programs usually has some criticisms to offer, just as he can find things to criticize in his

[5]Results of the study published in *Changing Public Attitudes* ..., 1959–1976.

favorite newspaper or magazine or in our system of public education. We do not expect perfection in life; we can find shortcomings even in institutions and agencies that, on the whole, win our hearty approval.

Every listener makes his own personal evaluation of the things he hears on the air. Primarily, he forms judgments with respect to individual programs. Some programs he especially likes; they arouse his interest or entertain him, and he tries to listen to them regularly. Others he accepts as being moderately good or at least satisfactory; he will listen to them when more attractive programs are not available and will derive some pleasure from listening—but he makes no special effort to "catch" them. Still other programs fail to interest him at all; some of them arouse his active dislike. Rather than listen to programs in this third group, he will turn off his radio or his television set completely.

In making his evaluations of programs—and possibly of the stations and networks that provide them—the listener is likely to base his evaluations largely on the *entertainment* values of the programs considered and the extent to which he personally finds them interesting and enjoyable. If radio and television supply a substan-

"Sure this is a lousy show, but I've got to watch something."

tial number of programs that, for him at least, have high entertainment values, then broadcasting is "doing a good job" and its weaknesses or failings are of minor importance. However, if he finds relatively few programs he enjoys and a large number of programs that he dislikes, then the listener tends to become highly critical of the entire broadcasting industry and of the service it provides the public.

Perhaps this tendency is logical and reasonable; most Americans think of radio and television as sources of entertainment, like motion pictures or the legitimate theatre. However, entertainment is not the only factor to be considered. Programs broadcast by radio and television stations exert some degree of influence on the tastes and attitudes and perhaps upon the behavior of the listening public; the nature of these influences necessarily must be taken into account. In many respects, radio and television have had a wholesome effect on our society, especially in the widespread dissemination of information. The American public today is probably better informed than ever before, and at least some of the credit must go to broadcasting.

On the other hand, broadcasting may have some less desirable side effects. Obviously radio and television have their weaknesses and imperfections, and all intelligent listeners have the obligation to examine critically the programs radio and television offer and the functioning of the system of broadcasting that makes such programs possible. They also have the obligation to use whatever means are available to help correct weaknesses in that system, so that broadcasting can better serve the people of this country.

The system of broadcasting in this country was established on the premise that the airwaves—the frequencies used by the broadcasters—are a natural resource. It was decided that any individual or corporation wishing to use these airwaves for commercial gain —wishing to broadcast and sell commercial time to pay costs and provide a profit—would be licensed to do so by the government. In exchange for this license and the profit potential it represents, a licensee is expected to use some broadcasting time to serve the public, without consideration of commercial gain.

Every intelligent citizen, then, has the right to listen to radio and television critically to be sure that the American public is getting a fair return from the exploitation of this natural resource. One should not simply accept whatever is offered by local radio and television stations, with a passive gratitude for a few moments of pleasure or entertainment in a welter of commercialism.

On the other hand, the intelligent listener cannot generate constructive and useful criticism without an understanding of the nature of the forces that shape and control the broadcasting industry. A certain level of commercialism, for example, is essential if a station is to stay on the air and provide *any* service to its public. In addition, Congress, the courts, and the Federal Communications Commission create situations in which broadcasters feel they must take actions that may antagonize some listeners—the preemption of popular programs for political conventions; the plethora of political advertising in the closing days of a campaign; the broadcast of informative documentaries of interest only to a limited audience. Further, economic forces may put such a premium on maximum audience size that genuinely good programming seems to give way to the lowest common denominator. Similar forces may increase the number of reruns on network television to almost 50 percent of the total schedule.

The critic of broadcasting, in short, can find many things to complain about. Intelligent, constructive criticism, however, can come about only through an understanding of the historic and economic forces that shaped broadcasting and the regulatory and social forces at work in the industry today. It is the purpose of this book to provide readers with an introduction to our complex system of broadcasting in the hope that they will be better able to see its strengths and weaknesses and to help maintain the former while helping correct the latter.

STUDY AND DISCUSSION QUESTIONS

1. Become aware of and assess the number of hours you devote to broadcast media by keeping a "Broadcast Media Log" for a typical week of your schedule. Organize it simply and try to keep it with you so it will not be necessary to trust your memory at the end of each day. An example of a simple log would be a small pad divided into columns with the following headings:

TIME	MEDIUM	CONTENT	FULL OR PARTIAL
(Start and stop or elapsed total)	(Radio or TV)		ATTENTION

2. Examine your completed Media Log and attempt to classify your time in various ways. Some possible classifications would be: nature of content (information, entertainment, background); degree of attention (full or partial); personal evaluation (enjoyable, informative, persuasive, routine, dull, better than nothing). Review these classifications (and any others that may occur to you) and begin to assess the impact of broadcast media on your personal life. Ask yourself:

   a. How important are they to me?
   b. What do they contribute to my life?
   c. How would my life be changed if they were no longer available?
   d. How could I make them more useful to me if I were in a position to do so?

3. Report on or be prepared to discuss your view of the impact of television on our society and culture in the light of some of the suggested readings and your own experience.

4. Choose a regular television series dealing with a profession or occupation that has representatives in your community (doctors, police, private investigators). Study a few episodes of the series and list the characteristics of the featured occupation as *you learned them from the series* with as little reference to your personal knowledge and opinions as possible. Then talk to a representative of the occupation. Report on or be prepared to discuss some of the differences between fiction and fact you discover.

5. Begin to evaluate the media of radio and television by listing the good and bad points of each as you see them now. Discuss these lists in class, and after the discussion reexamine your list to see if your mind has changed on any points or if any should be added. When you have created lists that satisfy you,

   a. Examine each of the good points to see if it could be improved in any way. Discuss these points in class to determine if any of them seem threatened by the attitudes of others or by government action.
   b. Examine each of the bad points and suggest what you would do to improve the situation. Discuss each of these points in class to determine their causes and whether or not the industry has any control over the causes.

6. Report on or be prepared to discuss the following:

   a. The impact of radio on vaudeville
   b. The impact of radio and television on the Broadway stage
   c. The impact of television on motion pictures
   d. The impact of television on professional and intercollegiate sports
   e. The impact of television on mass-circulation magazines
   f. The impact of electronic journalism on print media
   g. The effects of electronic media on politics
   h. Public attitudes toward news and entertainment on electronic media

---

SUGGESTED READINGS

Richard Adler, ed. *Television as a Social Force.* New York: Praeger Publishers, 1975.

Richard Adler, ed. *Television as a Cultural Force.* New York: Praeger Publishers, 1976.

Ben H. Bagdikian. *The Information Machines: Their Impact on Men and Media*. New York: Harper & Row, 1971.

Leo Bogart. *The Age of Television*. New York: Ungar Press, 1973.

Robert T. Bower. *Television and the Public*. New York: Holt, Rinehart and Winston, 1973.

James Combs and Michael W. Mansfield, eds. *Drama in Life: The Uses of Communication in Society*. New York: Hastings House, 1976.

George Comstock. *Television and Its Viewers: What Social Science Sees*. Santa Monica, Calif.: RAND Corporation, 1976.

W. Philips Davison, James Baylan, and Frederic T.C. Yu. *Mass Media Systems and Effects*. New York: Praeger Publishers, 1976.

The First Decade of Television in Videotown, 1948–1957. New York: Cunningham & Walsh, 1957.

George Gerbner, Larry Gross, and William Melody. *Communications Technology and Social Policy: Understanding the "Cultural Revolution."* New York: Wiley, 1973.

Bradley S. Greenberg and Edwin B. Parker, eds. *The Kennedy Assassination and the American Public: Social Communication in Crisis*. Stanford, Calif.: Stanford University Press, 1965.

Sidney Kraus and Dennis Davis. *The Effects of Mass Communication on Political Behavior*. University Park: Pennsylvania State University Press, 1976.

David LeRoy and Christopher Sterling. *Mass News: Practices, Controversies and Alternatives*. Englewood Cliffs, N.J.: Prentice–Hall, 1973.

Gary A. Steiner. *The People Look at Television: A Study of Audience Attitudes*. New York: Knopf, 1963.

Frederic Stuart. *The Effects of Television on the Motion Picture and Radio Industries*. New York: Arno Press, 1976.

2

Systems of Broadcasting

As radio broadcasting, followed by television, spread throughout the world, the questions of how to control and finance the service have been answered in many different ways. To simplify our discussion of the various systems of broadcasting that have evolved throughout the world, some terms should be defined.

Turning first to types of control, we find three major categories:

1. *state ownership:* broadcast facilities owned directly by the government with broadcasting activities under the immediate supervision of a government minister or a committee appointed by the state;

2. *autonomous corporations:* broadcast facilities owned and operated by a corporation that, although government owned, is almost completely independent of the ministry in power; and

3. *private ownership:* broadcast facilities owned and operated by private individual corporations or individuals, usually regulated in some manner by a government body.

We also find three major categories of financing plans:

1. *tax support:* supported primarily by taxes, ranging from the "general fund" to special taxes on set sales, imports, and the like;

2. *license support:* supported primarily by license fees paid annually by the owners of radio or television sets; and

3. *advertiser support:* supported primarily by the sale of advertising to businesses and services wishing to distribute their message to a large number of people.

Few of these control categories exist in their pure state in any one country. Some countries with state ownership, for instance, permit some privately owned broadcasting stations (for example, The Republic of Korea, Brazil). Other countries with predominantly private ownership also have some state-operated facilities (for example, Spain, most South American countries).

The financing categories also blend into each other. In most countries, one source of income is predominant but other sources are drawn upon. Tax money, license fees, and a combination of the two are the most common forms of support throughout the world, but as production expenses mount—especially for television—more and more countries are turning to some measure of advertising support. In virtually every country, though, one type of control and one financing plan predominate.

As one might expect in a world with as many diversities as ours, the student of broadcasting is faced by a bewildering variety of systems in other countries. When studying this variety, it is helpful to examine the cultural patterns, the traditions, and the philosophies of government of the various states.

In Europe, a strong, centralized government that evolved from the institution of monarchy is the political inheritance of most countries. In Western Europe, in the past century, this inheritance has been modified by a more democratic tradition. Most of these countries have selected for their broadcasting systems a combination of centralization and relative independence, the autonomous corporation. Spain, with its primary emphasis on private ownership, is the major exception to this generalization.

Eastern Europe, on the other hand, shows a different pattern. The Communist countries of this region—Bulgaria, Czechoslovakia, East Germany, Hungary, Poland, Rumania, the Soviet Union, and Yugoslavia—have retained a tightly controlled, centralized form of government. Similarly, all broadcasting facilities are owned and controlled directly by the state.

In North America, Canada is pulled between the traditions of Great Britain and the influence of the United States to the south.

"The Commissar of Ratings wants us to change the channel."

This country has developed a dual system that combines an autonomous corporation and private ownership operating in tandem.

With the exception of Cuba and Peru, all countries in Central and South America have followed the lead of both Spain and the United States and have developed broadcasting systems that are privately owned. In many Latin American countries, however, most stations are owned by a few powerful corporations.

In virtually all of the developing nations in Asia and Africa, broadcasting is considered an instrument of national unity and education and, as a result, governments have developed services run directly by the state. A few African countries with a British heritage (such as Kenya, Rhodesia, and South Africa) have retained the autonomous corporation, as have some well-established Asian countries (for example, Cyprus, Iran, and Israel). In other Asian countries that have felt a strong American influence, such as Japan and the Philippines, private ownership is predominant.

The world pattern that emerges may remain somewhat obscure; but, for the purposes of this discussion, we can reduce the confusion by focusing our attention on Europe (including the U.S.S.R.), North America, and a few other countries like Japan, Australia, and New Zealand. According to 1974 UNESCO figures,[1] the ratio of radio receivers to individuals is 5 per 100 in 26 African countries, between 1 and 8 per 100 in 19 Asian countries, and less than 10 per 100 in many South American countries. However, according to the same UNESCO report, by the mid-1970s, television still had essentially no impact in Africa and not much more in Asian countries, while in South America, only two countries had as many as 10 receivers per 100 persons. Since we are attempting to place the American system, with its virtually total penetration, in a reasonable context, little can be gained by further examination of systems that are still in their formative stages.

THE EUROPEAN SYSTEM

In the following pages, we will examine the general characteristics of systems of broadcasting in those countries that have well-developed broadcast services with high audience penetration. Further, we will compare these systems with the American system and discuss some advantages and disadvantages of various characteris-

---

[1]UNESCO, *World Communications: A 200 Country Survey of Press, Radio, Television, Film* (New York: Unipub, 1976).

Figure 2–1   a. The BBC Television Centre at Shepherd's Bush, London, England.
(Courtesy British Information Service, London)

b. Headquarters (under construction) of TV Globo, a Brazilian television network.
(Courtesy Rede Globo, Rio de Janeiro)

c. Broadcasting Center—NHK. (Courtesy Japan Broadcasting Corporation)

tics. Because most of the countries we are considering are in Europe, we will compare the American system with what can be called the European system.

Allowing for usually minor variations, government-owned broadcasting systems in Europe are essentially alike in five important respects. (1) Broadcasting facilities—including stations, network transmission lines, and usually studios and studio equipment—are owned by the central government or an autonomous corporation established by the government. (2) The system is monopolistic; all broadcasting operations are conducted by a single government agency with no competition for the attention of listeners from privately owned stations, at least from within the borders of the country operating the system. (3) Programming is highly centralized; virtually all programs originate in the nation's capital and are sent out over telephone lines, coaxial cables, or microwave relay systems for simultaneous broadcast by stations throughout the nation. In most European countries, no broadcasting originates at local stations; where local broadcasts are permitted, they take up an extremely small proportion of the average station's schedule. (4) Broadcasting is essentially noncommercial; at least it is not primarily a business enterprise operated for profit, although many countries allow paid commercial announcements on government-owned radio or television stations. (5) A major portion of the money used to maintain the government broadcasting system comes from a special license fee levied on each household in which a radio or television receiving set is used, from tax-generated funds, or from a combination of the two.

Except for Spain, in which virtually all stations are owned by private commercial companies, every major nation of Europe has a broadcasting system with all or most of these five basic characteristics: government ownership, monopoly, centralized programming, noncommercial operation, and support from taxes or license fees. Programming is not centralized in West Germany, where broadcasting stations are operated by the separate states making up the Federal Republic of Germany.

In an increasing number of countries, in both Eastern and Western Europe, the policy of noncommercial operation is somewhat modified by the fact that government-owned stations accept paid advertising announcements, but their number is limited and advertisers are not permitted to sponsor entire programs. Since 1965, the number of countries that do permit some advertising has risen from three to fifteen—even in the U.S.S.R., some broadcasting expenses are now met by income from announcements and information services. Only ten European countries continue to hold the line against any advertising: Belgium, Bulgaria, Czechoslovakia, Denmark, East Germany, Hungary, Norway, Poland, Sweden, and Switzerland.

State-Controlled Systems   Although European broadcasting services are in the hands of government agencies, the structure of organization and control varies from country to country. In all the Communist countries, broadcasting facilities are owned directly by the government, and broadcasting activities are under the immediate supervision of a government minister or an administration official directly responsible to a council of ministers. This system makes for immediate and complete control of all program content. In Communist countries, news and propaganda broadcasts and even entertainment programs conform rigidly to policies established by the government.

Autonomous-Corporation Systems   Many of the more democratic European countries have adopted the autonomous-corporation concept, which makes radio and television much less subject to pressures from the political party in control of the government. In these countries, broadcasting facilities are operated by a corporation, which, although largely government owned, is almost completely independent of the ministry in power. The officers and directors of the corporation are appointed on a long-term basis and continue in their positions regardless of political changes.

This system was first developed by Great Britain, where the organization in charge of broadcasting is the British Broadcasting Corporation (BBC). Most countries in Western Europe have adopted the same general system—some with modifications. The Netherlands has a system resembling in some ways the autonomous-corporation system of control. Stations and equipment are owned by the government, which also provides engineering services. Programs, however, are produced by private corporations or associations, with programming operations subject to periodic reviews by a government committee. Outside of Europe, New Zealand has adopted the autonomous-corporation system, while such corporations are responsible for broadcasts over government-owned stations in the dual-system nations of Australia, Canada, and Japan.

Broadcasting in Great Britain

As we have seen, Great Britain originated the autonomous-corporation system and most Western European countries have adapted the concept to their own needs. An analysis of the system as it exists in Great Britain will be helpful in gaining an understanding of the main features of this system of control.

Broadcasting in Great Britain began formally in 1922, with the creation of the British Broadcasting Company. Technically, this was a private company; its stock was owned entirely by British manufacturers of radio receiving sets and equipment. Otherwise, however, the company had all the characteristics of the European system. It had a monopoly on broadcasting activities; programming was on a centralized basis; its operation was noncommercial; and support was provided by license fees on radio receiving sets. In 1926, the British government took over the stock and facilities of the company, reimbursing the private owners for the amounts each had invested. To replace the company, the government created a new, government-owned agency, the British Broadcasting Corporation (BBC), which has had complete control over government broadcasting in Great Britain since.

In theory, the BBC is responsible to the British government. Directors of the corporation are appointed by the ministry in power; stations owned by the BBC are licensed to the Postmaster-General who, legally, has veto power over broadcast programs. In actual fact, however, the BBC is an almost completely independent organization. Directors are appointed for fixed terms and continue to serve regardless of changes in the party in power; policies are determined by the corporation's board of directors; day-to-day operations are carried on without regard for political considerations; and the veto power of the Postmaster-General has almost never been used. Operations of the BBC are noncommercial, being supported by license fees imposed on owners of receiving sets.

British Radio   Until 1973, radio in Great Britain was a government monopoly, with all programs originated and broadcast by the BBC. In that year, local commercial stations were approved and two opened in London—one devoted primarily to news and the other to light and popular music. By 1976, there were fifteen such commercial stations on the air in urban centers.

BBC Radio provides four national program services, each carried over a separate national network of stations. Radio 1 carries a continuous program of popular music. Radio 2 specializes in light entertainment—music, serials, sports, and women's programs.

Both carry hourly news summaries. Radio 3 concentrates on classical music and also offers plays, talk, special broadcasts, news, religious broadcasts, study courses, and commentary. Radio 4 provides the principal news and information services of the BBC, with parliamentary reports, political broadcasts, and a wide range of music and plays.

In the mid-1970s, programs on these four national networks included entertainment and music (42.9%), serious music (21.2%), talks (9.7%), news and outside broadcasts (9.1%), drama (4.8%), educational broadcasts (3.6%), minority broadcasts (3.1%), features (2.2%), and religious broadcasts (1.8%).[2] BBC also operates local FM stations designed to carry a full range of locally originated programs of interest to the communities served.

British Television   Television developed somewhat earlier in Great Britain than in the United States, probably because of the U.S. delay in deciding on engineering standards for the new medium. As early as 1936, a BBC station in London was providing regular, daily television to a limited audience. This station continued operating until 1939, when war conditions made it necessary for the BBC to discontinue its television broadcasts. After the war, however, television developed less rapidly in Great Britain than in the United States. Although the London station returned to the air in 1946, the BBC had only five television stations in operation by 1952, as compared with 129 stations in the United States at the end of the same year.

Television created a serious financial problem for the BBC. Virtually all its revenues come from an annual license fee levied on each receiving set, amounting at the end of the war to £1 (equivalent at the time to $2.80) for each home equipped with a radio set. Later, to pay the costs of increased television operation, the fee for a combined radio and television license was increased to £4. However, one quarter of this was an excise tax that went into the public treasury, so that, after costs of collection and the £1 allowed for radio were deducted, something less than £2 per home per year was available for the support of television. In the year ending in March 1953, the television tax was paid by set owners in approximately 2.15 million homes, providing revenues for BBC television of only about $12 million a year—not a very impressive figure when compared with the 1952 gross revenues of $324 million reported by American television networks and stations. In addition to this financial shortfall, BBC was faced with an increasing demand from its viewers for

---

[2]UNESCO, *World Communications.*

"I'm a two-time offender—listened to the BBC without a license."

a second television service to allow for a choice of programs. Such a service simply could not be provided with the money then available to BBC.

As a result, the British government was forced to abandon, for television only at that time, two of the principles basic to the European system: monopoly in broadcasting operations and noncommercial programming. In 1954, Parliament passed an act creating, side by side with the BBC, a second government corporation, the Independent Television Authority (ITA). In 1973, when commercial radio was approved, the name was changed to the Independent Broadcasting Authority (IBA). In conformity with the act's provision, the IBA has constructed and provides all engineering services for a system of television stations, one in each major population center in Great Britain and Northern Ireland. These stations are leased by IBA to private commercial companies or contractors; the contracting companies build and maintain their own studios, provide programs for broadcast, and sell commercial announcements to advertisers. For several hours each week most of the IBA stations are linked together for network broadcasting; at other times, stations are programmed independently with films, tapes, or locally originated programs.

During the spring of 1964, the British government authorized a second noncommercial BBC television service or channel, and provided for the construction of stations to carry the new network's programming. To finance the new network, the radio-television license fee was raised in 1965 to $14 a year. As a result, viewers in the larger cities of Great Britain have had access since April 1964 to three television services, or channels—two BBC noncommercial services and a commercial service offered by the IBA stations. So, since 1954, Great Britain has had a mixed, or dual, system of broadcasting for television—with radio becoming a dual system in 1973.

By the mid-1970s, program content on the two BBC channels included news, documentary, and information programs (31%); feature films and series (15.5%); outside broadcasts (14%); light entertainment and family programs (13.5%); educational broadcasts (11.1%); drama (8%); religious programs (2.2%); and music (1.6%). Average weekly composition of IBA programs is plays, drama, and serials (20%); news, documentaries, features, and outside broadcasts (18%); entertainment and music (14%); sports (13%); feature films (12%); education and school programs (10%); and religious (3%).[3]

Broadcasting in the Soviet Union

As the British broadcasting system has influenced most of Western Europe, so has the Soviet system been adopted by (or imposed on) most countries in Eastern Europe. An analysis of this system will parallel our study of Great Britain.

All broadcasting in the U.S.S.R. is state operated. Since 1971, control has been vested in a Union Republic State Committee of the U.S.S.R. Council of Ministers. The chairman of the State Television and Radio and Committee of the U.S.S.R. Council of Ministers is thus a member of the government.

Because of its vast size and the diversity of its states and autonomous republics, the U.S.S.R. does not have a completely centralized broadcast operation. Broadcasts originate from the capitals of all states and republics and from territory and district centers. In every other respect, however, the U.S.S.R. holds fast to the essential features of the European system—government ownership, monopoly, noncommercial operation and financing provided by taxes or license fees.

---

[3]UNESCO, *World Communications.*

Soviet Radio The Central Radio Service from Moscow broadcasts
seven program services, all in Russian. The first program service
provides information programs covering national and international affairs; news bulletins; talks and commentaries; interpreta-
tive features; programs for young people; literary, musical, and
children's features. The second service broadcasts 48 news bulletins
a day covering national and foreign events and, for the remainder of
the time, music and light entertainment. The third service is of a
general educational nature, including literature and music. The
fourth (FM) program service carries music, literature, and drama of
a somewhat higher quality than that provided by the third program. The fifth is a sociopolitical, news and music service intended
for Soviet citizens living abroad. The sixth and seventh program
services, designed for listeners in the eastern regions (Far East,
Siberia, central Asia, and Kazakhstan), are primarily repeats of the
first service, scheduled to allow for time differences.

   In the mid-1970s, the Central Radio Service's weekly schedule
included news broadcasts (13.2%); sociopolitical, economic, scientific, cultural, and sports broadcasts (15.5%); plays and literature
(9%); broadcasts for children and young people (13.7%); music
39.1%); and other broadcasts (8.5%).[4]

   Local broadcasting stations in the various republics, territories,
and regions operate their own stations, under the supervision of
television and radio committees, relaying programs from Moscow
and originating their own programs in one or another of the 67
national languages of the U.S.S.R. There are 10 main area, 200
municipal and 2,824 regional radio broadcast offices in Russia.

Soviet Television Russia was experimenting with television broadcasting as early as 1931, and by 1938 stations were operating in both
Moscow and Leningrad. A third station, in Kiev, was commissioned
in 1951. By the end of 1972, approximately 300 main stations and
1,000 relay stations were on the air, broadcasting either programs
from Moscow or locally originated material.

   The Central Television Service in Moscow offers five program
services. The first service reaches all parts of European Russia and
some parts of Central Asia and Siberia and carries information,
sociopolitical, cultural, and educational programs. The second service serves Moscow and the surrounding area with a large variety of
information and feature programs. The third service is educational,
related to secondary-school and university curricula and to the pro-

---

[4]UNESCO, *World Communications.*

fessional requirements of specialists in the national economy. The fourth service, also educational, is described by the Soviet government as a cultural and scientific university for the millions. Both the third and fourth services can be received only in and around Moscow. The fifth service is designed for the more remote parts of the U.S.S.R. and is transmitted by satellite. It seems evident from the above that the tightly controlled Soviet system of broadcasting deals with television more as an instrument of education, information, and culture than as a source of entertainment.

Advantages of the European System

For those countries in which it is used, the European system offers several obvious advantages. To begin with, the European system offers economy in programming. While many countries encourage a degree of local programming, the major emphasis of virtually all systems is on programs provided on a centralized network basis. A single program produced in national headquarters is carried by stations throughout the nation, instead of each station's having to provide its own programs. Money available for programming can consequently be spent to provide programs of better quality than would otherwise be possible. In addition, with only a single employer of broadcasting talent, there is no competitive bidding for the services of such personnel as writers, actors, producers, directors, and musicians. Artists' fees and program costs are kept at a much lower level than is possible in the United States. The combination of monopoly and centralized programming also contributes to national unity. The influence exerted by radio and television is applied in exactly the same way, and through the same programs, in every section of the country.

Government ownership and control also allow broadcasting to be used as an instrument of culture and mass education to an extent not possible under a commercial system. The government broadcast agency can present operas, concerts by major symphony orchestras, and dramatic programs using the classics of the theatre; it can provide talks by educators, scientists, and leading literary figures. Programs chosen for their cultural and educational values actually do make up a considerable portion of the offerings of both radio and television in nearly every country using the European system of broadcasting. There is no pressure from advertisers who demand large audiences, and for the most part there is no competition for listener attention from programs with greater popular appeal. With broadcasting a monopoly, the listener tunes in the one program offered at any given time, or he does not listen at all.

Disadvantages of the European System

In that same lack of choice on the part of the listener lies one of the weaknesses of the European system. In the United States, at least, program decisions are made by the management of stations and networks who are, in most cases, striving to attract the largest possible audiences. As a result, it can be said that most programs are aired because the public wants them. In countries where broadcasting is a government monopoly, on the other hand, the controlling agency decides what is to be broadcast, sometimes with little regard for the preferences or interests of the listening public. Sir John Reith, director general of the British Broadcasting Corporation for more than 15 years, expressed a common philosophy in the European system in these words: "It is occasionally indicated to us that we are apparently setting out to give the public what we think they need—and not what they want. But very few know what they want and very few what they need."

A second weakness in the European system is the lack of stimulus to experiment with new programs and new program forms—a lack resulting from the absence of competition. It must be admitted that in some countries, notably Great Britain, improvements in production techniques for dramatic programs came at least as rapidly as they did in the United States; however, overall, European broadcasting has been conspicuously slow to develop new types of programs. Until the end of World War II, the only radio program forms in use in most European countries were those that had existed in the United States before 1930. Comedy-variety programs, serial drama, quiz programs, situation comedies, audience-participation programs, panel discussions—these forms of entertainment were not provided by European stations before 1945. Since the war, European broadcasting has borrowed heavily from the United States, and most of the program forms that have been used in this country are also offered by European broadcasting systems; but, without competition between stations or networks for audiences, there is no particular reason for European broadcasters to experiment with new ideas or new forms in programming.

The introduction of commercial television in Great Britain had a decided effect on the television programming offered by the BBC. The government system has been forced to compete for the attention of listeners by offering a substantial amount of the same kind of entertainment programming provided on television in the United States.

A third and serious shortcoming of the European system, at least from the point of view of those interested in democratic government, is the ease with which a government-owned system can be made an instrument of political propaganda. Adolf Hitler, after becoming chancellor in 1933, made extremely effective use of radio to indoctrinate the people of Germany with his Nazi philosophies. In many Eastern nations today, radio and television are used heavily for propaganda in support of the group in power. On the other hand, in the countries of Western Europe, there is little overt propaganda in support of government policies, although the opportunity to use broadcasting for such purposes is always present. The charter of the BBC, for example, provides that the British Broadcasting Corporation is required to broadcast "any announcement" requested by "any department" of the government. Even without overt propaganda on the government-owned broadcasting facilities, news broadcasters in most countries are often somewhat cautious in their reporting of events that reflect unfavorably on the party in power. Also, although radio and television time is provided freely for speakers who support government policies, most European broadcasting systems—Great Britain is an exception—are less likely to provide time for speakers who are vigorous in their criticisms of current government activities. Even in highly democratic countries, there is always the possibility that the government-owned broadcasting facilities will become an instrument for direct or indirect propaganda in support of the party controlling the government.

THE AMERICAN SYSTEM

The commercial system of broadcasting in use in the United States contrasts strongly with the European system. Virtually all stations in this country are owned by private corporations or individuals, not by the federal government. A significant number—predominantly educational FM radio stations and educational television stations—are owned by tax-supported universities; others are owned by branches of state government—usually some form of educational broadcasting commission; still others are owned by municipalities or local school systems. No station engaged in domestic broadcasting, however, is owned or operated by the federal government.[5]

---

[5]A compilation from listings in the 1976 *Broadcasting Yearbook* showed that of 8,808 AM, FM, and television stations on the air in December 1975, only about 220 stations were owned by tax-supported state universities, local school districts, or other agencies of state and local government.

Not only are nearly all stations privately owned and operated, but also there is a high degree of diffusion of station ownership. In some countries with private ownership, such as Spain, Mexico, and Chile, 20, 30, or more important stations may be licensed to a single owning corporation. In the United States, by government regulation, no individual or company may own more than seven standard (AM) radio stations, seven FM stations and seven television stations. Consequently, the almost 8,000 commercial radio and televsion stations operating in this country at the beginning of 1976 were owned and controlled by nearly 6,000 separate individual owners or groups. Although a few large companies own several important stations each, station ownership, on the whole, is widely diffused in the United States.

Centralized programming or centralized control of programming simply does not exist in our country to the degree that it can be found in other systems. The national television networks do provide a degree of centralization since these networks provide most of our better programs, but they are owned by three separate companies that compete vigorously with each other. Certainly they do not cooperate in the planning of their programs. Moreover, the three television networks supply only about 60 percent of the programs broadcast by the nation's commercial television stations, and the four radio networks account for not more than 10 percent of the program time of our commercial radio stations. Most radio programs and a substantial proportion of the television programs broadcast in this country originate locally, with each station determining for itself what programs it will produce and what network or syndicated programs it will put on the air. Certainly, there is no centralized control over programs in America of the type that exists in countries operating under the European system.

American broadcasting is commercial. We do have noncommercial stations, but they are a decided minority. In 1976, nearly 90 percent of all American radio and television stations were commercial. These stations, like our national networks, depend for their revenues on the sale of time to advertisers. They receive neither appropriations from government nor funds from a tax on receiving sets. To survive in this country, under present law, broadcasting must operate on a commercial basis.

Finally, broadcasting in the United States is highly competitive. Stations compete both for advertising revenues and for audiences. To be attractive to advertisers, a station must first have listeners; to get those listeners, it must provide programs that can compete effectively with the programs offered by other stations. National networks compete with one another for advertising revenues, for outstanding programs, for the most popular entertainers and for affiliations with the best stations available in each community.

So, the American system of broadcasting is distinguished from the European system by five characteristics: (1) Stations are privately owned; (2) there is wide diffusion of ownership; (3) there is no central planning of programs or centralized control over programs; (4) stations are commercially operated; and (5) there is a high degree of competition between stations and between networks.

The above discussion of the American system, of course, refers only to commercial broadcasting in this country. A parallel but much smaller system of approximately 1,000 noncommercial stations has also evolved (mainly over the past 30 years) with somewhat different characteristics. Nearly all the stations are owned by educational institutions, by community or state organizations, or by religious groups. The stations are not commercially supported; they rely instead on outside sources—university budgets, direct tax appropriations, donations, foundations, and the like—for their support. There is little competition between noncommercial stations, for two such stations are seldom in the same market or after the same audience. A sense of competition for audience may exist between commercial and noncommercial stations, but the intense competition one finds between commercial stations simply does not exist in the noncommercial area.

On the other hand, the ownership of noncommercial stations is even more widely diffused than that of commercial stations. Some states do own networks of noncommercial television and FM stations but few other organizations are willing or able to assume the responsibility of supporting more than one or two such stations. The noncommercial system is also relatively decentralized. The Public Broadcasting Service (PBS) and National Public Radio (NPR) do provide some centralization of programming, but these organizations provide even less programming than do the commercial networks and they depend, in large measure, on programs produced by member stations.

The commercial and noncommercial systems in the United States, then, are similar in two particulars—diverse ownership and decentralization—and different in three—kind of ownership, sources of income, and amount of competition.

Advantages and Disadvantages of the American System

Like the system of broadcasting used in Europe, the commercial system that has developed in the United States has its advantages and its disadvantages. It cannot operate on any unified, predetermined plan; wide diffusion of ownership makes systematic central planning impossible. Especially for radio, lack of such planning has resulted in the establishment of far more stations than are needed to meet the real needs of listeners—in fact, there are more stations than can be supported adequately by the advertising revenues available. Such an absence of central planning and control is economically inefficient; there is tremendous duplication of effort by stations and networks; network competition for programs and for outstanding entertainers has forced program costs to levels far above those existing in countries with broadcasting monopolies.

Problem of Cultural Programs   Another major weakness is found in the field of cultural programs. No one would argue that the American system allows full use of the potentialities of radio and television for raising our standards of literary and musical appreciation. Symphonies, complete operas, and dramatic programs of outstanding literary value are common in European broadcasting but much less common in the United States. With relatively few exceptions, cultural programs in this country attract small audiences; therefore, advertisers who wish to reach the greatest number of listeners possible are not usually interested in sponsoring such programs. Lacking advertising support, cultural programs tend to be crowded out of the schedules of American commercial networks and stations by programs on the mass-entertainment level.

Most of our noncommercial television stations are members of a fourth network called the Public Broadcasting Service (PBS), and most noncommercial radio stations belong to National Public Radio (NPR), a radio network service. These noncommercial networks and the stations they serve do carry more cultural programming than do their commercial counterparts, but the audiences for these programs are usually quite small when compared with audiences for commercial entertainment. The Corporation for Public Broadcasting (CPB), for instance, estimated that during November 1976, only 26.7 percent of the television homes in the United States tuned in even one public television program in a given week.

Discussion of Public Issues   On the other hand, the American system of broadcasting does provide opportunities for the airing of controversial issues of public concern. Perhaps the greatest advantage of our system is the fact that it is a system of private ownership, with programs largely free from direct government control. True democracy demands an informed public, and broadcasting has become an important agency through which the public may be informed. Under a system of government ownership, information is not always provided on a two-sided basis; at worst, broadcasting may be used as a vehicle for out-and-out government propaganda and, at best, the broadcasting organization can hardly be expected to take positions highly critical of government policies. Here in the United States, however, broadcasters do not depend on the government for support: they are as free to criticize as they are to commend, and many take advantage of that freedom. Radio networks provide commentary programs, some of which are highly critical of the party in power. Television networks schedule many programs in which government spokesmen are called upon to answer the frequently embarrassing questions posed by a panel of informed interrogators (as in *Meet the Press*); in others, analyses of government proposals are presented in documentary form, with at least as much attention given to flaws as to possible virtues. In addition, owners of many stations use their facilities to present editorial opinions that are as often critical as commendatory of actions of the local or national government.

In short, the possibility of free discussion of vital public questions, and the resulting wide dissemination of information on issues of importance, is one of the major advantages inherent in the American system of broadcasting.

Listener Influence on Programming   One characteristic of the American system is considered by some to be an advantage and by others, a disadvantage. In this country, each listener selects from a considerable variety of programs those that satisfy his own special interest and tastes. On a larger scale, the public collectively selects the programs that best satisfy the public's collective tastes. If substantial numbers of listeners tune in a particular program each week, the program remains on the air. If, on the other hand, a program fails to attract a reasonably large audience, that program will usually be dropped, and networks and stations are not ordinarily inclined to introduce other programs of the same general type. In a European system, the public gets programs that those who control a government agency think listeners "ought to have"; in the system used in this country, listeners get the programs that they themselves select—or at least programs that are attractive to major segments of the total listening public.

It is often argued that, while the public does have the power to select or reject programs, it has virtually no control over the range of choices presented or the specific programs on the network schedules. While the American public does have a kind of "voting" power, the argument goes, it has little to say about the "nominating" process, which is entirely in the hands of network program executives. This argument may have some validity, but the fact remains that American broadcasting provides more program variety than any other system in the world.

Whether this listener influence on programming is an advantage or a disadvantage is a matter of individual opinion. It does result in the broadcasting of fewer cultural programs, and critics charge that radio and television cater to the tastes of the mass audience while ignoring the interests of intellectual minorities. Others feel, however, that this appeal to a mass audience is one of the strengths of the American system and is entirely appropriate in a country as committed to mass democracy as we are.

STUDY AND DISCUSSION QUESTIONS

1. Select a specific country and prepare a report on the system of broadcasting that developed in that country. Include in the report the following:

   a. The types of control of broadcast media, including a general description and the specific controlling body or bodies
   b. The method(s) of financing the system
   c. Sources of programming
   d. Degree of centralization of programming and production
   e. Methods of distribution
   f. The strength, number, and nature of local stations
   g. Policies relating to the use of programs from other countries
   h. Penetration of radio and television in the society

2. The system of broadcasting in the United States is devoted primarily to entertaining its listeners, with providing information decidedly a secondary goal. In other countries, broadcasting is seen as a means toward other ends—improving the cultural level of the people, raising educational standards and achievement, promoting national unity, presenting social goals and norms, and the like. Examine the system of broadcasting in a country that uses its system to advance one or more of these goals (Great Britain, the U.S.S.R., a third-world nation) and explore the differences between the system you selected and the American system. Consider the following:

   a. Differences in program content
   b. Degree of government control
   c. The amount of entertainment material available and its nature
   d. Available evidence indicating the degree to which broadcasting is succeeding in advancing the desired goals

3. Study the noncommercial radio system in Great Britain with particular emphasis on the period before 1973 when all radio in the country was noncommercial. Report on or be prepared to discuss the differences between radio broadcasting in the United States and in Great Britain. Consider the following:

a. Source(s) of financial support
b. Levels of financing
c. Programming philosophies
d. Kinds of program offered
e. Classification of programs by type
f. Public reaction to the service

4. Report on or be prepared to discuss the extensive public debate that preceded the addition of a commercial television system to BBC-TV in Great Britain. Consider the arguments for and against commercial television and the relative merits of each in light of the British experience with commercial television.

5. Report on or be prepared to discuss the differences between the system of commercial television in Great Britain and the system in the United States.

6. Discuss some of the advantages to the listener of centralization of programming decisions and production. Weigh these against the disadvantages you feel are relevant and decide whether or not you feel such centralization would be desirable in the United States.

7. There are critics of broadcasting in the United States who say that the dominance of the three major networks (ABC, CBS, and NBC) creates a situation in which broadcasting—at least television broadcasting—in this country is just as centralized as it is in the European system. Examine this position and see what support you can find for it. What argument can be made against the position?

SUGGESTED READINGS

T. J. Allard. *The C.A.B. Story: 1926–1946, Private Broadcasting in Canada.* Ottawa: Canadian Association of Broadcasters, 1976.

Robert F. Arnove, ed. *Educational Television: A Policy Critique and Guide for Developing Countries.* New York: Praeger Special Studies, 1976.

Arthur L. Banks, ed. *Political Handbook of the World: 1976.* New York: McGraw-Hill, 1976.

B. D. Dhawan. *Economics of Television in India.* New Delhi: S. Cahnd & Co., 1974.

Walter B. Emery. *National and International Systems of Broadcasting: Their History, Operation and Control.* East Lansing: Michigan State University Press, 1969.

Timothy Green. *The Universal Eye: The World of Television.* New York: Stein & Day, 1972.

Sydney Head. *Broadcasting in Africa: A Continental Survey of Radio and Television.* Philadelphia: Temple University Press, 1974.

John Lent. *Broadcasting in Asia and the Pacific.* Philadelphia: Temple University Press/Heinemann Educational Books, 1977.

Anthony Smith. *The Shadow in the Cave: The Broadcaster, His Audience and the State.* Urbana: University of Illinois Press, 1973.

Walter Taplin, *The Origin of Television Advertising in the United Kingdom.* London: Pitman, 1961.

UNESCO. *World Communications: A 200 Country Survey of Press, Radio, Television, Film.* New York: Unipub, 1975.

H. H. Wilson. *Pressure Group: The Campaign for Commercial Television in England.* New Brunswick, N.J.: Rutgers University Press, 1961.

3

The Development
of American Radio

Broadcasting in the United States did not become an important agency of mass communication overnight. Like other forms of communication and entertainment, it developed slowly, and after more than half a century broadcasting is still changing.

For several decades before 1900, scientists had experimented with the transmission of wireless signals. In 1901, Guglielmo Marconi succeeded in sending a signal in Morse code across the Atlantic Ocean, and in the next few years, wireless was increasingly used as a means of point-to-point communication. In 1910, radio had developed sufficiently that Congress passed a law requiring installation of wireless equipment on certain passenger vessels sailing under the American flag. In the same year, Lee de Forest, who had earlier invented the audion tube, which made possible the transmission of music or of the human voice, put on the air what was possibly the first *broadcast*—the voices of opera singers Enrico Caruso and Emmy Destinn from the backstage area of the Metropolitan Opera House in New York. For the next half dozen years, various types of program materials were transmitted by other experimenters, but, in the main, radio in these years was seen primarily as a method of wireless point-to-point communication for international and maritime use. Following our entry into World War I in 1917, however, the government took over all wireless installations and brought experimentation with radio temporarily to an end.

When radio transmitters were returned to their private owners early in 1920, equipment manufacturers and amateur radio enthusiasts renewed their experiments with the broadcasting of radio programs—talks, vocal music, or music from phonograph records. These transmissions, like the de Forest experiment in 1910, were early forms of *broadcasting*—the dissemination of radio signals intended for·reception by the general public, as opposed to point-to-point communication by wireless. Listeners were few, however, because broadcasting had yet to be successfully exploited as a medium of mass entertainment.

Most historians consider that *regular* broadcasting in the United States began on November 2, 1920; on that date station KDKA at Pittsburgh reported the Harding-Cox presidential election returns by radio and inaugurated a regular daily program service. By January 1922, a number of other stations were also broadcasting regularly, and radio was beginning to be recognized as an agency of mass communication.

THE NONCOMMERCIAL ERA

During 1922, interest in radio increased tremendously. By the end of that year, licenses had been issued to 666 stations,[1] and receiving sets were in use in nearly a million American homes. The new medium had little resemblance to the agency of entertainment and information it was to become even half a dozen years later. Equipment was primitive; most stations operated with power of no more than 50 watts; only a very few stations were broadcasting on a regular daily basis, and those provided programs for only 2 or 3 hours each day. During those early years from 1920 to 1922, American radio was nothing more than an interesting novelty.

Early Radio Stations

Between 1923 and the end of 1925, the Department of Commerce issued an additional 766 licenses, bringing the total number of stations authorized to more than 1,400. Fewer than half of this number, however, actually went on the air, and many surrendered their licenses within a few weeks or months after the authorizations were issued. The 1925 annual report of the Department of Commerce indicates that only 571 stations were actually operating at the end of that fiscal year. Even the stations that stayed on the air had financial problems; until the late months of 1925, radio was almost completely noncommercial, and operating costs had to be borne by station owners themselves. Perhaps 30 or 40 of the "big" stations of the period were relatively well financed; these were outlets licensed either to major electronic companies that manufactured radio receiving equipment or to insurance companies, large-city department stores, or major newspapers, which received advertising value from the operation of their stations. Most early radio stations were small-time affairs, licensed to local radio repair shops, hardware stores, small daily newspapers, sometimes to operators of ballrooms or local motion picture theaters, frequently to private individuals who were simply "interested in radio" or who wanted the satisfaction of presenting their ideas over the air. Up to the end of 1925, licenses had also been issued to no fewer than 153 schools and colleges and to 71 local churches or other religious organizations.

[1]*The First Decade of Broadcasting* (New York: Broadcast Pioneers, 1958).

These smaller stations frequently operated for only an hour or two each week, often on a completely irregular basis. While owners of major stations provided budgets of several thousand dollars a year for their broadcasting operations, the annual expenditures of smaller stations were usually limited to a few hundred dollars. Even this was more than many licensees could afford; throughout the period, scores of stations surrendered their broadcasting licenses each year, to be replaced by other small stations.

In spite of the limited service available to listeners, the radio audience continued to grow. During 1923, the number of receiving sets more than doubled; by the late autumn of 1926, an estimated 5.5 million families owned radio sets. Practically all of the radio receivers produced before the autumn of 1925 were battery sets, using one "wet" storage battery similar to those used in automobiles, and two smaller dry cells; "plug-in" alternating-current receiving sets were not yet in general use. Each set was equipped with a pair of earphones, allowing only one person to listen at a time. Tuning was a complicated operation, requiring accurate adjustment of three tuning dials to bring in the signal of any desired station. Reception was usually marred by static or by interference from signals of other stations. Primitive or not, these early sets did bring in programs provided by broadcasting stations, and during evening hours they could pick up stations hundreds of miles away.

Early Radio Programs

Radio programs of the early 1920s reflected the conditions existing at the time—equipment was primitive, listening conditions were unsatisfactory, and in particular, almost no money was available to be spent on programs. Since radio was noncommercial, radio stations had no outside sources of revenues; what money a station owner was willing to spend usually went for improved technical equipment. So for programs, station operators depended on materials that could be provided without cost: talks and amateur musical recitals. Some of the larger stations did provide programs of other types, such as remote pickups of band concerts or sometimes of concerts by symphony orchestras; many also placed microphones in hotel dining rooms and broadcast dinner music by string ensembles or small orchestras. Of course some stations in larger cities experimented with broadcasts of baseball and football games or boxing exhibitions; but for all stations, talks and musical recitals accounted for at least 90 percent of all programming.

THE RISE OF COMMERCIAL RADIO

If programs were to be provided on anything but an amateur-talent basis, stations had to find outside sources of revenue. The money might come from a government-imposed tax on receiving sets, following the precedent already established in Great Britain, or it might come from sale of time to advertisers. Use of the first method would involve either government ownership of stations or at the very least a high degree of government control over privately operated stations; neither seemed consistent with our theories of democratic government. So following a series of conferences arranged by the Secretary of Commerce, the idea of government support was definitely discarded; broadcasting stations were left to finance themselves by the only other alternative available to them, the sale of time to advertisers.

Possibly the year 1927 can be designated as the one in which American radio became really commercial; it was the first complete year of operation of permanent commercial radio networks. For some years before 1927, however, a few stations had operated on what was at least partially a commercial basis. Station WEAF[2] in New York broadcast advertising programs as early as the autumn of 1922; other broadcasters followed WEAF's example, and by the winter of 1924–1925 a number of advertisers in large cities were using radio on a regular once-a-week basis. However, sponsored programs made up only a small proportion of the total program offerings even of major large-city stations. During a typical week in January 1926, station WJZ, one of the two or three leading stations in New York City, broadcast a total of 123 programs, of which only 6 were presented on time paid for by advertisers. Radio was becoming commercial, but through 1926 no station had advertising revenues large enough to pay ordinary costs of station operation.

However, the fact that even a few programs were sponsored had a decided effect on owners of radio outlets. If advertisers were willing to pay stations to carry their advertising messages, then broadcasting might in time become a profitable business. So by 1925 or 1926 station owners had a dollars-and-cents reason to spend money for improved equipment and to increase the power of their stations, in the hope of making their operations attractive to advertisers.

---

[2]Now using the call letters WNBC; WEAF later became the key station of the NBC Red Network.

"These commercials won't last long—people won't put up with them."

Station Licensing

Before 1926, broadcasting stations operated under authorizations granted by the Department of Commerce and issued on the basis of a 1912 act of Congress, which required licenses for stations engaging in point-to-point radio communication. When hundreds of applications for *broadcasting* licenses were filed in 1922, the department, in an effort to hold interference to a minimum, adopted the policy of specifying for each new station the frequency that station might use and the hours during which it might stay on the air. In 1926, however, a federal court held that the Department of Commerce had no power either to require stations to broadcast on assigned frequencies or to limit their hours of operation.[3] The result was chaos; stations changed frequencies at will and broadcast whenever they chose, regardless of conflicts with signals of other nearby stations using the same frequencies at the same time. Interference became such a serious problem that Congress was forced to take action. The result was the Radio Act of 1927, creating the Federal Radio Commission (FRC) and giving the regulatory body authority to specify in each broadcasting license the frequency to be used, the hours during which the station could operate, and the transmitter power permitted.

[3]"Breakdown of the Act of 1912," included in Frank J. Kahn (ed.), *Documents of American Broadcasting* (New York: Appleton-Century Crofts, 1973), p. 17.

The newly created commission took immediate steps to correct the situation. Many stations were taken off the air entirely. Those remaining were forced to comply with the commission's restrictions on frequencies, power, and operating hours. By the end of 1928, broadcasting licenses issued by the commission were held by 620 stations, of which 325 shared time with other stations using the same frequency and located in the same general area, while the remainder were authorized to operate on a full-time basis. Among stations on the air during the autumn of 1928 were 53 outlets owned by colleges or universities, 7 operated by public school systems, and 49 others licensed to churches or other religious organizations. Practically all the educational or religious stations were part-time operations, on the air for only 2 or 3 hours a day.

Most broadcasting stations licensed before the end of 1922 used power of 100 watts or less. Between 1925 and 1927, many stations—a majority of those still on the air in 1928—made increases in the power used by their transmitters, to enable their signals to be heard over larger areas. By 1925, most of the larger stations broadcast with power of from 1,000 to 5,000 watts. In 1927, WGY, the General Electric outlet in Schenectady, became the first station to operate with power of 50,000 watts—the maximum permitted for standard AM stations today. When the FRC announced a general reassignment of stations to new frequencies in 1928, power increases were authorized for some 200 stations; 10 major stations were licensed to operate with power of 50,000 watts, and 17 others to use power of 10,000 watts or more. However, in December 1928, approximately 150 stations were still broadcasting with power of less than 100 watts and some used as little as 5 or 10 watts of power.

Improvements in Equipment

At the same time that operating power was being increased, stations were making improvements in transmitting equipment and in studio facilities. Many stations built studios large enough to allow the origination of programs by full orchestras; some also made provision for the seating of studio audiences of as many as 100 people. Typical of the improvements in equipment was the replacement of the early carbon microphones by more effective types; by 1930, velocity or "ribbon" microphones had become standard in all but the smallest stations.

Equally important were improvements made between 1925 and 1929 in home receiving sets. New sets offered for sale in 1925 and 1926 had much improved circuits, which lessened static and interference problems. By 1926, too, the earphones of earlier years were being replaced by loudspeaker systems, allowing the entire family to listen at the same time. Most sets sold after the summer of 1927 were built to use alternating current so that a receiving set could be plugged into any regular electric outlet in the home; in cities, at least, cumbersome batteries were no longer needed. Another major improvement was the introduction, around 1927 or 1928, of single-dial tuning, replacing the three-dial system required on earlier sets. All these modifications encouraged family listening; instead of merely attempting to tune in distant stations, people increasingly were listening to the programs that stations offered.

Development of Networks

With stations operating more efficiently, and with improved reception and resulting increases in total listening, conditions were favorable for the next bold experiment in the development of radio—the establishment in 1926 of the first permanent radio network. The idea of linking stations together by telephone lines for simultaneous broadcasting of programs was nothing new; as early as January 1923 the first recognized "chain" broadcast had been presented over facilities of WEAF in New York and WNAC in Boston. Five months later, a program originated by WEAF was carried over an experimental network that included WGY in Schenectady, KDKA in Pittsburgh, and KYW in Chicago. By 1924 network broadcasting had so far developed that during the winter of 1924–1925 and again during the following season two different groups of stations were operating on an informal network basis; stations in each group broadcast programs simultaneously three, four, or five evenings each week. One of these informal networks had WEAF, then owned by the American Telephone and Telegraph Company (AT&T), as its New York originating station; the other was under the leadership of WJZ, also in New York, and owned by the Radio Corporation of America (RCA). Most of the stations in each group were owned by electronics companies.

    The success of these informal networks or chains of stations led to the incorporation in November 1926 of the National Broadcasting Company (NBC), a wholly owned subsidiary of RCA created for the express purpose of engaging in network operation. The new company inaugurated service on November 15, 1926, with programs fed by telephone lines to a group of 20 stations making up what was to be known as the NBC Red Network. Originating station for the chain was WEAF in New York, which RCA had purchased

Figure 3–1 Guglielmo Marconi (right) with David Sarnoff of RCA in the 1920s. (Courtesy Broadcast Pioneers Library)

from AT&T a few weeks earlier. On January 1, 1927, 6 weeks after the start of NBC-Red, the NBC Blue Network [4] commenced operations, with WJZ serving as its New York key station. For the first few weeks this second network group consisted of only five stations, all in cities in the northeastern or north central states, as were the

---

[4]The Blue Network continued as a part of the National Broadcasting Company until February 1942, when it was formally organized as a separate corporation. In October 1943 the new company was purchased by a group headed by Edward J. Noble. The Blue Network name continued to be used until June 1945, when the corporation was officially designated as the American Broadcasting Company.

stations making up the NBC Red Network. During 1927, service from both network groups was extended to several stations in southern or southwestern states.

In September 1927, a second company, now called the Columbia Broadcasting System (CBS),[5] entered the network field, providing service to another group of stations. The first CBS program was fed to sixteen affiliates, more than half of them located in cities having NBC stations. During 1927, none of the three networks had lines extending farther west than Omaha or Kansas City in the Plains states or Dallas in the southwest, although NBC was establishing a Pacific Coast network with affiliates in major cities from Seattle to Los Angeles. Coast-to-coast network service was inaugurated by the NBC Red Network in December 1928; within a few months, both NBC-Blue and CBS were also linked up with stations on the Pacific Coast.

Programs before 1930

Before the winter of 1924–1925, practically all programs presented by radio stations fell within the broad categories of talks, musical recitals, and remote pickups, with some stations providing music from phonograph records. During the middle 1920s, as larger studios became available, several of the more important stations began to provide more elaborate types of programs. Four or five stations in the midwest and south developed late-night programs using a loose variety form. Others scheduled programs featuring local dance orchestras. A few—WGY in Schenectady in partic- ular—experimented with dramatic programs presented by ama- teur actors; materials used were in most cases one-act plays written for production in theaters. A new form for radio was the program featuring a "song-and-patter" team, borrowed directly from vaude- ville. Several such teams of entertainers traveled from station to station on a sort of organized circuit basis, each team remaining not more than a week or two in any one city. During 1927 and 1928, a few stations carried weekly or daily variety programs on a semi- sponsored basis; an advertiser paid the costs of presenting the program, which carried his advertising messages, but no payment was made for station time. The earliest sponsored programs for

---

[5]The company was originally incorporated as the United Independent Broadcasters. Before the network's inaugural program, the company was purchased by the Colum- bia Phonograph Company and given the name Columbia Phonograph Broadcasting Company. In 1928, the network company was sold again, and in January 1929 it officially became the Columbia Broadcasting System.

Figure 3–2 William Paley, who has managed the fortunes of the Columbia Broadcasting System (CBS) since 1928. (Courtesy Broadcasting Pioneers Library)

which advertisers paid for both station time and production costs were usually straight talks. However, for a year or more before the establishment of permanent networks, many stations in large cities were presenting weekly sponsored musical programs, usually featuring small orchestras or novelty musical groups.

When national networks were organized, it was natural that their schedules should include a number of the programs already being presented on the networks' key stations in New York, usually programs featuring musical organizations. In addition, several elaborate new programs were developed, some paid for by sponsors, others provided by the network company on a sustaining basis.[6] During January 1927, the weekly schedules of the two net-

---

[6]A sustaining program is not sponsored and contains no advertising announcements; consequently it brings in no revenue to the network or station. In some cases, production costs of sustaining programs are paid by the station or network presenting them. In other cases, they are produced by an interested agency (for example, the Treasury Department, religious groups) and donated to individual stations.

works operated by NBC included a total of 22 hours of evening programs, of which 16 hours were sponsored. Among the programs presented by advertisers were a 1-hour variety program, an opera broadcast by the Chicago Civic Opera Company, a concert by a symphony orchestra, 12 hours of popular or concert music and two half-hour talk programs. Evening sustaining programs included a 2-hour symphony program, a 60-minute musical comedy, 2 hours of concert music, a 30-minute hymn program, a religious talk, and a 15-minute commentary on Washington politics. Daytime programming was limited to 4 hours of sustaining religious programs on Sunday afternoons, and three 15-minute sponsored cooking talks on weekday mornings. There were no dramatic programs, no daily news broadcasts, no audience-participation programs.

As the number of network programs increased during the next 2 years, music continued to dominate evening network schedules, and daytime offerings consisted entirely of various types of talks. However, a few new program forms were introduced. By the winter of 1928–1929, evening programs included a minstrel show, two programs featuring comedy patter teams supported by popular orchestras, and seven or eight dramatic offerings. Patterns of network programming were beginning to show the types of changes that were to characterize the next decade.

Revenues from Advertising

Although during the middle 1920s some stations carried sponsored programs, station advertising revenues were small. During 1926, all radio stations combined probably received no more than $200,000 from sale of commercial time. However, after permanent networks had come into being, expenditures for radio advertising showed a rapid increase. In 1927, radio's revenues from sale of time totaled $4.82 million; in 1928, the figure had reached $14.1 million; and for the year 1929, network and station revenues totaled approximately $26.8 million, of which all but $7.6 million went to network companies. Probably by the end of 1929 the two network organizations were on a fairly sound financial footing. The same could not be said of individual stations, whether network affiliates or independents. With annual station revenues averaging only about $12,000 per station—in addition to whatever payments were made by the networks to their affiliates—it is doubtful whether more than 100 of the 618 stations on the air at the end of 1929 had revenues great enough to cover costs of operation. Broadcasting promised a bright future, but in most cases the operation of a radio station was not yet a profitable undertaking.

THE DEVELOPMENT OF AN INDUSTRY

However, by the beginning of 1930 the foundation had been laid for what was to become an important American industry. Stations provided program service for listeners from coast to coast; national networks had been organized; radio had proved itself an effective advertising medium; and, most important of all, people were listening to the programs that networks and stations were providing. From 1930 until this country's entry into World War II in December 1941, radio found itself in a period of phenomenal expansion, becoming probably the nation's most important source of entertainment, an increasingly used vehicle for the carrying of advertising, and in the later years of the decade a highly significant source of information for the people of the United States.

The Expanding Audience

Radio's possibilities as an advertising medium were naturally dependent on the number of prospective buyers of advertised products who could listen to broadcast programs. From 1930 to 1941, the number of radio-equipped homes increased steadily. In 1930, homes with radio receiving sets had reached a total of nearly 12 million (46%)—more than double the number reported four years earlier. In 1935, almost 23 million families (67%) had access to radio; by 1940, there were nearly 30 million receivers (81%) installed in listeners' homes, and more than 7 million automobiles were equipped with radio sets. As the number of radio homes increased, the amount of listening done by members of family groups was also becoming greater. In 1930, the average radio set was probably used no more than an hour or two a day, partly because networks and many stations offered only a limited amount of daytime programming and partly because the number of outstanding evening programs was still decidedly small. But by 1940, average listening per home had increased to at least 3 or 4 hours each day; more good programs were available, stations were operating on a full-time basis, and people had developed the habit of depending on radio as their major source of entertainment. In 1940, any evening network program of average quality attracted an audience of from 4 million to 6 million families, while such favorites as *The Jack Benny Show* or the *Edgar Bergen and Charlie McCarthy* program had listeners each week in 9 million or 10 million American homes.

Network and Station Revenues

As radio listening increased, so did network and station revenues from the sale of time to advertisers. As shown in Table 3–1, the industry's total revenues doubled over the 5 years from 1930 to 1935, and almost doubled again between 1935 and 1940, and again between 1940 and 1945. Almost equally important was the fact that throughout the period a constantly increasing proportion of the industry's revenues from advertising went directly to stations, instead of to network companies. National advertisers, during the early 1930s, began to divert some of their radio advertising dollars to what has become known as *national spot advertising*, buying time for programs or in some cases for commercial announcements directly from stations in the areas or "spots" in which special advertising coverage was desired. Use of national spot advertising continued growing, and local merchants kept increasing expenditures for local radio advertising, so that starting with the year 1935, station revenues from sale of time exceeded the amounts spent each year for network advertising.

Table 3–1   Revenues of Radio Networks and Stations from Sale of Time— 1930 to 1945 (in Thousands of Dollars)

	For Calendar Years			
	1930	1935	1940	1945
From sale of time by networks	27,694	39,735	73,789	133,973
From sale of time by stations				
National spot	—	13,805	37,140	76,696
Local advertising	12,806	26,074	44,757	99,814
Total net time sales for the year	40,500	79,614	155,686	310,483

From annual reports of the Federal Radio Commission and the Federal Communications Commission.

The Station Situation

For several years after 1930, the number of radio stations remained practically unchanged. The economic depression and bank failures of the early 1930s resulted in a serious drop in local advertising and in station revenues. At the same time, operating costs increased, in part because new engineering standards announced by the Federal Radio Commission required stations to install additional and improved equipment. Nearly all stations lost money; some were forced off the air. Although a number of new stations had received authorizations, only 605 radio stations were in operation in January 1935, as compared with 620 to which the FRC had assigned frequencies in the autumn of 1928.

However, after 1934 the economic situation improved, and from 1935 to 1940 the number of stations steadily increased. The 1940 issue of *Broadcasting Yearbook* shows a total of 754 stations within the continental limits of the United States on the air in January of that year. Although in 1928 more than half of all stations shared time with others in the same general area, only 90 operated on a time-sharing basis by 1940; however, 97 others in 1940 had licenses for broadcasting during daylight hours only.

As shown in Table 3–2, increases in station power during the 1930s more than kept pace with the increase in the number of stations. In 1928, ten stations had been authorized to use maximum power of 50,000 watts. In 1935, a total of 27 were in the 50,000-watt category, and another was blanketing half the nation with full-time power of 500,000 watts—the highest power ever used by a standard AM station in the United States.[7] Five years later, the number of 50,000-watt stations had increased to 39, and an additional 140 stations used 5,000 watts power or more.

The amount of power used is a matter of considerable importance to standard AM radio broadcasting stations. Although power is not the only factor determining a station's coverage, high-powered stations serve substantially larger areas and provide stronger signals in their home communities than competing stations with less power; as a result, they usually have considerably larger audiences than other stations in the area. This in turn makes the high-powered station more attractive to national advertisers, so

[7]For nearly 5 years between 1934 and 1939, station WLW in Cincinnati was licensed to operate experimentally with power of 500,000 watts. At the end of its period of special authorization in 1939, the station returned to its earlier power of 50,000 watts.

Table 3–2   Radio Stations in Various Power and Operating Time Categories, 1928 to 1940

Stations Using Daytime Power of	November 1928 (Authorized)			February 1935 (On the Air)			February 1940 (On the Air)		
	Full Time	Share Time	Day Only	Full Time	Share Time	Day Only	Full Time	Share Time	Day Only
500,000 watts	—	—	—	1	—	—	—	—	—
50,000 watts	8	2	—	22	5	—	34	5	—
5,000 watts[a]	35	30	—	26	14	4	114	12	14
1,000 watts	36	49	—	119	38	19	89	26	30
250 watts	65	131	—	79	55	18	270	21	41
100 watts[b]	151	113	—	85	75	20	60	26	12
Totals	295	325	—	332	187	61	567	90	97

[a]Power classifications of 5,000, 1,000 and 250 watts include a few stations authorized to use power somewhat higher than the amounts given; for example, a few stations using 10,000 or 25,000 watts power are included with those with power of 5,000 watts.

[b]This category also includes some stations broadcasting with less than 100 watts power.

Figures for 1928 from the *Second Annual Report* of the Federal Radio Commission; those for 1935 and 1940 from listings in *Broadcasting Yearbooks* for those years.

at least in the case of AM radio stations, increased power generally results in larger total revenues and substantially greater profits.

Networks

The economic depression of the early 1930s had little real effect on the two national network companies. The nation's major advertisers were becoming more and more convinced of the effectiveness of radio advertising; as a result, network revenues continued to increase in spite of the depression. As shown in Table 3–1, network revenues from advertising expanded considerably over the period from 1930 to 1935, and almost doubled between 1935 and 1940. In 1934, the two network companies already in the field were joined by a third, the Mutual Broadcasting System, originally consisting of only four stations, WXYZ in Detroit, WOR in New York, WGN in Chicago, and WLW in Cincinnati. In 1936, Mutual added already existing regional chains in New England and on the West Coast, and the new network became an active competitor with NBC and CBS in the sale of time to national advertisers.

By 1930, approximately 130 stations were affiliated with NBC or with CBS, including all the stations licensed for the use of 50,000 watts power. At the beginning of 1935, NBC's two networks provided service to 89 stations, CBS had contracts with 96 outlets, and Mutual still included only its four original stations.[8] By January 1940, a total of 386 stations were affiliated with networks, including all 39 of the 50,000-watt stations and 116 others with power of 5,000 watts or more. Most stations without network connections were stations with limited power or outlets operating on a part-time basis.

As the size of networks increased, so did the number of programs provided for affiliated stations. In January 1930, the three then-operating national networks offered a combined total of approximately 60 hours of sponsored programs each week, including 7 hours of daytime programming. Five years later, the four national chains supplied a total of nearly 125 sponsored hours each week to their affiliates; about 80 hours represented sponsored evening programs, and the rest were programs broadcast during the morning or in the afternoon. In January 1940, the four networks combined carried sponsored programs totaling 156 hours a week, including 87 hours of daytime programs. Time devoted to sponsored evening programs decreased somewhat between 1935 and 1940, but the increased number of affiliates meant that each program was broadcast by a larger number of stations and that network revenues from sponsored programs were correspondingly greater.

The figures given refer only to *sponsored* programs provided by the various networks for their affiliates. In addition, schedules of each network included a substantial number of *sustaining* programs, which individual stations could broadcast or not broadcast as they wished. For example, in January 1940 the four networks supplied approximately 40 hours of evening programs and 80 hours of daytime programs each week on a sustaining basis—three fourths of the number of hours devoted to commercial programs. Many of these sustaining network offerings were inexpensive presentations of talk or light music provided simply to fill gaps in the networks' schedules. Others were programs of considerable importance, produced each week at network expense. During the early months of 1940, for example, the networks' sustaining offerings in-

---

[8]At this time WLW in Cincinnati, broadcasting with 500,000 watts power, was a member of the Mutual network; however, the station also carried both NBC-Red and NBC-Blue programs and occasionally, by transcription, programs from the CBS network.

cluded 18 hours of serious music each week—a broadcast of a complete opera as well as concerts presented by ten of the nation's leading symphony orchestras. Also carried by the networks without sponsorship were several religious programs, four or five weekly discussions of important public issues, a farm information program 6 days a week, a few educational programs for children of school age, and about 30 news and commentary broadcasts each week.

The Expanding Industry

With four coast-to-coast networks, more than 700 commercial stations, and revenues from sale of time totaling more than $150 million a year, radio by 1940 had become a major business enterprise. Equally important, it had become a very complex business involving a wide variety of special services beyond those provided by networks and stations. To secure network time, and in many instances to develop and produce programs for their clients, the major advertising agencies were forced to create special radio departments. News-gathering agencies originally established to provide a wire service for newspapers expanded their activities to serve broadcasting stations.

Scores of new enterprises came into existence, some to act as sales representatives for stations in dealing with national advertisers, some to provide libraries of transcribed music for the use of broadcasters, some to develop and produce "package" programs to be carried on network schedules, and some to provide transcribed programs for use by stations on a syndicated basis.[9] Music-licensing agencies were established to collect royalties from networks and stations for use of copyrighted music; research organizations were set up to provide information concerning the number of listeners reached by sponsored network programs. Radio had its own national trade association, the National Association of Broadcasters (NAB), and most states had their own associations of broadcasters. Of course, as the industry's revenues increased, unions were organized to represent network and large-city station employees of almost every type, from actors to musicians and from writers and directors of programs to technicians and engineers. Administrative personnel and those engaged in sale of station or network time were not represented by unions.

---

[9]Functions performed by many of the most important components of the broadcasting industry are discussed in more detail in Chapter 6.

Industry Problems

The development of radio into an important industry brought new problems into being for operators of networks and stations. One such problem involved the use by broadcasting stations of news from the wires of national news-gathering agencies—the Associated Press (AP), the United Press (UP), and the International News Service (INS). Disturbed by the increasing number of news programs carried by stations and networks during the early 1930s, publishers of newspapers determined to cut off the supply of news materials used on such programs. Pressure was exerted on the three news services; the result was that in 1933 the three news agencies announced that they would no longer accept radio stations or networks as subscribers, and that the news materials they provided could not be used even by stations owned by newspapers. The following year, a compromise arrangement was worked out between broadcasters and the news services under which a newly created organization, the Press Radio Bureau, would supply a limited amount of headline news each day to broadcasting stations, which in turn were required to advise their listeners to read local newspapers for complete details. The arrangement did not satisfy the radio industry; networks moved in the direction of setting up news-gathering organizations of their own, and many stations subscribed to a newly created news service, Trans-Radio, which undertook to provide national news for the exclusive use of radio stations. Within 2 or 3 years, UP and INS gave up the fight and again made their services available to networks and stations. In 1939, AP formally withdrew restrictions on the use of its news on radio, and a year later activities of the Press Radio Bureau came to an end.

Another problem for broadcasters involved royalties to be paid for the use of copyrighted music. Even before radio became important in the economic field, holders of music copyrights had been organized in the American Society of Composers, Authors and Publishers (ASCAP) to collect royalties from theaters, ballrooms, and producers of motion pictures for public performance of music. When radio became a commercial undertaking, ASCAP issued licenses allowing stations to broadcast music in return for payment of annual fees usually based on station revenues. As revenues of stations increased during the 1930s, license fees also increased. In 1937, ASCAP officials announced that when existing contracts with radio stations expired in December 1939, the new contracts would call for annual payment of license fees equal to 5 percent of total station revenues. At this, the broadcasters rebelled. The NAB was authorized to set up a new licensing agency to provide music for radio use. The new organization, Broadcast Music, Inc. (BMI), came into existence in 1939; it entered into contracts with a number of composers and music-publishing firms designating BMI as licensing agent for the music they produced. However, very little BMI music had become available by the end of December 1939 when the ASCAP contracts expired; for several months during 1940 networks and stations were forced to depend primarily on music in the public domain for the programs they presented—music on which copyrights had expired and which was not under ASCAP control. The competition provided by BMI ultimately forced ASCAP to moderate its demands, and since 1941 most broadcasting stations have had licensing contracts with both organizations.

A third problem faced by broadcasters in the late 1930s involved relations with the most powerful entertainment-industry union of the period, the American Federation of Musicians. To make work for its members, the federation in 1937 announced its intention of requiring broadcasting stations to employ as regular staff members a number of union musicians, the number employed by each station to be determined by a quota arrangement based on the station's annual revenues. The following year, contracts were signed with most stations, putting the union's demands into effect. Networks and recording companies were forced, under threat of strikes, to refuse program service to any station failing to meet the union's requirements. The contracts with the union were declared illegal by the U.S. Department of Justice, so upon their expiration in 1940 they were not renewed. However, the pressures on networks and recording and transcription companies continued, so even without contracts stations found it expedient to employ their previously assigned quotas of union musicians. Finally, in 1946, Congress amended the communications act, specifically outlawing any use of threats to require any broadcasting station licensee to employ "any persons in excess of the number . . . needed to perform actual services."

An event of major importance to the broadcasting industry was the enactment by Congress of the Federal Communications Act of 1934, replacing the Federal Radio Commission with a new seven-member Federal Communications Commission (FCC) as the regulatory body for radio. The new agency was granted substantially the same powers over radio that had been exercised by the FRC; in addition, the FCC was given the responsibility of regulating interstate wire communication by telephone and telegraph.

Of importance, too, was the reorganization in 1938 of the National Association of Broadcasters, making the organization a much more powerful and influential representative of the broadcasting industry. In 1939, the NAB adopted a new and much more vigorous industry code of ethics, setting up standards with respect both to program content and to advertising and creating a code compliance committee to insure station adherence to provisions of the code. From the late 1920s to 1935, the NAB code had related only to fairness in advertising; in 1935, provisions were expanded to include some aspects of programming; the 1939 code was expanded even more, and included among other things specific limits on the time that might be devoted to advertising in any broadcast program.

Network Programs, 1930 to 1941

If radio's economic development during the 1930s was impressive, the advances made in network programming during the period were little short of spectacular. Broadcasting had become an important advertising medium; if network advertising was to be effective, programs carrying advertising messages had to capture the attention of large numbers of listeners. Networks were forced to develop more attractive programs than the talks and musical offerings provided during the first 10 years of radio's history. With advertisers willing to pay the bills, money was not a limiting factor. So beginning in 1929 and 1930, radio entered an era of program experimentation, invention, and development without parallel in any other period in the history of broadcasting, or of any other branch of the entertainment industry. Within 6 or 7 years, more than a dozen new program forms appeared on network schedules—new at least to radio, since some were borrowed from the theater, the motion picture, or the vaudeville stage. In fact, almost every type of program used on television today, from variety to situation comedy and from quiz shows to documentaries, had its broadcasting genesis in the radio developments of the 1930s.

A stimulus to program experimentation was the tremendous success of the *Amos 'n' Andy* series, first scheduled on the NBC Blue Network during the season of 1929–1930. The combination of comedy, excellent characterization, use of the same leading characters in a continuing dramatic series, and effective use of radio's ability to stimulate the imaginations of listeners brought *Amos 'n' Andy* a tremendously large and loyal audience; during its first two seasons on the air, it is estimated that the program was heard each evening in more than half of all radio-equipped homes.

 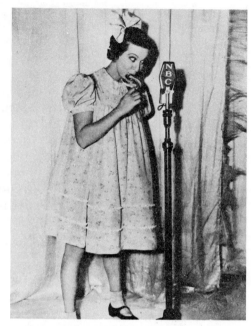

Figure 3–3 a. Rudy Vallee, host and star of an early variety program which introduced many radio performers who later became well-known. (Courtesy Broadcast Pioneers Library)

b. Fanny Brice moved from the Broadway stage to create the "Baby Snooks" character popular on radio for years. (Courtesy Broadcast Pioneers Library)

Variety and Music Almost as attractive to listeners were radio's new variety presentations. An early form of variety had been introduced on NBC's schedules before 1930; each week's broadcast offered a different general type of material, from short dramatic sketches to debates between congressmen. Closer to present-day forms on television were (1) a vaudeville type of variety, first introduced in the autumn of 1930 and using a different lineup of "guest" acts from vaudeville each week, and (2) the comedy-variety form, built around a featured "name" comedian and one or more permanent secondary characters, which appeared a year later. By the winter of 1933–1934, more than a dozen comedy-variety shows were presented by national networks each week, featuring such established comedy stars as Eddie Cantor, Al Jolson, Will Rogers, Ed Wynn, and Fred Allen, along with a comparative newcomer named Jack Benny. Other variety forms introduced during the early 1930s included the "barn dance" or "country and western music" type of program, the form of daytime variety used in the Blue Network's *Breakfast Club* (which started its long network run in the autumn of 1932), and the "amateur contest" form, of which the *Major Bowes Amateur Hour* was the most successful radio example.

No really new forms appeared in the field of musical programming, although by 1934 or 1935 the novelty musical groups of early network days had disappeared, their places taken by popular dance bands. A substantial number of concert-music programs were carried during the 1930s, but the form used was essentially that of the concert hall, transplanted to local and network radio in the middle and later 1920s. One new idea did make its appearance in the field of popular music with the introduction of the program *Your Hit Parade* in the autumn of 1935; in each broadcast, the *Hit Parade* program presented instrumental or sometimes vocal versions of the "top tunes" of the week. Possibly this program was the inspiration for the "Top 40" concept of formula program so widely used by radio stations since the late 1950s and early 1960s.

Dramatic Programs   Broadcasts of dramatic materials became increasingly popular during the 1930s as network program fare. Radio's first dramatic offerings were anthologies, using a new situation and a completely new set of characters in each broadcast. The earliest network anthology series was *Collier's Hour*, first presented in 1927–1928 and using dramatized adaptations of short stories appearing in current issues of *Collier's* magazine. But the dramatic anthology had by far its greatest success in the *Lux Radio Theater* program, which started a run of more than 20 seasons on network schedules in the autumn of 1934. The anthology idea was also used in a number of programs of the detective or adventure type, from *Empire Builders* and *True Detective Mysteries*, both carried on network schedules as early as 1928 and 1929, to the *Warden Lawes* series, *Gangbusters*, and *Famous Jury Trials*, all introduced several years later.

However, only a very small proportion of radio's dramatic programs during the 1930s and later were presented in anthology form. Far more successful were the new types of programs introduced during the 1930s; these programs, like *Amos 'n' Andy*, used the same leading character or characters in each broadcast in a series— situation comedies, adventure programs, crime-detective programs, late-afternoon "action" programs for children, and certainly women's daytime serials. Showing the prevalence of imitation in programming is the fact that although 30-minute situation comedies were offered in the late 1920s, the phenomenal success of the 15-minute *Amos 'n' Andy* caused network companies to offer situation comedies only in 15-minute serialized form until the pattern was broken by the introduction of *The Aldrich Family* in 1939. Although evening crime or adventure dramas—*Sherlock Holmes* in 1930 and the highly successful *Lone Ranger* starting in 1934—were presented as 30-minute programs, the 15-minute serial idea dominated late-afternoon "action" programs for children throughout the 1930s. Serials reached their greatest importance in daytime

"But if you listened to the radio all the time, what did you *look* at?"

dramatized stories presented for women listeners—programs presented in 15-minute episodes, five times a week, and usually with a woman character in the leading role. Interestingly enough, the earliest "daytime serials" for women were presented in early evening hours—*Myrt and Marge, The Goldbergs,* and *Clara, Lu and Em,* all introduced during the 1931–1932 season.[10] Serial stories for women, once introduced as daytime features, rapidly dominated daytime network schedules; by the beginning of 1940, no fewer than 57 different serials were being presented five days a week, all but four of them carried either by CBS or by NBC's Red Network.

Other Types of Programs Most of the program forms used on radio or later on television were direct borrowings from other and older agencies of entertainment: musical programs from the concert stage, the recital hall, or the ballroom; variety programs from the vaudeville stage or from the Broadway revue; anthology drama from the legitimate theatre; serial drama from the action-suspense two-reel serials presented in motion picture theaters. The continuing dramatic series used on radio and presenting the same leading characters in each broadcast was probably an adaptation of a similar form used in motion pictures, especially in western shorts and

[10]*The Goldbergs* had been carried on network evening schedules during the two preceding seasons, but as a once-a-week, 15-minute program, presumably not using serial form.

occasionally in full-length family dramas. However, one category of radio programs that developed during the 1930s was original with radio and had no counterpart in any other medium of entertainment—the group of programs involving audience partici-pation and depending largely on human-interest values to hold the attention of listeners. Some of these programs were simply inter-views with "ordinary people"; others, like *Professor Quiz* or *Old Time Spelling Bee*, both introduced during 1936–1937, made use of a contest or quiz element and were the forerunners of the "game shows" extensively used on daytime television later. Still others were presented for comedy values; *Truth or Consequences*, first broadcast in the autumn of 1940, made use of various "stunts" by people selected from the studio audience. A variant on the audience-participation idea was introduced in 1938 in *Information, Please;* the program used a quiz format with questions directed at a permanent panel of celebrities; it was the first of the panel shows, which were later to become popular on television.

Along with entertainment features, radio networks offered news and commentary programs. Such programs had been included on network schedules from the beginning of network operations in 1926. However, the programs of Frederick William Wile, H. V. Kal-tenborn, and David Lawrence were presented only once a week. They were limited to commentary concerning events in Washington and other capitals and made no attempt to provide up-to-the-minute coverage of the day's news. Network news broadcasting in the strict meaning of the term dates from the autumn of 1930, when NBC's Blue Network scheduled a 15-minute, early-evening news series five times a week featuring Lowell Thomas; CBS followed with a similar program a year or two later. News, however, did not become a really important part of network service until the late 1930s, when events in Europe created an intense interest in national and international affairs and when the ending of the "press-radio war" increased the availability of news materials for use both on networks and stations. One important innovation was the introduc-tion on CBS during the 1931–1932 season of the *March of Time*, a weekly 30-minute program dramatizing some of the major news happenings of the week. This program, modeled after the newsreels shown in motion picture theaters during the 1930s, was radio's first documentary series and was the forerunner of the broadcast documentary programs used on television today.

As might be expected, the introduction of a wide variety of new program forms combined with changing economic and political conditions brought about significant changes in the makeup of net-work schedules during the period from 1930 to 1940. As shown in

Table 3–3, music decreased in importance; there was a continuing increase in the use of variety programs and in various types of dramatic offerings; and in 1939–1940, 12 hours a week were devoted to quiz and audience-participation programs, forms not yet developed in 1930. Introduction of the daytime serial form during the early 1930s was followed by a tremendous expansion in the use of such programs to the point where they practically filled the daytime schedules of at least two of the four national networks. The threat of American involvement in the war in Europe stimulated interest in news and public affairs; by the beginning of 1940, networks were

Table 3–3   Hours per Week Devoted to Various Types of Network Radio Programs, 1930 to 1940

(During a typical week in January in each of the seasons indicated)

	Season 1929–1930	Season 1934–1935	Season 1939–1940
Evening or Sunday-afternoon Programs			
Variety, all types	8.0	21.0	21.0
Serious music	17.5	16.5	13.0
Popular music	33.5	37.0	22.0
Quiz programs	—	—	8.0
Human-interest programs	—	1.5	4.0
General drama	4.5	8.0	10.0
Informative drama	0.5	1.5	3.5
Comedy drama	3.0	2.5	5.0
Action, crime, mystery drama	1.5	9.0	10.5
Women's serial drama	—	3.0	—
Sports events	—	—	1.0
News, commentary	1.5	4.5	14.5
Miscellaneous talks	6.5	12.5	19.0
Daytime Programs			
Variety, all types	—	10.0	12.5
Popular or serious music	6.5	21.5	22.5
Human-interest programs	—	1.0	1.5
General drama	1.5	1.5	—
Informative drama	—	—	4.0
Comedy drama	—	3.5	1.0
Women's serial drama	—	12.0	75.0
Children's programs	3.5	8.5	7.0
News, commentary	—	—	3.0
Miscellaneous talks	12.5	24.0	11.5

Figures compiled from newspaper program listings for the weeks indicated and from programs listed in reports of national rating services; the table includes both sponsored and sustaining programs.

devoting more than 17 hours each week to news and commentary programs and presenting seven programs a week for discussions of important public issues.

Local Programming

Development in local radio programming was less spectacular than that on the network level; however, new forms were introduced and steady progress was made, especially after 1935 when stations were no longer seriously affected by the depression. Many of the program forms introduced on network schedules were originally developed by local stations; stations in turn borrowed many of the ideas made popular by the networks. By 1940, station programming was highly diversified. To begin with, station schedules included a wide variety of network offerings; more than two thirds of all stations had network affiliations and were devoting from 8 to 10 hours a day to network-originated programs. In addition, a number of syndication companies had been organized to provide nonnetwork musical programs, complete dramatic programs, and even daytime serials for station use. Network affiliates in 1940 devoted an average of perhaps an hour a day to the broadcasting of transcribed programs provided by these syndication concerns; nonnetwork stations, of course, made considerably greater use of syndicated materials.

Almost half of all station hours in 1940, however, were used to present locally originated programs. Nearly all stations carried several hours of live music each week; as a result of demands of the American Federation of Musicians, practically every station employed a few staff musicians on a regular basis, and used these musicians to present organ recitals, music by small orchestras, or in some cases fairly elaborate local variety programs. Many stations serving rural audiences scheduled live programs of country and western, or hillbilly, music. In addition, nearly all stations made considerable use of recorded or transcribed music. Most stations subscribed to a transcription library service; the music library included from 3,000 to 5,000 selections ranging from semiclassical and operetta music to novelty numbers and old familiar hymns; and most programs of recorded music were built from selections in these libraries rather than from recordings of current popular numbers. Around 1936 or 1937, many stations developed local amateur contest programs presented once a week; by 1940, however, most of these amateur programs had disappeared from local schedules.

Practically all stations depended heavily on the use of talk programs. Nearly every station had its women's program director who conducted a daily homemakers' program. Almost all stations that reached farm audiences had full-time farm program directors who presented farm market reports and other information of interest to farmers. Many stations had special programs for children, often combining storytelling and the singing of children's songs. A considerable number of radio outlets scheduled regular weekly programs developed in cooperation with local civic, educational, or women's groups. Interview programs were popular; perhaps half or more of the stations operating in 1940 carried a daily man-on-the-street program, in which a staff announcer interviewed passers-by from locations on downtown streets. Many stations also had regular programs that offered an opportunity for studio interviews with local leaders or with important visitors to the community. Of course, on Sunday every station broadcast at least one locally originated religious program and often one or more transcribed programs provided by national religious organizations.

News by 1940 was a staple in local offerings. Most stations scheduled at least three local news programs each weekday, in addition to the network news and commentary programs. A relatively small number of stations broadcast play-by-play accounts of local sports events on a regular basis; network commitments made such broadcasts difficult for affiliated stations except on Saturday afternoons. A few stations offered local weekly quiz programs; some also attempted locally produced dramatic programs, usually in cooperation with schools or colleges. In spite of the development of numerous new program forms on networks, stations for the most part depended on talks and musical programs to fill the time not required for network presentations, but these local offerings were of more varied types than those carried 10 years earlier.

Television before World War II

Although public attention was centered on radio during the 1920s and 1930s, the foundation was already being laid for a new form of broadcasting that after World War II was largely to replace radio as a source of home entertainment. As early as 1923, Vladimir Zworykin secured a patent on an experimental iconoscope tube using the principle of electronic scanning. Two years later, Charles F. Jenkins made the first wireless transmission of a motion picture—the earliest real television broadcast in this country—using the mechanical scanning method he had developed. In 1928, the General Electric Company broadcast the first television drama. Three years later, the Zworykin method of electronic scanning was being used in

Figure 3-4 David Sarnoff of RCA announcing the start of television broadcasting at the New York World's Fair, 1939. (Courtesy RCA)

York owned by RCA. By 1937, seventeen television stations were operating under experimental licenses; in 1939, the RCA station in New York presented regular daily broadcasts from the New York World's Fair and also experimented with television pickups of major league baseball and of a college football game. In 1940, a television station in Chicago broadcast portions of the Democratic national convention, held in that city; in addition, remote pickups were made from the Republican national convention in Philadelphia, with televised materials carried by coaxial cable to New York and broadcast by the RCA experimental television station.

Commercial television was introduced in 1941. In that year, the Federal Communications Commission issued orders fixing technical standards for visual broadcasting and establishing the channels on which stations might operate. In addition, the commission announced that it would grant licenses for stations desiring to broadcast on a commercial rather than an experimental basis; the beginning of commercial operation was set for July 1, 1941. Between July and November, five stations were granted commercial licenses: WNBT, now WNBC-TV, in New York, the former RCA-owned experimental station which had been transferred to NBC; WCBW, now WCBS-TV, also in New York, a CBS station; WPTZ in Philadelphia, owned by the Philco Corporation; WRGB, the General Electric

Company's station in Schenectady; and WBKB, owned by the Balaban and Katz motion picture theater interests, in Chicago. Other television stations continued under experimental licenses.

Although these five stations held commercial licenses, their operation during 1941 was only nominally commercial. WNBT in its first week of broadcasting in July had only four sponsors; from July through December the station took in less than $7,000 from its sale of time to advertisers. Other stations had even smaller commercial revenues. The reason was obvious: fewer than 10,000 television receiving sets were in existence even at the end of the year, and the audience that could tune in any television program was much too small to have commercial significance. With the entry of this country into the war late in 1941, commercial operation was practically abandoned; stations simply marked time, broadcasting for only a few hours each week until normal conditions returned and regular operation could be resumed.

RADIO DURING WORLD WAR II

During World War II, both industry and the American public were subject to wartime restrictions. Like most other forms of economic activity, broadcasting was directly affected by wartime conditions. Manufacturers of electronic equipment shifted entirely to production of materials used by the armed forces; private broadcasting stations were unable to secure new transmitters or technical equipment, and no new receiving sets or replacement tubes were produced for civilian use. In spite of shortages, there was some increase in the number of operating radio stations; by December 1945 approximately 940 stations were licensed and on the air. The number of radio-equipped homes also increased from an estimated 30.8 million in 1941 to almost 34 million (88%) in the autumn of 1945. Presumably some of the sets in the added homes had previously been second sets in the homes of relatives. In many of the 34 million radio-equipped homes, however, receiving sets were not in working condition by 1945, since in most communities radio tubes and other replacement parts were not available.

A major change in the network situation took place early in 1942. Complying with the "duopoly" order of the FCC that prohibited operation of more than one national network system by a single company, NBC turned over its Blue Network system to a separate corporation, which was later sold to a new group of owners. The new company ultimately became the American Broadcasting Company (ABC), while what had been known from 1926 to 1942 as the NBC Red Network remained simply as NBC.

Revenues from Advertising

In spite of the war, revenues from the sale of time to advertisers increased tremendously. As shown in Table 3–1, advertising revenues doubled between 1940 and 1945; of the approximately $310 million received by stations and networks in 1945, more than 43 percent went to the four national networks and another 24 percent represented spot advertising placed on stations by national advertisers. The increase in radio advertising was in part a result of a wartime shortage of newsprint that made it necessary for most newspapers and magazines to limit the number of pages in each issue and consequently the amount of advertising carried. Another highly important factor was the wartime federal tax structure, which imposed a tax of as much as 90 percent on excess profits of corporations. As a result, companies earning high profits from war production could buy broadcast advertising at an actual cost of only 10 cents for each dollar's worth of radio time; the remaining 90 cents would otherwise go to the government in taxes. Other factors undoubtedly contributed to the expansion in radio advertising as well, but no matter what the cause, during the war years radio networks and stations enjoyed the greatest period of prosperity that broadcasting had ever known.

Wartime Programming

Naturally, the war had its effect on programs. No major new program forms were introduced, but the fact that the nation was at war was strongly reflected in the content of programs offered, especially at the network level. A number of variety-program series were presented on a regular basis with servicemen as participants: *The Army Hour* and *Meet Your Navy* were typical titles. Service bands appeared each week on network schedules. Quiz shows and audience-participation programs had army and navy enlisted men as participants, almost to the exclusion of civilians. Documentary or informative dramatic programs dealt with activities of the Army Air Corps, the Army Service Forces, and various other military services; plot dramatizations made extensive use of wartime themes.

All entertainment programs, whether carried on network schedules or locally produced, carried "war messages" provided by the Office of War Information and the War Advertising Council urging listeners to conserve fats; to save copper, tin, and aluminum; to enlist in the various women's auxiliary military services; to contribute to the Red Cross or the United Service Organizations; or to buy government war bonds. At the same time, certain types of material were excluded from the air by broadcasters on the basis of guidelines provided by a government-established Office of Censorship; the ban covered information concerning troop movements, dates on which convoys were to sail, figures concerning production of war materials and supplies, even information concerning weather conditions. In addition, broadcasters were urged to take all possible precautions to see that unknown or unauthorized persons did not have access to microphones. As a result of government restrictions, all weather broadcasts were discontinued, as were interview programs of the man-on-the-street type and programs of recorded music in which either request numbers were played or in which numbers used were dedicated to friends of listeners who suggested such dedications.

War conditions also produced changes in the extent of use of programs of certain types on network schedules. In January 1941, the four networks devoted approximately 13 hours each week to news and commentary programs, all but 5 of these hours on a sustaining basis. Four years later, news accounted for a total of 34 hours a week—as much time as was used to present evening dramatic programs—with nearly 18 hours of the total sponsored. Almost equally dramatic increases were made in the areas of informative drama and of serious music; advertisers whose companies were engaged in war production showed a strong interest in sponsorship of prestige programs, with the result that by January 1945 networks were carrying nearly 5 hours of sponsored informative drama each week and more than 15 hours of advertiser-supported concert or classical music, including four weekly broadcasts by symphony orchestras.

As the war continued, however, network schedules also reflected the need for listeners to forget for a time the problems of everyday living, accounts of battles in faraway places, and the tragedy of casualty lists. Programs offering escape increased both in number and in popularity. Time devoted to evening comedy variety increased from 4½ hours to 8 hours per week between 1941 and the beginning of 1945. Situation comedy programs showed a similar increase, most of it after 1943. And evening "thriller" dramatic programs—

westerns, adventure stories, crime programs not related to the war situation—jumped from 9 hours a week in 1943 to nearly 15 hours in January 1945, although "problem" dramatic offerings decreased in nearly the same ratio.

Other changes in network and local station schedules were also taking place, some of which were to continue in the years ahead. By the start of the 1945–1946 season, the war had ended; but for the American radio industry, new and critical problems were ahead.

STUDY AND DISCUSSION QUESTIONS

1. Prepare a report summarizing the nature and extent of the contribution to broadcasting of an important figure in the history of the medium. The following are suggestions; there are many others.

   a. Heinrich Hertz
   b. Guglielmo Marconi
   c. Ernst Alexanderson
   d. J. Ambrose Fleming
   e. Lee de Forest
   f. David Sarnoff
   g. Frank Conrad
   h. Herbert Hoover
   i. John Brinkley
   j. Edwin Armstrong
   k. William Paley

2. Prepare a report on one of the following historical events of significance to the development of broadcasting.

   a. The sinking of the *Titanic*
   b. The conflict surrounding the acceptance of paid time (commercials) as the economic base of broadcasting
   c. The growth of radio networks
   d. Details of the settlement that led to the formation of NBC
   e. Details of the settlement that led to the formation of RCA
   f. The formation of CBS
   g. The formation of the Mutual Broadcasting System
   h. The formation of ABC
   i. The creation of the Federal Radio Commission
   j. The creation of the Federal Communications Commission
   k. Radio's troubles with ASCAP and the American Federation of Musicians
   l. The "press-radio war"
   m. The growth of advertiser control over network radio programming

3. The system of broadcasting that developed in the United States was based on individually owned local stations—many grouped into networks; financial support from the sale of advertising; and government regulation by a relatively independent regulatory body. As you saw in Chapter 2, this was not the only pattern that could have been followed in this country in the 1920s. Be prepared to discuss the following:

   a. The social and historical forces that contributed to the development of the system of broadcasting that evolved in the United States
   b. Alternative plans that could have been followed
   c. Your ideas on the restructuring of the United States' system (assume you have the power to do whatever is necessary to create a new system)

4. Report on or be prepared to discuss one of the following topics relating to radio programming in the 1930s and 1940s.

   a. The popularity and longevity of radio variety programs
   b. The development of the radio "soap opera"
   c. The development of radio drama as a unique form
   d. The use of radio for propaganda purposes in the United States during World War II
   e. The effects of "voluntary censorship" during World War II
   f. The growth in importance and popularity of radio news
   g. Changes in local programming in the decades of the 1930s and 1940s

5. Report on or be prepared to discuss the development of television in the United States before 1945.

SUGGESTED READINGS

Hugh G. J. Aitken. *Syntony and Spark: The Origins of Radio.* New York: Wiley-Interscience, 1976.

Erik Barnouw. *A Tower in Babel: A History of Broadcasting in the United States to 1933.* New York: Oxford University Press, 1966.

Erik Barnouw. *The Golden Web: A History of Broadcasting in the United States 1933–1955.* New York: Oxford University Press, 1968.

Frank Buxton and Bill Owen. *The Big Broadcast: 1920–1950.* New York: Viking Press, 1972.

Francis Chase. *Sound and Fury: An Informal History of Broadcasting.* New York: Harper & Row, 1942.

Herman S. Hetlinger. *A Decade of Radio Advertising.* Chicago, University of Chicago Press, 1933; reproduced by Arno Press, 1971.

Robert Landry. *This Fascinating Radio Business.* Indianapolis: Bobbs-Merrill, 1946.

Lawrence W. Lichty and Malachi Topping, eds. *American Broadcasting: A Source Book on the History of Radio and Television.* New York: Hastings House, 1975.

Christopher H. Sterling and John M. Kittross. *Stay Tuned: A Concise History of American Broadcasting.* Belmont, Calif.: Wadsworth, 1978.

Llewellyn White. *The American Radio.* Chicago: University of Chicago Press, 1947; reproduced by Arno Press, 1971.

4

Radio Makes Way
for Television: 1945–1965

At the close of World War II, in 1945, radio occupied an enviable position, both as an important and growing industry and as an influential American institution. Between 1940 and 1945, radio's revenues from sale of time to advertisers had practically doubled, reaching $310 million in 1945 (see Table 3–1). Even more important, radio enjoyed the confidence and approval of the American people to a degree rarely attained by any other institution in the nation's history. In a nationwide study in 1945, 82 percent of the respondents from coast to coast expressed the opinion that radio stations were doing either an "excellent" or a "good" job.[1] In comparison, churches received a similar vote of confidence from only 76 percent, daily newspapers from 68 percent, public schools from 62 percent, and local government agencies from 45 percent. Further, four out of five of those questioned believed that radio was "generally fair" in presenting both sides of public issues; only 39 percent expressed a similar feeling with respect to newspapers.

However, after the war, radio was confronted with serious problems, which were to produce revolutionary changes in programming and in the structure of the broadcasting industry itself.

THE POSTWAR ERA

Most historians of radio and television accept the year 1952 as marking the end of the era of radio dominance in American broadcasting and the beginning of the age of television in the United States. There were, of course, television stations and television networks before 1952, but in that year the Federal Communications Commission ended its 3½-year "freeze" on the licensing of additional television stations and permitted new stations to come on the air. Moreover, in 1952 the combined annual revenues of the national television networks were for the first time greater than those of the four long-established radio networks. The period between 1945 and 1952, then, was one in which television was growing in coverage and influence while radio—especially network radio—found itself faced with unaccustomed competition for the mass-entertainment audience.

World War II ended in 1945, and radio throve and expanded in the immediate postwar period. Receiving sets, not available during

---

[1] Paul F. Lazersfeld and Harry Field, *The People Look at Radio* (Chapel Hill: University of North Carolina Press, 1946).

the war, came on the market and the demand was tremendous. Between 1945 and 1950, approximately 67.5 million radio sets were produced by American manufacturers at a total retail value of almost $342 million. By 1952, almost 94 percent of all the homes in the United States had at least one radio and nearly half of the families in this country owned two or more sets.

Revenues from the sale of time also increased steadily during the postwar years, showing a gain of almost 50 percent between 1945 and 1950. This growth in total radio revenues continued after 1950, but the rate slowed, amounting to only 6 percent between 1950 and 1955. Radio was still an expanding industry, but the competition of television was making itself felt—primarily on network revenues.

Radio Network Problems

Networks in the postwar period were providing service to a constantly increasing number of affiliates. By 1952, the four major radio networks (NBC, CBS, ABC, and Mutual) were serving more than 1,000 stations. In addition, a fifth network, the Liberty Broadcasting System, had been organized in 1946 and by 1949 was providing a limited program service to some 300 stations. Radio networks, however, were hit hard by the rapid expansion of television after 1948. National advertisers shifted their accounts from radio to the newly organized television networks. As a result, the financially shaky Liberty radio network was forced to suspend operations in 1951, and the long-established radio operations of NBC, CBS, ABC, and Mutual showed serious drops in revenues. In 1948, radio network advertising revenues hit an all-time high of just over $141 million for the year—a figure never again reached by these networks. By 1952, radio network revenues had fallen by 22 percent (to $110 million) and for the first time were outstripped by television network revenues of $138 million.

Contributing greatly to the radio network problem was a decline in listener interest in programs offered on radio as television began to capture the public's attention. Ratings[2] of radio network programs dropped sharply as new television stations came on the air. In January 1948, the ratings of the ten most popular programs carried on national radio networks averaged 24.9; in other words, each program was heard each week in an average of approximately one

---

[2]A program rating is a figure representing the percentage of radio-equipped homes (or in the case of television, of television-equipped homes) in which, on a given date, sets are tuned to a specific program. A detailed explanation of the methods by which rating information is secured is given in Chapter 9.

fourth of all radio-equipped homes throughout the nation. Four years later, the ratings of the ten most popular radio programs then carried on network schedules averaged only 13.2—a little more than half the average reported in 1948.[3] Listeners were shifting from radio to television; inevitably, advertisers' interest in the use of network radio declined.

Radio Stations

While radio networks were suffering losses both in revenues and in public acceptance of programs offered, the situation of radio stations was, in the aggregate, more encouraging. The volume of advertising placed directly with stations rose from $176 million in 1945 to a 1952 total of $363 million. However, the increasing prosperity of radio stations was more apparent than real, since those aggregate revenues were divided among ever-increasing numbers of stations.

In January 1945, there were 933 standard (AM) radio stations on the air, virtually all of which had earned very substantial profits during the preceding 5-year period. Station operation, therefore, seemed a promising field for investors; and in the immediate postwar period, when transmitters and technical equipment were again available, there was a rush to secure authorizations for new broadcasting facilities. Frequencies were available, since the Federal Communications Commission (FCC) had modified its engineering requirements to reduce the mileage separation between stations assigned to the same channel. By the end of 1947, more than 1,000 new stations had been authorized; and, by the beginning of 1952, there were 2,331 AM stations on the air, with 70 others under construction.

At the same time, there was an equally impressive increase in the number of frequency modulation (FM) stations.[4] Frequency modulation was not new; as early as the summer of 1940 there were about 50 FM stations on the air, all operating on an experimental basis. Regular or nonexperimental FM broadcasting was authorized by the FCC in 1941. Because of the war, however, there was little FM development during the next 5 years, although by the end

---

[3]Averages in each case have been computed from rating figures reported in the National Nielsen Radio Index for the month indicated.

[4]Standard, or amplitude modulation, radio stations transmit on frequencies between 540 and 1,600 kilohertz; frequency modulation stations are assigned to much higher frequencies and also use a different method of modulating the signals transmitted. Radio stations are ordinarily referred to as AM and FM, depending on which kind of frequency they use.

of 1945 most of the existing FM stations held regular licenses. Postwar development of FM was impeded by a 1945 decision by the FCC to move this service to its present band of frequencies. All FM transmitters and receivers in service at the time were made obsolete by the decision.

Nevertheless, there was an expansion in the number of FM stations on the air in the postwar period. Established AM operations were encouraged by the FCC to open FM outlets; and, with permission to duplicate their AM programming on these stations, many did so. Some broadcasters, who feared the FCC might abandon the AM band entirely and permit only FM broadcasting, put stations on the air to protect themselves. Others wanted to take advantage of the higher fidelity and reduced interference of FM to broadcast "good music." Whatever the reasons, by January 1950, 733 commercial FM stations were in operation, in addition to a number of noncommercial FM stations.

The fact that many of the new FM stations were owned by operators of AM stations in the same communities and duplicated programming, however, worked against the rapid growth of this service. Stations that merely duplicated AM programming brought no additional revenues to their owners, many of whom were reluctant to invest in new programming in the face of the growing financial impact of television. After 1950, the number of FM stations took a downward trend that continued for several years. Even so, at the beginning of 1952, there still were 637 commercial FM outlets on the air, bringing the total number of AM and FM stations to nearly 3,000—three times the number of commercial stations in operation in 1945. Radio station revenue totals grew with the economy after the war, but the number of stations increased even more rapidly and average income per station showed a marked decline.

Postwar Radio Programs

Only one really new program form appeared on radio networks in the years following the war: the press conference type of public affairs program, of which *Meet The Press*, introduced in the autumn of 1945, was the most important example. However, important modifications were made in forms already used. The success of *Break the Bank* in 1945–1946 started a trend toward the use of "big money" in quiz shows. A year later, the audio-taping of *The Bing Crosby Program* marked the first use of prerecording in a national network program—until then virtually all network programs had been truly live performances. In 1947–1948, disc jockey programs were included for the first time on network schedules. Use of telephone calls to listeners as a feature of network quiz programs was introduced in the highly popular *Stop the Music* program in the autumn of 1948. In 1950–1951, *The Arthur Godfrey Digest* series on CBS inaugurated on network radio the use of recorded reruns of programs broadcast on earlier dates—a practice to become widely used on television networks a few years later.

Changes in Network Programming   Even more important were changes that took place in the relative use of various types of program between 1945 and 1952. Sponsored variety and musical programs showed a sharp decrease, largely as a result of the shift of advertiser interest to television. Quiz programs were more widely used from 1946 to 1950 than in any other period in radio network history; by 1952, however, only three such programs were sponsored each week on evening network schedules. The number of "thriller" dramatic programs increased tremendously; in January 1952, no fewer than 53 thrillers were presented each week during evening hours. Only half this number, however, were sponsored. Because thrillers could be produced at relatively low cost, they were used as sustainers to fill holes in network schedules created by the disappearance of sponsored evening variety and musical programs. The number of daytime women's serials continued to decrease, although in January 1952 more than 30 such programs were still carried by national radio networks. The canceled serials were replaced by daytime quiz and human-interest programs, which, by January 1949, filled thirteen half-hour periods a day on network schedules. Light variety programs were also used during daytime hours—such programs as *The Arthur Godfrey Program* on CBS and *Breakfast Club* on ABC occupied several hours of network time each week and continued to hold their attractiveness for listeners. In fact, daytime network radio had not been greatly affected by television in 1952, although evening radio network programs were rapidly losing popularity. The ratings of daytime programs showed only a slight decline, and the total number of sponsored hours of radio daytime network programming each week remained virtually unchanged between 1945 and 1952.

Local Radio Programming   Local radio station programming, like that of radio networks, changed materially during the 7 years following the war. The steady decrease in number of sponsored evening network programs created gaps in the schedules of local affiliated stations; and, in most cases, those gaps were filled by the least expensive and most easily produced kind of local programming available—

recorded music. For a time at least, loss of evening network programs created no financial problem for stations; revenues from sale
of spot announcements on the local record shows were usually
greater than the amounts networks had been paying the stations for
the time used by the canceled network programs. So, as sponsored
radio network programming decreased, network affiliates turned to
recorded music to fill the evening holes, while depending on networks to provide a variety of programs of other types, especially
during daylight hours.

The tremendous expansion in the number of radio stations,
however, meant that not all could secure network affiliations. A
majority of the more than 2,300 AM stations on the air in 1952
operated as independents. These nonnetwork stations were forced
to provide their own programs to fill their daily schedules, and they
naturally turned to the program material most readily at hand at
the lowest cost—recorded music. By 1952, on the basis of the programming they offered, radio stations fell into two basic groups.
The group affiliated with networks provided considerable variety in
programs and used recorded music only to fill the portions of each
day's schedule when network programs were not available. The
second group, made up of independent stations, used recorded
music all day long, almost without interruption. For these independents, program diversification of the type that had characterized
almost all radio stations before 1945 was simply impossible; they
broadcast "good" music or "popular" music or "Dixieland and
jazz" or sometimes "country and western" music—but their
schedules were filled with music.

Postwar Television

Television got off to a slow start in this country after the end of the
war. Between 1941 and 1945, ten television stations had been
licensed to operate commercially, but in January 1946 only six of
the ten were actually on the air. At the end of 1945, not more than
10,000 television receiving sets were in existence, all produced before 1942, and since tubes and repairs were not available during the
war period, few of these sets were still in working condition. During
1946, a few thousand additional sets were manufactured, but set
production on a large scale had to wait until final decisions were
made by the FCC on the channels to be used for television broadcasting. Originally, in 1945, thirteen channels in the "very high frequency" (VHF) band had been set aside for commercial television
operation, with the same channels to be shared with the military
and other nonbroadcasting services. The problem of channel alloca-

tions was not finally resolved until 1948, when the FCC dropped channel 1 from the list to which television stations might be assigned and reserved channels 2 to 13 in the VHF band for the exclusive use of television broadcasting stations. This allowed electronic companies to go ahead with the manufacture of television receiving sets. In 1948, a million receivers were produced, and more than 10 million additional sets were manufactured during the next 2 years. These early sets had very small picture tubes, usually only from 7 to 10 inches in diameter, although some of the higher-priced sets, costing from $350 to $400, featured 12-inch tubes. Receiving sets were available, however, and the way was open for the development of television as an agency of mass communications.

Since the consuming public owned very few receiving sets, construction of new television stations was slow for several years following the end of the war. At best, the construction of a television facility was not too promising an investment. To build and equip a station cost its owners from $750,000 to $1.5 million; and, after the station was on the air, it had to operate at a loss until enough receiv-

"What year was it that we moved from radioland to televisionland?"

ing sets were owned in the community to make the station attractive to advertisers. As a result, only one new station was added in 1946 to the six operating at the end of 1945, and only ten went into operation in 1947. However, with uncertainties about channels finally resolved and receiving sets in production, 1948 saw more broadcasters willing to gamble on the future possibilities of television and 33 new facilities were added. By the end of 1948, 50 stations were providing programs for viewers in major cities.

By 1948, however, the FCC had come to realize it had to make other hard decisions about television service for the nation. Even with only 50 stations on the air—many clustered in the crowded northeast—some interference between stations had already been noted. Further, the twelve channels in the VHF band simply would not be adequate to permit the number of stations needed to serve this country. Finally, color broadcasting was becoming commercially feasible and a choice between color systems had to be made. To allow time for the consideration and resolution of these questions, in October 1948, the FCC ordered a "freeze" on the processing of applications for new television stations. This freeze lasted until April 1952, almost four years, and during that period no construction permits were issued for new television stations. At the time the freeze was imposed, however, 109 stations were operating or had been authorized; and, by the early months of 1952, 108 stations had been constructed and were on the air.

Encouraging to owners of stations was the rapid increase, after 1948, in the number of television-equipped homes. By the end of 1949, receiving sets had been installed in an estimated 2.8 million homes (6%); and, by January 1952, 15 million families (34%) were able to receive television programs. The new sets were better adapted for family viewing than those available even a few years earlier. By 1952, manufacturers were producing sets with 20-inch screens; picture quality was much improved; "locked-in" tuning was standard on all sets, greatly simplifying reception of good pictures. Prices of the new sets were roughly the same as those charged in 1948; most of the 20-inch sets manufactured in 1952 were sold at retail for from $320 to $350, although some with smaller picture tubes could be bought for $275 or less.

Television Networks

National radio networks were not organized until hundreds of radio stations were already on the air. With television, however, the situation was different; networks existed before most stations. As early as 1945 and 1946, when fewer than a dozen commercial stations were on the air, television networks were being organized by four different network companies. One of the four was headed by Allen B. Du Mont, owner of one of the pioneer television stations in New York City. The other three were already operating as national radio networks: the American Broadcasting Company (ABC), the Columbia Broadcasting System (CBS), and the National Broadcasting Company (NBC). Each of the four television network organizations secured construction permits for network-owned stations in each of several major cities, and the radio network companies also urged their affiliates throughout the country to apply for television authorizations. Long before the new stations went on the air, their owners had signed television affiliation contracts.

By 1948, each of the four television network companies operated an eastern network linking together stations in cities along the Atlantic seaboard. In addition, ABC, CBS, and NBC had set up midwestern networks to provide television programs for outlets in Chicago, St. Louis, and Milwaukee. In January 1949, the American Telephone and Telegraph Company (AT&T) completed a coaxial cable connection between New York and Chicago, allowing eastern and midwestern networks to be linked together. In September 1951, AT&T completed microwave relay facilities to the West Coast for television network transmission so programs originating in New York could be broadcast simultaneously by stations from coast to coast. Not all network affiliates in 1952 had physical network connections in 1952, however. In many cases AT&T lines had not been installed to link these stations with the cable or relay systems used by the various networks. Network programs for these "noninterconnected" stations were provided in the form of kinescope recordings—films made from pictures appearing on the kinescope or picture tube of a television receiving set—shipped by mail or express to stations that used them.

The Television Industry

Television's rapid growth between 1948 and 1952 was stimulated by a number of conditions that had not existed during radio's early years. Radio in the 1920s was a new form of communication and its development as an advertising medium had to wait until receiving sets were available in millions of homes and until advertisers became aware of the advantages offered by radio. Services essential to the industry were developed slowly—even the *ideas* behind most of these services were completely new. Television, on the other hand, was simply an extension of radio, a somewhat different and perhaps improved form of radio broadcasting. The newly born televison industry of the late 1940s was built on a foundation created by radio. Its pattern of operation and most of its services had already been developed as parts of the radio industry. Of the 108 television stations on the air in the early months of 1952, 87 were owned by licensees of radio stations and three of the four television networks were operated by companies that owned established radio networks. Advertising agencies, station representatives, equipment manufacturers, program "package" production concerns, syndication companies—all of these already existed and had only to extend their operations into the television field. Even the program forms used on television had already been developed on radio.

Equally important, the financial support necessary for the establishment of television was provided in large part by radio. Profits earned by radio networks and major radio stations went into the development of television and the construction of television stations. When a new television station went on the air, it necessarily operated at a loss for several months, or even years, since the public bought receiving sets only *after* the station was on the air and was making programs available. Most of these losses were paid for out of earnings of radio stations whose owners had constructed the new television stations.

Television's development was at the expense of radio in other ways as well. Television was new and exciting while radio was already established. So network and station owners gave their first attention and devoted their energies to the new form of broadcasting; they largely ignored the needs of their radio operations. Advertisers were encouraged to shift their expenditures from network radio to television to help develop the new medium. Radio's most popular programs were moved to television networks—and few bothered to develop interesting new programs or new program forms to fill the places left vacant on radio network schedules. In financing, in program development, in interest and attention, the broadcasting industry robbed Peter to pay Paul and contributed directly to the decline of network radio and the drop in listener interest in programs that radio still provided.

Television benefitted from the situation, however; and the development of the new television industry was rapid, even though networks and stations were forced for several years to operate at a loss. In 1947, combined revenues of the seventeen television stations on the air at the end of the year were less than $2 million; expenses were many times greater. The following year, television stations and networks had a combined operating deficit of nearly $15 million; in 1949, with more stations, the deficit was more than $25 million. In 1950, television stations collectively had revenues large enough to equal expenditures, but networks still operated at a loss. Finally, in 1951, television operators were making money; networks reported net profits of $12 million on total revenues of $132 million; the 92 stations not owned by network companies had revenues of $107 million, of which $31 million represented profits.

Early Television Network Programming

In programming no less than in finance, television owes a tremendous debt to radio. Virtually all the program forms used on television were first developed on radio. Not only program forms but also actual programs that had won popularity as radio offerings were moved bodily from network radio to network television. During the first 2 years of television network operation, more than 20 of television's most popular programs, such as *Arthur Godfrey's Talent Scouts, Suspense, Studio One, The Life of Riley, Lights Out, The Goldbergs, The Fred Waring Chorus and Orchestra, Break the Bank, The Aldrich Family,* and the *Martin Kane* detective series were taken directly from radio network schedules. The use of programs already established on radio contributed in no small measure to television's early success in attracting loyal audiences.

Although television networks borrowed heavily from radio to fill their program schedules, television was a new medium, different from radio, and television producers were forced to learn from experience what types of programs the public would find most attractive. Between 1948 and 1952, network schedules changed tremendously from year to year. In 1948–1949, the first full season of network operation, more than 30 percent of all sponsored evening network programs were broadcasts of sports events—basketball, boxing, bowling and wrestling—perhaps reflecting the fact that during that season a large proportion of television receiving sets were located in bars and taverns. A year later, however, with sets installed in a much greater number of homes, sports broadcasting accounted for less than 5 percent of evening network hours. Emphasis had been shifted to early-evening children's programs, reflecting the greater use of television in the home. In January 1950, children's programs made up more than one fourth of all sponsored hours between 6:00 P.M. and 11:00 P.M. on schedules of television networks. Like sports broadcasts the previous year, however, they retained their position of importance for only a single season.

Network programming in 1950–1951 was strongly influenced by

Figure 4–1 a. Jack Benny, who starred on radio and television from the 1930s to his death in 1974. (Courtesy Broadcast Pioneers Library)

b. Red Skelton, another popular radio comedian who successfully made the transition to television. (Courtesy Broadcast Pioneers Library)

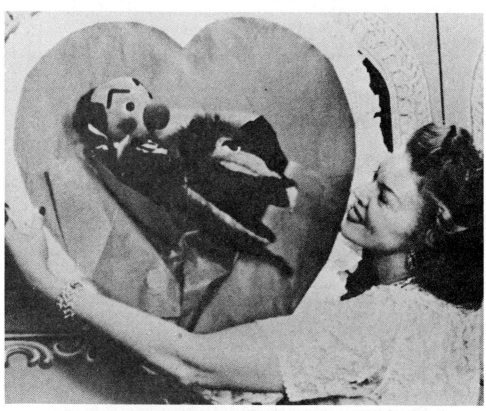

c. Fran Allison, with Kukla (left) and Ollie (right) of the *Kukla, Fran and Ollie Show*, popular on television in the early 1950s. (Courtesy Broadcast Pioneers Library)

the early successes of such variety shows as Milton Berle's program *The Texaco Star Theatre* and Ed Sullivan's *Toast of the Town.* In January 1951, no less than 24 hours on evening schedules were devoted each week to the presentation of sponsored variety programs. Once again, however, after one season programming patterns changed. Most of the network variety shows involved the use of vaudeville acts, and the supply of such acts was quickly exhausted. By January 1952, time devoted by national networks to evening variety shows had dropped to 15 hours a week, and the number of variety programs decreased even further in later years. In 1951–1952, dramatic programs replaced variety as the dominant form—during that season anthologies, thrillers, and comedy dramatic programs filled nearly 40 percent of the networks' evening schedules.

Local Television Programming

From 1945 to 1952, television stations provided a substantial amount of local programming—a larger proportion than in later years when network offerings had been increased and when large numbers of syndicated programs were available. With station revenues limited, the need was for programs that could be produced at a low cost, so stations experimented with many ideas. Some tried various types of disc jockey programs, without much success until a visual element was added by inviting local teenagers to the studio to dance to the music while on camera. Nearly all television outlets scheduled news broadcasts. Also widely used were programs of weather information, usually 5 to 10 minutes in length—weather maps and other reports were better adapted to use on television than radio. Most stations devoted from 30 minutes to an hour each day to homemakers' programs, usually originating from fully equipped kitchen sets. Another hour or more a day was used to present programs for young children, often featuring puppets. Many television outlets had daily programs of live music presented by small vocal and instrumental groups; a few provided fairly elaborate variety programs, often using amateur talent recruited in the community; several had daily or once-a-week local audience-participation shows. Other stations experimented with live coverage of "sports events" created solely for television coverage, like Roller Derby. Many of the stations on the air before 1952 invested in "remote" broadcasting equipment—trucks or buses carrying cameras and necessary equipment—to pick up local events of interest. In most cases, however, these failed to justify their costs and were little used past their first year or two.

Of course, even during the early years, stations made some use of syndicated film material. Many of the two-reel comedies and short subjects originally produced for use in motion picture theaters were available to television stations. The success on television of some of the early motion picture westerns—Hopalong Cassidy in particular—led to the filming and leasing to television stations of a number of adventure or western series produced especially for television use. In addition, in 1950 a few old theatrical feature films were released for television syndication—by the winter of 1951–1952, approximately 300 such complete features were available for broadcast. However, network programs and syndicated filmed materials filled only a part of the broadcasting day, and television stations in 1952 had to depend heavily on locally produced live programs.

BROADCASTING FROM 1952 to 1965

During the years after 1952 the same trends evident in the immediate postwar period of broadcasting continued. Television, with its networks reaching from coast to coast that year, grew steadily in popularity and in importance as an advertising medium, and radio became less secure as it struggled to find its place in the entertainment spectrum of the American people.

Radio Struggles to Adapt

The radio situation in the 1950s and early 1960s was filled with apparent contradictions as the industry attempted to compete with television. Sales of radio sets continued at a high level. From 1960 to 1965, an average of more than 20 million sets were sold each year, compared with an average of 12.5 million in the 1950–1955 period. The number of radio stations continued to grow, apparently reflecting a continued belief by many in the future of the industry. By January 1966, more than 4,000 AM stations and 1,400 commercial FM stations were on the air. Total industry revenues also increased steadily, as shown in Table 4–1, and by 1965 total revenues from sale of radio time amounted to more than $800 million—almost doubling the 1950 figure. These growth figures, however, concealed some internal inconsistencies that spelled trouble for many in the radio business.

Radio found itself the victim of circumstances that seriously injured many segments of the industry. As television developed, listeners spent more time watching television and less time listening to radio. As this decrease in audience size became evident during the early 1950s, national advertisers shifted their advertising expenditures from network radio to television, and as the attractive sponsored programs disappeared from radio network schedules, radio listening declined still further. On the surface, the situation for radio stations looked somewhat brighter, since local revenues almost tripled in the period between 1948 and 1965. However, the number of outlets to be financed by these revenues increased at virtually the same rate (from 2,079 to 5,083), and lack of balance in the distribution of this advertising money created serious financial problems for more than half of the radio stations on the air between 1958 and 1965.

Table 4–1 Annual Total Time Sales of Radio and Television Networks and Stations, 1948 through 1964   (in Thousands of Dollars)

	For Calendar Years				
	1948	1952	1956	1960	1964
Radio time sales[a]					
By networks	141,052	109,862	48,424	35,026	43,783
By stations					
National spot	104,760	123,658	145,461	202,102	232,038
Local	170,908	239,631	297,822	385,346	487,947
Total radio sales	416,720	473,151	491,707	622,474	763,768
Television time sales[a]					
By networks	2,500	137,664	367,700	471,600	562,800
By stations					
National spot	-0-	80,235	281,200	459,200	710,800
Local	6,200	65,171	174,200	218,800	275,700
Total television sales	8,700	283,070	823,100	1,146,600	1,549,300

[a] Figures represent gross billings, before deductions of commissions to advertising agencies and station representatives.

From annual financial reports released by the Federal Communications Commission covering the years indicated as reproduced in the 1975 *Broadcasting Yearbook*.

Even greater financial difficulties plagued the four national radio networks. As a result of television competition, the combined annual revenues of the four national network companies (plus, until 1956, income from regional networks) dropped from an all-time high of $141 million in 1948 to a low of $35 million in 1960. After that year, however, radio networks gradually gained strength, and, by 1964, revenues were approaching $44 million—more than $10 million below 1937 radio network revenues. This precipitous drop of revenues in the 1948–1960 period, of course, was the result of the steady disappearance of sponsored programs from network schedules. First to go were the popular programs of the pretelevision era. The winter of 1955–1956 found the four national networks providing a total of only 35 hours of sponsored evening programs each week. Even these disappeared over the next few years, and by 1960 only a few long-established news programs still remained on evening schedules.

Daytime radio programs survived a few years longer. As late as the autumn of 1955, the four radio networks still had sponsors for some 70 hours of daytime programming each week, but even these daytime programs were soon to disappear. By 1965, radio network service to affiliates was limited for the most part to headline-type news programs and short-talk features, with each network supplying an average of little more than 2 hours of programming a day to its affiliated stations, which were slowly recapturing some of their lost advertising revenues.

As television replaced network radio as a source of attractive programs, the amount of time devoted to radio listening naturally decreased. Reports released by the A. C. Nielsen Company show that, in the spring of 1949, receiving sets in radio-equipped homes were in use for an average of roughly 4½ hours a day. By 1953, average use of such home sets had dropped to 3 hours a day and by the spring of 1962 this average had dropped to slightly more than 1½ hours a day. Nielsen figures did not include out-of-home listening in automobiles or other places, of course, or in-home listening to transistor or other battery-powered sets; allowance for such listening would add considerably to the figures reported. (Indeed, a 1964 survey did indicate a total average listening figure of almost 2½ hours a day for out-of-home listening.) There is no question that, since the advent of television and the decline of network radio, in-home listening to radio has declined significantly.

The decline in radio listening, competition from television for advertising revenues, and the tremendous increase in the total number of stations among which radio's advertising revenues must be divided all contributed to the financial difficulties of many radio stations. Some radio stations still had substantial revenues from sale of time and still earned very satisfactory profits on each year's operation—especially those with high power and large-city locations. On the other hand, half or more of all radio stations eked out a precarious existence by cutting program and operating costs to the bone and either losing money on the broadcast operation each year or earning at most a few thousand dollars. Obviously, the difficulties of such stations had an effect on the quality of radio programming. By 1962, the situation had become so serious that the Federal Communications Commission attempted to deal with the problem of station overpopulation by ordering a partial freeze on the authorization of certain types of new AM broadcasting stations until more effective long-range policies could be formulated. The freeze, however, was by no means complete. New AM stations still came on the air at a rate of approximately 100 a year; and, in July 1964, the FCC ended its freeze on new authorizations and attempted thereafter to slow the increase of AM stations by tougher allocation rules. Even under these new rules, however, 342 applications for new AM stations were pending before the FCC in September 1965. This trend continued well into the 1960s, and by July 1968 the FCC felt the situation serious enough to impose another absolute freeze on AM allocations.

The explosive growth in the number of radio and television stations in the 20 years following World War II is illustrated in Table 4–2. The total number of radio stations more than doubled in the 4 years following 1946 and almost doubled again between 1950 and 1965. The rate of growth in the number of VHF and UHF television stations was much greater in the 1950s and 1960s. There were more than five times as many stations on the air in 1965 as in 1950.

Radio Network Programming, 1952–1965

In the years since 1952 the type of programming provided by radio networks and stations has changed almost completely. Networks had lost their once-popular evening entertainment programs by the late 1950s, and daytime network programs lasted only a few years longer. By 1956, radio networks were still offering affiliates some daytime variety shows, audience-participation programs, daytime serials, and sponsored religious programs on Sunday mornings. Most of these left the air during the next few years; and, by 1960, virtually the only programs remaining on daytime network schedules were ABC's *Breakfast Club*, Arthur Godfrey's program on CBS, a program or two of light music or chatter, some paid religious

Table 4-2 Broadcasting Stations in Operation on January First of Each of Six Selected Postwar Years

	On January 1st					
	1946	1950	1954	1958	1962	1966
Radio stations[a]						
Standard AM stations						
Commercial	913	2,051	2,487	3,156	3,653	4,018
Noncommercial	35	35	34	39	40	32
FM stations						
Commercial	48	733	560	537	960	1,466
Noncommercial	6	48	112	141	194	269
Television stations[a]						
On VHF channels						
Commercial	6	97	228	408	461	491
Noncommercial	—	—	1	22	44	61
On UHF channels						
Commercial	—	—	121	84	84	107
Noncommercial	—	—	1	5	18	44

[a] Number of stations in each case includes those licensed and on the air plus those operating with construction permits.

Figures supplied by the Office of Reports and Information of the Federal Communications Commission.

programs on Sundays, and a large number of news programs, most of them 5 minutes in length.

One network innovation that proved moderately successful for almost 20 years was the program form used in NBC's *Monitor*, a weekend combination of recorded music, news, and short features. Both CBS and ABC also provided a variety of short features to their affiliates, usually to be taped from the network line and inserted in local programs of recorded music; but network schedules in 1965 included little that resembled the type of entertainment programming provided for radio listeners during the 1930s and 1940s.

Local Radio Programming, 1952–1965

During the early 1950s stations affiliated with networks still depended on these networks for their most important programs. As network programs went off the air, however, stations filled their schedules with local programs of recorded music—the same type of programming widely used by nonaffiliated stations. A few well-established "old line" stations did attempt to preserve some degree of program variety by scheduling local talk shows, audience-participation programs, or even daytime variety, but these attempts were not usually long continued. By the late 1950s, probably 80 to 90 percent of all radio stations were filling most of their program time with recorded music, interrupted at intervals by short capsule news summaries either taken from network lines or provided by the station itself. Stations did differ, however, both in the type of music used and in the general manner of presentation. Most stations played nothing but currently popular music—the Top-40 records of the week; others made heavy use of "standards" (numbers popular in earlier years); still others featured country and western music. Some large-market stations used highly paid "personalities" as disc jockeys and included almost as much "chatter" as actual music in each program; others permitted only a minimum of talk by announcers. Many of the Top-40 stations tried to be different and to attract listener attention by using a variety of "gimmicks"—special sound effects to identify news programs or to accompany station identification announcements, giveaways, the organization of "record hops," shrill-voiced announcers, and elaborate contests used as station promotion.

After 1957 or 1958, however, a trend away from the dominance of Top-40 stations became evident. More radio stations throughout the country began to aim their programs at various special audiences. Some advertised themselves as "good music" stations and filled their schedules with show tunes, old standards, and, in some cases, semiclassical or even classical music. Others gave special attention to farm audiences, making heavy use of country and western music and expanding the time used for programs of farm information and weather reports. The country and western format also began to expand with considerable success into the medium and large urban markets. A considerable number of stations identified themselves as "Negro-appeal" stations, with much or all of their programming aimed at the interests of black listeners. A few stations even experimented with some success with an "all-request" format, but this seems to have been a short-lived phenomenon, at least as a format for the entire broadcast day.

Many stations gave increased emphasis to broadcasts of sports events and described themselves as "sports stations." Others expanded their local and national news coverage and broadcast several 15-minute or 30-minute news presentations each day while continuing to give 5 minutes of "news on the hour." In April 1965, a New York City station became "all news," filling its entire schedule with news broadcasts or commentary; and this format has been duplicated in other large markets, with varying degrees of success. Still others became "all-talk" stations, while at least one station in virtually every major market introduced daily all-talk programs ranging from 60 minutes to as much as 4 hours in length, including telephoned questions from listeners directed at speakers appearing on the programs. By the early 1960s, a few stations were even experimenting with dramatic programs, and a few syndication companies were supplying stations with taped or transcribed dramatizations of old network radio thrillers or once-popular daytime serials. Finally, in December 1965, a well-known broadcaster requested permission from the FCC to program an "all-classified ad" station in San Francisco. (Permission was granted in 1966, but the station was never a commercial success and the format was abandoned.) In short, it is difficult to characterize the radio programming of the early 1960s except to say that it was in a state of experimentation and change.

The Expansion of Television, 1952–1965

While radio was facing difficulties after 1952, television was experiencing a period of rapid development in number of stations, in size of audience, and in annual network and station revenues. In April 1952, when the FCC ended its freeze on the licensing of new television stations, it released at the same time an allocations table indicating the channels that could be used for commercial or educational television stations in each of about 1,300 communities. Since it was evident that the twelve VHF (very high frequency) channels already in use could not accommodate the number of stations that might be needed in the future, the allocations table provided for use by television of an additional 70 channels in the UHF (ultra high frequency) band. One channel in each of some 240 communities was reserved for use of noncommercial educational stations, and the remaining allocations were for stations to be operated on a commercial basis.

New Television Stations   By 1952, television was established as a potentially very profitable type of business enterprise. Consequently, when the FCC's freeze ended, there was a rush to secure authorizations for new stations, especially in larger cities in which VHF channels were still available. Within a month of the date on which the freeze ended, no fewer than 521 applications for new stations had been filed with the FCC, with many applicants competing for the same channel in most of the larger communities. By the end of the year seventeen new stations had gone on the air, and by January 1954, 356 commercial television stations were in operation. Expansion was less rapid thereafter, since the more desirable VHF channels in larger cities were already taken. By the beginning of 1966, though, a total of 598 stations were on the air.

Both revenues and net profits of television networks and stations increased tremendously in the years following 1952. In 1956, television revenues from sale of time and from other sources totaled $897 million, as compared with the $324 million received by networks and stations in 1952. Profits earned in 1956 were approximately $190 million, before federal taxes. By 1965, industry revenues had increased dramatically. Reports of the FCC showed network and station revenues for that year of almost $1.7 billion and total operating profits of more than $415 million.

Not all television stations shared in the industry's growing prosperity. Nearly all stations that had gone on the air before 1952 showed consistently high earnings, and, with few exceptions, they occupied the choice, large-market locations. Many of the newer stations, however, found conditions less favorable. Some had gone on the air in large cities as fourth or fifth stations, too late to secure network affiliations—with only three national networks after 1955, only three outlets in any one community could be network affiliates. Others were located in very small markets in which the advertising potential was limited, a few of them in small cities with populations of no more than 40,000.

Especially acute was the problem of the new commercial UHF stations. Many had been constructed in small, one-station markets; others were forced to compete with VHF stations located in the same communities. Unfortunately, the relatively limited coverage of UHF outlets, the greater susceptibility to interference and the fact that only a few receiving sets manufactured before 1964 had UHF tuning, all placed the UHF stations at a serious disadvantage. In fact, of the approximately 190 UHF commercial stations that had gone on the air between 1952 and 1964, only about half were still in operation in January 1965. The usually profitable business of operating a television station has not always proved profitable. Some stations have had extremely high rates of earning, but many others have had financial problems.

Network Developments   For the first few years after 1952, television stations received service from four networks: ABC, CBS, NBC, and Du Mont. The Du Mont network, however, encountered problems—as did the American Broadcasting Company to a lesser extent. During the early and middle 1950s, only half a dozen cities had more than three stations and many important markets only had two. From the beginning of television, with Du Mont starting from scratch and ABC struggling to become an independent entity rather than the ghost of NBC-Blue, NBC and CBS were the dominant networks and thus captured the most desirable stations. ABC had primary affiliations only in three-station markets, and Du Mont was placed in an even weaker position. Since Du Mont had never been able to offer many sponsored programs (and none of the big, outstanding "audience-pleasers" that other networks were providing), it was never able to secure more than a few stations willing to carry its entire commercial schedule. Naturally, lack of stations made it difficult for the network to find advertisers willing to sponsor programs. During the winter of 1953–1954, Du Mont was scheduling hardly more than a dozen sponsored programs a week, and a year later the number had dropped to only three or four. So after the middle of 1955, the Du Mont company gave up its network activities entirely, leaving only three television networks in the field.

In 1953, the competitive position of the American Broadcasting Company's network was improved when the company merged with United Paramount Theatres, thus acquiring a much-needed increase in operating funds. For almost 25 years, however, the ABC network was at a disadvantage in lining up primary affiliates. The steady increase in the number of major cities with three or more commercial stations did allow ABC to secure stations in most of the country's larger markets, but many of these affiliates occupied the less desirable UHF channels. In the 1976–1977 season, however, ABC's string schedule dominated the network prime-time rating race and, for the first time, ABC "won" in overall ratings for the season.

One result of this victory was the switch of several VHF affiliates from CBS or NBC to ABC, leaving the other two networks the choice of a UHF affiliation or no outlet in these markets. Analysts of network programming practices and performance estimated that the ABC schedule would remain strong through at least the 1978–1979 season. Such continued success should establish ABC as a virtually equal competitor to NBC and CBS in the network prime-time battle.

In an effort further to strengthen the financial position of the American Broadcasting Company, arrangements were completed in the autumn of 1965 for a merger with the International Telephone and Telegraph Corporation (ITT), a $2 billion concern. Unfortunately for ABC, this merger was opposed by the U.S. Department of

Justice, which managed to delay FCC approval for so long that ITT finally withdrew its request.

Color Television   The development of color television brought about another type of network rivalry. During the period of the television freeze, the FCC asked manufacturers of television equipment to demonstrate the color systems they had developed. In 1950, the FCC gave official approval to the system proposed by the Columbia Broadcasting System, which involved the use of a revolving color disc both on cameras and on receiving sets. Unfortunately, the CBS system was not compatible—programs broadcast in color could not be received at all on black-and-white receiving sets. Consequently, equipment manufacturers made virtually no attempt to produce sets using the CBS color system, and in the autumn of 1951 CBS gave up its efforts to secure industry and public acceptance of its color television technology. The Radio Corporation of America (RCA), meanwhile, had continued to work on its own color system—one using electronic scanning and producing color programs that could be received by both color and black-and-white

"I understand they had a very deprived childhood. Everything was in black and white."

sets. In 1953, the FCC gave official approval to the RCA color system; and, in November of that year, the National Broadcasting Company—owned entirely by RCA—transmitted an experimental program in color from New York to the West Coast. In the early years, when few color sets were on the market, NBC led the way in color programming, with a total of 35 to 40 hours a week in 1964–1965.

It can be said that color "turned the corner" for the networks, however, in the 1965–1966 season. Encouraged by the presence of color sets in nearly 3 million homes by early 1965 and by research reports showing that ratings of color programs were 80 percent higher in homes with color sets than in homes with black-and-white sets, NBC announced in the summer of 1965 that all but two of the programs on its evening schedule, as well as most of its daytime offerings, would be presented in color. The other two networks, which had made little use of color in earlier years, were forced to follow the NBC lead. In the autumn of 1965, CBS was presenting nearly half of its evening programs in color, and ABC used color for a little more than a third of its evening offerings.

Television Network Programs, 1952–1965

No entirely new program forms appeared on network television in this period, although some modifications had not previously been used on network radio. One was the talk-variety form, which combined rather lengthy interviews or talk features with variety materials; it was introduced in 1952 and was first used on NBC's *Today* and *Tonight* shows. Others were live-actuality broadcasts and filmed documentaries carried on a series basis; NBC's Sunday afternoon *Wide, Wide World* program, introduced in 1955, and the CBS *Twentieth Century*, which appeared two years later, were the earliest representatives of these types. Another new form, at least from the standpoint of emphasis, was what might be called satire-variety; the only example was the series *That Was the Week That Was*, a concept imported from Great Britain and carried on U.S. network schedules for two years starting in 1963. In addition, the "adult western" (a title created in the 1950s to describe westerns with more characterization and human problems than adventure) was first introduced on television network schedules in the autumn of 1955.

Major Program Trends

As might be expected, many important changes took place in the use of programs of different types on network schedules, as shown in Table 4–3. Nondramatic children's programs, sports broadcasts, and sponsored talk programs disappeared entirely from evening schedules; anthology drama was largely replaced by dramatic programs that used the same leading characters in each broadcast. Crime-detective programs and adult westerns reached a high point of popularity around 1960; following that year, the number carried on network schedules was considerably reduced. Major gains after 1960 were registered by general drama (already mentioned), variety programs, talk-variety—as

Table 4–3   Quarter Hours per Week of Sponsored Programs of Major Types on Schedules of Television Networks

	January 1950	January 1955	January 1960	January 1965
Evenings, after 6 P.M.				
Variety programs	38	48	20	42
Talk-variety	—	—	30	64
Musical variety, light music	19	14	22	22
Anthology drama	26	56	32	4
Other general drama	4	6	2	24
Crime-detective-mystery drama	12	24	46	28
Action-adventure drama	2	6	20	20
Adult western drama	—	—	66	22
Situation comedy	6	56	34	66
Theatrical feature films	—	—	—	24
Quiz, panel, or game shows	25	42	26	10
News broadcasts	11	24	11	26
Talks, forum discussions	7	7	—	—
Documentaries, informative drama	—	6	10	8
Play-by-play sports broadcasts	21	22	8	—
Children's programs, cartoons	24	19	6	10
Total quarter hours	195	329	333	370
Daytime, Monday through Friday				
Daytime variety or music	—	70	20	10
Talk-variety	—	80	40	40
General drama	—	—	20	10
Women's daytime serials	—	85	90	90
Reruns, filmed evening programs	—	—	70	100
Game shows, panels, human interest	10	80	120	120
News, 15 minutes or longer	—	—	—	10
Talks, miscellaneous	50	25	—	—
Children's programs	10	35	25	20
Total quarter hours	70	375	385	400

Figures for 1955, 1960, and 1965 based on sponsored programs listed in national Nielsen Television Index for months indicated; those for 1950 on sponsored listed in New York TV Nielsen Ratings for January 1950.

represented by NBC's *Tonight* show and unsuccessful attempts by
ABC and CBS to compete in the late evening (11:30 P.M. to 1:00 A.M.)
time period—and motion picture feature films. Time devoted to
news also increased, with two of the national networks expanding
their early evening news broadcasts to 30 minutes. Quiz shows,
panel shows, and audience-participation programs showed a consistent drop in evening use after 1955, although they continued as
popular features on daytime schedules.

One major change in television programming not shown in the
table was the extent of the trend toward longer programs. In
January 1955, the four networks then operating broadcast a total of
129 sponsored programs a week between 7:30 and 11:00 P.M.; apart
from sports broadcasts, 14 of these programs were 60 minutes in
length, 88 were 30-minute programs, and 22, including news broadcasts, were only 15 minutes in length. Ten years later, the three
national networks scheduled three 2-hour programs each week (all
motion picture feature film presentations), one 90-minute western,
49 hour-long programs, and 45 programs (most of them situation
comedies) 30 minutes in length. Between 7:30 and 11:00 P.M., 15-
minute programs had disappeared entirely from network schedules. The trend toward longer programs was undoubtedly related
to the decline in sponsorship of programs by a single advertiser
and the increasing use of multiple-sponsored or "participating"
programs—a development in network television advertising that is
discussed in Chapter 6.

A second major trend in network programming after 1952 was
the increasing use of programs produced on film, as compared with
live presentations. Particularly was this true in the case of evening
dramatic programs. Of the approximately 60 sponsored dramatic
programs carried on evening network schedules in January 1952,
only 18 were filmed programs, most of them of the action-adventure
type that could not readily be produced in television studios. By
1960, virtually all evening dramatic programs were on film; and, by
1965, according to figures in *Broadcasting Yearbook* for 1966, live
presentations accounted for only 24 percent of the networks' weekly
schedules with the remaining time divided equally between filmed
programs and those recorded on videotape.

Other Programming Features   Four other features of network television
programming in the 1952–1965 period deserve special mention.
One is the rise and fall of "big-money" quiz programs over the
period between 1955 and 1958. Programs like *The $64,000 Ques-
tion* achieved tremendous popularity during their first 2 years on

Figure 4–2 Hal March, host of *The $64,000 Question*, gives a contestant some reference books to study in preparation for his next appearance. (Courtesy Broadcast Pioneers Library)

network schedules, but audiences decreased rapidly, and programs of the type disappeared from the air after the discovery in the summer of 1968 that contests on some of the programs had been "rigged" in advance. A second feature was the increased use of special programs. In 1954, NBC broadcast the first of a long series of color "spectaculars"—a one-time musical comedy, *Satins and Spurs*, starring Betty Hutton. For the next few years, both NBC and CBS broadcast elaborate spectacular entertainment programs on a regularly scheduled basis. After 1957, however, such spectaculars were dropped from regular schedules; however, each of the national networks made frequent use of one-time entertainment specials featuring the top stars of Broadway, Hollywood, and network television, with a total of 170 such specials planned for the 1965–1966 television season on the three networks. In addition, networks made extensive use of documentary programs; during the winter of 1961–1962, five or six documentaries were presented in evening hours on a regularly scheduled basis. Since 1962, the trend has been away from the presentation of such programs in regular once-a-week series, but the networks usually managed to schedule a hundred or more documentary programs each year, in most cases as one-time special programs.

A third important trend in network television programming was the increased use of theatrical feature films in evening schedules. The trend started in the autumn of 1961 when NBC inaugurated a weekly *Saturday Night at the Movies* program; in 1962 ABC followed suit with a Sunday-evening program. By 1965–1966, feature films were scheduled on four evenings a week, and network companies were paying rental fees of from $500,000 to $750,000 per picture for the features presented. To insure a supply of first-run films for its programs, CBS in December, 1965 arranged with Warner Brothers to finance production of ten new theatrical features each year, budgeted at from $1 million to $1.5 million per picture; the films so produced were to be shown in motion picture theaters as well as on the network's programs.

A fourth conspicuous feature of network programming in this period was the tremendous increase in the broadcasting of sports events on Saturday and Sunday afternoons. Boxing and wrestling, popular as evening offerings in the early days of network television, disappeared entirely as network features; indeed, no regular broadcasts of sports events were included in evening schedules in the 1960s. But each of the television networks filled several hours of Saturday or Sunday afternoon time each week with broadcasts of major-league baseball, college or professional football games, and professional golf and bowling tournaments, with a variety of minor sports ranging from curling to European sports-car rallies thrown in for good measure.

Local Television Programming

The types of programs provided by individual television stations have reflected the changes in the availability of network and syndicated programs. In the very early 1950s, networks offered their affiliates a reasonably full schedule of sponsored evening programs but only a limited number of sponsored daytime shows. Consequently, stations had to depend on local live programs and syndicated materials to fill half or more of their total broadcasting hours. By the middle 1960s, however, network offerings had substantially increased; on weekdays during the winter of 1962–1963, NBC was providing its affiliates nearly 13 hours of sponsored programs a day, CBS nearly 12 hours, and ABC approximately 9 hours. In the late

1950s, the supply of syndicated materials available to stations also increased; in the early 1960s, however, few new filmed television series were produced for syndication, and the backlog of feature films available for first-run showing by stations was rapidly exhausted.

Surveys of station programming published in *Broadcasting Yearbook* for 1966 suggest the extent of changes that have taken place in the materials included in station schedules. In 1953, network affiliated stations were on the air for an average of 80 hours a week, and 49 percent of this time was filled by service from the networks. By 1965, total hours were up to an average of 119 and the percentage of network offerings had jumped to 64. In the same period, use of syndicated programs or feature films remained constant at about 26 percent. Network hours were taken from local-live hours. More than 21 percent of the programming of network affiliates had been live in 1953, while only 13 percent was live in 1965.

So, although the proportion of network programming rose from 49 to 63 percent in this period, and that of local programming dropped from 21 to 13 percent, local stations were still providing approximately the same number of hours of locally produced material in 1965 as in 1953. Virtually every station scheduled at least two local news programs a day, Monday through Friday, and many increased the length of at least one local daily news program to 30 minutes. Weather information was still important, and most stations offered separate sports news summaries once or twice a day. Some stations had farm information programs, usually scheduled before 8:00 A.M.; many more presented daily "women's interest" local programs, although the "kitchen" programs of earlier years were no longer extensively used. Nearly all stations devoted from 30 minutes to an hour of time daily to programs intended for younger children; clowns and puppets were still widely used and many of the children's programs included short filmed cartoons or short filmed subjects. A considerable number of stations experimented with live locally produced daytime variety shows on a daily or weekly basis; a few others carried local ad-lib dramatic courtroom programs; a somewhat larger number carried programs featuring interviews with local people or with important visitors to the community. Local television, then, was still varied and reasonably vital in 1965–1966, with a large number of stations still faced with the prospect of an expensive conversion to color equipment as the sale of color sets increased and the networks programmed more and more color shows.

STUDY AND DISCUSSION QUESTIONS

1. Report on or be prepared to discuss the reasons behind the rapid expansion in the number of AM radio stations in the period immediately following World War II.

2. Report on the rise and fall of the Liberty Network between 1946 and 1951.

3. Discuss the impact of television on radio. Consider the following areas:

   a. The shift of interest of broadcast professionals from radio to television
   b. The use by television, in its early days, of program forms and specific programs from radio networks
   c. The ability or lack of ability of radio "stars" to make the transition to the new medium
   d. The attempts by radio networks in the early 1950s to compete with television programming.

4. Report on or be prepared to discuss the development and growth of FM radio both before and after World War II.

5. Report on or be prepared to discuss one of the following topics relating to the early days of television.

   a. The emphasis on sports programming
   b. The "Golden Days" of live television drama
   c. The Kefauver and/or Army-McCarthy hearings
   d. Programming by independent television stations
   e. The causes and effects of the "freeze" of 1948–1952
   f. The development of color television
   g. The effects of rising production costs on patterns of advertising (sponsorship versus participation)
   h. The Du Mont network
   i. Local television programming
   j. The "quiz scandals" of 1958–1959
   k. The development of the "spectacular"

6. Report on or be prepared to discuss how local radio adjusted to the reality of television and retained its overall economic strength in the 1950s and 1960s.

SUGGESTED READINGS

Erik Barnouw. *Tube of Plenty: The Evolution of American Television.* New York: Oxford University Press, 1975.

Barry G. Cole, ed. *Television: A Selection of Readings from TV Guide Magazine.* New York: Free Press, 1970.

Paul F. Lazersfeld and Harry Field. *The People Look at Radio.* Durham: University of North Carolina Press, 1946.

Stan Optowski. *TV—The Big Picture.* New York: Collier, 1962.

Irving Settl and William Laas. *A Pictorial History of Television.* New York: Grosset & Dunlop, 1969.

Robert L. Shayon. *Open to Criticism.* Boston: Beacon Press, 1971.

Arthur Shulman and Roger Yorman. *How Sweet It Was: Television—A Pictorial Commentary.* New York: Shorecrest, 1966.

United States Congress, House of Representatives, Committee on Interstate and Foreign Commerce. *Network Broadcasting: Report of the FCC Network Study Staff* (often referred to as *The Barrow Report*), House Report 1297, 85th Cong., 1st Session. Washington, D.C.: U.S. Government Printing Office, 1958.

5

Broadcasting Faces New Challenges

In the previous two chapters we focused most of our attention on the history and growth of the broadcasting industry itself and touched only briefly on the regulation of broadcasting. In this country, of course, broadcasting has been regulated by some arm of government since 1912, and we will discuss specifics of regulation in Chapters 12, 13, and 14. In these earlier chapters, we emphasize the development of broadcasting as a business and the evolution of programming while touching only occasionally on matters of government regulation.

Since the mid-1960s, however, regulation of broadcasting by the Federal Communications Commission, the courts, Congress, citizens' groups and others has produced a series of challenges and changes that seem to go far beyond previous regulatory efforts in both breadth of issues and depth of effect. In the decade following 1965, the impact of regulation (taken in the broad sense discussed in Chapter 12) was felt in the areas of broadcast license renewal procedures, the length of license terms, ownership of broadcast properties, the relationship between station management and the community served, employment practices, coverage of controversial issues and political campaigns, limits on commercial time, control of programming by television networks, the content of network programming for the general public and for children, advertising on television, and network television news. In no other period in the development of broadcasting in the United States has the weight of regulation been felt, virtually simultaneously, over so broad a range of issues.

Because of this regulatory emphasis, we will begin this chapter in the middle of the 1960s and turn our attention first to a relatively brief overview of the major regulatory issues that broadcasters have faced since that time. The second half of the chapter will include the more familiar treatment of the evolutionary growth of the broadcast industry after 1965.

By the beginning of 1965, the structure of a broadcasting industry that would accommodate both radio and television could be seen fairly clearly. Television had established itself as the primary medium for entertainment, as measured both by audience size and total advertising revenues. Radio had passed through the worst of its adjustment to television and was finding a place by seeking specific audiences within the community and programming for them—primarily with music, but also with an ever-increasing emphasis on community involvement, fast-breaking news, and services during emergencies. (Many became particularly aware of this emergency service during the severe power blackout of November 1965, during which the only source of news and information for millions of people was battery-operated radios.) FM radio was showing signs of continued growth which was to be spurred by the approval of stereo broadcasting and a ruling by the Federal Communications Commission (FCC) requiring most stations licensed for both AM and FM to program at least 50 percent of the FM output independently of the AM—thus drastically modifying the common practice of an AM station simply duplicating its entire schedule on FM. As natural forces within a dynamic industry continued to bring about changes similar to those discussed in Chapters 3 and 4, color television, community antenna television (CATV), and satellite transmission grew in importance. Business continued to be good, overall (see Table 5–1); and, in the mid-1960s, broadcasting seemed destined to continue evolving in a familiar manner, shaped and influenced to a degree by the FCC, Congress, and the courts, but essentially determining its own future.

BROADCASTING AND ITS CHALLENGERS

After 1965, however, broadcasters were faced with a series of challenges and decisions that caused profound changes in the industry

Table 5–1   Annual Total Time Sales of Radio and Television Networks and Stations, 1965 through 1974[a] (in Thousands of Dollars)

	1965	1968	1971	1974
Radio time sales[a]				
By networks	44,602	54,700	55,100	60,300
By stations				
National spot	247,942	342,200	378,000	386,800
Local	535,238	733,400	954,600	1,308,800
Total radio sales	827,782	1,130,300	1,387,700	1,755,900
Television time sales[a]				
By networks	585,100	1,424,300	1,490,400	2,005,300
By stations				
National spot	785,700	1,009,800	1,022,800	1,336,100
Local	302,900	482,100	665,600	1,012,400
Total television sales	1,673,700	2,916,300	3,178,800	4,353,800

[a]Figures represent gross billings, before deductions of commissions to advertising agencies and station representatives.

From annual financial reports released by the Federal Communications Commission covering the years indicated.

and may continue to do so in the foreseeable future. The voice of the citizen, articulated by efficient and sophisticated groups, became an important factor in the regulation of broadcasting; the FCC found itself ever more intimately involved with the day-to-day operations of local stations and the networks; and the Federal Trade Commission (FTC) began moving with greater vigor and authority in its supervision of commercial practices. The courts, Congress, the administration, and, inevitably, in the face of such forces, the FCC took an ever-greater interest in program content; and the license that is the very backbone of any station operation seemed threatened by a series of court rulings and FCC actions.

All this activity on both the national and state level is closely intertwined and it is often difficult to separate the threads, but the natural evolution of broadcasting was channeled and shaped so persistently by these new challenges that we must consider them before turning to the more familiar questions of programming and industry growth. Since the stability of his license to operate is of such importance to any broadcaster, we will begin our exploration of this period of broadcasting history with a study of three court cases that seemed to place these licenses in some danger.

Threats to License Stability

The period between 1969 and 1971 has special significance to all broadcasters because in these years, the courts handed down three decisions that, in combination, would shake the industry to its roots. These decisions, *WHDH*, *WLBT*, and *CCC*, dealt with separate issues and were not closely related; but, when the dust settled, broadcasters found themselves confronting a host of new challenges and problems.

The WHDH Case   This long and complex case began in 1947, when several applicants filed for the same television channel in Boston, and it was not resolved until 1969. In 1957, WHDH, Inc. won a provisional right to operate on channel 5 in Boston, but a series of actions by the FCC and the courts involving, among other things, charges of improper influencing of an FCC chairman, had prevented WHDH, Inc. from securing final approval to operate on the channel. Then, in January of 1969, the FCC surprised virtually everyone by denying WHDH, Inc. the license and granting it to a competing group.

Some basis for the FCC decision derived from a 1965 policy statement that was designed in part to foster diversification of ownership of mass media.[1] Since WHDH, Inc. was also the licensee of WHDH-AM and WHDH-FM and was owned by a corporation that published two daily papers and one Sunday paper, the "concentration of media control" issue loomed large in the minds of many commissioners; and broadcasters in general saw the refusal to grant a license to WHDH, Inc. as a threat to all licensees—especially those owning AM, FM, television, and newspaper combinations.

The WLBT Case   While the *WHDH* decision really applied only to multiple-media owners, actions taken against the license of WLBT in Jackson, Mississippi, had implications for all broadcasters. Here again, the issues in the case are complex, revolving around allegations that the ownership of WLBT was not properly serving the minority citizens of its coverage area. Led by the Office of Communications of the United Church of Christ (UCC), groups of citizens from the Jackson area filed in opposition to the 1964 WLBT renewal and, after twice taking the case to the U.S. Court of Appeals in the District of Columbia, succeeded in blocking the renewal.[2]

The long-term significance of the *WLBT* case lies in the fact that it opened the door to the intervention of citizens' groups as parties before the FCC in renewal hearings. Before the *WLBT* decision, only other licensees alleging economic injury or electrical interference had been permitted to intervene in these hearings. Since the 1966 appeals court decision in the WLBT case, any interested group of citizens with the money and the desire has been able to come before the FCC, seeking to deny renewal to broadcasters they felt were not serving the public interest.

The CCC Case   The *Citizens Communications Center (CCC)* case,[3] decided in 1971, represented still another action by federal courts that had the effect of requiring the FCC to hear local groups that contested license renewal applications. Broadcasters had reacted to a sharp increase in the number of such contests after 1966 by turning to Congress for legislative relief. Before a license renewal bill satisfactory to both broadcasters and Congress could be passed, however, the FCC issued a policy statement to the effect that a licensee

[1]"Policy Statement on Comparative Broadcast Hearings," *in* Frank J. Kahn (ed.), *Documents of American Broadcasting* (New York: Appleton-Century-Crofts, 1973), p. 367.

[2]"*United Church of Christ I* and *United Church of Christ II*," *in* Kahn, p. 639.

[3]"The *Citizen Communications Center* Case," *in* Kahn, p. 666.

would be favored at renewal time if he could show that his programming had been "substantially" in tune with the needs and interests of his listening area.

The broadcast industry found this statement reassuring, but several organized citizens' groups disagreed and asked the federal appeals court in Washington, D.C., to overturn the statement. The court did just that in June of 1971 in its ruling on the *Citizens Communications Center* case. Broadcasters turned again to Congress for some relief, but by the mid-1970s no license renewal bill had been passed.

The *WHDH, WLBT*, and *CCC* cases have had a significant impact on the license renewal process. The *WHDH* decision seemed to indicate that the FCC was placing increased emphasis on the "concentration of media control" issue; the *WLBT* decision opened the door to the participation of citizens' groups in renewal hearings before the FCC; and the *CCC* decision forced the commission to hold hearings when there are competing applications at the time of renewal. Taken together, these three decisions gave a tremendous boost to the growth and actions of citizens' groups across the United States.

The Growth of Citizens' Groups   These groups moved slowly at first, uncertain as to how they should organize and what they should do. In January of 1967, the Office of Communications, United Church of Christ (UCC) announced a nationwide effort to force "balanced" programming by stations that carried "extensive propaganda" not balanced by opposing points of view, and it received grants of $85,000 from the Ford Foundation and others to support the program. Earlier, the Anti-Defamation League of B'nai B'rith had asked the FCC, without success, to deny license renewal to a station that had carried anti-Semitic material—even though the station had offered time to reply under the Fairness Doctrine. In 1967, however, the FCC acted on a petition filed by nineteen civic and religious groups and agreed, on the grounds of Fairness Doctrine violations, to hold hearings on the renewal of WXUR, a station in Pennsylvania owned by a theological school. An organization calling itself the Institute for American Democracy filed Fairness Doctrine complaints against several stations and began a campaign to educate the public to its rights under this doctrine. Commissioner Nicholas Johnson announced that he felt the FCC itself should be more active in encouraging and supporting citizens' groups on the local level.

Much of the early activity, then, focused on the Fairness Doctrine and program "balance." In 1969, however, a significant new pattern began to emerge. A number of viewer groups, aided by UCC, filed a petition to deny license renewal for KTAL, a local television station in Texarkana, Arkansas, because of alleged failure to meet the needs of blacks in the community. After a few months of negotiations, the groups agreed that they would drop the petition to deny in return for a number of promises by the station management. While much of the agreement involved services of the kind any station would be expected to provide, some of the promises included the hiring of black on-the-air reporters, regular announcements of the station's responsibility to consult with all community groups to determine needs and interests, and a policy of not preempting network programs of particular interest to any substantial segment of the community without previous consultation. For the first time a station, as a result of a petition to deny, had permitted significant input from the community in the formulation of basic station policies. The following year, in Atlanta, this strategy of using the threat of a petition to deny to back up a series of demands was successfully expanded to virtually all the stations in a single market. With varying degrees of success, the same strategy has been used in other communities since that time.

The FCC, while encouraging a "dialogue" between broadcasters and their publics, has looked with caution on these agreements. In a policy statement issued in December 1975, the commission declared itself "neutral" on the question of whether or not stations should enter into such agreements. Broadcasters were warned, however, that they must retain the responsibility for determining how to serve the public interest. No matter what the pressures, this is one responsibility, according to the FCC, that cannot be delegated to any group of citizens.

Citizens' groups continued to be active in the 1970s. "Women's Lib" organizations urged boycotts of products whose advertising they deemed degrading to the status of women. Community groups opposed changes of station ownership that would result in changes in programming format. Coordinated activities by viewer groups have resulted in agreements that more funds would be allocated to programming specifically for minority groups. Still other groups have filed petitions to deny, have seen some of their demands met, then have agreed to withdraw petitions if the licensees would reimburse them the cost of filing the petition in the first place.

The voice of the people has been heard and, as we will see in later sections, this voice has moved the FCC to an ever-greater involvement in the day-to-day operation of individual broadcast stations. Before turning to this, however, we will look at another series of threats to "license stability" that did not grow directly from actions by the courts or the public.

"When you get to that part about Nader, I want you to lower your voice and talk fast."

Diversification of Control and Multiple Ownership Since the early days of radio, Congress and the FCC have been concerned about the problems of concentration of control of mass media in too few hands. Indeed, one of the results of this concern was action to force NBC to sell one of its two radio networks in 1943. Concern with monopoly also lay behind the FCC rules prohibiting a licensee from owning more than one AM, one FM and one television station in a single market (the "duopoly rule") or owning more than a total of seven AM, seven FM and seven television stations throughout the entire country (the "multiple ownership rules"). Since 1965, however, the commission, the Congress, the courts, and the Department of Justice have expressed doubts about the adequacy of these rules.

In 1965, the FCC proposed limiting television ownership to a maximum of three stations in the Top 50 markets but this proposal was never applied to a transfer and was quietly dropped in February of 1968. The following month, however, the commission proposed another rule that would prohibit the licensee of an AM, FM or television station from acquiring a license for any other class of broadcast service in the same community. Under such a rule, an owner of an AM station could not purchase an FM or television station in the same market area. This proposal was adopted in 1970 and was promptly labeled the "one-to-a-customer rule." It was amended in 1971 to permit the transfer of AM-FM packages and stands today as an example of the commission's desire to achieve maximum diversification of media ownership with a minimum of disruption.

In this rulemaking, the FCC did not propose "forced divestiture" of holdings in a market that would have forced licensees to break up existing combinations. The "one-to-a-customer rule" applied only to transfers occurring after its adoption in 1970. Pressure from Congress, the courts, and the Department of Justice, however did force the FCC to consider such divestiture in a special category—multiple ownership that included newspaper ownership in the market—and in March 1970 it proposed a rule that would break up all such concentrations within 5 years of its adoption date.

This proposal was vigorously opposed by both newspaper and broadcast interests, and for 3 years the commission showed little inclination to pursue the matter. In January 1974, however, the Justice Department stepped in by asking the commission to deny the license-renewal applications of three newspaper-owned stations in the midwest. This action prompted the commission to resolve the matter, and in February 1975 it issued a ruling that pleased neither the Justice Department nor media interests. Backing away from the total break-up of all radio-television-newspaper combinations as "unduly disruptive," the commission banned any further acquisitions by any newspaper of a broadcast property in the same community; and it forced divestiture in only sixteen markets—those in which the only newspaper owner in town also owned the only radio or television station. The Justice Department felt this did not go far enough, and the owners of newspapers and broadcasting stations felt that it had gone too far, and both filed suit.

The United States Court of Appeals in Washington, D.C., overturned the FCC in 1977 and ruled that newspaper-broadcast cross-ownerships in the same market should be broken up unless it could be shown that such multimedia holdings were in the public interest. The court ruled further that the FCC must develop rules under which such "forced divestiture" should take place. Both the FCC and the National Association of Broadcasters sought Supreme Court review of this decision.

The FCC and Station Operation

The question of license stability was not the only problem to face broadcasters in the period after 1965. They also found themselves confronted by an ever-growing involvement of the FCC in the day-to-day operation of stations. Some of these incursions will be discussed below.

Ascertainment of Community Needs The responsibility of a broadcast licensee to serve *his* public is fundamental to the communications act, and the FCC has always placed great stress on the "local institution" concept of the broadcaster. In addition to entertaining his audience, each broadcaster is expected to know his community and its needs and interests and to devote some of his programming to those needs and interests. A concern that, in some cases, the voice of the public was not being heard, or attended to, by some licensees was expressed by the commission in a statement on programming policy issued in 1960.[4] This statement clearly spelled out the obligations of broadcast licensees: "The broadcaster is obligated to make a positive, diligent and continuing effort, in good faith, to determine the tastes, needs and desires of the public in his community and to provide programming to meet these needs and interests." In the same policy statement the commission announced its intent to modify a part of one of the forms used for license applications, renewals, and transfers to "require a statement by the applicant . . . as to (1) the measures he has taken and the effort he has made to determine the tastes and needs and desires of his community or service area, and (2) the manner in which he proposes to meet these needs and desires."

Many broadcasters found it difficult to grasp fully just what the commission was looking for in what came to be known as the "ascertainment" section of the application forms that were released in 1965 and 1966 and, for a few years, the FCC tried to clarify the situation with letters and public statements. In the late 1960s, however, the situation became so confused that the commission was persuaded to issue a "Primer" to answer the major questions raised by licensees. This 36-question Primer was released in 1971[5] and outlined in detail the steps a licensee must take properly to determine the problems of his community.

By 1971, of course, the turmoil introduced by the *WHDH, WLBT,* and *CCC* cases was creating an ever-growing backlog of contested renewal applications at the FCC, and the staff considered ways to reduce this burden. Reasoning that many petitions to deny stemmed

---

[4]"The 1960 Programming Policy Statement," *in* Kahn, p. 234.

[5]"FCC Ascertainment Primer," *in* Kahn, p. 316. The Primer was modified and reissued in 1976.

from a breakdown in the community dialogue that the ascertainment procedures were designed to encourage, the staff in 1971 made several proposals designed to encourage licensees and local groups to talk with each other and thus, perhaps, to resolve their differences before a dispute reached the commission level. Among these recommendations were regular announcements by all broadcasters encouraging comment and feedback from the public (these announcements, when adopted, were known as the "15-day announcements"); an expansion in the amount of material a station was required to keep in its "public file" (a file of documents and the like that must be made available to the public on reasonable demand); and a provision that television stations would be required to report annually on their programming related to community needs. These recommendations were adopted in 1973 and went into effect in 1974.

Equal Employment Opportunity   We have seen that after 1965 both the FCC and local minority groups, encouraged and assisted by well-organized citizens' groups, steadily increased pressures on broadcasters in the area of programming. Closely related to these programming pressures and to the "equal opportunity" spirit of the times, was the question of employment by broadcasters of members of minority groups. Reacting to a request from the United Church of Christ, the FCC in 1968 issued a policy statement declaring that license renewals would henceforth be denied to any station in violation of "national policy against discrimination in employment." At the same time, the commission proposed a rule that would require a licensee to demonstrate compliance with the principle of equal opportunity employment in a filing that would accompany any application for a new license, a license renewal, or a transfer. Finally, in what it called the most important part of its statement, the commission told broadcasters that "as a matter of conscience" they should go beyond simple passive compliance with the "national policy against discrimination" by taking affirmative action to seek out and train representatives of significant minority groups in their communities.

These rules were adopted, as were additional rules in 1970 requiring the submission of detailed equal opportunity policies and annual reports on job participation by minorities and women. These rules have been interpreted to mean that any licensee with a significant minority population in his listening area has a positive obligation to see to it that members of this group are employed by his station. Employment in menial or simple clerical tasks alone will not be satisfactory, nor will the commission accept the conten-

"I think I've found an Eskimo for that newscaster job."

tion that none of the applicants from the minority groups were qualified for a position of responsibility—in such cases, training programs must be established.

The Fairness Doctrine and the Local Station The ascertainment and equal opportunity issues discussed above affect both management and programming operations of local stations. The ascertainment rules set out a series of specific steps the licensee must take to keep in touch with his public and require him to devote some of his time to programming for that public. The equal opportunity rules go to the heart of management, dealing as they do with basic questions of hiring, promotion, and training. Still another FCC policy, the Fairness Doctrine, has an even greater effect on the day-to-day operations of a local station.

The evolution of the basic philosophy behind the Fairness Doctrine will be considered in some detail in Chapter 13. It is sufficient here to say only that the doctrine provides that if any licensee allows the use of his station for the presentation of one side of a "controversial issue of public importance," he is obligated to see to it that opposing views are also presented. The doctrine does not require that equal time be given to all groups holding opposing views. It tells the licensee instead that he must offer reasonable opportunity for the presentation of opposing views. He retains the right to choose who will present these views and how they will be presented.

This element of licensee discretion was restricted, however, in the late 1960s, when the FCC issued what came to be known as its "personal attack rules." Under these rules, a licensee whose station broadcasts an attack on the honesty, integrity, or the like of a group or person is required, within one week of the broadcast, to send a script, tape, or accurate summary of the attack, with an offer of time to reply, to the person or group attacked. These rules were upheld by the U.S. Supreme Court in a 1969 decision (*Red Lion*) that seemed to give even greater strength to the Fairness Doctrine and included the phrase "it is the right of the viewers and listeners, not the right of the broadcaster which is paramount."[6]

This latter phrase seemed to encourage both politicians and citizens' groups, and stations found themselves flooded by demands of individuals and groups demanding access to broadcast facilities. In 1970, the FCC ruled that licensees, if they wished, might decline to sell time for the discussion of public issues. The ruling was ultimately upheld by the U.S. Supreme Court, but this right to refuse access is limited. In the first place, it applies only to the first expression of opinion in a controversial case. The broadcaster, if he so desires, may decide that there will be no discussion of fluoridation on his station. However, if he allows one point of view on this issue to be discussed, he falls under the Fairness Doctrine and must seek out opposing views. Licensee discretion is further limited by the fact that the FCC has made it clear that it will not look with favor on a licensee who adopts a general policy of not permitting any discussion of "controversial issues of public importance."

The Federal Election Campaign Act of 1971   In 1971, the United States Congress took direct action that affected the operation of broadcast stations during election periods.

The act of 1971 limited the amount of money a candidate for federal office could spend on his campaign and the proportion of this money that could be allocated to electronic media. It required broadcasters who sold time to political candidates—federal, state, or local—to sell this time at the station's "lowest unit rate" for "the same class and amount of time for the same period." Finally, it required all licensees to provide a "reasonable" amount of time for candidates for federal office, without providing a definition of *reasonable*.

A 1974 amendment removed restrictions on the percentage of money that could be spent in broadcast media. Even as amended, however, the act enters the business operation of a station by forcing it to sell time for commercials to candidates at rates previously

---

[6]"The *Red Lion* Case," *in* Kahn, p. 412.

reserved for its best customers; and it includes the vague standard of "reasonable" access for federal candidates.

Limits on Commercial Time   From the days of the Federal Radio Commission, the regulatory body supervising broadcasting has been concerned lest individual stations devote too much of their time to commercials at the expense of service to the public. The National Association of Broadcasters has attempted to provide guidance to stations in the matter with its Code of Good Practices, which includes limitations on the amount of commercial time in a broadcasting hour. For radio stations, this limit is a flat maximum of 18 minutes. In television, the amount of time permitted for "nonprogram" material varies according to the class of time and station, but in no instance does it exceed 16 minutes per hour.

Subscription to this code is voluntary, however, with more than 60 percent acceptance by television stations and approximately 40 percent in radio. In 1963, the FCC attempted to adopt a rule that would force broadcasters to comply with the code limitations on commercials, but it was stopped by Congress. Not to be daunted, the commission then modified its license renewal forms to make clear that it expects broadcasters to adhere to the code limitations. Under some circumstances, slight variations from the time standards will be accepted, but the prudent licensee will keep his number of commercial limits in line with code requirements.

The FCC and the Networks

Most of our discussion to this point has focused on regulatory issues involving local stations and individual licensees. National networks, of course, are an integral part of the broadcasting industry, and, since 1965, they too have faced their share of challenges. The FCC can exercise no direct control over the networks, but it can regulate them through its authority over individual affiliated stations. Commission rules, for example, force the television networks to allow their affiliates to reject specific programs by a rule saying that no license shall be granted to a television station that has a contract with a network restricting such rejections.

Network Control of Programming   Most network challenges have focused on programming because, since the advent of television, the networks have assumed more and more control over the programming they carry. A study conducted by *Broadcasting* in 1965, for example, indicated that 91 percent of the prime-time network television programs were either produced or licensed by the major networks.

After wrestling with the problem through the 1960s, the FCC attempted to reduce this control by adopting what came to be known as the "prime-time access rule" in 1970. Under this rule, television affiliates in the Top 50 markets were prohibited from accepting more than 3 hours of network programming in prime time (7:00 to 11:00 P.M., Eastern Standard Time).

The 1970 access rule (dubbed "PTAR I" by *Broadcasting*) had a relatively short life. The FCC tried to revise it in 1973 but was stopped by a court ruling. In 1975, a third version (PTAR III) was approved by the FCC and was upheld by the court.[7] It retained the basic 3-hour limitations of PTAR I, but involved the commission closely in programming. The new rules would permit networks to carry, in the one "access hour" opened up between 7:00 and 11:00 P.M., children's programs, documentaries, public affairs programming, special news programs, half-hour news offerings following a local 60-minute news program, runovers of sports events, international sports events, New Year's Day college football, and special network programming filling the entire evening. By specifying that some programs would be approved and others disapproved in specific hours, the FCC took upon itself a measure of program control not previously exercised.

A suit filed in 1972 by the Department of Justice is aimed at reducing network control over programming on the grounds of possible antitrust violations. Tarred with the brush of "Nixon harassment," the original suit was dismissed by a federal judge. The suit was refiled, however, and is still pending.

Violence on Television   The question of violence in entertainment media, be they comic books, movies, or radio and television is raised regularly by concerned citizens and is usually debated to no useful conclusion. Television has not been spared this recurring inspection and has moved through several cycles of "nonviolent" programming prompted by congressional or FCC expressions of concern.

As violence spread across the country in the middle and late 1960s, the dominance and visibility of television made it a prime target of many seeking an explanation for the traumatic events of the period. The National Commission on the Causes and Prevention of Violence reported in 1969 that "research evidence strongly suggests . . . that violence in television programs can and does have adverse effects upon audiences—especially child audiences." In 1972, the

---

[7]*Broadcasting*, January 20, 1975, p. 5.

United States Surgeon General reported that televised violence has been shown to cause aggressive behavior in children who are already predisposed to such behavior. Following this report, the three networks united in saying that they were reducing the incidence of violence in all programming, with special attention given to children's programming.

Many were not satisfied with the network efforts, and in 1974 the move to curb violence took a new turn. Prodded by Congress to "do something" about violence and obscenity on television, FCC Chairman Richard Wiley entered into a series of discussions with network heads and the Code Authority of the National Association of Broadcasters (NAB). Presumably as a result of this "jawboning," the three networks, in 1975, agreed to the concept of a "family viewing hour," in which all programs would be appropriate for general family viewing. The NAB Code Authority followed suit by expanding this to 2 hours, from 7:00 to 9:00 P.M. (EST), and the 1975–1976 season operated under these restrictions. The lack of any clear definition of what constitutes material suitable for family viewing has made the networks uncomfortable and the producers of television programming unhappy; and a group of Hollywood writers, actors, and producers filed suit against the family-hour concept in late 1975.

Late in 1976 a court in Los Angeles ruled that the family-viewing self-regulatory concept was unconstitutional and that the policy had been adopted as the result of illegal government pressure. This decision, however, will be appealed and in the interim all three networks continue to adhere to its basic premises.

Network Programming for Children   Closely related to the question of violence is a concern for the nature of programming that is aimed primarily at children. Violence is not the only issue here; many suggest that the youth-oriented programming on Saturday and Sunday mornings amounts to an "intellectual wasteland," supplying the children with nothing of substance. Others complain about the amount, type, and tone of the advertising included in this programming.

Citizens' group activity on behalf of children's programming, led by a group calling itself Action for Children's Television (ACT), began to make itself felt in 1969, when the FCC was asked to take a close look at what *Variety* likes to call "kidvid" and to exert some control over this programming. Hearings were held, various congressional committies also expressed concern about children's programming, and in 1974 the FCC took action. Rather than issue the ACT-requested set of rules, however, it adopted a policy statement calling on stations to upgrade the quality of children's programming, to stop confining such programming to weekend mornings, and to pay special attention to advertising carried in the programs. The NAB Code Authority also moved at this time to tighten its restrictions on such advertising. ACT was not satisfied, however, and filed suit to force the commission to issue rules instead of a policy.

Network Advertising While local stations were harried by a Federal Communications Commission determined to limit the amount of commercial time they could carry, the national networks, all of which subscribe to the NAB Code of Good Practices, were faced with their own advertising problems.

Following the 1964 report by the Surgeon General that cigarette smoking could be dangerous to health of human beings, a ground swell of public opinion against cigarette advertising began to develop; and Congress ultimately banned all cigarette advertising on radio and television as of January 2, 1971. In mid-1967, however, the FCC had ruled that the subject of the relationship between smoking and health was sufficiently controversial and important to bring cigarette advertising under the requirements of the Fairness Doctrine. This action produced a rash of "anti-smoking" spot commercals that were carried in an approximate ratio of one "anti" to five "pro" commercials. Almost all of these were discontinued when Congress banned all cigarette advertising on radio and television in 1971.

By 1971, however, the FCC had discovered that it had opened something of a Pandora's box for itself with the 1967 cigarette ruling. In 1970, it had been asked to rule, under the cigarette precedent, that certain commercials for unleaded gasoline, detergents, high-powered cars, and some children's toys raised Fairness Doctrine questions. The commission consistently failed to so rule, but its decisions about unleaded gasoline and high-powered cars were reversed by the federal appeals court in Washington, D.C., in a ruling that further directed the FCC to restudy the entire Fairness Doctrine.

As a part of this mandated study, the FCC considered comments filed by the Federal Trade Commission (FTC). These comments urged the FCC to require broadcasters to carry "counter ads" in response to several types of advertising, including those making controversial claims or raising controversial issues, those based on controversial scientific premises, and those silent on negative aspects of the product.

In June 1974, the FCC completed its review of the Fairness Doctrine and issued a new policy statement. Among other things, the commission reaffirmed that it had never intended to establish the cigarette case as a Fairness Doctrine precedent, arguing that "we do not believe that the general product commercial can realistically be said to inform the public on any side of a controversial issue of public importance." The statement established a category of advertising known as "editorial advertising," which "actually consists of direct and substantial commentary on important public issues." Such advertisements would trigger the Fairness Doctrine, the commission said, but "standard product commercials, such as the old cigarette ads, make no meaningful contributions toward informing the public on any side of an issue," and the Fairness Doctrine should not be applied. The FTC proposals were quietly rejected in the same statement.

What one commission does, however, another commission can undo, and policy statement or no, the cigarette precedent still stands in history as an example for later "activist" commissions to see and study, as do the rejected FTC proposals.

Finally, during the decade after 1965, the Federal Trade Commission was given the power to require advertisers to support any comparative claims they make with hard evidence; to move decisively against any advertising it finds "misleading"; and to require advertisers to run "corrective ads" in cases in which it feels the misrepresentation has been extreme. These powers have been used sparingly, but their very existence has imposed a greater measure of responsibility and caution on the advertising industry. A national bakery, for instance, for a time advertised one of its bread products as suitable for diets, implying that its calorie content was lower than that of other brands. When it was determined that each slice of bread was low on calories simply because it was thinner than the normal slice, the company was required by the FTC to remove all advertising or to run "corrective ads" admitting the "error" and explaining that the bread really offered few advantages to weight watchers.

EVOLUTIONARY GROWTH OF THE BROADCASTING INDUSTRY

Buffeted by the winds of change blowing from Washington and local communities, the broadcasting industry also managed to evolve in more predictable directions in the years after 1965. We will conclude this chapter with a summary of such growth.

Television

New Television Stations In the period between 1958 and 1965, the number of VHF stations increased by 83—from 408 to 491—while the number of UHF stations increased by only 23—from 84 to 107. The practical limit in the number of available VHF channels, the "all-channel-receiver bill" that required all sets manufactured after April 1964 to permit tuning of both VHF and UHF channels, and increasing optimism about the future of UHF—all combined to reverse the figures almost exactly in the period 1966 to 1974. In that period, the number of VHF stations on the air increased by 21—to 573—and the number of UHF stations by 85—to 192.

Both revenues and profits of networks and local stations continued to increase as the industry grew; FCC figures show broadcast revenues of $4.09 billion (stations and networks combined) and profits of $780.3 million in 1975. The same FCC figures, however, also demonstrate the continued contrast between VHF and UHF operation. In 1975, 86 percent of the VHF stations reported a profit, compared with only 52 percent of the UHF stations. Optimism about UHF continues, however, and a 1974 NAB study showed that, based on data gathered from a sample of stations, a typical UHF station showed a profit of $95,700—not an overwhelming figure but certainly an improvement over the typical loss of $85,400 in 1971.

Network Developments Since 1965, there have been a few attempts to form a fourth commercial national television network. As we saw in Chapter 4, the original fourth network, the Du Mont Network, ceased operation in 1955. By the mid-1960s, an increase in the number of markets with four or more stations (50 by 1972) and the growth of multichannel cable systems encouraged some entrepreneurs to consider attempts at a fourth network service.

The most ambitious project of this type was headed by David H. Overmyer, who launched the Overmyer Network in 1966. Initial plans called for beginning with a nightly 2-hour variety program from Las Vegas and building to a total of 56 hours of programming each week. By December 1966, the new network claimed 123 affiliates, and it actually went on the air with the Las Vegas show in May of 1967. This effort lasted for 31 days; the venture reportedly lost $2.3 million for its investors; and nothing of this magnitude has been proposed since.

Before the Overmyer effort, there had been occasional suggestions that UHF stations across the nation should unite into a network of sorts. In 1967, Kaiser Broadcasting, owner of seven independent UHF stations, declared that its seven stations would be interconnected by 1970. However, by the mid-1970s, nothing had come of any of this, and a report issued by the RAND Corporation in 1974 concluded that the chances for a viable fourth network were slim as long as the then-current regulatory and economic climate persisted.

Another kind of network, the "occasional," or "event," network, has enjoyed some success. The Hughes Sports Network began in the mid-1960s by delivering special sports programs of national or regional interest by putting together one-time networks of interested stations. By the mid-1970s, the Hughes organization was being outbid by Television Sports (TVS)—also a special service network that built its success on a solid schedule of regional telecasts of college basketball and occasional "big games" of national interest. TVS had not tried to outbid any of the major networks for sports events they carried, but in 1974 it moved into the regular transmission of professional football when it covered the first year of the ill-fated World Football League. TVS also announced plans to offer an occasional movie—already seen on network but not yet released to syndication—but its main interest in the mid-1970s continues to be sports programming.

Color Television   In spite of a color set penetration of less than 10 percent in 1965, the three major networks—led by NBC which, through its connection with RCA, had a financial interest in the growth of color broadcasting—had realized that color was an idea whose time had come; and the networks moved quickly to convert. In the 1965–1966 season, virtually all NBC programs were in color, CBS programmed approximately 50 percent color, and ABC lagged behind at 33 percent. By 1967–1968, all network programming was in color, and local stations were quick to follow suit. Cost of conversion from local black-and-white operation to color was high; but, by 1970, 98 percent of the commercial stations in the country had at least a color videotape recorder capability and most were programming color all day—with the exception of some lingering reruns of such durable series as *Our Gang, I Love Lucy, Father Knows Best*, and old movies.

The American public was not so quick to convert to color and a 1970 report of the American Research Bureau showed only 43 percent penetration. By 1975, however, *Broadcasting Yearbook* reported an NBC estimate that this figure had jumped to 71 percent. Color set prices were going down, even in the face of inflation, and this, plus the growing impact of small-screen, foreign-made sets, indicated that the black-and-white set—at least as the "first" set —would soon be a thing of the past in most homes.

Network Television Programs after 1965   What might be considered a completely new program form had a brief popularity in the mid-1960s, but apparently did not have the staying power to survive and had virtually disappeared from network schedules by 1970. This was the "national test" format in which viewers were asked a series of questions on a subject, given an opportunity to respond at home, and then were shown the response to the same question previously gathered from a national survey sample. Interest in this form grew from the *Driver's Test* program scheduled in the summer of 1965 by CBS, which drew a rating of 28.2 and a 53 percent share of audience. Figures like these for a summer program will catch the eye of any network, and CBS and NBC were quick to announce similar tests for their 1965–1966 season. None of these achieved the success of the first program, however, and the idea quickly faded away.

Some more significant changes in the pattern of network programming developed after 1965, however. As could have been expected, increased reliance on theatrical feature films quickly depleted the stockpile of films available and this problem was compounded by the tendency of many major producers to make films with themes—or at least crucial scenes—that simply were not acceptable in the more family-oriented television medium. The networks took the logical step in the 1970s and became heavily involved in the production of movies that were shown on television first and then released for theatrical showing. In 1974, ABC went beyond the customary time restraints for a motion picture when it scheduled a six-hour, made-for-television film, *QB VII*, for 3-hour showings on two consecutive evenings. The programs received good rating figures, even in the face of a delay caused by a special Presidential address in the early evening. The success of this idea led ABC in 1975–1976 to offer a "novel for television," *Rich Man, Poor Man*, which ran for seven episodes, the number needed to complete the story. This "novel" was well received, and ABC followed with *Rich Man, Poor Man—Part II* in the 1976–1977 season. CBS and ABC followed suit with "short-form" series that year also, with less success than ABC. All three networks continued to express interest in dramatic series that utilize the number of hours needed to tell the story and are not locked to a 13- or 26-week schedule; and all three will work to have some on hand as replacements for scheduled programs that do not receive the ratings needed for continuation. Specific network time periods designated for "short-form" series over a full season did not appear on the 1977–1978 schedule, however, and seemed unlikely in the near future.

Made-for-television films have also become important testing grounds for proposed new series. A 90-minute pilot is made; it is run as a "movie of the week"; and it is brought back as a series if audience acceptance is high. ABC, for instance, scheduled three feature-length *Wonder Woman* films, and the program idea was held in reserve for the 1976–1977 "second season." These longer (90-minute) forms sometimes became significant vehicles for the introduction of a new series already scheduled by allowing for higher production costs in what amounts to the first episode of a series. The long-running *Ironsides* series and the more recent *Starsky and Hutch*, for instance, were introduced in this way.

In the 1970s, NBC also pioneered the introduction of the "revolving series" with its *Bold Ones* concept in which four different series, with different continuing characters and themes, were rotated through each 4-week period. This allowed more production time for each program and introduced an element of flexibility—allowing the networks to increase the number of programs produced for the strongest "miniseries," while reducing or eliminating other segments that demonstrated less strength. Both ABC and CBS experimented with this idea, but by the 1975–1976 season only NBC was using it in its *Sunday Night Mystery Movie*, which rotated *Columbo*, *MacMillan and Wife*, *McCloud*, and *McCoy* through the season.

Still another idea was introduced in the fall of 1974 when NBC ran five consecutive episodes of a complete production, *The Blue Knight*, on five successive nights. In the winter of 1977 ABC followed the same pattern with *Roots*. This 12-hour drama ran on eight consecutive nights in February and several episodes were viewed by more than 50 percent of all homes viewing television in the United States.

Major Program Trends Several of the programming trends noted in Chapter 4 continued in the years after 1965.

The balance between film, videotape, and live production has varied with little evident pattern since the mid-1960s, with film and tape continuing to predominate. According to a report in the 1974 issue of *Broadcasting Yearbook*, 32.6 percent of all network programming was on film in 1963. This rose to 44.2 percent in 1972, but dropped to 31.7 percent the following year. The use of videotape varied even more widely, from 41 percent in 1963 to 48.2 percent in 1968, down to 39.6 percent in 1972, and back up to 47.5 percent in 1973. Live programming stood at 26.1 percent in 1963, dropped to 15.8 percent and 16.2 percent in 1968 and 1972 respectively, and climbed again to 20.6 percent in 1973. The variations in live programming are affected, of course, by the frequency and duration of live coverage of such special events as space shots, the Watergate hearings, political election events, and the growing popularity of live sports programming, but film and tape continue to dominate, with only their relative balance varying from year to year.

In the decade following 1965, the networks expanded their news programming significantly. Details of this expansion will be covered in Chapter 9, but all three networks continue in an intense struggle for audiences for their regular news programs. In the 1970s, the networks continually maneuvered for advantage by shuffling in and out anchor and co-anchor persons and continually changing the assignments of and emphasis on the top-line network news correspondents. The result has been tight competition between CBS and NBC, with ABC News consistently running third. It is estimated that the three networks combined employ more than 2,500 people and spend between $140 million and $160 million a year on news alone. This network coverage, of course, is greatly aided by the system of satellites that now permit direct live "feeds" of news events from virtually any place on earth.

Another trend in network programming that continued to develop after 1965 is the ever-growing interest in sports programming. In 1973–1974, for instance, NBC alone programmed 361 hours of live sports coverage. Once confined almost exclusively to Saturday and Sunday afternoons, sports programming has spilled over to Monday nights during both the professional football and baseball seasons; and all three networks regularly preempt prime-time evening programming for coverage of such events as the World Series, bowl games, the NCAA basketball semifinal and final play-offs and professional basketball play-offs. In addition to this expansion into prime-time evening hours, more and more time is devoted to all forms of sports—especially football—on weekends. ABC-TV often schedules "double-headers," back-to-back college football games on Saturday afternoons, as do CBS and NBC with professional football on Sundays. So-called "long weekends" are fair game, and in the early 1970s ABC outdid itself with two games on Thanksgiving Day, a single game on Friday, and another double-header on that Saturday. Scheduling such line-ups has necessitated the juggling of college schedules and resulted in some unusual starting times, and there have been periodic complaints that television is "taking over" the game. Most colleges and universities are more than happy to make the necessary adjustments, however, in exchange for the national exposure and financial rewards.

Basketball has also grown steadily in popularity, with TVS and NBC offering a full schedule of college games and CBS carrying the National Basketball Association; and interest in professional baseball has always been high, with NBC and ABC both carrying games in 1976. Professional hockey and major horse races also receive coverage. Add the taped "anthology" sports programs covering everything from gymnastics to "demolition derbies," tennis and golf tournaments created solely for television, growing coverage of the professional golf tours, and periodic events like the Pan American Games and the Winter and Summer Olympics and the result is an emphasis on sports that far exceeds anything imagined in 1965.

General entertainment programming continues to experience cycles of various program forms. By the mid-1970s, the western seemed "out," with even the durable *Gunsmoke* gone from the prime-time schedule. At the same time, the number of detective and police programs seemed to be on the increase. In addition, the success of such adult, topical programs as *All in the Family* and *M.A.S.H.* had produced such successors as *Maude, Good Times*, and *Sanford and Son*. Running counter to this trend, apparently, was a feeling for nostalgia that resulted in such programming as *The Waltons* and *Happy Days*. Game shows were making a strong comeback in daytime television, but had yet to break back into prime-time schedules, although ABC did introduce *Almost Anything Goes*, a program pitting groups of people against each other in a series of outlandish competitions, in its summer 1975 and winter 1976 schedules.

Network television programming changed in two other significant ways after 1965. Early in the 1965-1966 season, ABC found itself running a poor third in overall, prime-time ratings. Rather than take a beating for the whole year, in mid-season the network made some drastic revisions in its schedule, moving programs around, dropping weak shows, and adding such new ideas as *Batman*. This "second season" concept succeeded in helping ABC make significant gains in the ratings; thereafter, all three networks adopted the policy of dropping weak programs in December or January and introducing new schedules for the "second season" each year. Indeed, most network advance planning came to include a few programs with high potential that were held in reserve for "second season" replacements.

By the end of the 1976-1977 season most observers of network programming had abandoned the "second" and "third" season concept and were speaking of a "continuous season." The term referred to the growing practice of taking a program with weak ratings off the air after only three or four episodes and replacing it immediately, instead of waiting for the beginning of a "second season." The traditional September to April "season" concept was further blurred by the growing practice of giving a trial run in the preceding spring to new programs tentatively scheduled for the new season. This practice pleased the critics of too many reruns, but the result is that episodes of some "new" programs in a given season have already been run before the traditional September "premier."

The second significant change in network programming patterns relates to the number of reruns included in the schedule. As television evolved from the patterns established by radio in the 1940s and 1950s, it carried with it the old radio ratio of 39 first-run programs and 13 repeat (or replacement) programs each year. Rising production costs, strikes, and the preemption of regular programming by specials caused an erosion in this ratio, but as late as 1964–1965 CBS was producing 36 episodes of *Gunsmoke* each year. By 1967–1968, however, this figure had dropped to 24 new episodes. A 1972 study by *Broadcasting* magazine indicated that only 59 percent of the 1971–1972 prime-time schedule was devoted to first-run material, with 41 percent devoted to reruns. In the same year, the average number of episodes of new, original series programming stood at 22.8 and the average number of reruns for those series was 22.7, a ratio that remained steady through 1974–1975.

The networks have maintained that rising production costs are the major cause for this trend, but a 1972 study ordered by President Richard Nixon and carried out by his Office of Telecommunications Policy concluded that while production costs were rising, in the previous decade network revenues had far outstripped expenditures on original programming. In 1975, the FCC was asked by Hollywood producers to require all networks to revert to 39 new episodes and 13 reruns per year, but the commission has not yet acted on this request.

Local Station Programming   Local station programming has not changed a great deal since 1965, with the exception of more extensive news coverage; but its sources have shown some variation. Reliance on network programming increased, jumping from 57 percent in 1963 to 61 percent in 1973, while live programming declined from 13 percent to 10 percent. At the same time, there seem to be signs of a move away from film to videotape. Between 1963 and 1973, the use of local film dropped from 25 percent to 15 percent while tape usage climbed from 2 percent to 9 percent.

It is evident, then, that filmed and taped programs continue to dominate the nonnetwork hours. With the increase in "off-network series" (network programs no longer scheduled in prime time and sold to individual stations for reruns), this programming has replaced conventional syndication as a primary source of material for local stations. With their restrictions on "off-network" reruns, the "prime-time access rules," however, have opened up some additional time to traditional syndicators. Some stations still carry local interview and talk programming, but the added expense of color has made such programming difficult for the marginal operation, which prefers to channel its available money into two areas of local programming, news and public affairs. FCC interest, of course, spurs the concern with public affairs; and licensees have come to realize in recent years that stations with the strongest, most popular local news programs have a built-in evening advantage over others in the market because of the strong local "lead-in" to the network schedule. This has led to such experiments as the "happy-talk" format in which the various members of the "news team" react to each other as individuals during transitions (and which has been criticized as taking too casual an attitude toward the events of the day); to an expansion in the number of local news programs to three or four a day; and to a lengthening of the early evening segment to 60 minutes, often "wrapped around" the network news. Indeed, local news has become so important that some major market stations are now planning an expansion to 2 hours of local news each evening.

Radio

Available financial data indicate that, as a whole, radio has continued to recover from the shock of television. Although it seems likely that only runaway inflation could ever raise radio network revenues to the dollar levels enjoyed in the late 1940s and early 1950s, local radio revenues have shown a decline from the previous year in only 2 years of radio history—1938 and 1954. Total radio revenues declined in only 3 years—1938, 1954, and 1961—and by the mid-1970s were more than $1.5 billion a year, almost four times as high as in the "golden years" of radio.

To be sure, this prosperity has not been shared by all. Overall, FM stations continue to be a red-ink commodity, with 55 percent of the independent FM stations in the country reporting losses in 1974. On the other hand, 65 percent of all AM and AM-FM combinations reported profits.

This prosperity has continued to attract investors and to persuade broadcasters to "try their luck"; events have forced them primarily into FM. The growth of AM came to a virtual halt in 1965 as the FCC continued its attempts to control an explosive growth— in 1945 there were 884 AM stations; in 1965, 4,012. After 1965, a series of "slow-downs," "freezes," and "partial freezes" resulted in the addition of only 448 new AM licensees in the period from 1965 to 1976. On the other hand, FM continued to grow, with the number of licensees jumping from 1,270 in 1965 to 2,648 in 1974. Many economists and broadcasters predict that the advantages of FM—a better quality signal, a lack of electrical interference, and stereophonic broadcasting—will eventually outweigh its primary disadvantage—a smaller coverage area—and that the real future of radio lies in the FM service.

Radio Network Programming The most significant change in radio network program patterns after 1965 was proposed by ABC-Radio in 1967. In August of that year, it asked the FCC for permission to offer four network services, feeding different lineups of programs to stations grouped according to their formats. The proposed services were the Information Network for talk and "middle-of-the-road" stations, the Personality Network featuring more conventional network programming, the Contemporary Network for contemporary (rock and roll, Top 40) stations, and the FM Network with programming designed specifically for FM stations.

A key factor in the request was the fact that ABC was also asking permission to affiliate with up to four stations in a given market—with each type of network service carried by not more than one station in any single market, of course. Other networks registered opposition; but, recognizing the changed nature of network radio since the days of NBC Red and Blue networks and noting that all services would be carried on one set of network lines, the FCC approved the plan, and ABC began its service in 1968 with an announced line-up of 300 stations.

The concept has been polished somewhat since that time, and the Personality Network was renamed the Entertainment Network; but the plan seems to have worked to the satisfaction of most affiliates, while allowing many more stations to offer a network service to their audiences. Mutual has since started up a separate Black Network and NBC, a News Network with an all-news format.

Aside from the ABC plan, network radio has changed little since 1965. The NBC *Monitor* concept continued to offer its weekend potpourri of news, music, and special features until its termination in 1975, while all networks continue to serve an essentially supplemental function by assisting their local affiliates with special features and international and national news.

From time to time, since the advent of television, some who remember the "golden days" of network radio attempt to revive radio drama, but until the 1973–1974 season these attempts met with limited success at best. That year, however, CBS began its *Mystery Theatre*, a regular series of new radio dramas with a mystery theme, and very soon the program was "sold out" to advertisers. Other networks watched this development with interest, but by the late 1970s no one cared to say whether or not it marked the beginning of a trend of any significance in network radio.

Local Radio Programming   As you would expect, most of the experimentation in radio programming has been at the local level as stations continue to seek out specific audiences and serve them with rather specialized formats. This evolution has produced a bewildering pattern of station programming, in which a few trends can be detected. Country and western music has increased in popularity, and few major markets now lack at least one outlet. The so-called middle-of-the-road (MOR) stations have shifted emphasis from the standards of the 1940s and 1950s to a mixture of the smoother contemporary selections and more acceptable arrangements of many of the Top-40 hits of the late 1950s and 1960s. "Underground" stations have experimented with varied success with a loose form featuring more off-beat records and the longer album cuts that would be unacceptable in a more tightly organized format. Automated and prepackaged music services, complete with breaks for local commercials, cues for news, and the like have become available and are widely accepted by FM stations, primarily. Black and ethnic radio continues to grow in popularity. Finally, the durable Top-40 format (now rechristened "Contemporary Format" and stripped of some of its more strident bells, whistles, and "shouters") has held up as a strong format for those aiming at the 18-to-34-year-old market and able to keep their fingers on the pulse of this mercurial and increasingly affluent group. In the years since 1970, however, it has become increasingly difficult to draw sharp distinctions among many of these formats, as country, ethnic, and MOR selections find their way into the Top-100 charts and recording artists experiment with new forms and new combinations. Easily discernable in the larger markets, on the other hand, are the all-news and all-talk stations, many of which have found a comfortable and profitable niche with these special kinds of programming.

The major exception to this proliferation of radio formats, of course, is the small-market station that serves only its own community, often in competition with signals coming in from nearby larger markets. These stations must depend on a localized service aimed at the entire community; as a solution, they often turn to "block programming"—a format in which various types of music, talk, news, and so forth, are "blocked" in at the same times each day to serve what is seen as the dominant audience at the time. If done well, this can be a successful format; and many of the daytime-only stations in this situation have expanded their service by opening an FM outlet for evening programming while simply duplicating on FM their AM service during the day.

In short, radio is a mixed bag, full of the complexities and pressures that produced such aberrations as "topless radio" in 1972 and such mistakes as an "all-classified ad" station in the mid-1960s. Basically, though, radio remains a local service with a flexibility and economy that allows it to spring into action quickly and efficiently in times of emergency and a local orientation that is needed to balance the domination of television by the networks. It may still be experimenting; but after being driven from the living room, radio has found its place in the study, the workshop, the bedroom, the kitchen, the car, the beach, and in the pockets or clipped to the belts of an increasingly mobile generation who simply want to stay in touch.

STUDY AND DISCUSSION QUESTIONS

1. Discuss the implications of one of the following cases on the development of broadcasting in the 1960s and 1970s.

   a. The *WHDH* case
   b. The *WLBT* case
   c. The *CCC* case
   d. The *Red Lion* case

2. Report on or be prepared to discuss the activities of citizens' groups in working to deny license renewals to licensees whom they felt were not serving the public interest.

3. Many critics of broadcasting in the United States feel that the Federal Communications Commission has not been sufficiently concerned about the issue of "concentration of media control." Report on or be prepared to discuss the following:

   a. The nature of the "concentration of control" issue
   b. The arguments for greater FCC attention to the issue
   c. The actions of the FCC, with its justification
   d. Reaction to and criticism of the commission actions in the area of "concentration of control"

4. Get access to the "ascertainment report" of a local station (it must be in the public file of every commercial station). Examine the report and evaluate the selection of problems in the light of your knowledge of the community.

5. Prepare a report on the evolution of the Fairness Doctrine. Include in this report the major differences between the Fairness Doctrine and the "equal opportunity" provisions of Section 315 of the Communications Act of 1934.

6. Report on or be prepared to discuss one of the following:

    a. The evolution of the prime-time access rules
    b. The effects of violence in television on children
    c. The nature and fate of the proposals on children's television by Action for Children's Television (ACT)
    d. Efforts by the Federal Communications Commission to limit commercial time
    e. The Overmyer Network
    f. The increase in the number of television network reruns

SUGGESTED READINGS

Harry S. Ashmore. *Fear in the Air: Broadcasting and the First Amendment — The Anatomy of a Constitutional Crisis.* New York: Norton, 1973.

Erik Barnouw. *Tube of Plenty: The Evolution of American Television.* New York: Oxford University Press, 1975.

Douglass Cater and Stephen Strickland. *TV Violence and the Child: The Evolution and Fate of the Surgeon General's Report.* New York: Russell Sage, 1975.

Edward J. Epstein. *News From Nowhere: Television and the News.* New York: Random House, 1973.

Fred W. Friendly. *The Good Guys, The Bad Guys and the First Amendment: Free Speech vs. Fairness in Broadcasting.* New York: Random House, 1976.

Henry Geller. *The Fairness Doctrine in Broadcasting: Problems and Suggested Courses of Action.* Santa Monica, Calif.: RAND Corporation, 1973.

William Small. *To Kill a Messenger, Television News and the Real World.* New York: Hastings House, 1970.

6

The Elements of Broadcasting

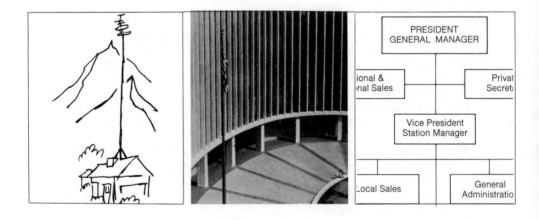

The broadcasting industry that has evolved in the United States since the 1920s is made up of a number of companies that provide a wide variety of services. In this chapter we will turn from history to a consideration of the major elements of our complex broadcasting industry, starting with the base of the industry pyramid—the local station.

BROADCASTING STATIONS

All broadcasting stations are alike in one basic respect: they put on the air programs or program materials to be received by the listening public. Commercial stations are alike in another important respect: they are operated by their owners for the purpose of earning a profit. Otherwise, stations are very different in the types of service they provide in the areas they cover, in their geographical locations, in the competitive situations in which they operate and in many other respects. Some are located in large cities, others in rural areas; some operate on a full-time basis, others are licensed only for part-time operations; some are affiliated with networks, others provide programming without network assistance. All these factors affect the kinds of program service that stations provide, as well as the stations' chances of earning a profit.

Types of Broadcasting Stations

Commercial stations may be classified in several different ways. First, of course, stations are divided into three basic groups: AM (standard-band) radio stations, FM radio stations, and television stations. Each group uses a different band of frequencies in the radio spectrum; AM stations are assigned to the standard band of frequencies from 540 to 1,600 kilohertz,[1] FM radio stations are assigned to frequencies between 88 and 108 megahertz, and television

[1]Broadcast frequencies traditionally were designated by the number of kilocycles (1,000 cycles) per second for the frequency. Thus a radio frequency of 540,000 cycles per second was called 540 kilocycles or Kc. As higher frequencies came into use, the term *megacycles* (1,000 kilocycles or 1,000,000 cycles) was adopted. The term *hertz* as a synonym for *cycles per second* has recently been agreed upon for national and international use and the terms *kilohertz* and *megahertz* mean the same as *kilocycle* and *megacycle*.

stations use channels in three separate bands of frequencies, 54 to 88 megahertz, 174 to 216 megahertz, and 470 to 890 megahertz.

AM Radio Stations In its Rules and Regulations, the Federal Communications Commission (FCC) establishes three classes of AM channel (frequency) and four classes of station. Channels are classified as "clear," "regional," and "local." A *clear channel* is one with a dominant station that is designed to offer service over a large area— often several states. Other stations may be assigned to the same channel, but these stations must operate with lower power and, if necessary, with directional antennas to avoid interference with the dominant station on the channel. A *regional channel* is one on which many stations may operate with a maximum power of 5,000 watts. These stations are expected to serve fairly large rural areas, in addition to their city of license—often a large city. A *local channel* is one on which many stations operate with a maximum power of 250 watts at night and, in most cases, 1,000 watts during the day. Such stations are expected to serve only their local communities and immediate vicinities. There are now designated 59 clear channels, 42 regional channels, and six local channels.

Stations are designated as Class I, Class II, Class III, or Class IV. A *Class I station* is the dominant station operating on a clear channel. Class I stations are protected from interference from all other stations on the channel. Minimum operating power is 10,000 watts and maximum is 50,000 watts. A *Class II station* is a secondary station operating on a clear channel. Operating power and times of operation of Class II stations are adjusted to provide maximum protection for Class I stations. Power can range from a minimum of 250 watts to a maximum of 50,000 watts. *Class III stations* are assigned to the regional channels, with minimum and maximum powers of 500 watts and 5,000 watts. Some Class III stations are also licensed for only daytime operation or are required to reduce power after sunset to minimize interference. *Class IV stations* are found on the local channels. Maximum power is 1,000 watts during the day and 250 watts at night. Minimum power today is 250 watts, but stations licensed for 100 watts before the establishment of this minimum are permitted to continue at this power if they wish to do so. Table 6–1 shows the number of stations in each power classification at the beginning of November 1974.

With as many as 60 or 70 stations assigned to each regional channel and from 160 to 180 operating on each local channel, interference between stations has become a serious problem. This is especially true at night, when AM signals can be heard over much

Table 6–1   Power Classifications of Standard-band (AM) Radio Stations
on the Air, November 1, 1974

Daytime Power of Station	Full-time Stations, Same Power at Night	Full-time Stations, Power Reduced at Night	Daytime Only or Part-time Stations[a]	Total
50,000 watts	73	53	14	140
10,000 watts	32[b]	54	49	135[b]
5,000 watts	342	345	339	1026
1,000 watts	152	1,096	1,105	2,353
500 watts	22	28	400	450
250 watts	35	3	289	327
100 watts	1	—	2	3
Total	657	1,579	2,198	4,434

[a]Includes stations licensed for operation only during specified hours as well as those operating only during daytime hours.

[b]Includes one station operating full time with power of 25,000 watts.

Figures compiled from radio station listings in *Broadcasting Yearbook* for 1975.

larger areas than in daytime.[2] To deal at least partially with this problem, the FCC makes use of three types of limitation in the licenses granted certain stations, providing another basis for classification of AM radio stations. First, as shown in Table 6–1, almost half of the standard (AM) stations on the air are licensed for daytime broadcasting only. Next, of those stations that do stay on the air at night, more than 70 percent use less power at night than during the day. Finally, almost all the regional stations on the air at night are required to use directional antenna systems, which reduce the strength of their signals in certain directions, in order to protect other stations on the same frequencies. Many Class II and Class III stations are also required to use directional antennas during the

---

[2]During nighttime hours, radio waves tend to "bounce back" from or be reflected back to earth by a layer of ionized atmosphere called the ionosphere or the Heaviside layer, from 30 to 250 miles above the surface of the earth, so that the reflected signals can be picked up by receiving sets much farther away from the transmitter than those reached by ground waves that parallel the surface of the earth. During the daytime, when the atmosphere is warmed by the sun's rays, the reflecting power of the ionosphere is much reduced; and radio signals are carried almost entirely by ground waves. The "bounce-back" phenomenon is particularly evident with respect to the medium-length waves used by AM stations; the degree of nighttime reflection of signals is considerably less for the shorter waves used by FM and television signals.

daytime. Table 6–1 shows the number of stations in each daytime power category operating on a daytime-only basis or required to reduce power at night as of the autumn of 1974. It may be noted, however, that even with the restrictions imposed by the FCC, night-time interference from other stations assigned to the same frequency remains a serious problem for almost all AM radio stations, except, of course, for the 50,000-watt facilities licensed as clear-channel stations.

A third possible basis of classification of AM stations is their affiliation or nonaffiliation with national radio networks. In 1976, 56 percent of all AM stations were listed as network affiliates. The distinction between network and nonnetwork radio stations is, however, of relatively minor importance in view of the limited program service the radio networks now provide. More meaningful, perhaps, would be classifications based on the size of communities in which stations are located—big-city stations, medium-city stations, and small-market stations.

Still another possible classification would be based on the types of program service, or format, that individual stations provide—Top 40, good music, country and western, talk, all news, black, farm, and the like. Such classifications are important to advertisers who are interested in reaching specialized audiences. Table 6–2 shows the distribution of formats in the Top 50 markets.

FM Radio Stations   Since 1962, the FCC has provided for three classes of FM stations, based on the amount of power each is permitted to use. *Class A stations* may use power of from 100 watts to 3,000 watts; *Class B Stations*, intended to serve larger areas, have power ranging from 5,000 to 50,000 watts; *Class C stations* are allowed to use power of 100,000 watts and antennas up to 2,000 feet in height. In 1975, more than 400 commercial FM stations used power of 100,000 watts or more and almost 400 others had power of 50,000 watts or more.

FM stations may be classified, too, on the basis of the extent to which they are independently programmed. More than 75 percent of all commercial FM stations are owned by licensees of AM stations in the same communities; until the mid-1960s, most of these FM stations simply duplicated the program schedules of the AM stations with which they had common ownership. In 1965, the FCC required all FM stations in cities of 100,000 or more to be programmed independently at least 50 percent of the time. During the following decade, the number of independent FM stations doubled and average revenues quadrupled. Reasoning that program duplication was a waste of a frequency and that the justification for duplication was greatly reduced, the FCC, in 1976, issued new non-

Table 6–2 Distribution of Formats among the Top-10 Stations
in the 50 Largest Markets, May 1976

Format	Number	Percentage
Contemporary	135	27.0
Beautiful music	88	17.6
Middle-of-the-road (MOR)	68	13.6
Country	45	9.0
All-news	20	4.0
MOR/talk/news	23	4.6
Talk/news	13	2.6
Contemporary/AOR	20	4.0
Black	24	4.8
MOR/contemporary	18	3.6
Album-oriented-rock (AOR)	17	3.4
All-talk	5	1.0
Golden oldies	6	1.2
Spanish	5	1.0
Mellow rock	2	0.4
News/beautiful music	2	0.4
Contemporary/MOR	1	0.2
Country/MOR	1	0.2
Disco	1	0.2
Classical	1	0.2
Hawaiian	1	0.2
Religious/black	1	0.2
Contemporary/talk	1	0.2
MOR/beautiful music	1	0.2
Big band	1	0.2

Based on figures compiled from April/May 1976 ARBitron radio figures by *Broadcasting* magazine,
September 27, 1976, with permission.

duplication rules, to take effect in 1977. According to these rules, duplication in cities of over 100,000 will be permitted for only 25 percent of the average broadcast week. Stations in communities of over 25,000 and under 100,000 can duplicate only 50 percent of the time.

Some FM stations, especially those in large cities, hold special authorizations from the FCC to engage in "multiplexing," the simultaneous transmission of two or more signals on different portions of the channel to which they are assigned. One signal must be used for ordinary broadcasting of programs intended for a general audience. Many stations use a second signal to provide stereophonic transmission of music. The second signal can also be used for non-broadcasting purposes, such as the provision of background music, uninterrupted by commercials, for the use of stores, offices, or other places of business.

FM stations are also used as relays to carry programs to members of regional AM radio networks; the FM signal of an originating station is picked up and rebroadcast by other FM stations whose signals are in turn picked up and rebroadcast by the AM stations that compose the network.

No mention has been made in the preceding sections of the noncommercial AM or FM radio stations that have been authorized by the FCC. The commission has set aside no special frequencies for the exclusive use of noncommercial AM stations, but at the beginning of 1975 about 40 noncommercial AM stations were on the air. Certain FM frequencies (88 to 92 megahertz) have been reserved by the commission for the exclusive use of noncommercial stations; and, by 1975, approximately 725 noncommercial FM stations were operating. Most of the noncommercial radio stations are licensed to universities, colleges, and local or state school systems and provide educational and cultural programs for listeners. A substantial number, however, are owned by religious organizations and are operated as religious stations.

Television Stations The Federal Communications Commission makes no provision for classes of commercial television stations; all are, in effect, local stations, each providing a service to a single community and the surrounding countryside. In fact, the area over which a television station has effective daytime or nighttime coverage is usually not much larger than the area served by a 250-watt AM radio station in the same community. An important difference between commercial television stations, however, lies in the fact that some are assigned to channels in the VHF bands (54 to 88 and 174 to 216 megahertz) while others use channels in the much higher UHF bands (470 to 890 megahertz), where signals can be received over a much smaller area and are more subject to interference. Partly to compensate for this variation in coverage, the FCC allows use of much greater power by television stations on the higher frequencies than by those on channels at the lower end of the band. Television stations assigned to channels 2 to 6 may use maximum visual power of 100 kilowatts (100,000 watts); stations using channels 7 to 13 may use maximum power of 316 kilowatts; UHF stations assigned to channels 14 to 69 may be authorized to use power up to 5,000

Figure 6–1 Typical of the exterior of many television stations in markets of moderate size is the low, rambling exterior of WBRZ-TV, Baton Rouge, Louisiana. (Courtesy WBRZ-TV)

kilowatts—power a hundred times as great as clear-channel AM stations are allowed to use. In actual practice, few UHF stations broadcast with more than a fraction of the maximum power permitted. Most VHF television stations, on the other hand, operate at the top power levels permitted by the commission.

A second basis of television station classification relates to affiliation with national networks. Most station operators *want* network affiliation; networks provide programs of types and of de-

"With all these new UHF channels, we now have twice as many reruns to choose from."

grees of popularity not otherwise available to the individual stations. In markets with four or more stations, however, there are not enough network services to go around. In addition, a few stations are located in communities so small and so far distant from existing network lines that network companies would not find it profitable to have them as affiliates. In any event, at the end of 1975, about 105 commercial television stations were operating as independents with no regular access to network programs. Of necessity, these nonnetwork stations have to be programmed in a manner considerably different from that of stations with network affiliations.

The Market Situation

A factor greatly affecting both the programming and the business success of broadcasting stations is the size of the market in which a station is located. Markets, or the home communities and surrounding trade areas served by stations, can be divided into three basic groups from the standpoint of their relation to broadcasting. First are the major markets—the 100 or so largest cities in the country, in most cases with three or more commercial television outlets and from five or six to as many as twenty or more radio stations. Almost all the powerful 50,000-watt radio stations are located in these major markets. An important subdivision of the major market category would include the 25 or so largest cities in the nation, since stations in these cities get a disproportionate share of all expenditures for radio and television advertising time. The second group includes what are known as secondary markets, usually cities with populations ranging from 50,000 to roughly 125,000 and their surrounding trade areas. Most of the secondary markets have service from two or three television stations and from four or five local radio outlets. Finally, we have a third group of still smaller markets with urban populations of less than 50,000, not large enough to support a commercial television station but with from one to as many as three or four local radio stations each. About 300 of these minor markets are served by two or more local radio outlets, but there are also many small communities which are "one-radio-station" markets—some of them small towns with populations of hardly more than 1,000 inhabitants.

Market size is extremely important in broadcasting. National advertisers buy time on stations in major markets and largely ignore those stations located in smaller communities. Approximately 44 percent of all national spot advertising on radio and television in 1974 went to stations in the nation's ten largest cities, and another

19.6 percent went to outlets in the fifteen cities next in size. Similarly, more than 38 percent of all money paid by networks to their affiliates went to television stations serving the 25 largest cities. The effects on average station revenues are obvious; the larger the city, the greater the average station revenues of stations in that city.

Naturally, size of the market is not the only factor that influences the economic success of broadcasting stations. For television stations, network affiliation is also highly important. In most large cities with four or more television outlets, nonnetwork or independent stations can charge only about half as much for advertising time as can the television stations in the same cities that have network connections. Average revenues of independent stations, as a result, are much lower than those of affiliates. For radio, however, station power is a more important factor than network affiliation. In selecting radio stations on which to place national spot advertising, a time buyer in New York tends to judge relative values of stations in the same market by the amount of power used; it is reasonable for him to expect that the station with greater power can cover a larger area and consequently attract a larger total number of listeners than can a station whose power is limited. In its financial summaries, however, the FCC does not break out radio figures by station power.

Ownership of Stations

As noted in an earlier chapter, ownership of American radio and television stations is scattered among nearly 4,000 different individuals or corporate groups. The FCC prohibits ownership by the same company of two stations of the same type in the same community, or in adjacent communities where station signals could cover much the same general area. However, the same licensee may own an AM radio station and an FM station in the same city, or an AM station and a television station or all three. Common ownership of this kind is frequent; more than 75 percent of all FM stations and nearly 25 percent of all commercial television stations are owned by licensees of AM radio stations operating in the same community. As noted in Chapter 5, FCC rules now prohibit purchase of a station or stations that would result in one licensee owning AM, FM, and television services in the same community. Because of this, the incidence of cross-ownership is going down steadily.

In addition, a number of corporations operate several radio or television stations located in different cities. In 1975, approximately 325 companies were "group owners" of this sort. Some owning groups operate small radio stations in several different cities in the same general area; others are large corporations with both television and radio interests in major cities from coast to coast.[3] All three of the national television networks are group owners of both radio and television stations; they own a total of 17 AM radio stations, and each owns five VHF stations in the nation's ten or twelve largest cities. Other important group owners include Westinghouse Broadcasting Co. (Group W); Storer Broadcasting Co.; Metromedia, Inc.; Cox Broadcasting Corp.; Taft Broadcasting Co.; and RKO General, Inc.—all with both radio and television stations. Other groups, such as Plough Broadcasting Co., Covenant Broadcasting, and Storz Broadcasting Co. own only radio stations. At the beginning of 1975, group owners were licensees of 96 of the 130 television stations located in the 25 largest metropolitan areas, along with some 130 AM stations in the same cities. Approximately 325 group owners owned or had interests in 459 television stations and more than 800 AM stations.

An interesting feature of broadcasting station ownership is the extent to which stations have been licensed to newspaper and publishing concerns. During the 1920s, a considerable number of the nation's more important radio stations were newspaper-owned. As broadcasting became more important as a disseminator of news and information, the interests of publishers in the ownership of broadcasting stations have increased. By the beginning of 1975, newspaper or magazine publishers owned or held substantial interest in 314 AM radio stations; in 241 FM stations; and in 176 television stations, of which 46 operated in the country's 25 largest cities.

Station Organization

Like other business enterprises, broadcasting stations vary in size, in number of employees, and in total annual revenues and net profits. Some small-market radio stations get along with no more than five or six full-time employees. At the other extreme, some radio stations have staffs of more than 100 people, and some large-city television stations have as many as 150 to 200 employees. In the circumstances, it is impossible to provide one employee organization chart that would fit all stations; organizational structure

---

[3]Regulations of the Federal Communications Commission limit the number of stations that may be licensed to one owner or one corporate group to not more than seven AM radio stations, seven FM stations, and seven television stations. Of the seven television stations, not more than five may operate on VHF channels.

of typical radio and television stations are shown in Figures 6–2 to 6–7. In every station certain functions must be performed, and these functions at least can be outlined.

First, there is the managerial function; every station is under the supervision of a station manager. While he exercises general oversight over activities of other station departments, he and his immediate subordinates are responsible for financial operations, handling billing and collections, and paying station expenses. In

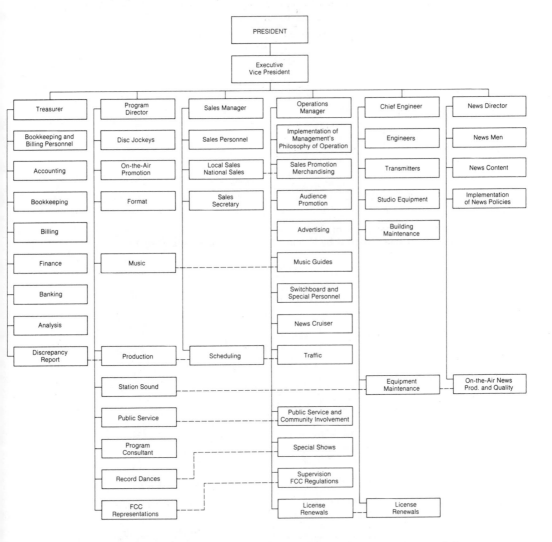

Figure 6–2 Organization of a radio station in a market of 2.5 million-plus population. (Data compiled by National Association of Broadcasters.)

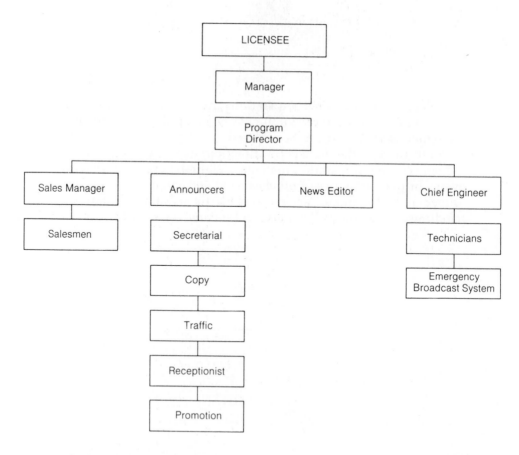

Figure 6–3 Organization of a radio station in a market of between 100,000 and 250,000 population. (Data compiled by National Association of Broadcasters.)

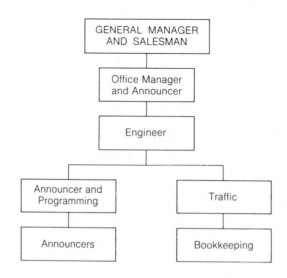

Figure 6–4 Organization of a radio station in a market of fewer than 10,000 population. (Data compiled by National Association of Broadcasters.)

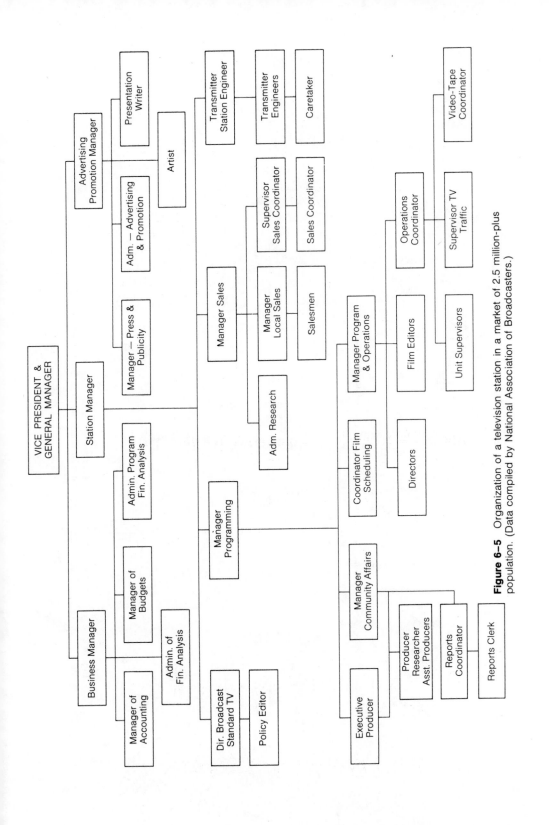

Figure 6–5 Organization of a television station in a market of 2.5 million-plus population. (Data compiled by National Association of Broadcasters.)

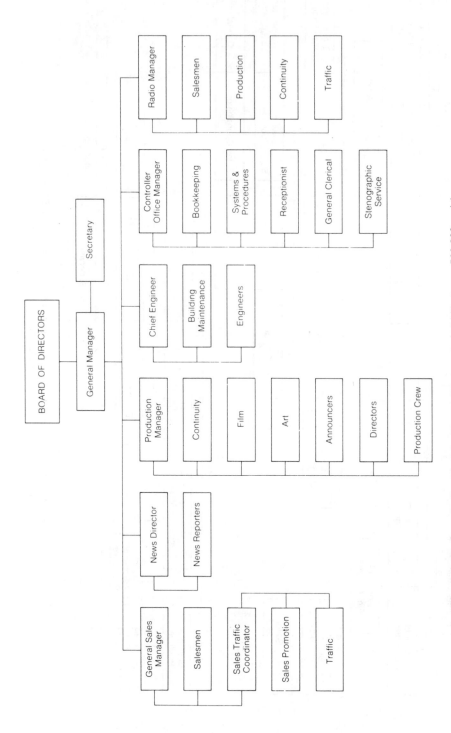

Figure 6–6 Organization of a television station in a market of between 500,000 and 1 million population. (Data compiled by National Association of Broadcasters.)

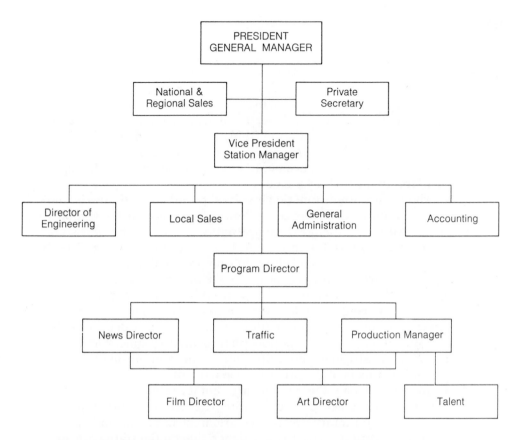

Figure 6-7 Organization of a television station in a market of fewer than 10,000 population. (Data compiled by National Association of Broadcasters.)

addition, the station manager prepares applications for license renewal and reports that must be filed with the FCC; he handles all dealings with national networks, negotiates contracts with employee unions, selects the men who serve as managers of the station's various departments, handles payments of music royalties and of charges for news services, and in a broad sense determines general station policies.

Next comes the engineering function, in the hands of a chief engineer and a staff of assistants. The engineering department selects, buys, and maintains all technical equipment; operates the transmitter; and handles control-room activities. In many television stations, engineering department personnel operate television cameras, videotape recorders, film and slide projectors, and also serve as members of the studio floor crews. In most stations, the chief engineer has supervisory control over building maintenance and janitorial services.

The sales function is performed by a sales department headed by the station's commercial manager. The department handles local sales and cooperates with the station representative concern in sale of time to national advertisers. In most stations, the sales promotion department and the traffic department are also under the control of the commercial manager—the traffic department maintaining an up-to-date log or schedule showing when each program and each commercial spot announcement is to go on the air and what spot positions are available for sale.

The programming function involves specialized activities on the part of a number of employees under the supervision of the station's program director. Included are staff announcers, news broadcasters and news editors, radio station disc jockeys, station "personalities" such as farm directors and children's program specialists, and continuity writers who provide program scripts or continuity and also write much of the commercial copy used by local advertisers. Program departments of television stations also include producer-directors of programs, film editors, members of art departments, and, in larger stations, motion picture photographers and processors of locally made film. Staff musicians and music librarians are also members of the program department.

In some stations, the news department is a separate entity and in others it is assigned to programming. General promotion, public affairs, and continuity acceptance are areas of responsibility that show up in various departments, depending on the station.

The variation in staff requirements are illustrated by the breakdowns of employees in the following examples. One AM-FM combination station in a city of moderate size employs twenty full-time and seven part-time people on the AM side. This includes three salesmen, five newsmen, six part-time announcers, four full-time announcers, three engineers, the general manager, the program director (who also takes the early-morning drive-time shift), a bookkeeper, a secretary, a receptionist and a maintenance man. The FM operation employs nine full-time and four part-time people—a traffic coordinator, three salesmen, five full-time and four part-time announcers. These figures are on the high side of a 1974 national average of twelve employees per radio station and are balanced by the many small stations with staffs of three or four in which the owner serves as manager and salesman, takes an air shift and, conceivably, also does engineering work when necessary.

One television station in a major market, on the other hand, has a total of 146 employees—12 in management, 37 in engineering, 9 in sales, and most of the remainder in programming. The general manager of this station also serves as program director, supervising the operation of news, public affairs, production, and operations departments. These figures are above the national average of about 70 employees per television station.

NATIONAL NETWORKS

National radio and television networks occupy an important place in American broadcasting. They perform special services with no direct counterpart in the operations of stations. For the national advertiser, they provide a nationwide interconnected system of stations that enables him to deliver his advertising message simultaneously to all parts of the country. For the affiliated station, they provide a program service that could not be duplicated locally. Television networks provide their affiliates with programs that are more expensive and of higher quality than would otherwise be available, and television and radio networks offer excellent national news service and coverage of special events of importance which no station could even attempt individually.

Network Operations

Each of the national television networks maintains studios for the origination of programs in Hollywood and New York; in addition, many of the networks' news programs come directly from Washington, D.C. The same cities serve as origination points for radio networks, with some network radio programs also produced in Chicago.

Each national network serves four basic functions. (1) It provides a schedule of programs ranging from 1 or 2 hours a day for radio networks to as much as 12 or more hours a day for each of the television networks. Some of these programs are produced by the network itself; others, especially evening-hour programs on television, are secured from outside production companies on a contract basis. (2) The network sells advertising spots within the programs to national advertisers. (3) The network distributes its programs over AT&T facilities to affiliated stations throughout the country and pays the affiliates for carrying the programs having commercial messages. (4) In an effort to attract larger audiences for its programs, the network carries on a continual promotion campaign to bring its offerings to the attention of the public.

Each of the network companies is organized in a somewhat different manner, and the organizational structure of even the same network is changed from time to time, especially when changes are made in top administrative personnel. However, on the basis of functions performed, the approximately 2,500 employees of a national television network company, other than top management, might be grouped into ten major departments, as follows:

Financial Department. Prepares and approves budget, handles accounting, billings and collections.

Legal department. Clears literary and music rights, handles contracts with talent and with program package producers, negotiates contracts with unions and handles other miscellaneous legal business.

Sales department. Sells programs, talent, program time, and spot announcement time to advertisers and handles all of the network's contacts with advertisers and advertising agencies. Usually includes or works closely with a *sales promotion department* and a *research department*, both of which prepare materials to be used by sales personnel.

Program department. Responsible for the network's weekly schedule of programs. Selects programs to be produced by packagers and develops and produces some programs for the network. Employees include producers, directors, writers, announcers, entertainers, casting experts, musicians, and others involved with presentation of programs.

News and public affairs department. Responsible for the planning, production and presentation of all news programs, public affairs programs, and special-events broadcasts. Usually includes a separate *sports department,* which handles all broadcasts of sports events.

Continuity acceptance or program practices department. The network's "censoring" agency; checks all scripts and all copy for commercials and screens all filmed materials to see that nothing is broadcast that is contrary to law or to network policy standards.

Operations department. Concerned with actually presenting programs and putting them on the network line. Includes engineers, camera men, sound technicians, lighting experts, sound effects specialists, floor men, ushers, maintenance men, and the like.

Information department. Provides program logs and program information to newspapers, handles on-the-air promotion for programs, and the like.

Station relations or affiliate relations department. Selects stations to be affiliated with the network and also handles all contacts with affiliated stations, secures clearances for commercial programs, and keeps affiliates informed about programs to be presented. Includes a *traffic department,* which orders AT&T circuits to connect affiliates with the network and procures the special circuits used for special-events broadcasts.

Owned-and-operated stations department. Supervises general activities of the stations owned and operated by the network company itself.

Network Program Service

The success of any national network organization depends on the quality and popularity of the programs it provides. Although radio networks offer a limited program service made up primarily of news reports and short features, each of the national television networks provides its affiliates with more than 100 hours of programming each week, at least 95 percent of which consists of commercial programs. This volume of programming must be maintained whether the network is able to sell all its available spots or not; affiliates depend on the television network to fill a large proportion of their broadcasting time. A major part of each television network's evening programming is provided by outside suppliers and usually is on film or tape. Network program offerings will be considered in a later chapter; however, one or two aspects of network service should be mentioned at this point.

Television networks are in vigorous competition with one another both for audiences and for advertising. In part, a network's success depends on the popularity of the programs included in its schedule, which of course reflects the ability of the network's program executives to select those entertainment programs that will best satisfy the public's tastes and to schedule them at hours when they have the best chance of reaching audiences. Equally important in its competition with other networks is the prestige each network enjoys—its image in the minds of listeners and of advertisers. Consequently, each network spends millions of dollars each year to enhance its corporate image. NBC's experiments with color programming over the years were encouraged, certainly, by the interest of its parent company, the Radio Corporation of America, in selling color television sets; but NBC's adoption of a virtually all-color evening schedule in the autumn of 1965 also added to that network's prestige with the general public—and forced its rivals to offer substantial amounts of color programming as well. Network prestige, the network image, depends also on the special programs it provides. Some are entertainment features of high quality or special audience appeal. Others are programs important for their cultural values—broadcasts of operas or programs featuring symphony orchestras or ballet companies.

Most of each network's prestige offerings, however, are in the fields of information and special events. In the 1974–1975 season, for instance, 21.5 percent of the 381 specials offered by the three television networks could be categorized as informative documentaries. The percentage of dramas offered, the second highest category in that year, was only 13.1. These informative documentaries provided by each network usually cost far more than could be covered by the sale of time within the programs. Coverage of special events—national elections, national political conventions, the various space flights, congressional hearings, and the like—entail production costs in each case of millions of dollars, in addition to loss of network revenues resulting from the cancellation of regular commercial programs. The three television networks, for instance, estimate they lost from $7 million to $10 million dollars in advertising revenues during their coverage of the Senate Watergate hearings of 1973 and from $4 million to $5 million during their coverage of the Nixon impeachment hearings of 1974.

Another factor in network prestige is the broadcasting of various sports events. *Broadcasting* magazine estimates that national advertisers spent more than $284 million during the 1974–1975 season for broadcasting rights to more than 1,100 hours of network sports. The three networks compete vigorously for the rights to various special sports events and ABC scored heavily in 1975–1976 with its exclusive coverage of the Winter and Summer Olympics; by outbidding CBS for rights to the Preakness, the second race in the so-called Triple Crown of horse racing; and by outbidding NBC for the right to carry some major league baseball and some World Series games, both once exclusive NBC properties. NBC fought back in 1977 by winning the rights to carry the 1980 Olympics in Moscow.

That the networks take seriously the prestige attached to specials of all types is illustrated by a 1974 statement by CBS claiming the crown as "specials network" formerly assumed by NBC. The CBS claim was based on the number of specials in 1973–1974 (70 CBS to 49 NBC), average ratings (23 CBS to 20 NBC) and the "superior quality" of their specials. NBC, however, did not agree and produced figures showing it with 46 specials in the September through December period in 1973 and an average rating of 22.2, compared with 38 specials for CBS with an average rating of 19.9. The two networks used different figures, of course; but the claims earned a story in *Variety*, and the very fact of the dispute shows the importance attached to specials by network executives.

Network-Affiliated Stations

With the exception of the Mutual Broadcasting System, each of the national network companies is the owner of a number of television and radio stations—a combined total for all three networks of 15 VHF television stations and 17 AM radio stations. In addition, each network provides program service to other stations in which network companies have no financial interest whatever—stations known as affiliates, linked to the network operating companies by affiliation contracts, in which the station agrees to broadcast certain commercial programs provided by the network. To enable national advertisers to reach the largest possible number of listeners, every network company attempts to secure affiliates in all or practically all of the nation's major markets.

However, there are three television networks, and not all major cities have as many as three commercial television stations; a few markets have only one. As a result, a television network is not always able to secure in every major city a "primary" affiliate—a station obligated by contract to give first preference to programs offered by that network. In markets with only one or two commercial television stations, then, a television outlet not only has a primary affiliation agreement with one network, but may also have a secondary affiliation with another. Such stations give preference to programs offered by the first network and also carry programs provided by the second network when they can be worked into the weekly schedule. In many instances, programs of the second network are supplied on film or videotape or are taped directly from the network "feed," and carried on a delayed basis at hours convenient to the stations. Table 6–3 shows the number of cities in which each national television network had primary affiliates during the latter part of 1974. In addition, CBS had secondary affiliation contracts with stations in 17 cities and NBC with stations in 24 cities; ABC, with fewer primary affiliates than either of its competitors, had secondary arrangements with stations in 43 different cities.

Network affiliation is much less important to radio stations than to television outlets, in view of the limited program service that radio networks provide and the relatively small amounts that stations receive for carrying network programs. During 1974, only about one AM radio station in four was affiliated with a national radio network.

Network Payments to Affiliates Affiliation contracts usually provide that the station is paid by the network for the time used to carry com-

Table 6–3   Television Stations Listed as Primary Affiliates
of National Television Networks, Fall 1975

Number of Stations per City	Number of Cities	ABC		Stations affiliated with CBS		NBC		Nonaffiliated Stations	
		VHF	UHF	VHF	UHF	VHF	UHF	VHF	UHF
4 or more stations	41	33	8	40	1	39	2	21[a]	52[a]
3 stations	71	45	26	55	16	52.	19	—	3
2 stations	51	15	12	22	8	28	7	2	8
1 station	155	28	7	38	10	35	15	6	16
Totals	319	121	53	155	38	154	41	29[a]	79[a]

[a] Figures include two Mexican UHF stations serving San Diego and one Canadian VHF station serving the Detroit area.

Figures are based on information given in station listings in the 1975 *Broadcasting Yearbook*.

mercial network programs. Since the four national radio networks have combined revenues totaling only $58 million a year, not much money remains after payment of rental on network lines and other network operating costs, so that most of the radio affiliates receive only nominal payments for carrying network programs. Many of the smaller radio stations receive no cash payments at all; they are simply allowed to carry the network's programs without charge and, if possible, to sell to local advertisers certain available minutes provided by the network. High-powered stations, especially those in major markets, fare somewhat better; in 1974, the network-affiliated radio stations in the 25 largest metropolitan areas—network-owned stations not included—received an average of approximately $12,500 each from the network companies with which they had contracts. However, 1974 network payments to the more than 3,000 affiliates in smaller communities averaged less than $1,500, and at least part of this amount represents revenues from programs provided by regional rather than national networks.

Television stations receive much more substantial payments for the time used to carry network programs; in 1974, national television networks paid more than $248 million to their approximately 500 affiliated stations, or an average of more than $473,000 for each affiliate. The amounts received by stations naturally vary, depending on the number of hours of commercial network programs each station carries and the rates charged for station time. Compensation for primary affiliates is determined on the basis of rather complicated formulas, varying from one network to another. In a standard contract of one major network, for instance, the payment to an affiliated station is calculated by multiplying its "affiliated station's network rate"—a figure jointly negotiated and agreed upon by both station and network—by various percentages assigned to different time periods—ranging from 7 percent for the 6:00 to 10:15 A.M. Monday through Friday period to 32 percent for the 6:00 to 11:00 P.M. period seven days a week—and then multiplying the product by the fraction of commercial availabilities unsold by the network within the commercial programs carried. Some networks also subtract from the total weekly amount paid to an affiliate a multiple of the station's "network rate," while others require their affiliates to carry a specified number of hours of programming without network compensation. Some stations in very small markets receive no payment whatever from the networks with which they are affiliated; they are simply allowed to carry the network's programs—commercials included—and to derive what revenues they can from the sale of spot announcements in station-break periods between programs. Stations with secondary affiliation contracts are paid a lesser amount for the time in which network programs are carried.

Other Contract Provisions   Almost all network contracts call for the network companies to pay the costs of delivering the network programs to the affiliated stations—that is, the rental on AT&T lines connecting stations with network originating points. Some network contracts also permit affiliates to tape "news excerpts" of news events as they are broadcast in network news programs and to edit these for use in their local news programs, within certain network-established limits. For this right, the affiliated stations allow a further deduction from their network compensation. Affiliates, of course, are permitted to carry network sustaining programs (those with no commercial announcements) without payment.

In addition, several contract provisions are standard in all contracts as a result of regulations laid down by the Federal Communications Commission. Affiliation contracts may not provide that any station is the "exclusive" outlet for any one network in its community; the network retains the right to allow other stations in the area to broadcast its programs, although, in practice, usually only those programs the affiliate does not wish to carry are offered to other stations.

The affiliated station on its part may accept programs offered by competing networks and does in fact accept a large number of such programs—at least if it is in a one- or two-station market and has a primary affiliation contract with one network and a secondary arrangement with another. Every affiliate has the right, by contract, to reject any program the network offers, either because the station's manager considers it unsuitable or of low quality or because he prefers to use the time period to present a locally produced or syndicated program, or even a program provided by a different network.

The network company may not determine the rates the affiliated station charges for advertising time, other than the rates charged for network programs. Before 1963, standard affiliation contracts gave the network an option on certain hours of the station's time each day, but this practice is now prohibited by a regulation of the FCC. Finally, by FCC regulation, network-affiliation contracts cover periods of not more than 2 years; at the end of any contract period, either the network or the station is free to make other arrangements.

THE BROADCASTING INDUSTRY

In addition to networks and broadcasting stations, literally thousands of other business concerns are involved in the process of providing radio and television programs for American listeners. Many of these companies were organized during the late 1920s or early 1930s to meet the special needs of radio. Others were developed as parts of the motion picture industry and have broadened their activities to include functions related to television. Still others have come into existence in more recent years to provide services connected with the expanding television industry. The business of broadcasting includes concerns engaging in specialized activities that range from the construction of antenna towers to the production and filming of commercial announcements.

Auxiliary Television Broadcasting Services

Several types of auxiliary services are used to extend the coverage of television stations. In 1955, the Federal Communications Commission authorized a service known as "satellite" television stations.

These are regularly authorized stations, occupying channels allocated by the commission to their respective communities and using as much power as used by other television stations. They are not required, however, to originate local programming or to maintain studios, although some of them do provide a limited amount of local programming. For the most part, the satellite merely reproduces the signal and the programming of a parent station located in a community 80 or 100 miles away, thus increasing the effective coverage of the parent station and bringing television service to communities too small to afford an independent television operation. Satellite stations, then, are considered by the FCC to be full-fledged television stations but freed from the responsibility of local programming.

In 1956, the FCC also authorized the operation of "translator" stations. Translators pick up the signals of regular television stations and rebroadcast them on a different channel, usually UHF. These use very low-powered, inexpensive equipment; they maintain no studios and originate no program materials; they are not even required to have an engineer in attendance while on the air. Many translators are operated by regular television stations to extend the coverage of the parent station over a larger area. Others have been constructed by nonprofit groups to bring television service to small communities. They are less expensive to build and operate than satellite stations and are most commonly found in such mountain states as Colorado, Montana, Utah, and Wyoming.

A third type of auxiliary television service is provided by "booster" or "repeater" stations. These are even less expensive to construct and operate than translator stations and serve substantially the same purpose of extending the coverage of a regular station over a larger area or providing a service in so-called "shadow areas" where reception is impaired by mountainous terrain. A booster station operates usually with very low power on the same frequency used by the parent television station. Since the FCC in past years has allowed boosters to be used only by stations on UHF channels and very few UHF stations operate in mountainous areas, boosters are less widely used than translator stations.

Cable Television

Satellite, translator, and booster stations all were designed to extend the signals of television stations to sparsely populated areas that would not support a commercial television station. Another device for expanding a station's coverage area is community antenna television, also called CATV or cable television. Indeed, cable has proven to be the most successful device for such extension, eclipsing the other services in recent years.

A CATV company provides television service to individual homes by connecting these homes by wire, or "cable," to the company's studio. Subscribers thus connected to these systems receive the signals from all local stations; from network, independent, and educational stations in distant communities; and, often, a variety of special services—local news, sports, education, feature-length movies, special visual displays of news wires, sports scores, weather reports, stock market figures, and so forth. For these services, typical subscribers pay from $6 to $9 a month, with a one-time installation fee averaging $15.

By 1975, there were 3,350 operating CATV systems in the United States, serving some 7,300 communities, with another 2,650 systems approved but not yet built. Systems operating by the mid-1970s reached approximately 10 million homes—15 percent of the nation's television homes. The number of subscribers per system ranged from fewer than 100 to almost 140,000. In 1975, total industry revenues totaled approximately $760 million—a figure not reached by radio until 1944 (and again, after the television slump, in 1964).

Cable television has had an interesting history in its brief quarter-century of life. Growing from the basic concept of a master antenna service in hotels and apartment buildings, CATV moved quickly through several distinct stages and emerged in the 1970s as a genuine competitor to the broadcast service as we know it.

What cable television set out to do first was simple enough. It began in Pennsylvania in 1949 as a service designed to bring television signals to communities that, because of distance or terrain problems, were unable to receive signals from television stations. Growth of this basic service continued through 1955, with cable systems springing up around the edges of coverage areas of existing stations, spreading their programming to an even larger number of homes.

By 1955, however, as the number of available unserviced markets declined rapidly, cable television operators began to look beyond this basic service and explore a new potential market for their services—communities without full network service because they had only one or two stations. Given permission by the FCC to construct their own microwave relays, CATV systems began bringing in stations from more distant communities, thus filling in the network gaps. As they did so, they began to compete significantly, for the first

time, with existing broadcasting stations—for audiences, if not for advertising dollars.

Five years later cable television had reached another plateau in its development as it approached a practical limit in the number of communities needing its services for full network coverage. By this time, technology had provided the answer in the form of equipment capable of carrying up to twelve channels to subscribers. With this added channel capacity, cable television systems could enter larger markets and offer additional signals brought by microwave from distant markets, as well as motion picture channels, syndicated programs, audio services, and a variety of specialized news and information services.

In 1959, the FCC had said it had no right to regulate cable and had later asserted its control only over systems with microwave links; but when faced with a threat of wholesale invasion of major markets, the commission announced in 1966 that it did indeed have the authority to regulate all aspects of CATV. Thereupon it issued a series of restrictions so stringent that the growth of cable was virtually halted for six years.

In the late 1960s and early 1970s, broadcasters and copyright owners had hoped that Congress or the courts would provide an effective way of dealing with CATV by requiring all systems to pay users' fees to the owners of copyrights. The U.S. Supreme Court, however, failed to do so and, in the *Fortnightly* case (1968) and the *Teleprompter* case (1974), ruled that cable television systems simply passed on signals and did not "perform" anything in the sense covered by copyright law.

The *Fortnightly* case demonstrated to the FCC that the courts were not going to help with CATV and it proceeded to reevaluate its position on the growth of the service. In 1972, the commission issued a comprehensive series of rules that, among other things, (1) sharply restricted the importation of signals from markets distant from the market being served; (2) limited the number of broadcast stations that could be carried on systems in markets of various size; (3) required all new systems to offer channels to local government, to educational bodies, and to the public for its free "access"; and (4) required all new systems to have the capability for some kind of feedback from subscribers to the cable system.

Under these rules, cable television resumed its growth in the 1970s, slowed somewhat in the early years of the decade by a shortage of investment capital caused by a sluggish economy. In 1976, a revision of the copyright laws passed by the Congress included the requirement that cable systems pay minimal copyright fees for the programs they carry.

Radio and Television Networks

Technically, the term *network* refers to any group of radio or television stations linked together by telephone land lines, microwave relay systems, or satellites for the simultaneous broadcasting of programs. However, the term is often used more loosely to apply to any grouping of stations making possible the broadcasting of the same program or programs by all stations in the group, regardless of the method by which the programs are distributed. Accordingly, we find a variety of types of networks in the broadcasting industry:

national networks; regional networks; special networks; and transcription, tape, or film networks.

National Networks By far the most important in volume of sales, in program service provided, and in influence, are the national networks already discussed.

As Robert E. Kintner, former president of NBC, once remarked, a network is "nothing but programs and telephone wires." While this description greatly oversimplifies the situation, a network company does no actual broadcasting of programs—at least not in its activities as a network; national network companies do own broadcasting stations, referred to as "O & O" ("owned-and-operated") stations. The network company's function is to create an organization of stations that will operate as a group and to provide facilities for linking those stations together for simultaneous broadcast of programs. For radio service, long-distance telephone lines are leased from the American Telephone and Telegraph Company (AT&T) to connect affiliated stations with network studios in New York, Washington, or other cities from which network programs are originated. For television, stations are linked together by coaxial cable or microwave relay systems also provided by AT&T. Network programs are then "fed" over these wire or relay connections to the various affiliated stations, to be broadcast in each local community.

The Public Broadcasting Service (PBS), an interconnected network of public television stations, was established in 1969 by the Corporation for Public Broadcasting (CPB). PBS provides a regular schedule of evening programs for most of the educational television stations in the United States. A similar service for public radio stations is provided by National Public Radio (NPR), also under the supervision of CPB.

The National Black Network (radio) has also been formed, with 75 affiliates in 1975, to provide specialized programs to radio stations aiming their programming toward the black community. Two national television networks, the Hughes Television Network and the TVS Television Network, provide live telecasts of sports and other special events. These networks have no regular permanent affiliates and line up groups of stations, many of whom have primary affiliations with one of the major networks, for specific events—most of which are aired at times that do not conflict with major network offerings. In 1975, TVS and NBC worked out an arrangement whereby the two networks would provide Saturday afternoon basketball double-headers during the 1975–1976 season, with TVS setting up a series of regional networks to carry games of local or regional interest and NBC producing a game of national interest between well-known collegiate "powerhouses."

Regional Networks   In addition to national network organizations, there are approximately 20 more or less permanent regional networks of television stations and almost 125 regional radio networks listed in the 1975 edition of *Broadcasting Yearbook*. A few of these are actively functioning organizations that provide a regular—though usually limited—program service on a year-round basis. Others are groups of stations operating as networks only when advertisers wish to secure coverage of a number of markets in a single state or a portion of a state. In addition to these regional networks, so-called sports networks are regularly formed during the appropriate season each year. Virtually every professional team has a network of both radio and television stations that carry play-by-play broadcasts of all or a significant portion of its schedule. Similar networks are formed for most college football and basketball teams and even some high school teams. The size of these sports networks, of course, generally depends on the success and popularity of the individual team. Some of the more important regional networks may be parts of national network organizations; because stations comprising these permanent regional groups are already linked together to form "legs" of national networks, it is a relatively simple matter for them to provide service for regional advertisers in a specified area in the same way that the national network carries programs for national advertisers on stations throughout the country.

Special Networks   Custom-built, or "special," networks may be created at times for national or regional spot advertisers who wish to present a program in a particular group of cities where no permanent regional net exists to provide the service desired. Such special networks are set up in most states during political campaigns to carry programs in support of individual candidates for office. Sometimes, too, stations join together in setting up special temporary networks to secure coverage of major news or sports events of particular interest to listeners in their respective communities. By sharing the time charges and the expense of originating the program, it is possible for even the smallest stations to broadcast eyewitness accounts of events taking place in distant cities, although the cost of providing such accounts might be prohibitive for any single station.

Noninterconnected Networks   National networks, regional networks, even special networks are literally networks or chains of stations; the stations comprising them are linked together by telephone line or microwave relay for simultaneous broadcast of programs. Transcription and film networks are technically not networks at all, since stations are not connected by telephone lines or microwave relay systems and since no simultaneous broadcasting of programs is involved. The transcription and film network companies do serve groups of affiliated stations, primarily as central sales agencies through which sponsored programs may be placed with the various affiliated outlets—the programs being prepared in taped, transcribed, or filmed form and distributed to the stations by parcel post or express before the time of broadcast. Only one regularly constituted national commercial transcription network is in existence: the Keystone Broadcasting System, with more than 1,000 affiliated radio stations, which are located for the most part in small towns and agricultural areas throughout the nation. With the reduced importance of interconnected national radio networks, Keystone in recent years has received considerable attention from national spot advertisers who are interested in reaching rural listeners.

One television film network, National Telefilm Associates (NTA), was in operation for a few years, attempting to provide a limited quantity of filmed programming to affiliates in a number of major markets. However, difficulties in clearing time for NTA programs on stations whose evening schedules were already committed to the regular television networks resulted in the failure of the project.

Noninterconnected networks were more successful in the educational field; the National Association of Educational Broadcasters inaugurated a taped program service for educational radio stations as early as 1950, and the foundation-financed National Educational Television organization provided several hours a week of taped and filmed programs for use by noncommercial television stations. Both systems have since been replaced by CPB and PBS.

American Telephone and Telegraph Company

Distribution of regular network programs is the special province of the long-lines division of the American Telephone and Telegraph Company (AT&T) and its associated Bell System companies. Hundreds of millions of dollars have been invested by AT&T in program transmission facilities—coaxial cable connections, microwave relay systems, and special long-distance telephone lines—and the company collects annual rentals of millions of dollars from the three national television networks for carrying their programs to affiliated stations, plus an additional million a year from national radio networks. Costs of cable or microwave interconnection are an important part of the television networks' expense of providing program service to affiliated stations.

Equipment Manufacturers

The manufacturing of equipment—receiving sets, transmitting equipment, television cameras, technical equipment of a thousand different kinds—is a fundamental part of the broadcasting industry. The statement has been made that the rapid development of radio during the 1920s was largely a result of the desire of manufacturers of radio receiving sets to create a market for their products. Certainly it is a fact that the technical excellence of radio and television today has been the result of the continuing research and experimentation carried on by electronics manufacturers, research that in recent years has given us transistor radios, color television, and satellite communications systems. One index of the importance of equipment manufacturers in the broadcasting industry is the fact that the American people spend as much money each year on new radio and television receiving sets and on parts and repairs for existing sets as the nation's advertisers spend for station and network time. During the 10-year period from 1964 through 1973, manufacturers produced, on the average, 13,400,000 new television receiving sets and 45,471,200 new radio sets a year; to buy these sets, the public spent a total of almost $3.5 billion a year.

However, radio and television receivers represent only a part of the output of equipment manufacturing companies. Stations and networks buy equipment of almost every type imaginable; how much is spent each year is almost impossible to estimate, but the figure must run into hundreds of millions of dollars. Many companies produce a general line of receiving and transmitting equipment. Others manufacture highly specialized products, such as, for example, antenna towers, magnetic tape used for audio and video recording, tape recorders, film used in motion pictures and in filmed television programs, studio lighting equipment for television and motion pictures, and automation systems for radio.

Advertising Agencies

Advertising agencies are important in broadcasting because all network and national spot advertising and at least 15 to 20 percent of all local radio and television advertising is placed by agencies. Advertising agencies serve as expert representatives of national manufacturing companies or of local distributors or retailers in the planning of advertising campaigns and the handling of day-to-day details of advertising, whether the medium used is television, radio, newspapers, magazines, billboards, or direct mail. When broadcast advertising is to be used, the agency gives advice on the amount of money to be spent, the stations or the network to be used, and the program or spot-carrier to be selected; it plans the commercial announcements, writes the advertising copy, and often produces the transcribed, filmed, or taped commercial spots used in the advertising campaign; it contracts for time on stations and networks and handles all details connected with the advertising activities of its client. Equivalent functions are performed when advertising is carried in newspapers or magazines, or is handled by other methods. For its services, the advertising agency typically receives a commission of 15 percent of the total amount the advertiser pays for station or network time, deducted when payment is made to the broadcaster. In addition, the agency collects from the advertiser the production cost of the commercials used in the advertising campaign. The typical advertising agency may have as clients fifteen or twenty different firms, no two of which are engaged in the same type of business.

Although there are many thousands of advertising agencies in the United States, most are small, local concerns with fewer than half a dozen employees each, with local advertisers as their only clients. Some national or regional agencies specialize in billboard or direct mail advertising, but most major agencies do not specialize. They handle all the types of advertising required by their clients—the important manufacturing and industrial enterprises, which include the heaviest users of network and national spot advertising. Some of the largest national advertising agencies spend for their clients collectively from $100 million to $250 million a year for network and station time.

Station Representatives

Extremely important in the handling of national spot advertising on radio and television are station-representative companies, usually referred to in the broadcasting industry as "station reps." Virtually every television station and important radio station employs a station-representative concern to act as the station's agent in the sale of time to national and regional advertisers. The "rep" company's salesmen call on time buyers for advertising agencies with clients planning national spot-advertising campaigns to attempt to induce the buyers to purchase time on stations the "rep" concern represents. In addition, station representatives assist their clients in determining the rates to be charged for time, in developing sales promotional materials and in planning advertising to be placed in industry trade papers. Some even assist stations in the selection of key employees. In return for these activities, the "rep" concerns collect commissions ranging from 7 to 17½ percent on amounts paid by national spot advertisers for time on the station or stations served.

While there are more than 200 station representative concerns in the United States, it is estimated that 23 firms place 99 percent of all national spot advertising. The typical television "rep" firm handles up to 70 stations, while the average radio firm represents between 100 and 200 clients. Virtually all "rep" companies specialize in handling the affairs of stations of one particular type. Some handle only 50,000-watt radio stations or 5,000-watt stations with large coverage areas; others handle only radio stations with a middle-of-the-road format; still others may represent only television stations. Naturally, the stations represented by any one concern are located in different cities and are not in direct competition with one another.

Program Production Companies

In the early days of network radio, practically all network programs were produced by the network companies themselves or by stations affiliated with the network. During the 1930s, a majority of sponsored network programs were produced by advertising agencies. Today, all network news programs and many television documentaries are produced by the networks, as are the NBC, CBS, and ABC morning programs (*Today, The CBS Morning News* and *Good Morning America*) and NBC's *Tonight, Tomorrow, Weekend,* and *Saturday Night* programs. Networks also produce most of the sports events on Saturday and Sunday afternoons and on Monday nights and some of the entertainment programs on daytime schedules. However, nearly 90 percent of all evening entertainment programs in prime time and a large number of the daytime entertainment programs come from independent companies known in the industry as "independent producers" or "package agencies." These are concerns that develop programs; employ writers, producers, directors, actors, entertainers, and entire production crews; and handle all of the details incidental to preparing a program for broadcast. Most "package programs" are produced on film or videotape. The package pro-

offered for use by other stations. The third major type of material consists of motion picture films, that is, features produced originally for showing in motion picture theaters; the rights to many theatrical feature films have been purchased by syndication companies, which lease prints of the films to television stations. The final type of syndicated material includes cartoons, travelogues, two-reel comedies and other "short-subjects" originally produced for showing in motion picture theaters. Many of these short films have been made available for syndication to television stations, which frequently use them as segments of programs produced locally for children. Perhaps the best known of this latter type of syndicated material is the *Our Gang* series of shorts, produced in the 1930s and still distributed under the title of *The Little Rascals*.

Some syndication companies handle only one type of syndicated materials; however, some major syndicators deal with both produced-for-television series and theatrical motion picture features. Often a single company holds syndication rights to as many as a dozen or more different television program series, each including from 26 to more than 100 episodes. The same syndication concern may also hold the rights to several hundred theatrical feature films, the latter usually sold to stations in packages including 40 to 50 features each. A station may contract for exclusive first-run rights in a given locality to a television series or to a package of theatrical films; rental fees will vary according to the size of the market and, of course, the quality of the material involved. Some of these contracts, usually for syndicated game shows like *Truth or Consequences*, are for only one run of the series in a single year. Other contracts allow for a certain number of runs over a specified number of years (for example, five runs of the series in a 5-year period). Following this period, rights for still more runs can be sold to another station in the same community, naturally at a much lower price.

For many years, industry trade publications emphasized the fact that the supply of theatrical feature films available for first-run showing on television was not inexhaustible. Of all the films produced in Hollywood over the years, by the mid-1970s only a relatively small number remained that had not already been released to television and therefore presumably had already had first-run showings on stations in most major markets. In addition, as mentioned in an earlier paragraph, only a few new program series have been produced especially for television syndication in recent years. However, there are numerous programs still available that were originally carried in series form by television networks, and new programs are appearing on network schedules every year.

One important source of revenue for syndication and production companies is the leasing of program series, including programs currently being carried on our own national networks, to television stations in other countries. Schedules of national networks and of commercial stations in Great Britain, Japan, Australia, and literally dozens of other countries include many of the same American-produced, made-for-television programs that viewers see in the United States, with sound tracks in the appropriate languages dubbed in.

Since national networks frequently are part-owners of syndication rights to television program series carried over their facilities, each network company once had its own program sales division to handle the sale of some or all of the network-controlled programs to American and foreign television stations. The same FCC ruling that produced the prime-time access rules discussed in Chapter 5, however, forbids the networks domestic syndication of their own programs, although they can still deal with foreign nations.

Program Services

Program packagers and program syndication companies deal in finished, complete programs; but both radio and television stations also buy materials for inclusion in their own locally produced programs—for example, news, recorded music, sound effects, and special production effects. Most of the national and international news materials included in radio or television news programs are supplied by Associated Press (AP) and United Press International (UPI), although the three major networks have built sizable news operations of their own in recent years. The news services provide a daily wire news service to broadcasting stations and a sound-film service to television stations; UPI also offers a special newsfilm service for television; and both services provide live audio news "feeds" for radio stations. Several smaller concerns also supply special types of news material to radio stations; these include sports news features, on-the-spot reports from overseas reporters, news of interest to blacks and other minorities, reports from Washington, farm news, religious news, and the like. In addition to the three national television networks, which provide electronic "feeds" of news stories to affiliates for use in local news, several firms supply specialized news and features on film and tape.

Music Suppliers   While of minor importance in local television, music is the essence of local radio programming. Music in recorded form has long been available from music library services that supplied stations, for a regular monthly fee, from music libraries including from 3,000 to 5,000 separate selections. These libraries offered a wide variety of types of music ranging from standards to semiclassical and from familiar hymns to music by military bands. The popular numbers most heavily played by present-day radio stations, however, are on records or in albums produced by the major recording companies. For promotion purposes, most of the record companies distribute a limited number of recordings to radio stations without charge, but for most stations the best records and albums are usually available only upon the payment of a nominal service fee. This service brings the latest recordings to stations at 10 to 20 percent of the market price, however; and most radio stations subscribe to the album-and-record services of one or more record companies to provide material for programming in the area of popular music. Other independent concerns offer a low-price record service designed to provide contemporary stations with the most popular albums and records of the day.

The introduction of automation in radio stations—FM stations in particular—made necessary the supplying of another type of music. As noted earlier, the automated station uses music recorded on long-playing tapes, including "cue" devices that, at the proper times, automatically switch in other tapes or tape cartridges on which commercial announcements or station identification materials have been recorded; several concerns distribute these long-playing tapes to automated stations on a rental basis. Various music formats are available, ranging from "good music" through "middle-of-the-road" to " 'Solid Gold' contemporary."

Suppliers of Special Materials   Several companies specialize in providing music in forms other than complete selections—music bridges, transitional music, theme music for programs. Some produce made-to-order jingles for station identifications, weather reports, lead-ins for news programs, or commercial announcements for local advertisers. Still other companies offer special sound-effects recordings or complete libraries of sound effects. A number of concerns make slides or films for station identification visuals for television stations or provide art work used in television commercial announcements; some specialize in the production of animated-cartoon commercials. A few companies maintain stock-film libraries, selling stock-film footage of places or events or film clips from old newsreels to television stations for use in the production of documentary programs or as filmed "signatures" for local programs of other types. A few concerns sell comedy routines for use by radio disc jockey personalities or by masters of ceremonies of audience-participation programs. Two or three companies specialize in providing prizes to be given participants in quiz and audience-participation programs, supplying brand-name goods at prices very much below those that would be paid if the items supplied were purchased separately. Almost any type of material required for the presentation of local radio or television programs is available from some supplier connected with the broadcasting industry.

Music Licensing Organizations

The function of music licensing organizations is only dimly understood outside of the industry, but they perform an important service. The first such organization, the American Society of Composers, Authors and Publishers (ASCAP), was formed before broadcasting existed to insure that the creators of the words and music of songs, and the publishers who made them available, were reimbursed in some way for the performance of their music for profit. Before ASCAP existed, the creators and publishers lost control of their product after it was printed and sold, while users were free to make as much money as they could from the performance of this material.

Simply stated, ASCAP changed all this by collecting "license fees" for any performance for profit of a musical number written or published by an ASCAP member. Fees thus collected were redistributed to these members in a manner that reflected the relative popularity of their works. When radio broadcasting ceased to be a novelty and began showing signs of making a profit, ASCAP moved quickly and negotiated a fee schedule that allowed it to collect from broadcasters for the right to play music licensed to the firm.

As noted in Chapter 3, another licensing firm, Broadcast Music, Incorporated (BMI), was formed in 1939 by broadcasters who objected to a new ASCAP contract proposal. Since its formation, BMI has developed into a genuine competitor to ASCAP and both organizations work vigorously to sign new artists to their contracts. The national networks and virtually all radio and television stations hold licenses to perform both ASCAP and BMI music, paying license fees for the right to use copyrighted music. A similar organization known as SESAC (Society of European State Artists and Composers) holds the rights to much music of European or Latin American origin and to enough religious and martial music to force most broadcasters into signing still another contract.

Pay Television

During the late 1950s and early 1960s a number of experiments were conducted involving "subscription" or "pay" television (which *Variety* likes to call "feevee"), in which programs were delivered to subscribers who paid for the service on a per-program basis. In some systems, the programs were delivered over a coaxial cable to receivers in the homes of subscribers, the number of programs viewers selected were metered, and the subscribers were billed at the end of the month. In others, like the experiment in Hartford, Connecticut, authorized in 1962 by the FCC, the programs were broadcast by a regular television station, but the use of a "scrambler" device made reception possible only in homes having a metered "unscrambler" attached to the set.

Most providers of "feevee" have promised to make available programs of types not usually available from "free" television stations: concerts, operas, ballet, current Broadway productions, outstanding sports events, and the best of current motion pictures. Most of the pay-television experiments lasted only a few months and were apparently not too successful, although detailed financial information has not been available. The pay-television companies have had the same problems of high production costs that have plagued the commercial television networks, with the result that very little of the promised high-quality programming has actually been provided.

In spite of this, Zenith Radio Corporation and RKO General Inc. continued their experiments with on-the-air pay television in Hartford, and in 1965 they were happy enough with results to ask the FCC to approve a nationwide pay-television system. The FCC, on the other hand, was faced with a strong element of congressional opposition to "feevee," especially in the House of Representatives, and moved very slowly. After proposing rules in 1967 and then agreeing to delay them for a year at the request of the House, the commission in 1968 refused a second request from the House for a one-year delay and finally issued its pay-television rules.

As issued, these rules placed restrictions on the age of feature films that could be shown; limited the carriage of regular sports events that were also being carried on "free" television; and banned series-type programming with connecting plots. In March 1977, however, the Court of Appeals in the District of Columbia threw out any such rules as unconstitutional. The FCC considered an appeal.

"Feevee" became related to cable television when a provision of the 1972 CATV rules allowed CATV systems to "lease" channels to those who wish to use them. Current technology permits the use of these leased channels as a pay-television system, and many cable operators feel that the real future of their operation lies in pay-cable television. Broadcasters, on the other hand, are vigorously opposed, arguing that extensive growth of pay television or cable television would take programs away from "free" television and ultimately force viewers to pay for programs they now receive free.

While over-the-air pay television remains confined to a limited number of subscribers in a few major cities, pay-cable television systems are having more success. *Broadcasting* magazine's *Cable Sourcebook* for 1976 indicated that approximately 100 CATV systems had a pay-cable television channel and that these reached 273,000 subscribers in eighteen states. Home Box Office, Inc., a supplier of programming for pay-cable television, initiated in 1975 the first interconnected—by satellite—pay-cable television network and by the end of the year was serving 27 cable systems.

A successful variation of pay television has been an enterprise called "theater television." Outstanding sports events, like heavyweight championship fights, are picked up by regular television cameras and transmitted by satellite and AT&T facilities to theaters in major cities throughout the country. The events are projected on large screens for audiences who have paid up to $50 for the privilege of watching events not otherwise available on television. Promoters of heavyweight championship fights so televised received many times as much money from the sale of theater television rights as from paid admissions to the fight itself. The same closed-circuit television idea is also frequently used for sales meetings of major corporations; programs originate from a "main" meeting in a major city and are carried to regional meetings in theaters or hotel ballrooms in a number of other cities. Some hotels and motels also offer feature films to guests willing to pay extra to have them piped to the television sets in their rooms.

Industry Groups and Associations

As in any other type of business that operates on a national scale, the broadcasting industry has a number of trade associations and other groups representing people who engage in broadcasting. The most important industry trade group is the National Association of Broadcasters (NAB), which speaks for the broadcasting industry in national policy matters, in matters related to legislation and government regulation, and in the establishment of acceptable industry practices. The NAB includes as members most of the commercial television stations and approximately half of the commercial radio stations in the nation. Responding in the mid-1970s to complaints that NAB placed too much emphasis on the interests of its television members to the detriment of radio, the independent National Association of FM Broadcasters (NAFMB) renamed itself the National Radio Broadcasters Association (NRBA), opened its membership to all radio stations, and launched a program of legislative activity for the benefit of radio broadcasters only.

State associations of broadcasters have been formed in the various states, not directly a part of NAB but serving as extensions of the national association in matters of common concern. Other management groups operating on a national basis include TvB (the Television Bureau of Advertising), RAB (the Radio Advertising Bureau), and TIO (the Television Information Office). The first two are organizations formed to promote the sale of broadcast advertising time; TIO is a public relations body that attempts, by the use of

Figure 6-8 Headquarters for the National Association of Broadcasters (NAB), the major industry trade group, is located in the heart of Washington, D.C., only blocks from the offices of the FCC and from the White House. (Courtesy National Association of Broadcasters)

large-scale publicity and promotion, to create a more favorable public image for the television industry.

In addition to organizations representing stations and station management, there are several professional groups whose members are station employees working in specialized fields. Among them are such associations as American Women in Radio & Television, the National Association of Television and Radio Farm Directors, the National Association of Television Program Executives, the Radio & Television News Directors Association and the Broadcasters Promotion Association, whose members are in charge of the promotional activities of their stations. Probably one of the most influential groups is the news directors association, which works closely with the NAB and with the newspaper industry in efforts to arrange for greater access to news sources for news broadcasts and reporters.

The National Academy of Television Arts and Sciences is made up of writers, producers, directors, technicians, and featured entertainers involved in the production of television programs. The Academy gives annual awards of "Emmys" for outstanding achievement in writing, acting, directing, music scoring, and technical work in network television programs presented during the year.

Broadcasting Unions

Like other industries, broadcasting has labor unions representing employees of stations, networks, and program production concerns in their relations with employers. In all, nearly 50 different unions are involved entirely or in part with broadcasting activities. Most engineers and technicians are members of either the International Brotherhood of Electrical Workers (IBEW) or the National Association of Broadcast Employees and Technicians (NABET); combined, the two organizations represent more than 10,000 network and station employees. Another major broadcasting union, the American Federation of Television & Radio Artists (AFTRA), has a membership of announcers, actors, vocalists, dancers, and other performers who appear on broadcast programs or in commercial announcements. Many AFTRA members also belong to the Screen Actors Guild (SAG), a much larger organization made up of actors and other entertainers who appear in motion pictures made for theatrical use or in filmed television programs or commercial announcements. The International Alliance of Theatrical Stage Employees (IATSE), originally a union of stagehands in theaters and of motion picture projectionists, is also active in television; IATSE represents stagehands and studio floor crews and, in some parts of the country, motion picture cameramen and operators of motion picture projection equipment. Musicians who provide live or recorded instrumental music for use on the air are represented by the American Federation of Musicians (AFM). Certain types of industry workers are organized into "guilds," rather than formal unions. Writers of network or syndicated programs are members of the Writers Guild of America; television directors employed by networks or by package production concerns belong to the Directors Guild of America. In addition, numerous smaller unions or, in some situations, specialized locals of IATSE represent such varied groups as scenic artists, film editors, studio carpenters, wardrobe attendants, makeup artists, hair stylists, and even parking lot attendants.

Unions are an important factor in the broadcasting industry; to a large extent they determine the wages and working conditions of those involved in the production of network and syndicated programs. However, their activities are confined for the most part to the large production centers, and their memberships are made up mostly of employees of networks, package agencies, and large-city stations. Almost all the engineers employed by radio or television stations in major population centers are members of IBEW or NABET; announcers and other on-the-air personalities employed by the same stations are members of AFTRA. However, in smaller communities, few employees of broadcasting stations are union members, aside from musicians and a limited number of station engineers.

Miscellaneous Services

In addition to organizations and business concerns of types already mentioned, there are numerous others providing a variety of services connected with broadcasting. Most of the important network entertainers and writers are represented by *talent agents* who attempt to sell the services of their clients to producing companies, networks, or advertising agencies.

As in other industries, trade papers serve an important function in broadcasting by providing news and feature articles relating to the industry. Publications such as *Broadcasting, Radio-TV Daily, Variety, Billboard, Advertising Age,* and *Television Digest* are widely read by broadcasters and others concerned with special aspects of radio and television, and they exert a considerable amount of influence in industry affairs.

Many other organizations or individuals offer specialized services to broadcasters. A number of research companies provide national ratings for network programs or detailed information about the buying habits of listeners; activities of research organizations will be discussed at length in Chapter 11. Several firms act as station brokers, handling sales of radio and television stations to new owners. Between 1954 and 1974, 5,842 radio stations, 569 television stations, and 235 radio-television combinations changed hands; the amount paid by buyers totaled almost $3.5 billion. There are more than 125 consulting engineers to assist stations with their technical problems. More than 800 attorneys specialize in communications law; they give legal advice to stations, especially on matters relating to federal regulation, and they appear as representatives of their station-clients in hearings on license applications or in presenting oral arguments before the Federal Communications Commission. Some concerns serve as management consultants; others as consultants on station programming and news. In short, whenever a need for specialized services exists, there are companies available to provide those services.

A final but exceedingly important element in the broadcasting industry is the Federal Communications Commission itself, the federal agency charged with the responsibility of regulating American radio and television. The FCC grants licenses to stations and also licenses the engineers who put the stations on the air and keep them on; it determines general policies for broadcasting; it sets technical standards for television; it assigns television and FM radio channels to various communities; it makes recommendations to Congress concerning new legislation relating to broadcasting. More than any other single organization involved in broadcasting activity, the Federal Communications Commission determines the overall nature of broadcasting service and the patterns that characterize broadcasting in the United States. The commission will be considered in greater detail in Chapter 12.

STUDY AND DISCUSSION QUESTIONS

1. Secure a copy of *Broadcasting Yearbook* and determine the classification of each AM station in your immediate area, in the following categories:

    a. Clear, regional, or local channel

    b. Class I, II, III, or IV station

    c. Daytime only or 24-hour authorization

Study the programming and schedule of a representative of each type of station you identify and see if you can come to any conclusions about the following:

a. Types of programming and music format
b. Number of commercials
c. Proportion of national, regional, and local commercials
d. Amounts and types of news and public affairs
e. Target audience

2. Examine the FM stations in your market also. Determine the maximum power authorized for each. Study their programs and schedules and see if you can reach any conclusions about the following:

a. Types of programming and music format
b. Number and frequency of commercials
c. Proportion of national, regional, and local commercials
d. Amounts and types of news and public affairs
e. Target audience

3. If there are any commercial television stations in your market that are not affiliated with a network (or if a cable system in the market carries such a station) study the schedule and determine to the best of your ability the sources of programming used on the station. The most common sources will be the following:

a. Off-network syndication
b. Network programs rejected by affiliates in the market
c. Theatrical motion pictures
d. Programs made exclusively for syndication
e. Local production

4. Report on or be prepared to discuss one of the following topics:

a. The growth of community antenna television (CATV; also called cable television)
b. The impact of cable television on your community
c. The varieties of programming provided on cable television
d. The development of pay-television
e. The development of "special" networks for sports and other programming
f. The possibilities of a fourth national (commercial) network
g. The function and operation of advertising agencies, local, regional, and national
h. The role of the station representative
i. Factors affecting the development and success of independent television program producers
j. The importance of program syndication
k. Music services available to radio stations

5. Report on or be prepared to discuss the evolving relationship between the major Hollywood producers and television. Begin with the attitude of those producers to television in the late 1940s and trace the changes in these attitudes—and changes in the relationship—since those years.

6. Report on or be prepared to discuss the evolution and growth of the major music licensing services in the United States (ASCAP and BMI).

SUGGESTED READINGS

Joseph S. Johnson and Kenneth Jones. *Modern Radio Station Practices.* Belmont, Calif.: Wadsworth, 1978.

Ward L. Quall and James A. Brown. *Broadcast Management: Radio and Television.* New York: Hastings House, 1976.

Yale Roe, ed. *Television Station Management.* New York: Hastings House, 1964.

Edd Routt. *The Business of Radio Broadcasting.* Blue Ridge Summit, Pa.: TAB Books, 1972.

7

The Economics of Broadcasting

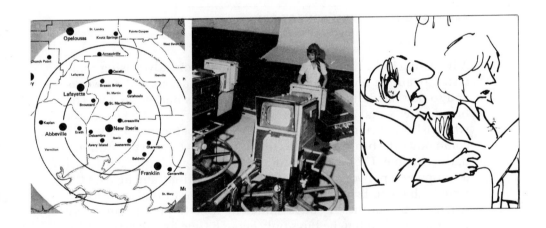

Under the system of private ownership and operation of broadcasting stations that exists in the United States, broadcasting is a business undertaking. The licensee of a broadcasting station is a businessman. Like other businessmen, he naturally hopes to make a profit on his broadcasting operations; in any event, he must at least break even financially to stay in business. If radio or television stations fail to earn enough money to meet their expenses, sooner or later they will be forced to go off the air.

The business character of broadcasting is somewhat unusual in our economic society. Unlike other business enterprises, the broadcasting station "gives away" its primary product—programs—to be "consumed" by listeners who pay nothing whatever to the station for the privilege of listening to the programs presented. The listener, as a result, is not really the broadcaster's "customer" at all, nor are broadcast programs the major commodity the station has for sale.

RADIO AND TELEVISION ADVERTISING

Advertising is the lifeblood of broadcasting. From advertising come virtually all the revenues needed to operate stations and networks and to pay the costs of programs that stations put on the air. The broadcaster's real customer is not the listener, but the advertiser who wishes to bring his wares to the attention of the public; the only commodity the broadcaster has to sell is time—time in the station's daily schedule. The advertiser merely buys the use of the facilities of a station or a network for specified periods of time, and he uses the time he buys to bring his advertising message to the attention of listeners. Sometimes he buys sufficient time to present an entire program; more often, he buys only enough time for advertising announcements 60 seconds or less in length.

A station's time, however, is valueless unless that station has listeners. So the station presents programs to attract a listening audience. For practical purposes it might be said that the broadcaster is engaged in two separate enterprises: (1) providing a free program service for the benefit of the nonpaying public, and (2) selling time in his schedule to advertisers to pay for this free service. Since each of these enterprises involves somewhat different procedures, we will examine them separately, looking first at the ways in which advertising is handled on radio or television.

Types of Broadcast Advertising

Some of the advertisers who buy time on networks or stations are big concerns, with products marketed in every part of the United States. Others are small, with operations limited to a single community. On the basis of the size of the area to be reached and the manner in which advertising time is purchased, broadcast advertising falls into three general classifications, all referred to in earlier chapters. First we have *network advertising*—advertising carried over the facilities of a network that is made up of a number of different stations linked together for the simultaneous broadcasting of the same program in a number of different communities. The second type of broadcast advertising is that known as *national* (or regional) *spot advertising*—that placed by a single advertiser on stations in a number of different markets, but not using network facilities. The advertiser using "national spot" may buy time for complete programs or for merely selected spot announcements. The term *spot advertising* comes from the fact that the advertiser selects the markets to be reached and the stations he wants to use and so is able to "spot" his advertising in the particular areas where he thinks it will do the most good. Network and national spot advertisers are necessarily those big concerns whose products are distributed on a national or a regional basis. The small Main Street merchant who sells only to customers in a single city buys time only on his home town station; the advertising carried in his behalf falls into the third category, that of *local advertising*.

Local advertising is highly important in the radio broadcasting industry. In 1975, of a total of $1.89 billion spent by advertisers for radio time, 74.1 percent or more than $1.4 billion represented expenditures by local advertisers, as compared with 22 percent spent by national spot advertisers and only 3.9 percent spent for network advertising. A different situation, however, exists in television. Advertisers spent approximately $4.72 billion in 1975 for time on television networks and stations—almost triple the amount that went for radio time—and of this total only 23.6 percent came from local advertisers. Network advertising accounted for 45.8 percent of all sales of television time, and the remaining 30.6 percent represented expenditures for national spot advertising.

Types of Sponsorship

Advertising time on radio and television may be purchased in units of varying length. Historically, stations have divided the time they

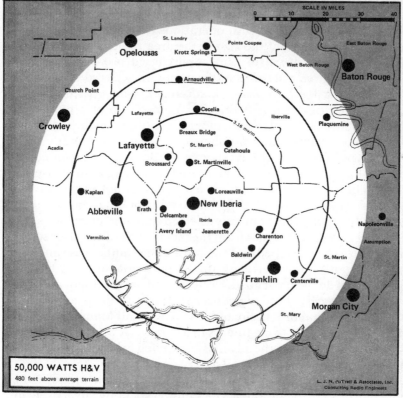

Figure 7–1 Local sales are important to radio, and stations prepare elaborate promotional pieces to aid such sales. (Courtesy KDEA Stereo Radio, Inc.)

offered for sale into two classifications, program and announcement time. Program time comes in units of 5 minutes or more, permitting the presentation of a complete program. Announcement time comes in units of 2 minutes or less—usually no more than a single minute—suitable for the presentation of a commercial message.

An advertiser wishing to sponsor all or part of a program, then, can purchase an entire program or series—called *full* or *single sponsorship*, in which he pays the entire cost of producing and presenting the program or series—or split the cost with other sponsors by paying for portions of each program or for a specified number of programs in the series—called *split* or *shared sponsorship*. In these situations the advertiser is closely identified with the program he sponsors.

An advertiser wishing to buy available units of commercial time within a program simply purchases the announcement time and is said to be a *participating sponsor*. Such advertisers do not pay the costs of producing the programs but merely buy time within the program. Program production costs are paid by the station or network on which the program is carried, with commercial time priced so as to recover these costs, plus a profit, if a substantial percentage of the commercial minutes are purchased.

During recent years there has been a decided trend away from program sponsorship, as such. In the days before television almost all radio network programs were presented on a single-sponsorship basis, and the same was true in the early days of television. Rising costs of programs and increased charges for network time, however, produced tremendous changes in patterns of sponsorship of television programs, and by the 1972–1973 season virtually all regularly scheduled network programs during prime time (8:00 to 11:00 P.M., eastern standard time) were sold on a participating basis. A few

"I know it's silly of me, but I miss the days when I knew exactly who sponsored what."

advertisers continued to buy full sponsorship in special broadcasts (*The Hallmark Hall of Fame*, for example) and partial sponsorship of sports events or news programs, but by the mid-1970s full or split sponsorship of prime-time television series had ceased almost entirely. Some daytime programs retained full or partial sponsorship, but their number decreased each year.

One reason for the virtual disappearance of program sponsorship is obvious. In 1951–1952, production costs of evening network programs averaged only about $28,000 for each hour of programming; by 1965–1966, this figure had risen to nearly $137,000; and, by 1974–1975, costs per hour were approximately $235,000. Charges for network time increased as production costs rose. In 1951–1952, the one-time rate for a 60-minute evening period on the NBC television network of 62 stations was a little less than $50,000; in 1965–1966, the charge for an hour's time on NBC's full 201-station network was more than $145,000; and by 1975–1976, this figure had jumped to more than $166,000 for 213 stations. More importantly, NBC was getting $100,000 *per minute* for its top-ranked prime-time program, *Sanford and Son*, $9,900 for 30 seconds in an afternoon "soap opera," and $8,700 for 30 seconds in an afternoon game show. With production costs and network time charges so tremendously inflated, virtually no advertisers could afford to carry the full load of presenting a network program week after week; participating sponsorship became the only feasible method of dealing with the problem.

Most daytime television network programs are also handled on a participating-sponsorship basis, and trends in sponsorship on individual stations have followed approximately the same pattern as those on national networks, although full and partial sponsorship of local programs has not completely disappeared. In radio, participating sponsorship was widely used even before the advent of television; aside from news broadcasts and occasional short features, few programs on radio stations today are sponsored by single advertisers.

Spot Announcements

With the virtual disappearance of full or split sponsorship from broadcasting, a once-meaningful distinction between types of advertising also disappeared—that between spot announcements, commercials, and participating announcements. Originally, spot announcements were considered to be commercial messages scheduled in station-break periods between programs; announcements within programs were simply "commercials" if the program was sponsored, or "participating announcements" if messages for several sponsors were included in the same program. As distinctions blurred, however, a spot or a spot announcement was considered to be any announcement sold independently of a program, whether inserted in a multiple-sponsorship program or in a break between programs.

Spot announcements come in a variety of shapes and sizes. On radio, those for local advertisers are usually live announcements read by a station announcer. National spot advertisers usually provide their spot announcements to stations on audio tape. On television stations, spots for local advertisers may be presented live with the announcer on camera or with the announcer unseen and with slides or pictures on the screen, but most commonly they are recorded by local talent on videotape for easy replay during the run of the spot. Some of the more important local advertisers have their commercial messages produced on film or tape by advertising agencies in larger cities. Few television markets, of course, lack one or more advertisers who feel they can do as good a selling job as local talent and insist on appearing in their own commercials, sometimes doing the entire selling job. Spot announcements used in national spot advertising campaigns are produced and distributed on film or on tape, as are the great majority of announcements used in network television programs. Through the 1960s, the customary length for all commercials—both radio and television—was 60 seconds, with 10-, 20-, and 30-second spots also available. Economic pressures, however, worked to change this, and by the mid-1970s, 30 seconds was the basic length of radio and television spot announcements. By 1975, the 60-second spot announcement for a single product or service had all but disappeared from national network and nonnetwork television advertising, and 60-second "availabilities" were filled with two 30-second announcements— often for totally unrelated products.

There are many variations from this norm, however. Very short announcements are often used on radio, usually in connection with time signals or brief weather summaries. Television spots shorter than 30 seconds are also seen and occasionally longer announcements are used, usually in cases of single sponsorship of specials. A form of local television advertising that was once popular but seemed to lose favor later, is the 8-second "ID" or station identification commercial, in which visual commercial material shares the screen with station call letters or channel number.

Radio and television stations are required by FCC regulations to give station identification announcements at regular intervals. To

allow enough time for these identifications, the practice developed
in the early days of network radio of shortening each network program by 30 seconds. Since the identification itself could be given in
only a few seconds, this practice made time available for the inclusion at each station break of short commercial spot announcements.
Announcements in these breaks have always been attractive to local
advertisers who wanted their messages in close proximity to popular network programs. All programs on television are similarly
shortened, whether network presentations, filmed syndicated programs, or programs produced locally, with the station breaks between programs used to present spot announcements as well as
station identifications. At certain times during the day and evening,
television networks provide a 62-second break between programs.
More commonly, however, the breaks between television network
programs are 32 or 42 seconds in length.

On both radio and television stations, however, the greatest use
of spot announcements is within participating programs, and in
these programs the 30-second commercial announcement is nearly
always used. Aside from newscasts, almost all of the commercial
programs on radio stations are of the participating sponsorship
type. Television stations offer many local or syndicated programs
of types in which participating announcements can easily be
placed—children's programs, motion pictures, local news, and the
broadcast of local sports events. These, like many of the longer variety and dramatic programs on network television schedules, are
often referred to as "spot carriers," since they are so well suited to
the inclusion of spot announcements for a number of different advertisers.

The National Advertiser

Although many thousands of business concerns market their products on a national or regional scale, not all these companies engage
in large-scale advertising. In 1974, approximately 500 companies
bought time on national television networks, spending an estimated
$2.3 billion, with 30 of these companies accounting for slightly more
than half of that total. In the same year more than 1,500 companies,
representing more than 5,000 brands of products, engaged in national spot advertising on television. Approximately two thirds of
all the money spent for network television advertising goes for announcements scheduled during evening hours. In national spot advertising, on the other hand, more than half of all expenditures go
for advertising carried during the daytime.

Most of the money spent by national advertisers is used to promote the sale of low-cost, mass-consumption types of goods. In
1974, network television advertising was dominated by producers
of food products, cosmetics, drugs, and laundry products. Since
many companies produce and market a wide variety of products, all
of which must be brought to the attention of the public by advertising, a few major corporations spend enormous amounts of money
for television advertising each year. Procter & Gamble Company,
the largest buyer of television time, spent more than $234 million
for television time in 1974.

Every national advertiser has a different marketing problem; he
attempts to use broadcasting in a way best suited to his special
needs and objectives. He is concerned with the problem of geographical coverage, to see that his advertising reaches every major
community in which his product is offered for sale. Obviously, the
use of network time has many advantages; the advertiser is assured
of full national coverage with a minimum of effort. On the other
hand, if his product is not distributed equally throughout all sections of the country, the advertiser may find national spot advertising more satisfactory, although buying time on a large number of
individual stations is more complicated than buying a segment of
time on a national network. The advertiser must decide which markets he wishes to reach, which station or stations to use in each
market, and how much money he should spend on advertising on
each of the stations selected.

The Local Advertiser

The owner of a business concern that serves only a single community does his radio or television advertising on a local basis. It is
impossible to make more than a rough estimate of the number of
local business establishments that buy local advertising time on
radio or television each year, but the number must be over half a
million. Some are regular, year-round advertisers; many others use
the broadcasting media only during certain seasons of the year.
Although some department stores and local drug or grocery chains
spend substantial amounts of money for radio and television advertising, most local advertisers operate with decidedly limited
budgets, especially as compared with those of companies that sell
their products on a national scale.

Although the amount of money involved is relatively small, as
compared with the amounts spent for network and national spot
advertising, the local retail merchant must make the same basic

decisions as the national advertiser in his efforts to get the
maximum result for the money he has to spend. He must decide how
much of his total budget should go for broadcast advertising and
how much should be spent on billboards or direct mail or for space
in the local newspaper. He may sponsor a program or buy spot
announcements; he may buy time on television or on radio; he may
use two or three stations in his market or spend his money for time
on a single station; he may spread his advertising budget fairly
evenly over a 52-week period or concentrate his expenditures for
station time during the month or two of each year offering the
greatest sales potential·for his product. In one respect, of course, the
local advertiser has a tremendous advantage over the concern that
operates on a national scale; he has a firsthand acquaintance with
the local market and a much more intimate knowledge of the relative values of the stations that serve the market. As a result, he is
usually able to plan his advertising more intelligently than the
larger company located in a city 1,000 miles away.

Many retailers, too, benefit from *dealer cooperative*[1] advertising
allowances offered by national manufacturers of the brands the
retailers handle. It has been estimated that as much as one fifth of all
local advertising on radio and television involves some dealer co-op
plan under which the national manufacturer or a regional distributor pays a part of the cost of the time used by the retailer on the
local station.

The dealer cooperative system is popular because it enables the
local distributor to use advertising messages prepared by national
agencies and to tie his efforts directly to a national campaign. Some
stations also sell local advertising at lower rates than those charged
for national spot advertising, and in these circumstances the
national advertiser is able to purchase spots at the lower rates.
On the other hand, co-op advertising has the disadvantage of being
available to the local merchant only if he advertises in a certain way
at a certain specified time, in most cases using advertising copy
supplied by the manufacturer. Major users of co-op plans in television are manufacturers of automobiles and of home furnishings and
appliances, but co-op arrangements are commonly used by nearly
every type of manufacturer of brand-name merchandise.

---

[1]Not to be confused with network "cooperative" or "co-op" advertising, in which
network-produced programs are fed to affiliates over network lines with the express
understanding that each affiliate is permitted to sell the program, or spots in the
program, to local advertisers. Each station selling the program is expected to pay the
network a small amount to help pay the program's production costs; this charge is, of
course, passed on by the station to the local sponsors of the program.

The Machinery of Time Sales

Every spot announcement or sponsored program, whether it is presented in behalf of a local advertiser, a national spot advertiser, or an advertiser using a national network, comes ultimately to the local television or radio station to be put on the air. The process of getting that spot or that program to the station follows one of four distinct routes, as indicated in Figure 7–2. Local time sales may be handled directly by the local advertiser and the station with no intermediaries involved; a member of the station's sales staff calls on the advertiser and sells him the time. Sometimes the local advertiser is a larger concern that employs a local advertising agency to buy newspaper space or broadcasting time; in that situation, the sale of time is handled through the advertising agency.

The buying of national spot or network time is a more complex affair, involving many stations in a number of different cities. Almost all national advertisers employ large national advertising agencies to look after their advertising interests. Stations, of course, are not usually able to have their own sales employees call on national advertisers or agencies located in cities from coast to coast, so each station employs the services of a national station-representative concern[2] to act as its sales representative in selling time to national advertisers planning national spot advertising campaigns. So, in national spot advertising two intermediary organizations are used; an advertising agency representing the adver-

---

[2]Functions performed by advertising agencies and station representative companies were explained in greater detail in Chapter 6.

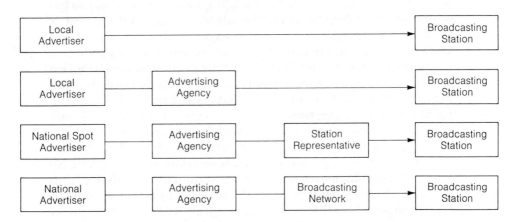

Figure 7–2   The four processes followed in the purchase of broadcast time.

tiser and a station-representative company working on behalf of the station. If the advertiser buys network time, the advertising agency deals with the network organization, and the network in turn reserves the necessary time on its affiliated stations. No station-representative concern is involved, but there are still two intermediaries between the advertiser and the station that carries the advertising message.

Placing Commercial Announcements Of course, the sale of time does not complete the process of putting advertising on the air. With the exception of news and short features, radio has few programs, as such, and commercial spots are placed in the schedule according to the commercial policy established by management. Most advertisers, of course, want their commercials to be heard when audiences are the largest, and many stations charge a premium for spots placed in peak listening periods. For a lower rate an advertiser can usually purchase "run-of-schedule" (ROS) spots, which are scattered throughout the broadcast day with no specific time guarantees. When news and other programs are available, like the coverage of special events or sports activities, salesmen will attempt to sell spots for these programs—with the commercials priced so as to cover the cost of production, line charges, and station profit.

The syndicated and locally produced programs on television stations are purchased or planned by the station's program director. The station sales staff then tries to find advertisers to purchase spots in the programs. As in radio, rates for these spots are set so as to cover costs and produce a profit.

Occasionally an advertiser or the advertiser's agency may come to a radio or television station with a program or series ready to put on the air. In these instances, the advertiser has paid the cost of producing the program(s) and also pays the cost of station time. Once a common practice, such "full sponsorship" is rare today.

More common in the 1970s is a type of program distribution known as barter. A barter series is one to which an advertiser has purchased the rights with the intention of distributing it to individual stations. The advertiser fills all but a specified number of commercial slots (usually all but two) with his own commercials. Stations that use the programs do not purchase or lease them but get them free with the right to sell the two open slots in the program. No money changes hands between the station and the distributor (thus it is called a barter deal). Instead, the advertiser places his commercials in the markets that accept the program and the stations make money if they are successful in selling the open commercials to local

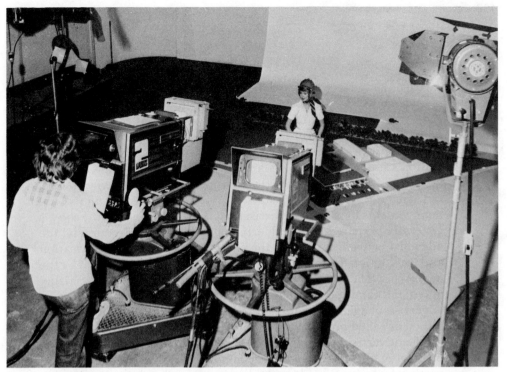

Figure 7–3 Many local television commercials are produced on tape by stations in the market, with production expenses paid by the advertiser. (Courtesy WBRZ-TV, Baton Rouge)

advertisers. Examples of barter programming include *The Lawrence Welk Show, Hee Haw,* and *Wild Kingdom.*

Network television programs are handled in much the same way as local commercial programs. In the case of program series, the network itself may produce the program or may pay an independent production agency to develop the show and handle all phases of production, paying the production company an amount agreed upon in advance to cover all costs of production and give the production company a reasonable profit. A similar arrangement exists when the network is presenting a sports program or a one-time special broadcast. In many instances, the network and the production company agree on the price the network is to pay before production of the program is even started, and the network may even advance the money to pay for all or a part of the program's production costs. After the program has been definitely scheduled, network salesmen go "out on the streets" and try to sell participating spots in the program.

Commercial Announcements   One other element in broadcast advertising remains to be considered—the commercial announcement that carries the advertising message. In smaller communities, announcements for local advertisers are often written, without extra charge, by continuity departments of the stations over which the announcements are to be broadcast. This is especially true of radio, where copy for the local merchant is read over the air by one of the station's staff announcers. In larger cities and on national networks, however, advertisers supply the commercials at their own expense. Occasionally, a television station produces filmed or taped announcements for a local advertiser using its facilities, but the copy is generally prepared by an advertising agency. More frequently, the advertising agency assumes the entire burden of copy preparation and production. In either situation, production costs are paid by the advertiser. The spot announcements used in network advertising and in national spot campaigns are always planned and written by advertising agencies; and, for television advertising, the actual filmed or taped production of the announcements is either handled by the advertising agency itself or by a concern that specializes in producing filmed or taped advertising materials. Naturally, the advertising agency is paid for the services it performs in the preparation of announcements used.

ECONOMICS OF STATION OPERATION

Broadcasting stations differ in size and in physical character; they also differ widely in earning potential. Station owners hope, of course, to operate at a profit. A station that earns substantial profits can afford to pay high wages, employ competent personnel, and provide programs of high quality for listeners. When revenues barely meet expenses or when a station operates at a loss, efforts to reduce costs result in lower pay for employees, the hiring of less qualified personnel, and deterioration in the quality of program service. If losses continue, of course, the station will sooner or later be forced off the air.

Station Revenues

Every station's revenues depend on the amount of time the station sells and on the prices charged for the time. Since the total time available for sale is substantially the same for every station, revenues depend largely on the rates the station is able to charge. Naturally, the station operator charges as much as he thinks advertisers will pay. The advertiser, in turn, wants to reach as many listeners as possible for each dollar he spends. Consequently, a station's charges for time must be roughly in proportion to the size of the audience the station can deliver. More specifically, the base rate a radio or television station is able to charge for its time is determined by the size of the community, by the amount of power the station uses—a measure of its coverage and its ability to reach listeners outside its city of license—and the attractiveness and popularity of the station's programming. Large-city stations can charge more for time than can stations in rural communities; high-power stations can fix rates at a higher level than those with less power, even in the same community; very popular stations are more attractive to advertisers than are those with small audiences. Finally, since less total time is devoted to radio listening than to watching television programs and since the television audience is divided among fewer stations than is the radio audience in any community, a television station can fix its rates at a much higher level than can a radio station with which it competes in the sale of time to advertisers.

Rate Structure   The term *base rate* used in the preceding discussion refers to the highest rate charged by a station—usually the one-time 60- or 30-second rate charged at peak audience times. In most stations, the factor of audience size causes variations in the rates at various times of the day and creates a rate structure in which the charges reflect differences in audience size. More people are at home and available for television viewing in the evening than during the daytime; as a result, television stations make their highest charges for so-called prime evening hours, usually between 7:00 and 10:30 or 11:00 P.M. With fewer listeners available during the daytime, rates charged for daytime advertising on television stations are lower in proportion—usually about half as much as the prime-time rate. Charges for time on Sunday afternoons and between 6:00 and 7:00 P.M. are usually set somewhere between the prime-time rate and the lower daytime rate.

The same pattern of varying charges was used by radio stations until evening listening was so largely taken over by television and "in-car listening" became an important factor for radio; then radio stations changed their rate structures. Many radio stations now charge less for advertising time during evening hours than for that used during the daytime, while others use a single rate for all their hours of operation. Many stations in metropolitan areas, capitalizing on radio's ability to reach motorists during peak traffic hours, have established their highest rates during "drive time," the hours when many people are driving to or from work. On the rate card of

"We have to schedule Whitlow's program. What's the opposite of prime time?"

one large-city station, "Class AA" time is the period between 6:00 and 10:00 A.M., Monday through Saturday, with top rates of $55 for a minute of advertising time. Evening "drive time" falls between 3:00 and 7:00 P.M. and is priced at $50 per minute. The lowest priced spots available, $20 a minute, are in "Class C" time, from 7:00 P.M. to midnight, Monday through Saturday, and 6:00 P.M. to midnight on Sundays.

In television, the cost of a prime-time 30-second spot has become the basis for most time charges, although some stations still list rates for sponsorship of programs of 60 minutes or less. Because the 60-second spot has virtually disappeared, many stations no longer list a 60-second rate or simply add a note saying that 60-second spots go at twice the 30-second rate. Many stations charge a premium spot rate for "adjacencies" in the station-break period preceding or following an unusually popular network program. In radio also, the sale of program time in units longer than 5 to 15 minutes has become so infrequent that station rate comparisons are made on the basis of the charge for spot announcements in the station's prime-time period, but on radio rate cards, the basic rate is still the 60-second spot.

Discounts   To induce advertisers to buy greater amounts of time, stations also offer discounts, based on the frequency of use or the volume of advertising bought on the station. A television station will sell a 10-second spot, five times a day on a 52-week contract, at a price substantially lower than the 10-second, one-time rate. Discounts ordinarily range from 5 to 25 percent, although some stations give discounts of as much as 40 or 50 percent for unusually large time purchases. In radio, conventional discount patterns are widely supplemented by "package" plans offering heavy discounts to advertisers who buy large numbers of spots each week over a period of from 4 to 8 weeks.

Station Profits

Radio and television station revenues come mostly from sale of time to local and national spot advertisers; television stations also receive considerable amounts from network payments for the use of station time to carry commercial network programs. Stations also have some revenues from other sources: sale of station-produced programs to advertisers, fees paid by advertisers for services of station announcers and other talent, payments for production of filmed or taped commercial announcements, and the like.

As shown in Table 7–1, total revenues of the average television station are nearly ten times as great as those of the average AM radio station. From the gross revenues from sale of time, of course, commissions to advertising agencies and to station representatives must be deducted and, from what is left, station operating expenses must be paid.

The distribution of these expenses among various categories differs between radio and television stations, as shown in Table 7–2. From this table it can be seen that sales and administrative costs represent almost two thirds of the expenses of the average radio station and less than half of the expenses of a typical television station. More than half of the expenses of a television station fall in the programming and technical areas, while these areas create only about one third of the expenses of a radio station.

Variations in Station Revenues   Average figures for station revenues and profits do not tell the entire story. As already noted, revenues of AM radio stations, and profits as well, are strongly affected by two factors: the power the station is authorized to use and the size of the market in which it operates. As shown in Table 7–3, more than half of all the money spent for national spot radio advertising goes to stations located in the nation's 25 largest cities, as well as about 30 percent of the amount spent for local advertising. A sharp contrast is

Table 7-1   Average Per-Station Revenues and Net Profits of Non-Network-Owned
Radio and Television Stations for the Year 1974

	Average of 4,361 AM radio stations	Average of 679 television stations
Revenues from:		
National networks	$ 2,108	$ 310,309
Regional networks	617	—
Sales of time to:		
National or regional advertisers	69,492	1,545,949
Local advertisers	255,135	1,306,627
Total gross revenues from time sales	327,352	3,162,885
Sales to other than advertisers	2,827	42,562
Total broadcasting sales	330,179	3,205,447
Less commissions to agencies and representatives	29,629	473,195
Total broadcasting revenues	300,550	2,732,252
Total broadcasting expenses	279,251	2,133,873
Net profit before federal taxes	21,299	598,379

Averages as reported by the Federal Communications Commission.

Table 7-2   Distribution of Expenses among Various Categories
by Radio and Television Stations

	Percentages for	
Expense Categories	Television	Radio
Administrative	31	41.1
Programming	44	29.9
Technical	13	8.7
Time Sales	12	20.3

Figures released by the Federal Communications Commission.

Table 7-3 Sources of Revenues of Television and Radio Stations
During 1974 in Markets of Various Sizes

	Number of stations	Total revenues in thousands of dollars[a]		
		Network payments	National spot advertising[b]	Local advertising[b]
Location of Television Stations				
Ten largest cities	63	60,655 (962.9)	588,110 (9,335)	295,697 (4,693.6)
Fifteen next largest cities	67	35,719 (533.1)	260,659 (3,890.4)	182,941 (2,730.4)
Markets with three or more stations	360	125,691 (349.1)	418,418 (1,162.3)	426,319 (1,184.2)
Markets with one or two stations	179	26,179 (146.2)	62,830 (351)	74,399 (415.6)
All television stations	669	248,244 (371.0)	1,330,017 (1,988.0)	979,356 (1,463.9)
Location of radio stations				
Ten largest cities	222	3,925 (17.7)	131,370 (591.7)	205,617 (926.2)
Fifteen next largest cities	253	2,675 (10.6)	54,715 (216.3)	143,602 (567.6)
Other metropolitan areas	1,758	4,606 (2.6)	113,306 (64.4)	449,347 (255.6)
Nonmetropolitan areas	2,128	1,508 (0.7)	41,727 (19.6)	331,229 (155.6)
All radio stations	4,361	12,714 (2.9)	341,118 (78.2)	1,129,795 (259.0)

[a]Figures in parentheses are per-station averages for each category.

[b]Figures for advertising revenues are gross billings before deduction of agency and station representatives' commissions.

Figures are compiled from annual reports for 1974 released by the Federal Communications Commission, based on financial reports filed by stations operating during the calendar year 1974.

also evident between revenues of AM radio stations in the Top 25 markets and those in the remaining markets. Average revenues for radio stations in the Top 25 markets were five times higher than average revenues for all other AM stations. No separate figures are provided by the FCC on the revenues of high-power stations compared with low-power stations, but it is a recognized fact in broadcasting that advertisers show strong preferences for the 50,000-watt and 5,000-watt stations—usually the prestige stations in each market—and that advertising revenues of such stations are always much higher than those of their low-power competitors.

Revenues of FM radio stations are somewhat lower than those of AM outlets. The 2,552 FM stations in operation during 1974 had average revenues of $97,257 per station. Of course, more than 75 percent of all the FM outlets were operated in conjunction with AM stations under common ownership; and, in many such situations, time on the FM stations was not sold separately. The 678 FM stations that operated independently during 1974 showed average total revenues of a little less than $189,000 per station.

The average television station, as shown in Table 7-1, has revenues far in excess of those of radio stations. Television station revenues are affected strongly by three factors: (1) whether the station is affiliated with a network or is independent, (2) the size of the market in which the station is located, and (3) whether it is assigned to a VHF or UHF channel. In markets with four or more commercial television stations, the rates charged for time by independent stations are usually only about half as high as those of network-affiliated stations.

The effects of market size are clearly indicated by the figures given in Table 7-3; in 1974, more than 60 percent of all money spent for national spot and local advertising went to the 130 stations operating in the nation's 25 largest cities. The situation is reflected even more strongly by the average total revenues of stations in those large cities. In 1974, television stations in the ten largest cities had total revenues averaging almost $15 million each; stations in the next fifteen cities in size had average total revenues of about $7.3 million each. At the other extreme, stations in smaller cities with fewer than three television stations had total revenues averaging only about $912,000 each.

Not quite so striking, but still impressive, are the differences in the revenue figures reported for VHF and UHF television stations. In 1974, average total broadcasting revenues of 494 VHF television stations were slightly more than $4 million each; revenues of the 175 UHF stations operating during the year, however, averaged only $1.3 million each, although many of the UHF outlets were located in the 25 largest cities in the United States.

Profits Earned by Stations   The amount of revenues received, of course, is not the final test of successful station operation. Radio and television stations are operated for the purpose of earning profits for their owners. Most broadcasting stations do return a profit on their operations, as indicated by the average figures in Table 7-4. As one would expect, amounts earned vary with different types of stations and with different market situations—and a considerable number of stations each year operate at a loss. As shown in Table 7-4, in 1974,

Table 7–4   Average Station Profits by Class of Station

Class of Station	1974 Average Profit
AM Stations	
All reporting	$ 21,000
Stations in Top 10 markets	141,000
Stations in nonmetropolitan areas	9,009
FM Stations	(-10,030)
TV Stations	
All reporting (not owned by networks)	$ 598,000
Stations in Top 25 markets	2,420,000
Stations in smallest 179 markets	87,500
VHF Stations	1,000,000
UHF Stations	(-28,000)

Figures compiled by the Federal Communications Commission.

AM radio stations showed average net earnings of a little more than $21,000 before federal taxes, but this net income was not equally distributed. Some stations had decidedly larger earnings, especially those located in large cities. On the other hand, almost 35 percent of the stations reporting profit and loss figures to the Federal Communications Commission in 1974 lost money on their broadcasting operations—the losses averaging a little more than $48,000 per station. In addition, another 11 percent of all AM stations operated on a marginal basis, earning less than $5,000 each for the year.

As might be expected, stations located in major cities have largest total revenues and report the largest net earnings. In 1974, radio stations operating in the Top 10 markets reported average profits of more than $141,000 per station before federal taxes. At the other end of the scale, the 271 AM stations in nonmetropolitan areas had average net profits of only a little more than $9,000 each.

FM stations, once in a difficult competitive position with only 20 to 30 percent of all homes equipped with FM receivers, improved their position somewhat in the late 1960s and early 1970s. In 1964, only 30 percent of the 306 FM stations that operated independently reported a profit. By 1975, FM penetration was estimated to be more than 40 percent, and 44 percent of the independent FM stations on the air were reporting profits. Even so, the FM stations that reported separately from AM stations in 1974 (some of which were co-owned with an AM station and were not independent) showed an average loss of more than $10,000 per station. Although some FM stations show moderately good earnings, and a few earn more than some AM stations in their market, commercial FM has failed to show a collective profit since it was authorized in the 1940s.

The profit position of television stations is considerably better than that of radio outlets. The 1974 figure for average earnings in Table 7-4 represents an increase of more than $35,000 per station over 1973. As with radio, some stations lost money on their broadcasting operations—about 15 percent of all VHF stations and 50 percent of the UHF stations reporting to the FCC. The 15 network-owned stations, all located in large cities, had average earnings of more than $7 million each. The stations operating in the nation's 25 largest cities showed profits averaging about $2.4 million each. At the other extreme, stations in the smallest markets showed profits four times higher than those shown for the average AM station in Table 7-4—and these tabulations include those television facilities that operated at a loss.

Of course, the situation was not so bright for UHF stations as for those using the more desirable VHF channels. While VHF profits were high, the average UHF station lost $28,000 in 1974, an improvement over the 1973 average loss of $43,500. Not all UHF stations lost money, of course; 48 percent reported a profit and 52 percent, a loss.

Before 1964, a major problem faced by UHF stations was the fact that in most areas only a small proportion of television-equipped homes had sets that could bring in UHF signals. Congress came to the aid of UHF by passing a law requiring all-channel tuning on all sets marketed after April 1964. In the subsequent decade, UHF penetration jumped from 22 to 86 percent.

That this act of Congress was not a cure-all is illustrated by the fact that in 1964 the 92 UHF stations on the air reported a small average *profit* ($29,300), while in 1974 the 175 UHF stations then on the air reported the average loss of $28,000. Unfortunately, UHF continued to face other problems, including smaller coverage area, greater susceptibility to interference, and difficulty in tuning; and most of these stations continue to look with envy at the profits reported by their VHF brothers.

NETWORKS AND ADVERTISERS

National advertisers buy time on networks partly because of the convenience of being able to have a single sponsored program or commercial message broadcast by stations throughout the country and also, in television, because network programs fill the most desirable hours of station time and attract larger audiences than the advertiser could reach by national spot advertising. Whether the advertiser buys time to present his own sponsored program or buys time for spot announcements, his dealings with the network company are handled through his advertising agency. In most instances, spot announcements are purchased on a 13-week, 26-week, or 52-week basis; the contract covering the purchase gives the advertiser an option on renewal for an additional period or allows him to cancel at the end of any 13-week cycle. When business conditions are unfavorable, of course, these contracts are adjusted by the networks. To make the sale more attractive to a potential advertiser, short-term contracts are offered with the right to cancel under certain conditions. Occasionally an advertiser may purchase time for a special one-time program, usually an hour or more in length. To make room for such programs, the network cancels, or preempts, for that date the regular program normally broadcast during the time period the special program is to use.

Costs of Network Time

Network salesmen always attempt to sell an advertiser a "full network" of stations—all the stations with which the network has affiliation contracts. After all, most costs of presenting the program—administrative, selling, and technical expenses and costs of the program itself—remain the same whether the program is broadcast by only 50 stations or over the facilities of a full network. The advertiser, however, is not required to buy the full network. He can omit affiliates in markets less important in his advertising campaign, provided he buys enough stations to bring his total up to a network-stipulated figure. Stations not "bought" may let the commercial run without compensation or "cover" it with a Public Service Announcement. If a large portion of the spots in a particular program are not bought for a given market, the network affiliate in that market has the right to refuse to carry the program and to substitute a syndicated program or a program from another network.

The average rate for a 30-second announcement in prime time in 1976 was about $45,000 for a full network of television stations, with a highest rate of $62,000 and a lowest rate of approximately $28,000. Although the basic unit for television advertising is the 30-second spot and although program sponsorship has virtually disappeared, published rates for the major television networks list the charges for advertiser-supplied programming for a one-half hour period. This published material, however, can provide some interesting comparisons to demonstrate how hour of broadcast and volume of purchase can affect costs.

The cost of one half hour of evening time on one major network in 1976 (ABC) ranged from $65,000 for the 11:00 P.M. to sign-off period (Eastern Standard Time) to $95,000 for the 8:00 to 11:00 P.M. period. Daytime rates ran from a low of $25,000 to a high of $75,000, depending on the time of day. Charges for broadcast periods of greater or lesser duration than 30 minutes—but at least 5 minutes—would be directly proportional to the half-hour rate. A 15-minute program would cost half as much and a 60-minute program, twice as much.

The above figures are for one-time use only. Networks also provide discounts for quantity purchases. An advertiser buying 12 consecutive weeks in the 9:00 to 10:00 P.M. period would pay one network (CBS) 54 percent of the one-time rate. Another advertiser buying for only 4 consecutive weeks in the same time period would pay 64 percent of the one-time rate.

Radio network rates are, of course, considerably lower than those demanded by television. Only one radio network company still lists rates for full sponsorship of a 30-minute program, and these range from $5,800 to $8,500—about one tenth of television rates. On this network, 30-second spots sell, at a one-time rate, for from $950 in the evening to $1,150 in the daytime. These, of course, are the top rates; quantity discounts can reduce them to $600 and $800.

Network Revenues and Expenses

Network revenues, of course, come primarily from the sale of time to national advertisers, although television networks do have revenues from such sources as the sale of programs and foreign syndication of programs. In 1974, the three national television networks had combined revenues of $1.5 billion from sale of network time and announcements, according to the financial report issued by the Federal Communications Commission. From this total gross income, expenses had to be paid. Something more than $300 million went to advertising agencies as commissions on the sale of network time. Another $244 million was paid to network-owned and affiliated stations for the use of station time to broadcast network commercial programs. Payments totaling $43 million were made to the American Telephone and Telegraph Company for rental of cable and relay facilities used to transmit the networks' programs to affiliated stations. More than $675 million was spent for programs—a part of the total representing production costs of network-produced programs and a larger amount representing amounts paid for programs supplied by outside agencies. Other expenses—salaries, administrative costs, purchases of equipment, costs of selling, promotion, and the like—reduced net profits of the three national networks before federal taxes to a combined total of $225 million or about 14 percent of total revenues for the year. In comparison, the fifteen network-owned television stations reported combined net profits for the same year totaling $105.2 million, before federal taxes.

The radio networks find themselves in a much less desirable financial position. During 1974, the four national network companies had total revenues of only a little more than $40 million, of which $38 million came from sale of network time. Operating expenses, on the other hand, including payments to affiliated stations, totaled more than $46 million, so that for the year 1974 the four companies showed a combined net loss of about $6 million on their network activities. Fortunately, the radio stations owned by three of the network companies had combined earnings of $8,445,000 in 1974.

The operation of a television network, involving tremendous risks and the expenditure of hundreds of millions of dollars each year, has proved to be a highly profitable undertaking. In recent years, however, the same has hardly been true of the operation of radio networks.

STUDY AND DISCUSSION QUESTIONS

1. Seek the cooperation of a local radio or television station and determine the relative proportion of the station's advertising time that is devoted to national network, national spot, regional spot, and local advertising. If you can locate a station with a reasonable distribution of these types of advertising, analyze those commercials that fall into each category. Consider the following:

   a. The types of product or service in each
   b. The nature of the commercials in each category (hard-sell, dramatizations, celebrity endorsement, and the like)
   c. Your subjective evaluation of the quality of the writing and production of the commercials in each category

2. Report on or be prepared to discuss the following:

   a. Dealer cooperative advertising
   b. "Double-billing"

    c. Barter programming

    d. Sources of revenue for radio and television networks

    e. The evolution of participating sponsorship in programming on radio and television

    f. The decline of full sponsorship

3. Analyze the rate cards of radio stations in your market (secure them from the stations themselves or use national spot rates as published in the *Spot Radio* editions of the Standard Rate and Data Service) to determine the different kinds of commercial time included in these cards. Identify, define, and discuss the relative costs of:

    a. Run-of-schedule spots

    b. Fixed position spots

    c. Preemptable spots

    d. Prime and marginal times

    e. Frequency discounts

4. Study the most recently available FCC figures on radio and television station revenues (these summaries are published once a year in *Broadcasting*) to determine the degree to which market size affects relative revenues of these stations.

5. Analyze these revenue figures further to determine the relative financial strength of:

    a. FM compared with AM radio stations

    b. UHF compared with VHF television stations

    c. Network affiliates compared with independent stations

SUGGESTED READINGS

Elizabeth J. Heighton and Don R. Cunningham. *Advertising in the Broadcast Media*. Belmont, Calif.: Wadsworth, 1976.

James E. Littlefield. *Readings in Advertising: Current Viewpoints on Selected Topics*. St. Paul, Minn.: West Publishing Co., 1975.

Roger G. Noll, J. Peck Merton, and John McGowan. *Economic Aspects of Television Regulation*. Washington, D.C.: Brookings, 1973.

Bruce Owen, Jack H. Beebe, and Willard Manning, Jr. *Television Economics*. Lexington, Mass.: Lexington Books, 1974.

John S. Wright and John E. Meetes, eds. *Advertising's Role in Society*. St. Paul, Minn.: West Publishing Co., 1975.

8

Programs

Most Americans take for granted the fact that at almost any hour of the day or night they can turn to radio or television sets to select from a variety of offerings presented by their local stations. They have come to expect this service and probably give little thought to the way these programs are produced or get on the air. They are concerned only with whether or not they enjoy the programs they hear. However, programs of the kind to which we are accustomed do not just happen by accident. They must be created, produced. People must develop the ideas on which the programs are based and must shape those ideas into the product that finally goes on the air.

THE DEMAND FOR PROGRAMS

Networks face one set of programming problems, their affiliates another set, and independent stations still another. Radio stations have different needs in program development from those of television stations; but, in one respect at least, the situation is the same for all. Every network and every station must constantly be looking for new program ideas and new concepts of programming if they wish to capture and hold the attention of listeners.

Local Station Programming

As contrasted with nonaffiliated outlets, television stations with national network affiliations have relatively simple requirements for the planning and developing of programs. Since an affiliated station can count on more than 100 hours of network programs each week and has access in addition to a wealth of syndicated filmed program material, it needs to produce no more than 2 or 3 hours of locally originated programs a day to complete its weekly schedule. Most of these local presentations are standard "service" shows— news, weather, sports, religious broadcasts, and public affairs discussion programs. Of course, some stations in larger markets go considerably further with their local programming, scheduling locally originated variety shows, interview or audience-participation programs, or broadcasts of local sports events. A considerable number of major television stations throughout the country produce occasional documentary programs on a special-program basis; a few offer local dramatic shows. Most affiliated television stations fill most of their nonnetwork hours with syndicated filmed materials—theatrical feature films and produced-for-television syndicated programs. In any event, development of new and original program ideas is not a critical problem, since the affiliated station can depend on network programs to carry much of the load of attracting listeners to the station.

Figure 8–1 shows the extent to which affiliated stations depend on national networks to fill their weekly schedules. The station used as an illustration is an NBC primary affiliate located in a three-station market. During the week analyzed, the station was on the air for nearly 133 hours between the hours of 6:00 A.M. and 1:00 A.M. The weekly schedule included a little less than 100 hours of network programs and 17½ hours of syndicated program materials.

The independent television station, lacking programs provided by a national network, has a much more difficult problem than that of the network affiliate. Not only must it fill its entire schedule with either locally produced programs or syndicated materials, but it must find or develop programs attractive enough to compete with the network programs offered by other stations in the community. Oddly enough, the networks assist the independents in this task by making available off-network series that have run their course on network schedules and are sold to interested stations. Such long-running, durable series as the original *Perry Mason, Bonanza, I Dream of Jeannie,* and *The Brady Bunch* often turn up on the evening schedules of independent stations and compete directly with current network fare.[1]

Local radio stations also need programs and program ideas; even those with network affiliations are forced to depend primarily on local offerings to attract the listening public. At a time when listeners have access to the signals of perhaps eight or ten different stations, each station must look for effective ways to make its own programming distinctive and different. Most radio stations try to meet this need by finding a music format that is different from others in the area and that will attract an audience. If all available popular formats are already in use, a station will strive for individuality by selecting one of them and trying to do it better by developing stronger personalities on the air and by a greater sensitivity to the tastes of the audience served. Not all stations adopt music formats, of course; some are all-news, others all-talk and still others schedule different kinds of programming at different times of the day.

---

[1]For a discussion of syndication and syndication companies see Chapter 6, p. 172.

Time	Sunday	Monday	Tuesday	Wednesday	Thursday	Friday	Saturday
6:30 A.M.							
7:00							
7:30							
8:00							
8:30							
9:00							
9:30							
10:00							
10:30							
11:00							
11:30							
12:00 NOON							
12:30 P.M.							
1:00							
1:30							
2:00							
2:30							
3:00							
3:30							
4:00							
4:30							
5:00							
5:30							
6:00							
6:30							
7:00							
7:30							
8:00							
8:30							
9:00							
9:30							
10:00							
10:30							
11:00							
11:30							
12:00 MIDNIGHT							
12:30 A.M.							
1:00							

	Syndicated film and tape
	Local-live
	Local film and tape
	Network

Figure 8–1 Sources of programs carried on the schedule of an NBC-affiliated station.

Successful stations also try to provide unique and different features in the programs they present or new approaches to programming, and to find such different elements calls for the use of imagination and creative ingenuity. As a rule, coming up with an elaborate production is less important than finding a novel way to present the conventional or inserting striking and unusual materials in programs to intrigue the listeners. Some disc jockeys have used the technique of placing long-distance telephone calls to persons of prominence or persons figuring in current news stories. If not handled with skill by the on-the-air personality, telephone interviews could lose their appeal as soon as the novelty wears off; but some radio performers have used the technique with success for years. One such broadcaster in New Orleans, in an attempt to vary this format a bit, would, on occasion, dial the number of a pay telephone in the San Francisco airport simply to get the reaction of the person who answered. Such telephone-call devices illustrate the importance in radio of the use of fresh, new ideas and the extent to which success in radio programming depends not merely on use of personalities but on the availability of a variety of program ideas.

Program Needs of Networks

Television networks in the United States operate under highly competitive conditions. To hold its affiliated stations, to make its services attractive to advertisers, and to capture the attention of listeners, each network must provide a reasonably well-rounded program service with a wide variety of programs of different types. To compete effectively, a network must offer at least some programs that are unique and distinctive and that in some way are more attractive than are most of the programs of rival companies. Moreover, the network must, of course, strive to keep abreast, and if possible even a little ahead, of the public's constantly changing program tastes— to anticipate the kinds of programs that will be most attractive to listeners a year or two in the future. To provide the needed quality of uniqueness in programs and to offer enough change to keep ahead of the competition, network program executives are constantly looking for new talent, new personalities, new program ideas, new types of programs, new approaches to programs of familiar types, and new plot situations for dramatic shows.

Regular Program Series During a typical week, each national television network carries from 45 to 55 different program series presented on a regularly scheduled basis. During the 1975–1976 season, the three networks combined offered a total of almost 75 different evening programs each week, from 25 to 30 different daytime program series on weekdays, and nearly 40 other programs during daytime hours on Saturdays and Sundays.

Almost all evening programs are presented in regular series form, with one episode or broadcast presented each week. Daytime programs, aside from those on weekends, are scheduled "across the board"—five days a week, Monday through Friday. In the early days of television, a typical weekly nighttime series presented 39 new episodes each year. In the summer, variety or musical shows were replaced by a less expensive program, while dramatic series and situation comedies filled the summer months with reruns. Rising costs and other factors have combined to reduce the number of new episodes and to increase reruns to the point that, by the mid-1970s, the average dramatic series contained only 21 to 24 original episodes, with reruns and preemptions for specials filling the remaining weeks. Variety programs in the 1970s also used reruns for part of the year, with replacement programs filling the summer months. Since daytime programs are usually of less expensive types, most daytime series run for a full 52 weeks without interruption and without the use of taped reruns.

New Program Requirements   As already noted, network programming is highly competitive. Each network tries to build a weekly schedule that will be stronger and more attractive to listeners, program period by program period, than that of either of its rivals. As a result, each new season brings a considerable number of changes in the program lineup of each network, as the network's program executives try to find programs that will be tuned in by greater numbers of listeners. During October and November, network executives review the ratings of their various shows and study popularity trends and the comparative standings of the three networks. If major weaknesses appear, some schedule changes may be made; strong programs may be shifted to bolster weaker time periods, and weak programs may undergo changes in format or some may be canceled outright to be replaced by other new programs that network officials hope will be more attractive to listeners.

As the season continues, other changes are planned, to become effective in January, April, or the following year. A surprisingly high proportion of the new evening program series introduced with high hopes each year are canceled before the next season gets under way. In the 5-year period from 1969 through 1974, an average of 31 new programs each year were added to network schedules at the beginning of the new season in the fall or as mid-season replacements. In this period, according to the A.C. Nielsen Company,[2] 63 percent of these new programs did not return for a second season. Programs surviving the first season, however, had a better chance of returning. From 1969 through 1974, 69 percent of the programs on for 2 to 5 years, and 75 percent of those on for more than 6 years were

---

[2] A. C. Nielsen Company, "Selected Current Events in Television Audience Research," *The Nielsen Newscast* (Northbrook, Ill.: A. C. Nielsen Company, 1975), p. 6.

"The acting is perfect, the script is superb, and the production is excellent. But it won't catch on. We need a gimmick."

returned. Network program executives are kept busy 12 months of the year, trying to discover or to develop new programs or program ideas that will meet the test of competition.

Plans for Specials Of course, in addition to regular program series, each network presents many entertainment or informative special programs during the course of each season. In the late 1950s and early 1960s, this term had real meaning—usually representing something really special in the way of entertainment or information. By the mid-1970s, however, the term *special* was being applied to "blockbuster" motion pictures like *The Poseidon Adventure*, long-form introductions of new series like *Kojak* and *Rockford* and special events in a series, like "Rhoda's Wedding."

In the 1974–1975 season, the three commercial networks presented a total of 381 special programs. As summarized in Table 8–1, the 1974–1975 season included 50 special dramatic programs, 61 variety programs, and 30 animated cartoon specials, in addition to 82 documentary-type programs. Also included were 15 awards ceremonies, 5 beauty contests, and 23 "pilot" films for new programs. Table 8–1 includes a breakdown of the specials by networks as well, showing that CBS carried the most such programs (143) and NBC the fewest (110). The planning of such special broadcasts places an additional burden on network program executives in their search for new ideas for programs to be offered for the approval of listeners.

Radio networks have a much less serious problem than do the national television network companies, since most of their program offerings are in the form of news, short talks, or music. However, even the radio networks must discover new talent and new ways of presenting familiar materials. There is still a demand for new program ideas, especially for programs that can be produced at low cost but that can attract substantial audiences in the face of competition from television.

Network Programming Patterns Programming competition among the television networks over the years has produced some interesting trends and patterns. Some of these were studied and analyzed by two researchers at the University of Georgia, Joseph R. Dominick and Millard C. Pearce. The results of their study were summarized in an article published in the Winter 1976 issue of the *Journal of*

Table 8–1 Special Programs Broadcast during the 1974–1975 Television Season

| Program Type | Network | | | |
	ABC	CBS	NBC	Total
Informative documentaries	31	35	16	82
General drama	20	14	16	50
Musical variety	14	13	11	38
Sports events	18	8	11	37
Animated cartoons	7	18	5	30
Comedy variety	6	5	15	26
Series pilots	6	7	10	23
Series: expanded episodes	5	10	8	23
Multipart drama	1	12	9	22
"Blockbuster" movies	13	2	3	18
Awards ceremonies	5	7	3	15
Miscellaneous	2	3	2	7
Beauty contests	0	4	1	5
Series highlights	0	5	0	5
Totals	128	143	110	381

Information compiled from data published in *Variety*, September 10, 1975.

Communication.[3] They have granted permission to use their findings, and this section is based on their published results.

Using listings and descriptions in *Broadcasting, Sponsor, Variety,* and general newspapers, the authors compiled a schedule of all programs on television networks in October of each year from 1953 to 1974. Specials and "second-season" programs were not included unless they turned up again as regular programs the following October. The completed listing included approximately 2,100 different programs over the 22 years covered. Fourteen program categories were then established and the percentage of total network prime-time minutes for each program type in each year was computed. Highlights of this analysis are found in Table 8–2.

A few programming trends emerge from such an array of data. The most obvious, of course, is the emergence of the action-adventure form as dominant. In every year since 1957, this category has accounted for the largest percentage of prime-time programming. A study of the year-by-year figures reveals also that the per-

[3]Joseph R. Dominick and Millard C. Pearce, "Trends in Network Prime-Time Programming, 1953–1974," *Journal of Communication,* Vol. 26 (Winter 1976), pp. 70–80.

Table 8–2   Percentage of Prime Time Devoted to Major Program Categories by All Television Networks in Selected Years

Program Categories	1954 %	1959 %	1964 %	1969 %	1974 %
General variety	6	4	7	3	—
Musical variety	7	9	6	12	—
Comedy variety	7	3	5	7	3
Dramatic anthology	14	8	1	—	—
Action-adventure	9	43	29	27	42
Situation comedy	17	13	26	19	12
General drama	4	3	10	6	13
Theatrical feature films	—	—	9	22	26
Sports	12	3	—	—	3
Talk-interview	6	3	1	—	—
Quiz and game	11	8	3	2	—
Documentary and public affairs	2	—	2	1	—
News	3	—	—	—	—
Miscellaneous	1	4	3	1	2

Compiled from data in Joseph R. Dominick and Millard C. Pearce, "Trends in Network Prime-Time Programming, 1953–1974," *Journal of Communication,* Vol. 26 (Winter 1976), pp. 70–80.

centage of action-adventure programs seems to reach peaks and valleys at 7-year intervals, climbing over 40 percent in 1959 and 1960, in 1966 through 1968, and in 1974, and dropping below 30 percent in 1962 through 1964 and 1969 through 1970.

Other program categories show less variation. The percentage of situation comedies has remained fairly stable since 1953, with only one sharp increase in 1964. In fact, after 1967 in this category there was no more than 3 percentage points of difference between any two consecutive years. Of the three types of variety program listed, only comedy variety remained on network schedules, but these categories rarely represented more than 10 percent of the programming in any given year. The percentage of general drama also remained fairly stable, rising over 10 percent only in the 1961 through 1965, 1970, and 1974 seasons.

Seven categories that existed in 1953 had disappeared by 1974; musical variety, general variety, dramatic anthologies, talk-interview, quiz and game, documentary and public affairs, and news. Only one new category—theatrical films—was added after 1953.

Examining the data more closely, Dominick and Pearce found what they termed a "follow-the-leader tendency" among the television networks. For example, when ABC stepped up its action-adventure programming by 800 percent from 1955 to 1960, NBC quickly followed suit by increasing its programming in this category by 1,200 percent from 1956 to 1960 and CBS increased its action-adventure programming by 100 percent. Similar patterns were seen in the other two peak periods of action-adventure programming, with ABC and NBC moving simultaneously in 1965 and NBC moving first in 1970. In both cases, the other networks were quick to follow with similar increases.

The same pattern can be seen with situation comedies, with NBC not following the crowd. In the 1958 through 1960 period, CBS increased its programming in this category by 82 percent, and ABC followed quickly with a 100 percent increase in 1959 through 1961. Again, from 1967 to 1970 CBS increased situation comedy time by 28 percent, and ABC again followed suit with a 60 percent increase from 1968 to 1971.

This tendency to follow the leader is also seen in the middle-to-late 1950s when CBS led the way in big-money quiz programs and again in the early 1960s when ABC and CBS followed the NBC use of theatrical feature films in prime time.

Finally, Dominick and Pearce set up what they called "systems indicators" to detect other trends in network programming in the 1953 through 1974 period. The first of these was the *instability indi-*

cator, which measured "how much change occurred from season to season in program categories." They found here that network programming is marked by relatively short and regular periods of change and stability with major changes coming on every 2 or 3 years after short periods of greater stability. Over the years, however, the trend was toward greater season-to-season stability.

A second indicator was the *diversity index*, which measured "the extent to which a few categories dominate prime time." The trend here was quite clear. With the exception of two brief periods—1961 through 1963 and 1969 through 1970—this indicator declined sharply after 1953. In other words, the trend was toward fewer program types in virtually every year, reaching a 1974 low in which three categories—action-adventure, feature films, and general drama—accounted for 81 percent of prime time.

A third system indicator, *homogeneity*, "measured how much the content of one network resembles the content of the other two." Again, the 1953 through 1974 trend was toward less variety and more similarity, with CBS remaining the most distinctive because of its devotion to situation comedies.

This analysis of programming by Dominick and Pearce reveals three relatively clear trends between 1953 and 1974. The first is a series of follow-the-leader changes in the percentages of various program categories from year to year, with a trend toward less change each year. The second is a steady decrease in the variety of programming types available to viewers in network television prime-time schedules. Finally, we can see an ever-increasing similarity in the kinds of programs carried by the three networks.

HOW PROGRAM NEEDS ARE MET

Radio and television programs come from three possible sources: local stations, networks, and independent producers. These sources serve both radio and television, and each medium has its own peculiar problems. In the section that follows, we will examine some of the ways programming needs are met.

The Local Radio Program Situation

Radio networks provide only a limited amount of programming. Consequently, 80 to 90 percent of all radio broadcast time is local and live—produced by the local station—or is purchased from program syndicators who can provide a full schedule of music in virtually every format.

More than 75 percent of the radio stations in the United States rely on local-live programming, filling their time with material produced by the station itself. Most of this time is devoted to the station's chosen format—music, news, talk, or whatever—and it is difficult to single out portions of the broadcast day and call them programs. If one thinks of a program as a specified segment of time with a unifying theme and a distinct opening, body, and close, this form has virtually disappeared from local radio. Its place has been taken by a continuous flow of broadcast material, interrupted by commercials, news summaries, and occasional short features. Some programs of the old type—public-service shows, farm information, local discussions, and the like—do continue to exist, but their numbers are few.

Production of this kind of broadcast material is relatively inexpensive, requiring a minimum number of employees and only a few outside sources. There are, of course, some expenses in addition to salaries of staff announcers, even for stations that adhere rigidly to a news-and-music programming formula. Stations must secure the recorded music to be used on their disc jockey programs, and they must subscribe to a wire news service provided by one of the national news-gathering agencies; but these costs may be held to a very low figure. Often recordings are provided without charge by music distributors or local music stores; albums usually can be purchased by stations at a fraction of their retail cost. News-gathering organizations will provide a limited news service to a small-market station at a cost no higher than the amount the station pays as a salary to an inexperienced new announcer.

On the other hand, some stations in large cities spend substantial amounts of money for their news broadcasts, with expenditures for other types of material in proportion. They may employ a staff of news writers and editors; they may have a number of special roving reporters in mobile units; they may arrange for correspondents who cover the news in outlying areas or in other cities in the state; they may develop three or four highly paid "news personalities" who devote full time to presenting the news. These elaborate provisions for news coverage or for the presentation of expensive programs of other types are found only on large stations operating in major markets. The standard pattern of programming in hundreds of small radio stations throughout the country is the so-called "combo" operation in which the announcer on duty acts as his own control engineer, plans and handles all of his own programming, and in effect serves as a one-man programming, production, and engineering staff.

A growing number of radio stations in this country are turning from local-live music to the purchase of their music from program syndicators. These firms can provide on tape all the music a station wishes to put on the air. Many syndicators also offer the option of music with or without announcers, allowing the stations to decide whether or not to use local announcers to introduce the music. The cost of such full-time syndicated programming varies with the size of the market, beginning with $400 to $500 a month in small markets.

Radio Network Programs

The national radio networks are in much better position than are local stations with respect to the availability of talent and facilities. However, network budgets are limited; commercial offerings consist almost entirely of news broadcasts and short features—the same sort of one-man shows provided by local stations. The networks, of course, do have much better facilities at their command for handling such programs—nationally known entertainment or news personalities to put materials on the air, news correspondents in all parts of the world, much larger budgets for programming than are available to local stations. Even with these resources, the radio network companies concentrate on low-cost programs; their limited revenues in recent years have made elaborate programs impossible.

Local Television Programming

The programming situation in television is decidedly different from that in radio. If the local television station is a network affiliate— and all but about 100 do have network connections—it depends primarily on network programs to fill its weekly schedules. In addition, television stations have access to a tremendous supply of syndicated materials—theatrical feature films, motion picture short subjects, filmed or videotaped programs produced especially for television, and off-network series. The result, as previously mentioned, is that most television stations devote only 2 or 3 hours a day to the broadcasting of locally produced programs. In the spring of 1973, stations with network affiliations were on the air more than

122 hours a week and devoted 64 percent of their time to network programs, 22 percent to syndicated programs, and 13 percent to local materials. Independent stations were on the air, on the average, 101 hours a week, with 12 percent of their time devoted to carrying network programs rejected by the affiliates in the market. Syndicated programs filled 71 percent of their time, with live programming at 17 percent.[4]

Production Cost Considerations   To fill these local hours, the aim is of course the same as in radio—to develop simple, low-cost programs. Even for these programs, costs in television are tremendously greater than are the costs of similar programs on radio, largely because of television's much greater technical requirements. Compare the television local news program with its counterpart on radio. In radio, the news broadcaster can come to the station, check the late news-wire reports, make a few telephone calls to secure up-to-date information on local happenings, select and organize the materials he wishes to present, and then go on the air, requiring at most the services of one control-room engineer and possibly of an announcer to introduce the program and read the commercials. However, if the program is to be presented on television, a special set is needed and news photographs must be provided, as well as short filmed or taped sequences of local or national news events. Consequently, one or more news photographers must be employed to cover local news stories; their filmed materials must be developed, edited, and cut to appropriate lengths; the services of an ''t department are required to prepare visual headlines and captions for pictures as well as special production effects. When the newsman goes on the air with his copy, he still needs an announcer to introduce him; a director, a technical director and an audio operator must be in the control room; another technician is needed to handle film, tape, slides, and other visual material; and two cameramen and a floor director will make up a crew in the studio.

To keep their total programming costs at a reasonable level, virtually all television stations depend heavily on programs that make use of staff "personalities"—usually appearing on the air one at a time, as in news, weather, and sports programs. Even a one-man show on television represents the work of a dozen or more individuals whose combined efforts may involve as many as 50 man-hours in preparing and presenting an ordinary 30-minute program.

---

[4]Lawrence W. Lichty and Malachi C. Topping, *American Broadcasting: A Sourcebook on the History of Radio and Television* (New York: Hastings House, 1975), p. 443.

Frequently interview shows or children's programs are included in the daily schedule; even these are essentially one-man shows, since each program is built around a staff "personality" who works with unpaid guests—local adults or children. In any local production, every effort is made to hold production costs to minimum levels. As often as possible, such programs are taped when production crews are available, to avoid the necessity of scheduling crews at odd hours for short periods—news, of course, being the major exception to this practice. Most local programs are ad-libbed, presented without the use of written scripts. Participants are expected to follow a predetermined format for each broadcast, but to provide their own dialogue; rehearsals are held to a minimum, with on-camera rehearsals almost never arranged. Permanent sets are designed and used over and over again to save the costs of new set construction.

Program Development at a Television Network

Networks are in a much more favorable situation than are local television stations in program development, since they have plenty of money to spend and almost unlimited access to new program ideas, to outstanding talent, and to production resources. However, the network problem is extremely complex. Individual programs are less important to the network than the development of a strong, overall program schedule. While a local station can depend on its network for its most popular program offerings, the network must develop a new schedule of programs every season, with sometimes as many as fifteen or twenty entirely new series included; and of course, the program line-up for each season must surpass that of the preceding year.

Planning the Network Schedule   The planning of the network schedule and the selection of programs for each new season begins as much as 2 years before the time the new programs are to go on the air. The network's program executives meet, discuss suggested new ideas, review program weaknesses of past seasons, evaluate the offerings of competing networks, and consider possible changes in programming philosophies or program objectives for the seasons ahead. These strategy sessions continue at frequent intervals, with special attention given to changes in the popularity of programs currently being broadcast and to indications of trends in listener acceptance of programs of various types. Current schedules are examined to determine which programs are strong enough to be continued and which ones must be replaced. Of course, ideas for new programs are also considered, evaluated, and weighed in an effort to find replacements to strengthen the network's schedule.

Probably several hundred possible new program ideas are examined by the network's program staff each year. Most have little merit and are dropped without further consideration. Perhaps 70 or 80 of the ideas presented to the network's program executives seem to justify further examination and investigation—most of them ideas submitted by outside production agencies, others possible programs suggested by employees of the network itself. By the autumn preceding the start of the season for which plans are being made, the number of ideas under consideration will have been cut to perhaps 40 or 50, selected on the basis of the variety, freshness, and novelty offered, the success of programs of similar type in attracting audiences, the proven creative ability of the producer who will develop the program, and the stature of the featured entertainers involved.

These ideas, of course, must be studied further and more hard decisions must be made before a few are chosen to be included in the network schedules. To aid them in making these decisions, network executives ask for more detailed treatments or outlines of those series ideas that seem most promising. At this point in the development process, the network and the production firms begin paying for work done on the ideas, and decisions begin to have financial implications.

The series outlines—often called "bibles"—include the major premise of the series (a test pilot is badly injured in a crash and is "reconstructed" in such a way as to give him certain superhuman abilities that must be kept secret); the nature of continuing characters (the "Six Million Dollar Man," his Washington contact, a few scientists, and an old girlfriend who appears occasionally, is also "reconstructed" and "bionic" and has her own adventures); and specific script restrictions imposed by the concept of the series (both legs and one arm are "bionic" and have extra strength, one eye has telescopic abilities, hearing can be supersensitive, the man is vulnerable to bullets, and so forth). Such a series treatment gives the executives a better idea of its nature and becomes essential in the production of any scripts.

In addition to the series outline, specific program outlines—often called "stories for scripts"—are also prepared. These are rather detailed narrative summaries of the content of programs in the series. They are used in conjunction with the "bible" to determine whether or not the series idea is to be developed any further.

If a series is approved for further development at this stage, the next step is the preparation of a script or scripts and the shooting of an episode—called a pilot. The pilot film for a series carries a considerable burden. It must introduce the series concept and all the main characters in addition to giving an idea of the nature of a "typical" program—and it must do so in an interesting and dramatic manner. Because of this, pilots are often longer than other programs in the proposed series and more money and more time are devoted to them. If the series is placed on a network schedule, such pilots are often shown as two-part or long-form specials to attract audiences for subsequent episodes. Unsuccessful series pilots sometimes turn up on network schedules as well—often as made-for-television movies.

In the planning for the 1975–1976 season, according to *Broadcasting* magazine, a total of 84 pilot programs were ordered by the three commercial networks. NBC ordered 31, ABC 28, and CBS 25. Only 27 of these pilots were ultimately sold to the networks, 9 to each.

In most situations, final decisions on a series are made on the basis of reactions to the pilot by network executives and, sometimes, by test audiences. Each year, some series are accepted outright and orders are placed for a specific number of episodes—perhaps five or six. If the program is well accepted, the order is extended for the remainder of the season. If not, production is stopped and a replacement is sought. To insure that such replacements will be available, all three networks also accept some series ideas and order a few episodes so they will be ready when the inevitable cancellations and readjustments begin in October and November of each season.

Networks try to establish their schedules for the coming year by mid-April or early May to allow producers time for the production of programs. In recent years, efforts have been made to increase the time available to producers by settling schedules earlier and starting the "season" in late September. Giving the producers more time, it is hoped, will result in programs of higher quality for the fall.

The financial arrangements between the networks and the program producers during this selection process vary from series to series. Someone must pay for "bibles," stories for scripts, scripts, and the production of a pilot. In some cases, the networks carry the costs; in others, the producers do so. Most commonly, however, networks and producers share the costs, with the proportion borne by each determined by negotiation.

This development of new programs calls for the expenditure of millions of dollars each season by each of the network companies. Much of this expense represents payment for the production of pilot programs on film or tape. Because of their importance, and because contract arrangements with talent and production crews are different, pilots cost more to produce than a single episode of an established series. A half-hour pilot can cost $250,000 and an hour pilot more than $500,000—probably twice the cost of an average episode of the same series. If the series is then rejected, much of the money spent is lost. The advertising receipts of a single showing of a pilot as a movie will not cover production expenses. If the series is successful, of course, the network easily recaptures its investment and makes a profit on reruns, on repeats in morning, afternoon, or late evening slots and on foreign syndication.

Sources of New Program Ideas   Ideas for new television network programs come from a variety of sources. While programs on local stations are usually developed within the station itself, most network shows are the products of outside professionals. Sometimes an idea for a series may grow out of the program-planning sessions of the network staff, or occasionally even from a suggestion made by an advertiser or an advertising agency. As a rule, however, the new series owes its existence to ideas developed by individual writers, producers, or agents, working with independent production companies. If an idea generates any interest within the staff of the production company or advertising agency or network, a tentative format for the series is developed, possible entertainers considered, and a "treatment," or detailed description of the program, is prepared to serve as the basis of discussions with network executives.

While most network series are developed in the routine manner described, some are developed to utilize the services of an available "name" entertainer. Efforts were made by NBC in 1976, for example, to develop a series for Raymond Burr—of *Perry Mason* and *Ironsides* fame—solely in an effort to get that successful actor back on the network schedule. For many variety programs built around such established entertainers as Carol Burnett, Tony Orlando, and Dick Van Dyke, the network first contracted for the services of the star entertainer, and worked out details concerning the format used in the program sometimes weeks or even months after the star had signed the contract.

Requirements in New Programs   The network companies naturally attempt to hold their risks to a minimum. One already mentioned

device is to work out some kind of cooperative arrangement with the producer under which both expenses and profits are shared, reducing the amount of possible financial loss to either party. Even more important is the selection of programs that offer the greatest promise of success. As a rule, the network deals only with outside producers with established reputations, on the assumption that a company with an established record of success is much less likely to produce a weak program than would be a less experienced concern. Regardless of source, each proposed program series must satisfy network executives on a number of major counts before that program is finally scheduled for network presentation. It must have audience appeal—the ability to attract large numbers of listeners. It must show originality and novelty value. It must not offer any unusually great production problems—in other words, it must be feasible from the standpoint of production. There must be certainty that the entertainers needed for the program are available. There must be agreement between the network and the producing company on program costs and budgetary arrangements. The program must offer features that give it good publicity and promotion potentials. Finally, it must be the type of program that, on the basis of past experience, is likely to attract advertisers.

Failure to meet network requirements in any one of these areas is usually enough to result in the abandonment of any program idea, even though its prospects otherwise seem excellent. A program with limited audience appeal is not likely to justify its cost of production or its place in the network's schedule; one too much like other programs already on the air may fail to attract a large enough following of listeners and is also likely to injure the network's reputation through its very lack of originality. Some program ideas call for extensive production in remote locations, likely to create major technical problems and possibly causing unexpected production delays and expense. Competent writers who fit the program's requirements may not be available; perhaps the series may call for the use of particular stars who are already committed to other programs or who demand an excessive price for their services.

There may be circumstances that make the proposed series difficult to sell. Few advertisers are greatly interested in documentary programs, in "arty" drama, or in programs of classical music; the scandals connected with network quiz shows completely destroyed for years to come any chance of selling an idea for a new "big-money" quiz or give-away program; oversaturation of network time with western programs greatly reduced the salability of any new western series. Unless the network is reasonably confident

of the success of any new program in terms both of attracting listeners and of satisfying the requirements of advertisers, that program is not likely to find its way into the network's tentative schedules.

Production of Network Programs

Most of the programming on commercial television networks is provided by independent producers, most of whom work out of Hollywood. Some of these production companies are subsidiaries of major motion picture firms; others have no connection with companies producing feature films. Some companies maintain their own studios, while others lease the space and equipment they need. Some companies work primarily with film, others with tape. Some specialize in variety programming, others in situation comedies, and still others in action-adventure. The result is an enormous and diverse concentration of facilities, equipment, and talent on the West Coast from which comes most of the programming seen on commercial television.

Headquarters for the three major networks, on the other hand, are in New York, as were most production facilities until the mid-1960s. It can be said that television grew up in New York—in 1963, CBS alone maintained twelve studios in New York and only four in Hollywood. By the mid-1970s, however, Hollywood was dominant to the degree that a decision by CBS to produce in New York some episodes of *Kojak*—a series about a Manhattan police lieutenant—merited headlines in *Variety*. Only news and informational programming now originate regularly from New York.

Live Production

In the early days of television, live production meant just that— the program viewed by the audience was being performed in a network television studio before live cameras and transmitted directly to the homes, errors and all. Many programs famous from the "golden days" of television drama in the 1950s—such as *Studio One, Philco Playhouse, Robert Montgomery Presents, The United States Steel Hour,* and *Playhouse 90*—were live, and a remarkable level of quality was maintained. From a production standpoint, however, the disadvantages of live production far outweighed the advantages and by the late 1950s film was becoming dominant.

Some of the reasons for this are obvious. A dramatic program can be shot on film over a period of days instead of concentrating

production into the available 60 or 90 minutes. Action can be staged outside more easily, with "stock shots" of almost any location available. Mistakes can be corrected, and many technical special effects are available to film and not to television.

Another reason for the shift to film was the question of "residuals." Programs done live were seen once and lost forever. "Kinescope recordings" on film were of poor quality and were used primarily by stations with no network interconnection. Production on high-quality film, on the other hand, allowed for reruns, repeats, and later syndication, all of which meant more money for all involved in production.

The result is the situation we know today in which, aside from sports, truly live programming is virtually extinct. Parts of NBC's *Today, Tomorrow,* and *Saturday Night Live* programs are live, as are parts of ABC's *Good Morning America*. The evening news broadcasts of all three networks are live—although some markets may receive network "feeds" of the programs that are tape recordings of the original broadcasts. With a few scattered exceptions, everything else on television network schedules is on either film or tape.

Producers and networks still use the term "live," though, and apply it primarily to variety programs that are recorded on tape before a live audience. Such programs appear live and minor errors are permitted to stay to heighten this appearance. That major mistakes are corrected, however, is made evident by the fact that producers often use shots of these mistakes (called "out-takes") for comedy effect before presenting the accepted version of a performance.

Production on Film   By the mid-1970s, the great majority of all dramatic programs on network television were produced on film, using traditional motion picture techniques. Programs produced in this way are put together in piecemeal fashion. Each scene is rehearsed and shot as a separate unit; actors run through the scene in rehearsal until the director is satisfied, then do the scene again with the camera running. If the director is not satisfied with the result, he orders a retake of the scene. The individual scenes are shot out of order, with all those using the same set or location filmed in groups, to reduce costs. Only one camera is used and each scene is shot several times, with the camera moved each time to focus on a different principal, on a wide shot, or on a medium shot.

The shooting is only one stage in the production process. At the end of each day's filming, exposed film is developed; during the evening, the film footage produced during the day is reviewed by the director and chief cameraman, who select the "take" of each scene to be used. Then the film goes to the film editor who cuts out unwanted footage and splices the remaining scenes together in proper sequence. When all the scenes for the program have been shot and edited, the finished product is timed and cut to required length; titles and credits are added; and the complete program is reviewed again by the director and producer of the series to determine whether last-minute changes are needed. After this, the filmed episode goes to the film editorial department, which "dubs" sound effects and musical backgrounds into the sound track. Finally, the film in its completed form is sent to the laboratory where prints are made of the complete program, ready for use in the projection room of the network or of individual stations.

Film production using traditional motion picture techniques obviously takes a great deal of time, and some producers have developed multiple-camera techniques to speed up the process and reduce the number of retakes. Producers of *The Mary Tyler Moore Show*, for instance, used a three-camera technique with cameras placed in strategic locations and all running at the same time. This produced three versions of each scene with each take, which the director and editor later cut and pieced together to produce the best effect.

Production on Tape   The advent of videotape resulted in another medium for the recording of television programs. As already noted, most musical and comedy variety programs are produced on television tape. The development of smaller television cameras and more sophisticated editing procedures in the 1970s has led some producers to use tape in the production of dramatic programs as well.

Taped programs use two, three, or more cameras and the director does much of his "editing" on the spot. With monitors displaying all of his video sources before him, he selects the camera or cameras that will be recorded on tape at a given moment while the recording is in progress. The result is a tape in which much of the routine editing has already been completed.

Usually, a program produced in this way is recorded more than once. At the very least, both the dress rehearsal and the performance before a live audience (or the final performance) are put on tape. In addition, some scenes that are still unsatisfactory to the director will be shot again for inclusion in the broadcast version. These are called "pickup scenes." The director and the tape editor, then, still have a job cut out for them before a final version of the program satisfactory to the producer, the director, the network, and the stars is put together. They must select the best segments from each recording, put them together smoothly, and add necessary music, sound effects, audience reactions, and the like, to produce a polished product.

Tandem Productions, the producers of such programs as *All in the Family, Maude,* and *One Day at a Time,* uses a multicamera tape process for most of its programs. For *All in the Family,* for instance, several hours of camera blocking, two show tapings, and some "pick-up" scenes normally were edited down to a final version. To expedite this editing, each of these versions was dubbed from master, broadcast-quality tapes to ½-inch videotape for "trial editing" before actual electronic editing of the originals. The editing process for a 30-minute program usually took from 12 to 15 hours and occupied the last 2 days of the production schedule.[5]

Use of Reruns   The high production costs of evening network programs are responsible for the practice of making extensive use of reruns of programs broadcast earlier in the season. Since the early 1960s, reruns have filled the entire 13-week summer schedule of nearly every evening dramatic program series; in addition more and more reruns have been inserted into the other 39 weeks, with the result that, over a year, some series now include more reruns than new episodes. The reason for the practice is a matter of simple economics. Network executives maintain that production and other costs have risen to the point that, in many cases, they cannot recover all of their costs from the advertising revenues derived from the first run of a series episode. Profits are made, they say, on the reruns, in which advertising rates drop by 30 percent while production costs are down by 90 percent—the payment of residuals being the only major cost. Thus the rerun has become an important factor in network economics.

THE SHORT LIFE OF A PROGRAM

One factor that causes headaches for network executives is the exceptionally short life span of the average television program series. A few network programs seem to go on forever—*Gunsmoke* ran 19 years before being cancelled; *The Wonderful World of Disney* is well into its second decade; *The Carol Burnett Show* had its tenth birthday in 1975—but these are the exceptions. Relatively few television

[5]For an interesting discussion of the production of one such program, see James E. Lynch, "Seven Days with 'All in the Family'—Case Study of the Taped TV Drama," *Journal of Broadcasting,* Vol. 17 (Summer 1973), pp. 259–274.

"The program originally scheduled for cancellation at this time is being switched to Tuesday at 9:30 P.M. It will be cancelled at that time."

programs last for more than three or four seasons; one can be reasonably sure that two out of every five evening programs carried on network schedules during any year will be replaced before the start of the next season.

The Survival Pattern

As has already been noted, television networks originate an average of 31 new programs each season, most of them new nighttime programs. On these new programs rest the network's hopes for increasing its share of the viewing audience, its prestige as a developer of new program ideas, and most important of all, its economic future. In network programming, nothing succeeds like success, for if a network's new program offerings fail to win the approval of listeners, both sponsors and affiliated stations are injured, and the network will find it difficult to sell next season's shows.

What happens to the new programs added each year to the network's evening schedules? According to performance records over the period from 1969 through 1974, some of the new programs will be canceled before the end of the season, after network runs of not more than 6 or 13 weeks. Others will be dropped at the start of the following season; in all, at least nine or ten of each year's new evening program offerings will not be carried into a second year. These, with six or eight "old" programs dropped, make it necessary for the network to develop another fifteen or sixteen new programs for the start of the following program year.

Why this tremendously large number of programs dropped each year—from 35 to 40 percent of the network's entire evening schedule and nearly two thirds of the new programs the network develops each year? Does it mean that all the programs dropped were hopelessly bad, incapable of holding the interest of listeners? Or that network executives lack knowledge and understanding of audience tastes and are unable to develop successful shows? Not necessarily, by any means. Many factors contribute to a program's success, or to its failure.

Why Programs Fail

Some new programs, certainly, fail to measure up to expectations and to the demands of listeners and of network advertisers. They attract too limited audiences and consequently must be dropped. Producers may have shown poor judgment in gauging the responses and interests of the listening public; or a program that held forth excellent promise as a pilot film may have failed to show the strength expected as a continuing once-a-week series; or a program idea may have built-in limitations that make long runs impossible. The *Union Pacific* series, carried by one of the networks several years ago, illustrates this problem. A series built around an important method of transportation would seem to have excellent dramatic possibilities. However, after the series was on the air came the realization that there is a limit to the number of dramatic situations in which a train crew may reasonably be involved; after those situations had been exploited, there was nowhere for the series to go but off the air. Built-in limitations rarely are responsible for the dropping of a new series, but they do quite often limit the network run of a program to one or two seasons. A situation comedy built around smaller children loses its appeal rapidly as the children grow up or grow out of the "cute" stage, as happened to *The Brady Bunch;* when Jeannie married her astronaut in *I Dream of Jeannie*, the program lost some of its appeal.

Sometimes a change in the production situation is responsible for the failure of a program series. The illness or death of a leading character creates serious problems for the producer, to say the least; the same result can occur when a popular entertainer leaves a series because of contract difficulties or simply because he wants a change of scene. NBC's long-running *Bonanza* weathered the loss of one son when Pernell Roberts left the show for a better variety of roles but could not survive the later death of Dan Blocker, who played the popular "Hoss" Cartright. Then, of course, we have had other types of changes in conditions: when, some years ago, accusations were made that two of the popular quiz shows on network evening schedules were "rigged," every other quiz show was automatically "dead," as far as audiences were concerned; within two months, all of the six or eight "big-money" shows, which previously had attracted large numbers of listeners, had been dropped from network schedules.

Programs fail for other reasons, also. Some, like *The Ed Sullivan Show*, may enjoy long runs, but audiences eventually tire of any program and even this Sunday night tradition was finally cancelled as ratings fell. Other programs are cancelled because network executives feel they are appealing to the wrong audiences. In 1970, for instance, CBS dropped *Petticoat Junction* and variety programs hosted by Jackie Gleason and Red Skelton. All three programs were getting good ratings, but surveys determined that their audience included too many residents of rural counties and too few young adults to be retained on the schedule. (Adults aged 18 to 35 living in urban centers have been determined to be the "biggest spenders," and advertisers prefer to concentrate their efforts on this group.) A program like *Laugh-In*, seen at first as a refreshing new approach to comedy, found itself canceled after a few years because of cast attrition and the enormous demands for material that a 60-minute comedy program produces.

The Problem of Saturation   One factor that accounts for the failure of many network programs is the scheduling of too many programs of similar types during a given season. Programming runs in cycles; a new or relatively new form is introduced; it becomes successful; a few months or at most a year or two later, half a dozen programs using a similar basic idea are on the air. We have had, on network television, cycles of variety programs, of quiz programs, of musical shows. We have had "private-eye" detective programs, "real-life" police detective shows, "costume-type" adventure programs, courtroom dramas, medical dramas, and, of course, dozens of situation comedies. The television western provides an excellent illustration of this tendency in network programming. The success of *Gunsmoke* and *Wyatt Earp* during the 1955–1956 season found other producers anxious to develop programs with a western setting that could achieve the same high levels of popularity. Five years later, no fewer than 29 western series were being presented by the networks each week. Unfortunately, the number of possible plot situations and the number of possible hero characters were not unlimited—so every series began to resemble every other western series on the air. Producers resorted to "gimmicks" in an effort to make their own programs different; *Bat Masterson* wore a derby hat and carried a cane; the leading character in *The Rebel* wore a Confederate uniform; *The Rifleman* used a rifle instead of a pistol; *Shotgun Slade* carried a shotgun and had only one arm. However, these devices could not change the fact that each story was largely the same as the stories used on other series—and most of the western programs introduced on the networks were dropped at the end of a single season. The same tendency is seen in police drama and by the mid-1970s we had *Columbo* looking as though he slept in his clothes, *McCloud* riding his horse down Fifth Avenue, *Ironsides* in a wheelchair, *Kojak* sucking lollipops, and *Baretta* with his bird. Overuse of any idea for a series reduces listener interest.

The Problem of Scheduling Another important factor in the success or failure of a program is the place given the new series on the network's schedule. If it follows a very popular program on the same network and has only weak competition from programs on the other two networks, a program of only average attractiveness may be quite successful; but the same program may be a complete failure if forced to compete with a highly popular program broadcast during the same period. In the early to middle 1970s, CBS developed a series of powerful situation comedies (led by *All in the Family* and later by *The Mary Tyler Moore Show*) against which NBC and ABC had little success no matter what programming they tried. In the same period, NBC developed a strong Friday night schedule, and competing programs from the other two networks found good ratings virtually impossible.

Occasionally a new program catches the fancy of the audience and displaces what had been a dominant program in the time period—as *The Waltons* did to *The Flip Wilson Show*—and the networks keep trying, usually with unfortunate results. On the other hand, some new programs have been helped by the time at which they were scheduled. When CBS introduced *Phyllis*, they positioned it between *Rhoda* and *All in the Family*. This scheduling virtually guaranteed its success. However, lead-in and following programs are usually not enough to carry a show alone, especially when competition is strong, as evidenced by the NBC venture in 1975 with *Ellery Queen*, following *Walt Disney* and followed in turn by the high-rated *Sunday Mystery Movie*—but with *Sonny and Cher* and *The Six Million Dollar Man* competing for listeners on other networks.

The time at which a program is scheduled, the attractiveness of the program it follows, and the strength or weakness of competing programs, all have much to do with the success or the failure of every new program series.

The Penalty of Success   A factor often contributing to the demise of a well-established and still-popular program series is the spiraling cost of production, created by the program's very success. Most new dramatic programs make use of relatively unknown actors. Frequently "regulars" in a series may be paid as little as $200 to $250 a week during the program's first season on the air, with leading characters receiving a little more. If the series proves successful, the $250-a-week actor demands and can get more money for his services each year the program continues on network schedules. Actors and writers are almost always represented by business agents whose major function is to negotiate salary contracts and to secure as much compensation as possible for their clients. Thanks to the success of the program, by the time the series goes into its fourth season on the air, the once unknown actor may be receiving $10,000 or more each week. Or in some cases, he may quit the show entirely to accept a part in a Broadway play or in a motion picture—or in another television series.

One great fear in the life of television actors is that of being "typed" to the point where they cannot find other employment for their talents. Unfortunately, the stars of nearly every television series are closely identified with the roles they take on the air, with the result that later they all too often have difficulty in finding other types of roles to play. Fear of being unable to break away from a "type" was considered to be at least one reason for Pernell Roberts' leaving *Bonanza*, for Michael Douglas' dropping out of *Streets of San Francisco*, and for numerous other actors leaving established programs at the height of success.

So the success of a dramatic program—its continuing on the air for more than a single season—creates serious problems for the producers of that series. Production costs go up, almost in proportion to the show's success. Actors and writers, established by their participation in a successful series, may leave the program for more lucrative work in other fields. Of course, what is true of dramatic programs applies equally for variety shows, musical programs, audience-participation shows —every type of entertainment shown on network television.

Not all the programs that leave the air may properly be classed as failures. Even some of the programs that fail to attract a sufficient number of listeners may possess a considerable amount of merit. At the same time, we should note that few really strong programs, with sound ideas, good writing, and excellent production, go off the air at the end of a single season. Some of those cancelled should never have been presented in the first place. Some rest upon the abilities of an entertainer with too little personality to "carry" his own show. Some fail because of poor production, poor writing, poor acting; an even larger number fail because of poor basic program ideas.

Whatever the reason, only a very few programs possess the ingredients necessary to keep them on the air more than three or four seasons. The fact that so few do survive emphasizes the need for new programs, new ideas, and new talent; and the search for successful programs continues unabated with little change from year to year.

STUDY AND DISCUSSION QUESTIONS

1. With a few exceptions, each of the radio stations in your market is aiming its programming at a specific segment of the population, which can usually be identified by age, income level, and taste in music. Study the radio stations in your market or in one nearby and determine as well as you can the nature of the audience sought by each. For each station, also indicate how successful you feel it is in programming for this audience. To the degree possible, check your judgments through interviews with the management of the various stations.

2. Analyze the schedule of one of the major television networks for a recent year. Report on or be prepared to discuss the following about regularly scheduled programming:

   a. The number and nature of new programs at the beginning of the season
   b. The number and nature of carry-over programs, including the number of previous seasons each has been on the air
   c. The strengths and weaknesses of the schedule as revealed by rating figures in early to middle November
   d. Programs cancelled in the course of the season and the date of the last regular airing of each
   e. Sources and nature of replacement programs
   f. The number and nature of programs switched to different times to strengthen the overall schedule
   g. The relative strengths and weaknesses of various categories of program (situation comedy, westerns, and so forth) in the network schedule
   h. An end-of-season "box-score" of successes, marginal programs, and cancellations for the entire season

3. Report on or be prepared to discuss the specials offered by the three networks during a recent television season. Consider the following:

   a. The number of specials offered by each network
   b. The various categories of special offered and the number of programs in
   each
   c. Average ratings of various categories of special
   d. The number and content of those specials that could be considered
   extensive coverage of special events.

4. Using the program categories developed by Dominick and Pearce, study
network programming in the years following 1974 and report on:

   a. New and continued program trends
   b. The emergence and disappearance of program forms
   c. The follow-the-leader trend
   d. Whether or not the trends established by "systems indicators" have continued

5. Report on or be prepared to discuss the following:

   a. The growth of radio program syndicators
   b. Sources of program concepts for new programs appearing in a given
   year
   c. The comparative advantages and disadvantages of program production
   on tape and film
   d. The increase in the number of reruns on the network schedules
   e. The effects of scheduling on program life (lead-in and lead-out programs,
   competing programs, audience flow, and the like)

SUGGESTED READINGS

Muriel G. Cantor. *The Hollywood TV Producer: His Work and His Audience.*
New York: Basic Books, 1972.

Nina David. *TV Season, 1974–75.* Phoenix, Ariz.: Oryx Press, 1976. (1973–
74, 1975–76 and subsequent volumes may also be available from the
same source.)

William Kuhns. *Why We Watch Them: Interpreting TV Shows.* New York:
Benziger, 1970.

Bob Shanks. *The Cool Fire: How to Make It in Television.* New York: Norton,
1976.

9

News and Information

While commercial broadcasting places most of its emphasis on programs that entertain, news and information occupy a portion of the schedule of virtually every commercial radio and television station in the United States. The quantity and quality of this news varies, of course. In radio it ranges from "rip and read" stations, in which news headlines are taken directly from wire service machines and read with little or no effort at understanding or interpretation, to all-news stations in major markets that devote their entire broadcast day to international, national, state, and local news and features. The television range is not so wide, but some stations are far superior to others in their news coverage.

In a democracy, citizens who participate in the political process must be informed. Radio and television are the most popular—the most "used"—mass media in our society today and, as a result, are natural vehicles for the movement of information to the public. Partially in recognition of this fact, the Federal Communications Commission insists that news coverage is part of the public-service responsibility of all broadcast licensees. Most broadcasters agree, recognizing the importance of information to the political process, for the soundness and intelligence of opinions formed by the voting public depend on the extent and nature of the information received by individual voters—information on which their collective decisions are based.

Not everyone agrees, however, that the broadcast media provide the kind and amount of news and information that concerned citizens need. Broadcast news media have been, and will continue to be, accused of distortion, superficiality, and hidden bias. The fact remains, though, that radio and television do provide most of the news to most of the people in the United States. Good, bad, or mediocre, electronic journalism is an important fact of life today and deserves description and analysis.

Sources of Public Information

In any society, the public depends for its information about public issues on many media of mass communication—newspapers, magazines, motion pictures, books, television, and radio. The effectiveness of any single medium of information, however, is limited by certain obvious factors. Print media can be effective only if people know how to read and have the money and motivation to buy printed materials. As a result, in countries with high illiteracy rates and with low average family incomes, books, newspapers, and magazines are inefficient as media of *mass* communication. Even in countries such as the United States that have high average annual incomes and high levels of technical literacy, the effectiveness of print media in providing information at all levels of society is highly debatable. Most Americans are literate, but relatively few devote much of their time to reading. Studies of reading habits suggest that the average American adult reads no more than three or four books a year and devotes an average of not more than 30 to 35 minutes a day to magazines and newspapers; other studies indicate that average newspaper "reading" in the United States is largely limited to the picture pages, comic strips, front-page headlines, and amusement features. Of course, even in a nation as prosperous as ours, not all families have access to magazines, books, or even daily papers. It has been estimated that only about 70 percent of all homes receive a daily newspaper; aside from best sellers in fiction, very few books are sold to more than 3,000 readers; and the combined circulation of the three major newsmagazines, *Time*, *Newsweek*, and *U.S. News & World Report*, is only 7.5 million. It is an interesting fact that of all the magazines and journals available to American readers, since the mid-1950s the one with the largest average circulation has been *TV Guide*, the publication that lists the programs to be seen on television during the coming week.

Advantages Offered by Broadcasting

Radio and television do have limitations as agencies for the conveying of information, but when compared with print media they also have certain advantages. First, with receiving sets in about 98 percent of all American homes, radio and television can reach listeners on every educational, cultural, and economic level. Again, because of the existence of national networks, radio and television can ignore geographic barriers; the materials in network programs reach listeners in every section of the United States. Third, in delivering the news or in covering special events, radio and television have a distinct *time* advantage over print media. Broadcast stations can provide up-to-the-minute news almost as it happens, while there is a necessary delay of several hours before a newspaper can bring a news story to its readers—and of several days or even weeks before a magazine's coverage of a news event reaches the public. Finally, the average radio or television listener in this country may make a choice among programs offered by several different radio and television stations, so that he has available a variety of sources of information and the possibility of hearing expressions of a variety of different points of view.

Broadcast information is presented by *people* and by means of the human voice. On television, viewers see the speaker and, more often than not, what he says is supported by pictorial evidence. Whether on television or radio, broadcast information has a personal quality and a sense of "realness" the print media cannot offer, with the result that people find it easier to give attention to materials on radio or television than to read the same materials in their daily newspapers.

As an agency of mass information, broadcasting can bring the listening public a wider variety and a greater quantity of information than can be provided effectively by any other medium. The question is, how well does broadcasting actually perform in satisfying the public's need for information—how much information is broadcast and what kinds of information are provided? To answer this question, it is necessary to analyze the activities of networks and stations as they present general information (news and public affairs) and the ideas and opinions of national and local leaders on the issues confronting the nation or the local community.

GENERAL INFORMATION

Since broadcasting is primarily a medium of entertainment, most programs on radio and television are designed to entertain the listeners. Stations and networks also provide information, some of it in the fields of news and public affairs and some of it general information on a wide variety of subjects.

Local Informational Programs

Much of the general information offered by radio stations relates directly to listener needs. Every radio station gives up-to-the-minute weather reports a dozen or more times a day—short capsule announcements of current temperature readings with the weather forecast for the rest of the day and for the day following. In fruit-growing areas in Florida and California, stations broadcast special frost warnings at frequent intervals; in areas where tornadoes are frequent, radio assists the local weather bureau by broadcasting emergency tornado warnings; radio and television stations along the Gulf and Atlantic coasts are especially alert during the hurricane season each year—often preempting all regularly scheduled programming in communities in the predicted path of the damag-

Figure 9-1 Some local television stations install varieties of weather forecasting equipment to supplement information from the National Weather Service. (Courtesy WWL TV Weather Center, New Orleans)

ing storms; during winter months stations give information about road conditions when icy streets or heavy snowfalls make automobile driving hazardous. In times of weather emergencies in any part of the country, listeners depend on radio to learn about plans for the closing of schools or whether factories and local businesses are suspending operations.

Most high-power radio stations and regional stations serving farm areas carry daily programs of farm information—prices being paid at livestock and produce markets, details of pending farm legislation, and advice on marketing or on the planting of crops or the times when fruit trees should be sprayed. Other stations offer regularly scheduled programs with information on buying foods, planning menus, home decoration, fashions, vacation traveling, and the planning of household budgets, as well as interesting local people or visitors to the community. Some radio stations carry programs giving the time and place of meetings of local organizations; others give names of those admitted to hospitals. Many large-city stations give regular reports on traffic conditions on congested streets or freeways during morning and afternoon rush hours, using information relayed directly from helicopters or airplanes circling the city.

In addition to service broadcasts of the types noted above, virtually every radio station presents religious programs on Sunday, some in cooperation with local churches, others from tapes or transcriptions provided by religious organizations. Some schedule weekly taped reports from such public officials as congressmen and senators, the governor of the state, and the mayor of the city, to keep listeners informed of the activities of national and local governments. A number of stations in larger cities devote from 2 to 5 hours a day to blocks of 60-minute talk programs on each of which an expert on some subject presents a 10- to 12-minute talk and then is available for another 40 to 45 minutes to answer questions phoned in by listeners. Only a small number of radio stations devote more than a couple of hours a day to such informational programs, although some stations in the largest markets have successfully adopted an all-talk format. Because the average listener has access to a number of stations, local radio has become an important source of general information.

Local television stations also contribute to the listeners' stock of information, although on television the emphasis is usually different from that on radio. Nearly every television station schedules three or four local weather programs each day, usually 3 to 5 minutes in length and giving much more detailed information than is supplied on radio about the national picture and the meterological conditions that affect the weather. Many television stations carry regular early morning programs of farm information, with some employing full-time farm directors to supervise such programs. Television stations also broadcast a number of religious programs each week, in addition to offerings of the national networks. These often include at least one program produced in the station's own studios and two or three filmed or taped presentations—some using the dramatic form—supplied by various religious organizations.

Many television stations also include live daily informative programs on their schedules. Most of these programs feature interviews with interesting local people or with visitors to the community, especially those who are authorities on subjects that lend themselves to visual demonstrations like home decoration, fashions in clothing, sewing, and cooking. Widely known actors, writers, musicians, entertainers, local people who "made good," and men and women in public life are also frequent guests on these shows.

Most television stations present some sort of program for children on weekdays. Sometimes these are syndicated programs, on film or tape, that require little or no production effort. In most larger markets, however, stations also present children's programs that are locally developed and produced. Many such programs are planned to include a considerable amount of information for children.

Since the early 1960s, many television stations in the larger markets have been producing local documentary programs, primarily on film, that are broadcast at irregular intervals throughout the year. Subjects of these documentaries range from such items as an examination of the reasons for a shortage of lids for home canning to the problem of alcohol abuse by minors. Some stations also carry documentary programs made available by nearby universities. A few provide instructional programs on such subjects as driver education or fire prevention, sometimes prepared in cooperation with local school systems.

Network Informational Programs

Aside from news, the informational materials made available by radio networks in recent years has been limited almost entirely to short (5-minute or less) talk features that affiliates can tape off the network line and insert in their local programming of recorded music. Television networks, however, offer a variety of informational programs to their affiliates, some on a regularly scheduled basis, others as special broadcasts.

Since the early 1950s when many stations carried the documentary series *Victory at Sea*, dealing with the Pacific phase of World War II, network schedules have included such outstanding historical re-creations as *Crusade in Europe, The Valiant Years, Air Power, Alistair Cooke's America*, and other programs of general information.

Typical of network offerings in recent years are programs presented in the 1974–1975 season. Although regular, weekly informational programs had, with one or two exceptions, disappeared from network schedules, many special informational programs were presented. A 1975 summary of network prime-time specials carried in the 1974–1975 season, published in *Variety*, showed that 82 of the 381 specials listed for the season could be considered newsinformational. These ranged from the *National Geographic* specials and the Jacques Cousteau specials through such historical programs as *Sandburg's Lincoln* and *Benjamin Franklin*, speculative features like *Magnificent Monsters of the Deep*, topical reviews like *Vietnam, A War That Is Finished*, network reports on such subjects as *The White Collar Rip-Off, And Who Shall Feed This World, Prescriptions—Take With Caution*, and *Crashes, The Illusion of Safety* to coverage of the joint Russian-American space venture in 1975.

Network offerings in the religious field, like *Look up and Live* and *Lamp unto My Feet*, were usually programs of general information that used dramatic, documentary, or discussion forms to deal with current social problems. The NBC *Today* program, although emphasizing news, devoted from 45 minutes to an hour each weekday morning to interviews with authorities on subjects ranging from foreign travel to environmental problems, and from advances in medical science to art exhibits and style shows. CBS tried for years to compete with the *Today* program by scattering a mix of informative features throughout its *CBS Morning News*, but by the mid-1970s had yet to find the proper mix to offer any effective competition to NBC at this hour. In 1975, ABC entered the early-morning competition with a 2-hour mixture of entertainment, information, and news, first called *AM America* and later *Good Morning America*, which provided still a third source of information for the early-morning viewing audience. Moving into very late-night programming in 1973–1974, NBC has been successful with its *Tomorrow* program that leans heavily on an interview format focusing on informative and controversial subjects.

There can be little question that television makes an important contribution to the public's stock of general information.

Incidental Information

The informational programs that stations and networks provide are undoubtedly important, but it would be a mistake to assume that only by tuning in these programs does the radio or television listener add to his store of information about the world. Included in any person's stock of what we call general knowledge are thousands of bits of unrelated information that have come from personal experience, from casual reading, from conversation with friends, and from a variety of other sources. Certainly included among these sources of general information are those broadcast programs—television programs in particular—presented not to give information but to entertain.

Listeners pick up some odds and ends of information by listening to musical programs or talk shows. They get bits of information from materials presented in the daytime game and panel shows. In fact, when respondents in the 1940s were asked to name their favorite "educational programs," two thirds of the programs named were radio quiz shows.

It can be argued further that audiences also gain some general information from the programs that fill most of the evening schedules of television networks. The value or reliability of such information, however, is open to question. Some programs, like *Police Story* and the short-lived *Medical Story*, do receive fairly high marks for accuracy from the professions involved. On the other hand, fans of *Marcus Welby*, *Starsky and Hutch*, and *The Rockford*

Files would find real-life doctors, policemen, and private investigators to be a far cry from their television counterparts. The fact remains, however, that television audiences *do* take some general information from the programs they listen to. Accurate or not, this information can contribute significantly to the formation of public attitudes.

NEWS AND PUBLIC AFFAIRS

Broadcasting's greatest contribution to public enlightenment, however, has been in the field of news and public affairs. From the time they were first organized in the late 1920s, radio networks gave their listeners weekly reports on happenings in Washington. By the autumn of 1930, one network was providing its affiliates with five-times-a-week, 15-minute, early evening news programs, and since that time emphasis on news and public affairs has steadily increased. In recent years, so well accepted has been radio and television news coverage that in 1977 the Elmo Roper research organization reported that 64 percent of its respondents stated in a survey that they got "most of their news about what is going on in the world today" from television. The same survey showed that 19 percent depended primarily on radio for news.[1]

The importance of television in particular in providing news firsthand to the American people was dramatically illustrated on November 22, 1963, when millions of Americans sat silently before their television sets watching the events that followed the assassination of President John F. Kennedy. Ten minutes before the first announcement was made that the President had been shot, television sets were in use in approximately 23 percent of all homes in the United States, according to the A. C. Nielsen Company. An hour later, the proportion of homes with sets tuned to reports of the tragedy had doubled; and, between 6:00 P.M. and 10:00 P.M. that Friday evening, the event in Dallas held the attention of viewers in from 65 to 90 percent of all American homes. Another dramatic

---

[1]Newspapers were named by 49 percent of the men and women interviewed, since many of the respondents named more than one medium as the most important news source. In the same study, when asked which medium they would be most inclined to believe if conflicting reports of the same event were given by radio, by television, by newspapers, and by magazines, 51 percent indicated that they would believe the television account, while only 22 percent had a greater faith in the accuracy of the account given by newspapers. *Changing Public Attitudes . . . 1959–1976* (New York: Television Information Office, May, 1977).

illustration of the importance of television is provided by the estimate that 125 million Americans watched the first moon landing on
June 28, 1969. In both instances, television allowed its viewers to see
events while they were happening in a way no print news medium
could attempt to equal.

News on Radio

Of course, events like those of 1963 or 1969 are rare exceptions.
However, radio and television provide reports on news for their
listeners in less spectacular fashion on regularly scheduled news
programs, day after day, year after year. Virtually every radio station, no matter how small, carries a dozen or more news programs
on its daily schedule. Since the middle 1950s, radio news has usually been presented in short, 5-minute capsules at hourly intervals.
In addition, many radio stations schedule "news-hours" during
both morning and evening drive times. These so-called "hours"
often run through virtually the entire drive-time period, and, of
course, news is not their only content. In these periods, however,
stations greatly reduce the amount of music played and fill the time
with weather reports, reviews of the traffic situation, sports summaries, and large quantities of hard news—national, state, and
local—in an effort to capture and keep the attention of people as
they get ready for and drive to and from work.

Network affiliates frequently schedule their short, capsule programs of local news immediately following the programs supplied
by the networks. For national and regional news, most radio stations subscribe to a news wire service from the Associated Press or
United Press International—the two major news-gathering organizations in the United States. Local news is often limited to what can
be learned from routine telephone calls to public officials, police
and fire departments, hospitals, and mortuaries. On many radio
stations, most of the 5-minute newscasts are given by whatever staff
announcer happens to be on duty, and in the same language in
which it comes from the service to which the station subscribes.

Larger radio stations and those in major cities, however, tend to
give much more attention to local news. Practically all have full-
time news directors, many of whom are persons with journalism
training. On larger stations, the news director may be assisted by a
staff of as many as five or six men and women who serve as reporters
in gathering local news, rewrite wire copy, and present most of the
station's regular news programs. Many radio stations have regular
correspondents in outlying communities or in the capital city of the

state. Some make extensive use of taped interviews with people involved in news events, including audio-taped telephone calls to public officials in other cities. In many situations, the coverage of major stories by large-city radio stations compares favorably with that of local newspapers. Radio stations also have the advantage of being able to bring their listeners on-the-spot accounts of local events that warrant such coverage—community-wide celebrations, fires, or police emergencies.

News is heavily emphasized by radio networks; in fact, the service provided to affiliates consists largely of news broadcasts. Five-minute news summaries are presented by national networks ten or a dozen times each day, in addition to two or three longer news, sports, or commentary programs. Radio networks also provide extended coverage of special events of national importance— such as astronaut flights, national political conventions, and government reports on military actions abroad.

This coverage of news by radio is not without its weaknesses. In most instances, the medium depends on brief summaries of the news—often little more than headlines—and does not provide the depth needed to understand a complex story or issue. Because of the portability of audio-tape recorders and the emphasis placed on "actualities" (taped comments from witnesses to or participants in the story), many radio newsmen tend to favor stories that lend themselves to this kind of coverage and ignore others. The very immediacy of radio can be a disadvantage when a story is rushed to the air without adequate background research or time for a reasoned consideration of its implications.

These weaknesses are real, and those individuals who depend on radio for most of their news are probably ill-served. Other, more complete news sources are available, however. Used in conjunction with these sources and with an understanding of its strengths and weaknesses, radio news can perform a valuable service. It can provide capsules of information from which listeners can select the stories they wish to explore in other media; it can alert the public to fast-breaking stories and provide warning of impending disasters; and it can be a presence during times of emergency and crisis, often giving otherwise isolated people a source of ready information unavailable through other media.

Local Television News Programs

Television coverage of local news in most markets is generally more thorough than that provided by the larger radio stations, although

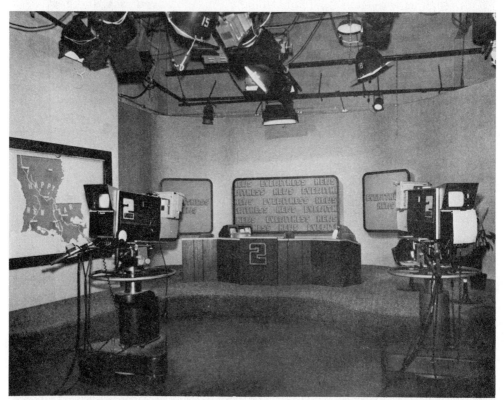

Figure 9–2 News sets used by two local television stations. Details may differ but basics—a desk, chairs and a weather map—vary little from station to station. (Courtesy WWL, New Orleans, and WBRZ, Baton Rouge)

news programs are presented at less frequent intervals. Nearly all television stations have included local news programs in their schedules almost from the time they first went on the air; by the late 1950s many had strong news departments. By the mid 1960s, most stations had independent news departments with substantial staffs devoting full time to the gathering, editing, and presentation of news. A substantial number of stations scheduled a 30-minute local news program preceding or following the network evening news. Many carried programs of similar length at 10:00 or 11:00 P.M., and a large number also carried shorter local news programs in the morning or at noon.

By the early 1970s, many local television stations had expanded their early evening news programs to 60 minutes—often "wrapped around" the network news with 30 minutes before and 30 minutes after. Indeed, some larger stations in major markets have expanded

" 'The 11 O'clock News', 'The 11 O'clock News', 'The 11 O'clock News'—say, here's one that sounds interesting! 'The Eleventh Hour News'."

their local news to a full 2 hours in the evening. Late-evening news, more restricted by network entertainment programming, has not seen the same expansion, but some independent stations have gone to a full hour at that time of the evening.

A 1973 study of television news operations conducted at the University of Wisconsin[2] reported that the median weekly news budget for all stations surveyed was $2,500. When analyzed by market size, median budgets fell into a wide range—from $9,750 for large markets to $1,500 for small markets. Size of staff also varied according to market size. Median staff for all stations was 10; for large stations it was 23 and for small, 5.

Virtually every commercial television station subscribes to the wire services of either Associated Press (AP) or United Press International (UPI) as a source of national and regional news; many also receive the sports news service provided by Western Union. Most stations also arrange for a variety of visual services. Both AP and UPI offer a service to provide still pictures or slides or both to television stations. A number of stations subscribe to services that ship news film to subscribers by air express. The television networks offer to subscribing affiliates coverage of eight to ten stories a day, which are delivered over network lines during hours when no network program service is provided and are videotaped by stations for inclusion in their local newscasts. In addition to this special news service, the three television networks, for a consideration, permit their affiliates to tape portions of their regular evening news offering for editing and later use in local news programs.

News programs produced locally, of course, give major emphasis to local news events, especially since most stations also carry network news programs. Pictorial coverage of local happenings is provided most commonly on 16mm sound film. A film crew usually accompanies the television newsperson covering a local story, shoots pertinent scenes, and often provides footage of the reporter opening and closing the story on the scene. Stations using film in news programs must have facilities for processing this film, and members of staffs of station news departments devote many hours to editing and selecting the sequences to be used on the air.

In recent years, the availability of small, hand-held color television cameras and smaller and lighter videotape recorders has encouraged an ever-increasing number of stations to shift completely

---

[2]Vernon Stone and Deborah Hayes, "Television News Needs, Finances and Staffing Are Surveyed," *Broadcast Financial Journal*, Vol. 4 (February 1976), p. 4.

from film to tape for the recording of local news stories outside the studio. Reports from these stations show them enthusiastic about what has come to be known as electronic news gathering (ENG), claiming reduction in costs and the size of the crews along with an increase in the average number of "remote" stories in each local newscast.

As a result of their less flexible schedules, television stations are not so likely as radio outlets to break into their regular programs to give on-the-spot coverage of local news happenings. Except for instances of major disasters or emergencies, reporters and photographers are dispatched to the scene of the local news event and their accounts and pictures are inserted in the station's regular news programs. When events of outstanding importance occur, of course, stations in the locality cancel their regular programs to provide listeners with immediate coverage. In addition, special news programs are frequently arranged to present the filmed highlights of a state political convention or of an unusually important meeting of the city council, school board, or zoning commission. Evening network programs are often canceled to allow the station to broadcast a local basketball game or a high school football game, especially when championships are at stake. Many television stations provide special coverage of local news events—usually, however, on a complete-program basis.

Network Television News

If the element of prestige is important in the field of local news, it has become an even stronger factor in the news activities of national television networks. With nearly all the major network entertainment features produced by outside production companies, news and public affairs programs offer almost the only remaining opportunity for a network organization to develop its own "personality" or to give outlet to the creative abilities of its executives and employees. As a result, competition between network news departments is keen; each network organization attempts to outdo its rivals in the thoroughness of its news-gathering activities and attractiveness of those who present the news, and in the development of special programs in the area of public affairs.

To support its news and public affairs operations, ABC had an approximate annual working budget in 1974 of between $35 million and $40 million, depending on activity. In a presidential election year, with attendant primaries, this figure is even higher. Similar figures for CBS and NBC are not available, but the Television Information Office estimates that the three networks combined spent between $160 million and $170 million in the 1973–1974 season. Assuming that NBC and CBS spend approximately the same amounts, we can estimate that each spends between $62.5 million and $65 million on its news operation. Contrast this with the reported expenditure of $30 million by the NBC news department in 1963.

These budgets can vary widely according to the number of newsworthy events in a given year. As early as 1968, for instance, the three networks spent an estimated $150 million in news coverage in a year which included the Apollo 8 space flight, the Tet offensive in Vietnam, the assassinations of Martin Luther King and Robert Kennedy, the Republican and Democratic nominating conventions, the primaries, and the 1968 presidential and congressional elections.

The three networks combined employ nearly 3,000 people in their news and public affairs departments—NBC, 1,400; CBS, 1,000; and ABC, 600. Not all these employees are concerned solely with the gathering and presentation of news as such; network news departments are responsible for most of the informational programs mentioned earlier in this chapter, for weekly discussion or interview programs, for news documentaries, for appearances of candidates during political campaigns, and for live coverage of important special events, as well as for the network's regularly scheduled daily news programs.

Regularly Scheduled News Programs   The chief function of a network news department is to provide a news service for the public, and television networks provide excellent coverage of national and international news. During the winter of 1976–1977, NBC, CBS, and ABC each scheduled 30-minute early evening news programs—the NBC and CBS programs appearing seven nights a week and ABC program, six. CBS also scheduled a 15-minute Sunday news program in the late evening. *The CBS Morning News* was presented for an hour each weekday morning and the same network offered a news feature program, *60 Minutes*, on Sunday evening. The ABC morning program, *Good Morning America*, included news summaries on the hour and half-hour and features and interviews in the body of the program. News, features, and news interviews also filled about half of the time in NBC's 5-days-a-week, 2-hour *Today* program, and interviews with interesting and often controversial figures of national interest occupied a significant portion of NBC's *Tomorrow* program. On Sunday afternoons, all three networks offered a regular 30-minute interview program focusing primarily on current events; and, when events warranted, these were occasionally expanded to 60 to 90 minutes. In addition, each of the networks scheduled short, 5-minute news summaries during the daytime hours on weekdays, while NBC inserted an even shorter *News Update* once each weekday evening between prime-time programs. In all, in a 7-day period, the three networks made more than 100 news programs available to their affiliated stations, accounting for a weekly total of approximately 33 hours of broadcasting time.

News Specials   The regular news programs of the television networks have the advantage already noted of bringing news to the public without the time delay required for the printing and distribution of daily newspapers. They also have the advantage of allowing viewers to *see* newsworthy events recorded on film or tape. They are, however, subject to one serious disadvantage; in a single 30-minute period, a television news program can deal with no more than ten or a dozen news happenings and can give little more than the highlights of these. So networks supplement their regular news reports with frequent news specials. Sometimes these are documentaries to provide detailed background information about important news situations and sometimes they are on-the-spot coverage of significant news events as they happen. Most commonly these special news reports are provided by canceling regularly scheduled entertainment programs, and such cancellations are more frequent than most viewers realize.

For an extreme example, consider the week of January 20 to 27, 1973. On January 20, a Saturday, President Nixon was inaugurated for his second term and coverage of the ceremonies and allied events spilled over into the early hours of Sunday. On Monday evening, January 22, word was received of the death of former President Lyndon B. Johnson—with a telephone message giving the information to Walter Cronkite carried live on the regular *CBS Evening News*. All three networks followed with special programs in honor of the late President. On January 23, unofficial word was received that final agreement had been reached in the Vietnam cease-fire negotiations in Paris and that evening President Nixon went on television and radio to announce the event. The next day, Wednesday, January 24, Secretary of State Kissinger held a 95-minute briefing on the agreement, which was carried live by all three networks and ended

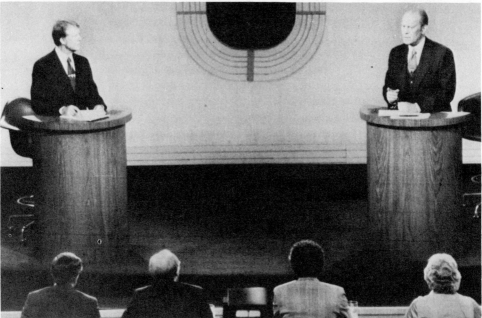

Figure 9–3 The Kennedy–Nixon (1960) and Carter–Ford (1976) debates are examples of network news coverage of noteworthy news events. (Courtesy Compix, United Press International)

only minutes before the arrival of Mr. Johnson's body in Washington and the televised procession to the Capitol. On Thursday both the funeral services in Washington and the burial services at the LBJ ranch were carried live, and on Saturday all the networks devoted considerable time to the signing of the Vietnam peace agreements in Paris.

By any measure, this was a hectic week for the network news operations. On one day alone—Wednesday, January 24—special news coverage took up more than 7 hours of the NBC-TV schedule, more than 6 hours of CBS-TV's, and approximately 3½ hours of ABC-TV's. According to an estimate published in *Broadcasting* magazine immediately thereafter, the cost of that week of news coverage alone—aside from the losses in commercial program preemption—ran between $7 million and $10 million.

This, however, was only the beginning of one of the busiest news years in our history. Starting with the inauguration of a President and the end of a war in Asia, 1973 included all those events known as "Watergate"—including 319 hours of live coverage of the Senate Watergate hearings; the Skylab orbital space station; accusations against and the resignation of the Vice-President; war in the Middle East; the firing of the Watergate special prosecutor, the U.S. Attorney-General and his assistant; and a Middle East cease fire. The year also included a sharp jump in the inflation rate, announcements concerning wage and price controls, a sudden fuel shortage, and other items of the sort one would expect in any year.

Indeed, under normal circumstances a year like 1973 would be expected to be a relatively "quiet" news year—at least on the national level—with no November elections of national importance and no conventions or primary races on the national level. In 1972, on the other hand, the three networks had devoted approximately 20 hours to November election night coverage, 54 hours to the Democratic national convention and 46 hours to the Republican convention. In view of the record, it is hardly surprising that the three networks spend a combined total of more than $160 million a year to provide information about national and international happenings for television viewers.

The Weaknesses of Television News

As with radio news, television news is not without its weaknesses. Network and local television stations program longer segments of news than do their radio counterparts, but they also cover more stories and seldom linger on one event for more than a minute or two. Thus the stigma of superficiality can also often be applied to television news. As radio news shows a favoritism for stories with "actualities" and an audio slant, so does television news favor stories with a strong visual element—a fire, a wreck, casualties of battle, and the like—and tend to avoid less visual and more complex stories.[3] At times, television can also be faulted for rushing a story to the air without proper consideration of its implications.

Because of the penetration of television and the large audiences for television news, many politicians and others find it tempting to create news events for the sole purpose of getting their faces, or the faces of their client, on television. Candidates for public office, especially candidates for reelection, are often adept at this technique, wearing unusual hats, visiting nursing homes, greeting visitors, plowing fields, throwing footballs, and the like. Indeed, there are some who say that the Senate Watergate hearings were just such an event, staged by a Democratic Congress and designed to give the senators maximum exposure while embarrassing a Republican administration.

Television has also spawned the news "personality" who seems to be a skilled performer and skilled news reader first and a professional journalist second, if at all. This accusation is directed more often at local talent than at the network news personnel, and it seems justified in many instances. Most television stations are competing with other news operations in the market, and audiences do seem to prefer the polished performer who can give the appearance of professionalism and concern in news delivery. Unfortunately, many of these "personalities" lack the training and experience to recognize, analyze, and interpret a significant news story and, unless supported by a staff with a sound and professional journalism background, they can make serious errors on the air.

Other potential problem areas also exist. Broadcast advertisers could, and in some cases probably do, influence the selection and placement of certain news stories and the content of editorials, a possibility that also exists for newspapers and newsmagazines. Irresponsible coverage of riots or demonstrations can make the disturbances even more serious by drawing people to the scene. Neglectful or unprincipled management can create a consistent news bias. Television, in short, is not a perfect news medium. Some critics even see television as having the potential of doing serious harm to

---

[3]In retrospect, television has been given high marks for its coverage of the events surrounding Watergate. Actually, broadcast media coverage of these events was poor at first because no clear-cut issues had emerged and the lines of the story were tangled and complex. Only after print media had helped bring the issues to a head and the Senate Watergate hearings had begun—a distinctly visual event—did television news come into its own. Issues came into better focus and events like Mr. Nixon's speeches in his own defense, the firings, the impeachment hearings of the House Judiciary Committee, and Mr. Nixon's ultimate resignation lent themselves directly to the immediacy and presence of television.

democratic processes.[4] Like radio, however, when approached with an understanding of its strong and weak points, it can be used in conjunction with other media to provide a reasonable summary of the news and issues of the day.

IDEAS AND OPINIONS

Broadcasting has contributed in no small measure to the listener's stock of general information and to his knowledge and understanding of important events taking place throughout the world. To meet his responsibilities as an intelligent citizen, however, the listener must also be acquainted with ideas—with the opinions of national and local leaders on the vital issues that confront the American people or the people of his community. Newspapers and national magazines provide a valuable forum for opinions on public questions, but broadcasting also makes its own contribution in presenting points of view concerning issues of the day. Often the views of the nation's leaders are set forth in news or documentary programs, in interviews or in two-sided forums; occasionally programs are presented that attempt to give a cross-section of the opinions held by ordinary citizens, and many broadcasters voice their own views in editorial presentations.

Broadcast Editorials

In the early days of radio, editorials by station licensees were relatively common; indeed, some stations apparently were operated for

---

[4]For example, political scientist Michael J. Robinson advances the following theory: "I have begun to envision a two-stage process in which television journalism, with its constant emphasis on social and political conflict, its high credibility, its powerful audio-visual capabilities and its epidemicity, has caused the more vulnerable viewers first to doubt their own understanding of their political system. . . . But after these individuals have passed this initial stage they enter a second phase in which personal denigration continues and in which a new hostility toward politics and government also emerges. Having passed through both stages of political cynicism, these . . . individuals pass their cynicism along to those who were, at the start, less attuned to television messages and consequently less directly vulnerable to TV malaise." For expansion and support of this theory, see Michael J. Robinson, "American Political Legitimacy in an Era of Electronic Journalism: Reflections on the Evening News," in Douglass Cater and Richard Adler (eds.), *Television as a Social Force: New Approaches to TV Criticism* (New York: Praeger Publishers, 1975), p. 97.

the sole purpose of giving their owners an opportunity to express extreme views on political matters, on religion, or even on the evils of chain stores. As radio became commercial, however, editorial expressions became less frequent; advertisers were not interested in using the facilities of stations whose owners' outspoken opinions aroused the resentment of large numbers of listeners. In addition, the expression of editorial views was discouraged by the Federal Radio Commission, which refused to grant license renewals to what were regarded as "propaganda stations." The Federal Communications Commission took a similar position and in 1941 flatly banned all editorial presentations by the owners of radio stations. In 1949, however, the FCC abandoned its earlier position and, in a new ruling on editorializing, held that a licensee had the right to present his views over the facilities of his station, but warned that the station owner who expressed editorial opinions on controversial issues should also provide time for supporters of opposing points of view—a policy which came to be known as the Fairness Doctrine.

Encouraged by the favorable attitude of the FCC, an increasing number of radio and television stations now present editorial opinions on various community matters or on national or local issues. A survey of broadcasting stations reported in *Broadcasting Yearbook* for 1976 indicates that more than 65 percent of all AM radio sta-

"Remember, this channel is always pleased to give air time to a broad spectrum of editorial responses which agree with us."

tions, 54 percent of all FM stations, and 58 percent of all television stations editorialized at least occasionally during 1975. Their editorials were usually presented by the station manager or by the station's news director. In some instances, the opinions offered were the joint product of a committee of station employees—the manager, the news director and one or two other responsible staff members; on most stations, however, editorials presented the views of the station manager or the licensee himself. The *Broadcasting* survey indicated that about a third of the radio stations and nearly half of all television stations that carried editorial comment did so on a regularly scheduled daily or weekly basis; operators of other stations expressed editorial opinions less frequently—waiting, as a spokesman for one station put it, until "something comes up that is important enough to justify an editorial."

It must be admitted that only a small proportion of editorials on radio or television deal with highly controversial issues. Stations urge their listeners to contribute to the local United Givers or to register and vote; and they deplore the increase in crime; they call for more vigorous enforcement of traffic laws. Sometimes they may endorse or oppose the adoption of a specific ordinance by the local city council or express disapproval of some action of a zoning commission. In other instances, a radio or television station may campaign vigorously for the installation of traffic lights at street intersections near schools, or for the modernization of the city's firefighting equipment, or for the elimination of a hazardous grade crossing on a heavily traveled street. Most broadcast editorials deal with purely local conditions; rarely does a station take a definite stand on any highly controversial issue.

Particularly is this true when listeners in the community have strong feelings with respect to some local or sectional issue. In the 1960s, not many licensees of stations in the south were willing to take an editorial stand either for or against school desegregation or on restrictions placed on voting rights of blacks in the region. Nor have many station owners editorialized on partisan political issues. Some stations have endorsed candidates for local office, but only a very small number are known to have urged their listeners to support a particular candidate for the Presidency or for election to Congress. Radio and television stations are not usually identified, as are most newspapers, as having Republican or Democratic leanings, as being liberal or conservative, or as being consistently for or against a national administration.

The same is true of national radio and television networks. Networks simply do not editorialize—at least in any direct manner. On only one or two occasions in broadcasting's history has any network official gone on the air to express his personal views or those of the corporation he represents, and then only to discuss some matter affecting broadcasting. A few news commentators on radio and television networks do take editorial positions on national issues, but their comments reflect their personal views, not those of the network on which they appear. The same is true of local commentators on a few radio and television stations in large cities. The opinions expressed are their own, not the editorial expressions of their employers.

Documentaries as Editorials

A documentary program is, presumably, an objective report in depth on a single topic of general concern or importance. Even the most unbiased documentary, however, may have an editorial effect. A documentary special that actually shows illegal gambling establishments in operation in a large city certainly would have some effect on viewer attitudes and an equally evident impact on the zeal of city officials in seeing that laws are properly enforced—probably much more marked an impact than any number of editorial statements by the manager of a television station. Network documentary programs on the Vietnam War and its effects on the United States and South Vietnam did much to stimulate the resistance to the war that developed in the late 1960s and early 1970s. Programs showing conditions in prisons or mental hospitals have sometimes helped to bring about improvements; the same has been true when local documentaries have dealt with problems of public housing, drug addiction, or inadequate inner-city schools. On rare occasions, networks have presented documentary programs that have reflected an obvious editorial purpose, at least on the part of the program's producer. The classic example of this is Edward R. Murrow's CBS program of the 1950s on the treatment of witnesses by the late Senator Joseph R. McCarthy and his Senate permanent investigations subcommittee. Other examples include the CBS documentary on the plight of migratory workers, *Harvest of Shame*; the NBC documentary on pension plans, *Pensions, The Broken Promise*; and, possibly, CBS's *The Selling of the Pentagon*, which dealt with the public relations activities of the U.S. Department of Defense and angered many congressmen and senators.

The deliberately slanted or editorial version of the documentary is, fortunately, not too common. For one thing, the Fairness Doctrine would force the broadcaster to make time available for the presentation of opposing views or to present them in a later program produced by the station. Under these circumstances, presentation of a documentary that presents a balanced view of an issue enables a licensee to avoid the necessity of dealing with later Fairness Doctrine demands on his time.

The Fairness Doctrine, however, is not the only factor working against editorial documentaries, at least with responsible broadcasters. The Fairness Doctrine requires only that a licensee make time available for the presentation of opposing views; it does not require the production by the station of such replies. When producing a documentary, most broadcasters take pride in their ability to use the medium skillfully and to make their points in a convincing and entertaining manner. Few citizens' groups, no matter what their dedication and knowledge of the subject, could produce a rebuttal that would have the impact of the program produced by the station. The responsible licensee, then, avoids taking advantage of this apparent weakness of the Fairness Doctrine by taking care to see that all the major sides of an issue are presented with equal effectiveness.

Even an objective documentary program may often have an unintended editorial effect, however. It is manifestly impossible in a 60-minute or 30-minute program to include all of the significant facts concerning a complex problem such as race relations or foreign policy; a selection must be made. The process of editorial selection, of determining which facts to include and which to leave out, of deciding which aspects of the problem are to be given special emphasis—the very elements that make for the effectiveness of the documentary form—tend to affect the listener's conclusions concerning the problem.

Broadcasting as a Public Forum

In addition to their editorial programs, radio and television stations provide a public forum for the expression of the views of community leaders. In most instances, these views are presented on regularly scheduled news programs and in news specials that deal with important events or problems of the day.

Controversy is an important element in news. When national leaders disagree about vital issues, the public is interested; when these leaders express their varying opinions, their statements are included in radio and television coverage of the news. If the President of the United States or the Secretary of State expresses an opinion concerning our country's foreign policy, that opinion is included in the regularly scheduled news programs—often with opposing comments by minority leaders in Congress. Similarly, network news programs report the views of advocates of federal intervention to reduce unemployment, of increases in military spending, or of changes in Social Security legislation; they also include the opinions of those who disagree.

The same is true with respect to local issues. Local news programs include the opinions of those who favor and those who oppose the adoption of state or city income taxes, bond issues for the construction of new schools, or salary increases for policemen. Inclusion of statements of opinion has been facilitated by the use of audio-tape on radio and film or videotape on television.

Controversy on Regular Programs A number of radio and television stations in major cities carry regular forum or discussion programs in which the advocates and opponents of proposed state or local projects can present opposing views in face-to-face situations. National television networks schedule weekly programs of the "press conference" type, in which national leaders or representatives of foreign governments answer pointed questions posed by members of a panel of journalists from print as well as electronic media. Special programs on free time are provided for such newsworthy happenings as presidential press conferences and less frequently for leaders of the opposition party in Congress to voice opposition to some major administration proposal. National networks, however, prefer to handle expressions of opinion in regularly scheduled news or interview programs—understandably, since the grant of a half-hour period for a special sustaining network program of opinion means the cancellation of a regularly scheduled commercial program and a resulting loss of $90,000 to $100,000 in network revenues. Local stations, with few exceptions, follow the lead of the networks in preferring to limit expressions of opinion on public issues to their news programs or to scheduled programs in which advocates of opposing points of view appear in face-to-face situations.

Controversy on Paid Time Although radio and television stations are reluctant to provide free time for programs in which only one side of a controversial issue is to be presented, many will *sell* time for such one-sided presentations. Almost without exception, stations sell time for appearances by candidates for national or local office during political campaigns. Indeed, the Communications Act of 1934 was amended in 1972 to provide that a station's license can be revoked for "willful or repeated failure to allow reasonable access to or to permit purchase of reasonable amounts of time for the use of a broadcasting station by a legally qualified candidate for Federal elective office on behalf of his candidacy."

In addition, most stations are willing to make time available for public utilities to argue for franchise renewals or the development of nuclear power or for state or local medical societies to express their opinions on national health insurance. Many stations—radio stations in particular—are also willing to sell time for taped commentary programs, scheduled on a regular weekly or daily basis, in which featured speakers give their views on various social, economic, or political questions. Some of these programs are sponsored by religious organizations, others by ultraconservative groups, some by labor organizations.

Stations that sell time for one-sided, controversial presentations, however, run the risk of being forced to provide free time for the presentation of opposing points of view. As presently interpreted, the Fairness Doctrine requires any licensee who allows the use of his facilities for the presentation of one side of a controversial issue of public importance to make an "affirmative effort" to present opposing views, either by seeking out appropriate spokesmen or using personnel already on the staff to present the opposing views. Even more important, from the point of view of the licensee, the Fairness Doctrine has been interpreted to mean that a broadcaster who carries one side of a controversial issue on a paid program cannot reject presentations of other sides solely on the grounds that sponsorship cannot be found for the rebuttal.

In most cases, the licensee retains the right to determine *who* shall present the opposing views, but he cannot require payment for a legitimate response to a one-sided presentation. The rights of the licensee are restricted even further if, in the course of any presentation of a controversial issue of public importance, the honor, integrity, etc. of an individual or a group is attacked. Under these circumstances a special set of rules, called the "personal attack rules," come into play; and the licensee is required to notify the person or organization attacked, provide a transcript, tape, or reasonable summary of the nature of the attack, and offer time for a reply.

BROADCASTING IN POLITICAL CAMPAIGNS

Radio and television play important roles in both national and local political campaigns. During the early months of presidential election years, candidates for the Republican and Democratic presidential nominations are given wide exposure on network news programs and those of the press conference or interview type. Network coverage of primary election campaigns includes additional appearances of leading candidates before the microphone or the television camera, so that by the time the national political conventions are held the listening public has had dozens of opportunities to become acquainted not only with each candidate's views on major issues, but with many facets of his personality as well. Broadcasts from the conventions themselves, including coverage of meetings of platform and credentials committees, allow the listener to learn far more about the actual principles each party organization supports than is possible from formal platform statements. Finally, during the 8 or 9 weeks before the election, candidates for the nation's highest office are seen and heard repeatedly over network facilities, not only in special broadcast programs on time paid for by political organizations but on news specials documenting the progress of the campaign and on the regular network news programs.

Candidates for election to Congress or to state and local offices appear less often than do the presidential aspirants, but most of them are given opportunity to present their views over local radio and television stations. Nearly all candidates buy time for special programs designed to reach listeners in their respective areas and, under the provisions of the Federal Election Campaign Act of 1971, during the 45 days before a primary or run-off election and the 60 days before a general election, stations selling time to any legally qualified candidate for any public office must do so at the "lowest unit charge of the station for the same class and amount of time for the same period." In addition, stations donate time to candidates for the more important offices, and those voters who care to take the time are given opportunity to form individual judgments about the qualifications and the personal strengths or weaknesses of the men who seek to represent them in Congress or in the state legislature or to serve as city or county officials.

Costs of Political Broadcasts

In every national election, each of the two major political parties spends millions of dollars for radio and television time. During the 1968 campaigns, including both primary and general elections, Republican national, state, and local party organizations spent a total of almost $27.8 million for programs and spot announcements; Democratic party expenditures in the same campaign amounted to approximately the same amount, with roughly two thirds of the funds spent in television by both parties. Two years later, with no presidential election involved, Republican expenditures for broadcast time totaled approximately $21.7 million, while $26 million was spent in behalf of Democratic candidates. These figures illustrate the dramatic increase in campaign expenditures in electronic media since 1960. In that election campaign—the John F. Kennedy–Richard Nixon race—the Republicans spent only $7.5 million and the Democrats, $6.2 million

The 1972 election was the first affected by the Federal Election Campaign Act, which limited the total amount a candidate could spend campaigning and said further that no more than half of this could be spent in electronic media. The combination of this spending limitation and the fact that an incumbent President was running for reelection reversed the upward spiral of campaign costs somewhat. Republicans spent only a total of $20.7 million; but the Democrats, because of heavy expenditures in the primary campaigns, spent a total of almost $35.5 million. Primary elections cost the Republicans only $3.2 million, while the Democrats, in their search for a candidate, spent almost $17 million. Both parties spent just about the same amount, $17.5 million, for the presidential campaign itself.

Free Time for Candidates

In each of the campaigns considered above, candidates probably appeared as frequently on news programs and on time donated by stations as on time purchased in their behalf by political organizations. During the 1972 campaign, radio stations broadcast almost 9,000 unpaid hours of programming in which rival candidates for office appeared and offered almost 5,000 hours of free time for candidates in sponsored programs. Television stations broadcast 1,900 unpaid and 645 paid hours of such programming. Thus radio and television stations combined, according to a report issued by the Federal Communications Commission, provided a grand total of over 16,000 hours of free time for political candidates in 1972. These figures do not include taped or filmed statements by candidates on regular news programs.

Although stations often invite candidates to appear over their facilities without charge, network organizations are careful to avoid giving free time to candidates for the offices of President or Vice-President after their nomination by party conventions. Section 315 of the Communications Act of 1934 provides that "if any licensee shall permit any person who is a legally qualified candidate for any public office to use a broadcasting station, he shall afford equal opportunities to all other such candidates for that office in the use of such a broadcasting station." Consequently, if during the course of a campaign a network were to make sustaining time available to the Democratic Party's presidential nominee, it would be required by law to provide an equal amount of free time not only for his Republican rival but also for the presidential candidates of perhaps ten or a dozen minor parties—such as the America First Party, the Socialist-Labor Party, the Prohibition Party.

In 1960 a special act of Congress temporarily waived this provision of the Communications Act as it applied to candidates for the offices of President and Vice-President of the United States. This allowed the national networks to bring their listeners a series of four hour-long "Great Debates," or confrontations between Republican candidate Richard M. Nixon and Democratic candidate John F. Kennedy, and also to present both candidates on other sustaining programs filling more hours of network time than the total purchased by the two major parties. In subsequent years, Congress has failed to act on a similar proposal. In 1976, the FCC ruled that coverage of debates between candidates for elective office was coverage of a bona fide news event and thus not subject to the "equal-time" rules—if the debates were covered live in their entirety and if they were planned and produced by an organization other than a network or an individual station. This ruling led to the Carter-Ford debates of 1976, but networks were still unable to offer other kinds of free time to major candidates without opening the door to demands from the so-called "minor" candidates. Filmed excerpts from the campaign speeches of both major party candidates, however, were extensively used on network news programs and on numerous network special reports on the progress of the campaign.[5]

Although the national networks do not provide free time for presidential candidates in the period following their nominations by national conventions, the network organizations usually arrange for the appearance, on sustaining programs, of the leading contenders for the presidential nomination of each major party during the months before the conventions. Up to the time of the actual convention vote, these aspirants are technically candidates for their party's *nomination*, rather than for election to the Presidency; as a result, the problem of splinter-party candidates does not exist. Similarly,

---

[5] A 1959 amendment to the Communications Act exempts from the "equal opportunity" provisions of Section 315 appearances of candidates on regular news programs, regularly scheduled news interview programs, and documentaries, the subject of which is incidental to the individual's candidacy.

since with few exceptions the various minor parties do not nominate slates for state and local offices, stations usually have no minor-party difficulties when they offer free time to Republican or Democratic candidates for Congress or for the office of governor of a state or mayor of a city. As a result, radio and television stations often allow such nominees of the two major parties to present their views on a sustaining basis, instead of limiting the unpaid appearances of such candidates to items in local news programs and appearances on regularly scheduled news-interview programs.

THE CRITICS OF ELECTRONIC JOURNALISM

Stations and networks do provide an impressive amount of broadcast information for their listeners. Most responsible licensees believe that a broadcaster, having been granted a government-created monopoly in the use of a particular frequency or channel, has a responsibility that goes beyond the provision of entertainment. Most of them also feel that the carrying of informational programs enhances the image of their station in the communities they serve. In any event, virtually every station includes a substantial number of informational programs on its schedule, some taken from network lines, others produced by the station itself.

Volume aside, however, electronic journalism does have its weaknesses, as we have seen, and it is not free from criticism. For instance, we know that accusations of bias and distortion naturally arise every time a news editor or producer makes a judgment as to what shall and shall not be included in a news story or documentary. Such charges were common during the radio and television coverage of the disturbances in cities and on campuses in the 1960s, during the Vietnam War, and following the Democratic national convention in 1968. During the Nixon administration they were made by the President, the Vice-President, and the Chief Justice of the U.S. Supreme Court. Producers of specific programs like the CBS documentary *The Selling of the Pentagon* were accused of deliberate distortion, and books were published charging all three networks with a deliberate slanting of news to favor the liberal wing of the Democratic party.

It is not surprising to see such charges and complaints aimed at media as pervasive and as widely used as radio and television. Because so many people use broadcast media as their primary or sole source of news, critics and those with special interests are constantly on the alert for any material or treatment of material that seems to reflect bias. The media, on the other hand, can only devote a certain portion of their time to news and information and must constantly deal with selection, rejection, and condensation of stories. This editing process is further affected by what is seen as a need to simplify complex issues to make the broad outlines understandable to a general audience. These processes of selection, condensation, and simplification necessarily involve choice, interpretation, and human judgments. Under these circumstances, charges of bias and distortion seem inevitable.

News Consultants·

In recent years, as the competition for news audiences between local stations has grown more intense, a phenomenon known as the "news consultant" has come into being. These organizations contract with a television station to come into its market to study and analyze its existing news organization, format, and personnel; to examine the competition and the nature of the market; and to make recommendations for changes and modifications. The consultants express confidence that, if followed, these recommendations will improve the image of the station's news operation and bring higher ratings—possibly the position of "number one" in news in the market.

In many situations, these recommendations include changes in personnel, both on and off the air; the introduction of a different format for the news; changes in the ratio between filmed (or taped) and live stories; limitations on the length of stories; and even advice on the kinds of stories that should be emphasized. While not successful in every instance, these organizations have an impressive record of securing higher ratings for their clients, and they have become a significant factor in the development of television news.

The news consultant, however, has also become a focus for much of the criticism leveled at television news. Some critics argue that the consultants have created across the country a series of plastic, virtually identical, "Eyewitness News"-type formats that seem like stale imitations of each other instead of reflections of the cities they serve. Others criticize what has come to be known as "happy-talk" presentation of the news—a format in which transitions between members of the "news team" are accompanied by light banter that is meant to indicate that the news persons like and relate to each other as friends both on and off camera. To some critics, "happy-talk" degrades journalism and turns a news program into a form of entertainment. Still others maintain that the emphasis on ratings and surface appearance supposedly instilled by the consultants turns the attention of a news organization from its most important function—gathering and presenting news.

There is an element of truth in all of these criticisms, with some stations "guiltier" than others. Television is perceived by most viewers in the United States first and foremost as an entertainment medium. The ratings successes of the consultants in many markets would seem to indicate that audiences are drawn to news presentations that include a certain element of showmanship. Since licensees would prefer a profit to a loss in their news operation, it is not suprising to see many of them turning to the techniques that build the audiences that can be sold to advertisers.

The news consultant has met a real need in the television industry. The result may not be journalistically pure or sound—it sometimes is not even journalistically good—but it seems to be the combination of news and show business that "works" for many local television stations and their audiences.

Reaching the Mass Audience

While coverage of such events as the first manned lunar landing can reach more than 100 million Americans, the average news or public affairs or general information program presented by a television network is probably not heard by more than 8 million or 10 million people. Consequently, some critics contend that the audiences of such programs are made up largely of the more intelligent and better educated elements in the population, while those most in need of information devote most of their listening time to television action-adventures or contemporary music on radio. While there may be some basis for this criticism, audiences of informational programs are by no means limited to the intellectual elite in our society.

To begin with, some programs have considerably more than 8 million or 10 million listeners; at least 50 million people listen to television network news every night, for example, and certainly not all can be classified as intellectuals. Even when audiences are smaller, it is hardly possible to assume that exactly the same 8 million or 10 million people who listen to a documentary dealing with abortion also heard a program on the military situation in Africa on the preceding evening and will give their attention a day or two later to an expose of political corruption. The total number of individuals who tune in and listen to at least *some* informational programs is decidedly more than 10 million—probably closer to 60 million, and many of that total number are men and women with limited educational attainments. The information provided in broadcast programs reaches people on nearly every economic and social level.[6]

It is probably true that the American people have access to more information than do the people of any other nation in the world. Many factors have played a part in creating such a situation: our books, our newspapers and magazines, our libraries, our churches, our system of public education, and the training our children receive in the home. Radio and television, with their weaknesses and their strengths, have certainly made a contribution to the enlightenment of the American people.

STUDY AND DISCUSSION QUESTIONS

1. Examine the complete schedule of the television networks for a typical month in the regular season and make a record of all the programs that could be classified as news and information in that period. Record the following:

   a. The name of each program
   b. The time of its broadcast and its length
   c. The nature of the material covered in the program
   d. The form of the broadcast (live coverage of an event, documentary, regular news broadcast, news-interview, and so forth)
   e. Your estimate of the target audience for each program
   f. Your evaluation of the relative merit of the program

2. Prepare a similar report on the nature of the informative programming offered by a radio station in your market during a typical week. Radio schedules are often difficult to come by, but you may be able to gain access to the logs of a station for such a study. If this is not possible, the class, working together, may be able to collect the information by assigning portions of the broadcast day to individuals and preparing a class report. Informative programming on

---

[6]Indeed, some critics argue that the media reach an audience that will not read a newspaper or a newsmagazine but will sit through 30 minutes of news on television or a documentary. It is argued further that this "inadvertent audience," many of whom watch the news with only the half-remembered information from an eighth-grade civics course to guide them, simply do not have the background to understand or interpret the news and are not enlightened by radio and television at all. Instead, they become frustrated and apathetic, feeling there is nothing they can do about politics or government or anything else. See Robinson, "American Political Legitimacy," p. 137.

radio is less likely to be confined to specifically designated programs, but estimates of the amount of time devoted to news and information should be possible.

3. Prepare a report on one of the following:

   a. Radio news before World War II
   b. Radio news during World War II
   c. The informative documentary on radio
   d. The development and evolution of the television newscast
   e. The development of the "dual-anchorman" concept
   f. The expansion of network television evening news programs to 30 minutes—and longer
   g. The development of electronic news gathering (ENG)
   h. Local television news programming
   i. The rise of the "news consultants"

4. Report on the coverage by the radio and television networks of the following or comparable events:

   a. The Kefauver hearings
   b. The Army-McCarthy hearings
   c. The assassination and funeral of President John F. Kennedy
   d. The suborbital and orbital flights of the United States space program
   e. The NASA "moon-shots"
   f. The Watergate hearings
   g. The Nixon impeachment hearings

   Include in your report as much information as you can find on the total number of hours devoted to the coverage, estimates of audience size during peak hours, cost of production, financial losses from preemptions, critical reaction, and the like.

5. Report on or be prepared to discuss the relative strengths and weaknesses of radio news when compared with the following:

   a. Television news
   b. Newspapers
   c. Newsmagazines

6. Report on or be prepared to discuss the relative strengths and weaknesses of television news when compared with the following:

   a. Radio news
   b. Newspapers
   c. Newsmagazines

7. If a radio or television station in your market editorializes consistently, do a study of these editorials over a period of a month. Consider the following aspects:

    a. The subject of each editorial
    b. The number of times each was carried
    c. The degree to which you judge each subject as controversial
    d. Your subjective evaluation of the impact of the editorials

8. Report on or be prepared to discuss the influence of broadcast coverage of and commentary on political campaigns.

SUGGESTED READINGS

Ben H. Bagdikian. *The Effete Conspiracy and Other Crimes by the Press*. New York: Harper & Row, 1972.

William A. Bluem. *Documentary in American Television: Form, Function, Method*. New York: Hastings House, 1965.

Daniel J. Boorstin. *The Image: A Guide to Pseudo-Events in America*. New York: Harper & Row, 1964.

Edward J. Epstein. *News From Nowhere: Television and the News*. New York: Random House, 1973.

David LeRoy and Christopher Sterling, eds. *Mass News: Practices, Controversies and Alternatives*. Englewood Cliffs, N.J.: Prentice-Hall, 1973.

Robert MacNeil. *The People Machine: The Influence of Television on American Politics*. New York: Harper & Row, 1968.

William Small. *To Kill A Messenger: Television News and the Real World*. New York: Hastings House, 1970.

Robert Vainowski. *In Our View*. Belmont, Calif.: Tresgatos Enterprises, 1976.

10

Public Broadcasting

Although commercial broadcasting makes a significant contribution in providing news and information to the American people, its service in supplying educational or cultural programs is less impressive. Advertisers naturally want their programs or their advertising messages to reach the largest number of listeners possible, and the so-called cultural programs—those that deal with art or literature or that present the works of great composers—generally fail to attract substantial audiences, with the result that the number of cultural programs offered is definitely limited. Similarly, commercial broadcasting provides little programming that might be described as educational in character—programs providing instruction on a systematic basis either for adults or for children. Information may be given on a variety of subjects, but rarely is a program series presented in an attempt to provide a thorough treatment of any selected body of knowledge.

As the "baby boom" of World War II moved through high school and college in the 1960s, school enrollments increased, shortages of teachers and classrooms developed, and educators sought ways to relieve the pressures building on the educational facilities in the United States. One solution was the use of broadcast programs to supplement instruction in primary and secondary schools as well as in college and adult education. Commercial broadcasters could hardly be expected to provide such programs on a regular basis, at least not to the extent educators felt necessary.

From the earliest days of radio, many influential groups of Americans have believed that education and culture should receive the same attention in broadcasting in this country that they are given in Europe, and that if commercial broadcasting stations are unable to provide programs to meet our educational and cultural needs, some other means must be found to make such programs available. The ideal solution to the problem, in the opinion of many who are convinced of the need for such programs, is to be found in the creation of a "second broadcasting service," independent of our present commercial system, supported by educational interests, and operated for the sole purpose of providing cultural, educational, and informational programs for listeners. Anything less, they argue, would be an unsatisfactory compromise, incapable of meeting either the cultural and educational needs of the public or the practical requirements of successful commercial operation. The Public Broadcasting Service we know today approaches this ideal, but educational broadcasting had a long history before PBS appeared on the scene.

EDUCATIONAL RADIO

The idea of such a "second service" had its beginnings in the early 1920s when scores of schools and colleges applied for licenses for radio stations. According to records of the Department of Commerce, authorizations were granted between 1921 and 1925 to 153 educational institutions. Not all the stations authorized were actually constructed; some that did go on the air suspended operation within a year after receiving their licenses, so that by the end of 1925 probably not more than 100 school-owned stations were attempting to provide service.

In the subsequent decade the number of these stations dropped by more than two thirds and by 1935 only 31 were still on the air. The reasons for this decline are numerous and varied. After the creation of the Federal Radio Commission (FRC) in 1927, stations were required to meet more rigid technical standards, and few educational operations could find the money to equip themselves properly—often because neither the faculty nor the administration of many schools could see the potential of radio as an educational force. At the same time, the rapidly growing commercial broadcasting industry was pressuring the FRC (and later the Federal Communications Commission) to turn over the frequencies occupied by these educational radio stations, arguing that commercial broadcasters could use them more effectively; and the commissions often agreed. Finally, it can be argued that the FRC was not at all sympathetic to educational stations and did little to assist them or protect them from the pressures of commercial broadcasters.

By 1935, then, only 5 of the 31 educational stations still on the air were licensed for full-time operation; the others shared time with commercial stations and were allowed to broadcast for only 2 or 3 hours a day. About a dozen religious stations also operated on a noncommercial basis, most of them limited to broadcasting religious services on Sunday mornings. By 1940, the number of noncommercial educational stations had dropped to 26, and only a handful of these survivors were being adequately financed by the schools to which they were licensed.

During the 1920s, nearly all radio stations operated on a part-time basis, sharing frequency assignments with other stations in the same general area. This arrangement created serious problems for the then-existing educational stations; the commercial broadcasters with whom time was shared naturally wanted to increase their authorized hours of operation at the expense of their noncommercial neighbors. In 1930, after several educational stations had almost literally been pushed off the air, a National Conference on Radio and Education, convened by the United States commissioner of education, demanded that Congress should adopt legislation reserving 15 percent of all broadcasting facilities for the exclusive use of educational institutions. Congress asked the Federal Radio Commission to study the proposal and, if it saw fit, to recommend suitable legislation. The FRC showed little interest in the 15 percent idea, however, and made no recommendation. Four years later, the idea of educational reservations came up again, this time in the form of a proposed amendment to the communications act then under consideration by Congress. The amendment failed to receive the necessary support, and the proposal was not incorporated in the Federal Communications Act of 1934.

The Federal Communications Commission (FCC), however, took a more favorable attitude than had the earlier FRC toward the idea of reserving facilities for noncommercial use. In 1945, the FCC designated twenty channels in the frequency modulation (FM) band as "educational channels," to be used only by noncommercial educational stations.

The FCC's decision to reserve these educational channels was largely a result of the activities of various interested educational groups. In the early 1920s, the National Association of Educational Broadcasters (NAEB) was a leader in the movement to secure educational reservations; the same organization, backed by the United States Office of Education, had much to do with the commission's action in setting aside FM channels for educational station use.

At the end of World War II, some 35 standard-band (AM) stations were operating on a noncommercial basis, including several licensed to religious organizations. After 1945, the number of noncommercial AM stations increased slightly; by January of 1975, 40 AM stations were functioning on a noncommercial basis. Of these, 18 stations were operated by tax-supported colleges or universities, 13 were licensed to private colleges or other educational agencies, 7 were operated by religious organizations, 1 by a municipality, and 1 by a state organization.

There has been a tremendous expansion in the number of noncommercial radio stations using the FM band. In January 1975, a total of 717 noncommercial FM stations were on the air, virtually all on frequencies reserved for education. Of the total number, more than 150 were licensed to tax-supported colleges and universities; approximately 300 were operated by private colleges and junior colleges; and 125 served the needs of local public school systems. The remainder were licensed to various state agencies, to private educational groups, or, in a few instances, to religious organizations. About 40 percent of the noncommercial FM operations were low-power 10-watt stations, costing little to construct or operate. On the other hand, more than 55 of the educational FM stations used power of 50,000 watts or more.

Programs provided by educational radio stations vary widely. Many of the noncommercial stations are relatively well financed and have competent program staffs; other stations, especially those in the 10-watt category, have very limited budgets, and some are operated entirely by students. A few stations owned by local boards of education limit their programming activities to the presentation of instructional materials for use in the classroom. Other stations aim their programs at a general audience, and as with commercial radio stations, recorded music forms the backbone of their program schedules. By 1975, a substantial number of these stations were being programmed, at least in part, by students and were scheduling regular blocks of "contemporary" music representative of the period. Many still provide listeners with programs of show tunes and middle-of-the-road music, with substantial amounts of time each week devoted to broadcasts of classical and semiclassical music. Some stations also present programs of jazz and folk music. Most of the educational radio stations use an hour or more a day to present talk programs, ranging from educational lectures to discussions of public controversial issues. College- and university-owned stations usually carry play-by-play broadcasts of local sports events, especially those involving teams representing their own institutions. Some educational radio stations owned by state or private colleges, like those licensed to local school systems, offer instructional programs for use in classrooms of elementary and secondary schools. Although the larger university stations include news broadcasts in their daily schedules, most of the smaller educational FM outlets give almost no time to current news, probably because their operating budgets are too small to cover the costs of a wire news service.

Little is known about the audiences reached by educational radio stations; such stations are not usually mentioned in local rating reports of commercial rating services, and in any case, the number of listeners to most of the educational stations is probably small. However, educational radio stations are providing a "second broadcasting service" in radio, and one of particular value to those listeners who are interested in serious talks or in music of somewhat better quality than that provided by most commercial radio stations.

THE RISE OF EDUCATIONAL TELEVISION (1952–1967)

In 1950, the NAEB and the United States Office of Education were responsible for the formation of the Joint Committee on Educational Television (JCET), representing such important educational groups as the American Council on Education, the Association of Land-Grant Colleges, the National Association of State Universities, the National Council of Chief State School Officers, and the National Education Association. Under the guidance of JCET, dozens of educational leaders appeared at hearings before the FCC to urge that specific reservations be made for the educational television (ETV) stations that might later come into being.

In spite of the objection of many commercial broadcasters, the commission, in its Sixth Report and Order, issued in April 1952, reserved a total of 242 channels for the exclusive use of educational television stations, 80 VHF (very high frequency) channels and 162 UHF (ultra-high frequency) channels. The commission's 1965 revision of its allocations table for television more than doubled the number of reserved channels for noncommercial use—from the 242 assignments in 1952 to a total of 604 reservations in 559 different communities, including two assignments each in 45 major cities. Of the noncommercial channel assignments in the 1965 allocations, 102 were in the VHF band and 502 were UHF stations. Hardly had the FCC's Report and Order of 1952 been released when plans were being made by educational institutions to construct stations on channels that the commission had reserved for the exclusive use of educational television outlets. By the end of 1953, only two educational television stations had gone on the air, one of which suspended operation during the following year; by the end of 1954, however, eight additional stations had been constructed. During the next four years, the number of educational outlets had increased to 34; and, by the beginning of January 1966, a total of 105 noncommercial television stations were in operation, 61 using VHF channels and the remainder assigned to channels in the UHF band. Nine years later, in the fall of 1974, the number of these ETV stations had more than doubled, reaching 241.

Rules of the FCC provide that noncommercial educational stations may be licensed only to "nonprofit educational organizations upon a showing that the proposed stations will be used primarily to serve the educational needs of the community." Under this rule, licenses have been issued to a variety of types of organizations. Of the 241 stations in operation in the autumn of 1974, 52 were licensed to state colleges and universities, 12 to privately owned colleges, 29

"There was no Sesame Street or Electric Company? Then how
did you learn to read and write?"

to local boards of education and comparable units, and 58 to local
non-profit groups. Of considerable significance in this period is the
growth in the number of stations licensed to state boards of education, ETV commissions, and their equivalents. Since 1965, this
number has mushroomed from 16 to 85 with twenty states establishing some sort of ETV commission to establish and supervise the
growth and development of educational television within the state.
The number of stations administered by such state agencies ranges
from thirteen in Kentucky to only one each in Arkansas, Idaho, and
Rhode Island, but this pattern of growth demonstrates increasing
recognition of the value of educational television by the various
states.

The development of educational television since the FCC's Report and Order of 1952 can be divided neatly into two periods:
before and after establishment of the Corporation for Public Broadcasting (CPB). The signing in November 1967 by President Lyndon
B. Johnson of the bill creating the Corporation for Public Broadcasting changed the ETV situation so significantly that one must look at
educational television in pre-CPB years as a very different service
from that available to a large number of American citizens today.
On the other hand, the present system had its roots in the structure
that developed in the 1950s and early 1960s, and these years bear
some examination.

Educational television grew in the 15 years between 1952 and
1967 for several reasons. One was the concern of college and university administrators over expanding college enrollments. With little

chance that faculties and physical plants could be expanded rapidly enough to keep pace with the increased numbers of students, officials of some tax-supported institutions saw in television a possible method of coping with the problem. In this they were encouraged, as were public school administrators, by findings of dozens of research studies investigating television's effectiveness as a classroom teaching tool; in nearly every instance, researchers reported that while instruction by television was not significantly more effective than that provided by teachers in a face-to-face situation, television instruction was at least no less effective than that provided by conventional methods, at least in some subject-matter areas. As a result, many university and public school administrators saw television as a means of providing instruction for students, without adding large numbers of highly qualified instructors to teaching staffs.[1]

For community stations, the motivating factor was somewhat different. Community leaders who were active in the development of these stations expected them to use a part of their time to broadcast programs for use in public school classrooms, but they were interested primarily in the possibilities that educational television offered in the area of adult education and in the providing of cultural programs. Probably many organizers of community groups hoped that the educational television stations to be built would be able to devote several hours a week to broadcasts by symphony orchestras, to operas, to serious drama, to programs dealing with art or literature, and to other cultural materials not provided by commercial television.

Financial Assistance

An important factor in the rapid growth of educational television in this period was the financial assistance given to prospective licensees of educational stations by outside agencies. In cities in which educational stations were constructed by community groups, funds for construction and operation of the educational outlets came

---

[1] In those years, many colleges and universities installed closed-circuit television systems to provide in-school instruction for students, often with classrooms in a dozen or more buildings linked by coaxial cable with the originating television studio. Similar systems were also in use in many high schools and elementary schools. Where the school buildings to be served were scattered over a large area, however, as in major cities or when schools were located in several different communities, open-circuit or "broadcast" television was required. This form of instructional television continues to this day.

largely from public subscriptions; local business concerns were often heavy contributors. In many communities, commercial broadcasters donated money or equipment to help get the new educational stations on the air. In one situation, the owner of a commercial outlet in a two-station market bought the rival commercial VHF station in that city and turned it over to an educational institution—channel, transmitter, antenna tower, studios, and technical equipment—with the understanding that the station would be operated on a noncommercial basis. In many other communities, commercial broadcasters donated amounts ranging from $50,000 to as much as $250,000, or provided studios, antenna towers, or equipment worth thousands of dollars. Contributions of commercial stations and networks to new educational stations between 1955 and 1967 probably totaled $15 million or more.

Even more important was the financial support provided the infant educational television stations by foundations—the Ford Foundation in particular. The Fund for Adult Education, using money provided by the Ford Foundation, made substantial grants of money to early educational stations for purchase of equipment. At least 30 new stations received donations of $100,000 or $150,000 each from the fund, with the proviso that a part of the money received be used to buy equipment for kinescope recording. Later, foundation money was made available for the purchase of videotape-recording equipment; educational stations were among the first to install such equipment. Probably the most important contribution of the Ford Foundation and the Fund for Adult Education, however, in terms of long-range development of educational television at least, was the financing of the National Educational Television and Radio Center,[2] an agency organized to produce educational and cultural programs on film or videotape for distribution to noncommercial educational stations. By the end of 1965, the Ford Foundation had contributed more than $96 million, either directly or through organizations it financed, to help establish educational television. Other foundations had contributed smaller amounts toward the construction or support of individual educational stations.

The growth of educational television was also aided by actions of the federal government. The National Defense Education Act passed by Congress in 1958 authorized the spending of up to $110 million a year for 3 years for the encouragement and improvement of the teaching of mathematics, the sciences, and foreign languages.

---

[2]In 1963 the last three words of the original title were dropped and the organization came to be known simply as National Educational Television.

Many of the grants approved by the Department of Health, Education and Welfare under provisions of this act involved research studies or other experiments in the field of educational television. In May 1962, Congress passed a second measure, this time authorizing the use of $32 million of federal funds for construction of educational television stations. By the summer of 1964, $8 million of this amount had actually been appropriated and made available; in each instance, an amount equal to the federal grant had to be provided from state or local funds. While no financial aid was involved, the construction of educational stations on UHF channels was stimulated by the enactment by Congress of the law requiring all television sets manufactured after April 1964 to be equipped with all-channel tuning and to be capable of bringing in signals of UHF stations as well as those of stations assigned to VHF channels.

By 1967, the United States had a "second television service," albeit without direct interconnection, operated for the specific purpose of providing educational, informative, and cultural programs for listeners. More than 100 noncommercial educational stations were already on the air—roughly one educational station for every six commercial outlets—and the number of stations was increasing at the rate of six or eight each year.

Programming

Programs offered by educational outlets fall into two major classes. During school hours, a major part of the schedule of the typical station consists of instructional programs intended for use in classrooms of elementary and secondary schools. Frequently the same lessons are broadcast twice or even three times each day, to make them available for classes meeting at different hours. Most of these daytime instructional programs are locally produced; variations in courses of study from state to state and even from city to city make it difficult to make the same instructional materials fit lesson plans in use in different localities. In most situations, the specific sequence of materials used in each broadcast course is worked out by station producers in cooperation with committees of teachers from the local school system or with assistant superintendents responsible for curricula. Instructors or "experts" appearing before the cameras in televised courses for the most part come from the instructional staff of the local school system and are selected jointly by local school authorities and by representatives of the television station. Almost all the instructional programs planned for classroom use follow the "lecture and demonstration" pattern, with "master teachers" who appear on the program and who prepare and present their own materials. This "extension of the classroom" technique has sometimes been criticized as not making full use of the possibilities offered by television, but no better method of instruction has been developed that could be used for subjects ranging from physical science to driver education—and that is economically feasible for use by a single station. Apparently local school authorities have felt that televised instruction is effective; in any event, the number of school systems using educational television programs in the classroom has increased steadily.

The second group of programs provided by noncommercial educational stations included those intended for out-of-school listening, usually by an adult audience. Through these programs educational television had its opportunity to offer instruction and inspiration for the general audience and to serve the cultural needs of the community—to provide the "second television service" that is one of its major objectives. A limited number of cultural programs were provided by most stations, but a major part of the non-classroom offerings consisted of adult educational programs of the "how to do it" type, of roundtable or panel discussion programs, and of talks on a wide variety of subjects.

The published schedule of WNDT (now WNET), the noncommercial VHF television station in New York City, for a typical week in February 1965 was fairly representative of the offerings of educational stations throughout the country. The station was on the air Monday through Friday from 9:30 a. m. until 11:00 p.m.; like most other educational television stations, WNDT did not broadcast on Saturday or Sunday. Daytime hours were devoted largely to classroom instruction, using programs developed in cooperation with the board of education of the city of New York. Schedules for the late afternoon and early evening during the 5-day period included eight half-hour programs for young children, five half hours of instruction in basic English for Puerto Ricans, three program periods providing instruction in advanced French, two programs dealing with gardening, two talks on French cooking, and three programs of vocal music. Programs scheduled later in the evening included a documentary on life in the "old West"; two half-hour dramatic presentations by a little theatre group; an hour-long British-produced dramatization of short stories by Guy de Maupassant; a 30-minute piano recital from Lincoln Center; interviews with composers of "new music," a famous photographer, and the art editor of a national magazine; and two presentations dealing with the art of motion pictures. The prime-time schedule also included no fewer than eight panel discussion or "conversation" programs on topics rang-

Figure 10-1 Many local educational television stations aired with some success analyses and showings of classic motion pictures. Pictured are Rudolph Valentino and Lila Lee in *Blood and Sand*. (Courtesy Public Broadcasting Service)

ing from the rights of blacks in northern cities to conditions in Red China and at least a dozen talks or interviews on such subjects as narcotics addiction, the use of computers, oceanography, air pollution, recently published books, and chess masterpieces. Ten 5-minute periods were devoted to news and five longer programs to news commentary. Of the approximately 37 hours of nonclassroom programming, more than 12 hours consisted of repeats of broadcasts that had been carried on the station before, many only a few days earlier.[3] This WNDT programming of 1965 undoubtedly ben-

---

[3]Contrast the above with the following summary of the schedule of WNET-TV (formerly WNDT) printed in the January 22, 1975, issue of *Variety:* "By comparison WNET-TV's seven-week prime-time schedule today includes such highlights currently as 'Nova,' the science show from Boston; 'Soundstage,' the contemporary musical concert show from Chicago; 'Special of the Week' ('A Rachmaninoff Festival' this week); 'Masterpiece Theater' (currently the BBC's 'Upstairs, Downstairs'); 'Monty Python's Flying Circus,' the zany comedy half-hour from the BBC; 'Theatre in America,' this week featuring the Trinity Square Repertory Co. of Providence, R.I.; 'Bill Moyer's Journal: International Report'; 'Gerald Ford's America,' Top Value Television's half inch vidtape telementary series; 'Behind the Lines,' the media show; 'World Press' and 'Washington Week in Review'; 'Black Journal'; 'The Ascent of Man,' ambitious historical series from England; not to mention 'Yoga for Health,' and a lot of cooking instruction."

efited from the wide cultural and educational variety of New York City and the content of some programs may not have been typical of other ETV stations of the time—few of which would have had reason to schedule 2½ hours of education for Puerto Ricans. The schedule is typical, however, in its emphasis on instructional programs, panel discussions, talks, interviews, repeats, and prime-time reliance on the offerings of the ETV "network" of that period, National Educational Television.

National Educational Television

The National Educational Television organization—or NET, as it was more commonly known—was created in 1952 as the National Educational Television and Radio Center. Financial support came largely from the Fund for Adult Education or directly from the Ford Foundation. The organization engaged in a variety of activities, from lobbying in Washington to encouraging schools and local community groups to apply for licenses for educational stations; NET's main function, however, was that of supplying programs. Practically all of the educational television stations in the country were NET affiliates and part of the tape network made possible by magnetic videotape recording. For an annual membership fee of only $100, each affiliate was provided with 5 hours of new programming each week and an additional 5 hours of programs taken from the organization's program library. Additional programs from the NET library, which included 3,000 separate programs, were secured by affiliates on payment of a rental charge of $5 for each half hour of material.

During the first 10 years of its existence, the network secured most of its programs from member stations, which produced them under grants from the network organization. Additional programs were purchased from the British Broadcasting Corporation and a few were produced by private contractors. In 1963, however, the Ford Foundation increased the amount of its annual subsidy to the educational network to $6 million, with the proviso that practically all of this amount was to be used to produce programs of high quality. Officials of NET, as a result, adopted the policy in 1964 of having nearly all of the network's new programs produced by independent professional program packagers instead of by affiliated educational stations. The network organization did continue to use programs produced by the British Broadcasting Corporation and occasionally programs secured from state-owned television systems in other countries.

Figure 10-2 While it leaned heavily on panel discussions and topical interviews, National Educational Television did provide viewers with cultural programs of the kind pictured above. (Courtesy Public Broadcasting Service)

The National Educational Television library served a purpose and, by the mid-1960s, it was central to the loosely knit "network" of ETV stations in the United States. Unfortunately, NET was able to supply its affiliates with only a limited number of the more elaborate cultural programs—operas, symphonies, plays of outstanding literary merit—that proponents of educational broadcasting wanted to see included on the schedules of educational stations.

THE CARNEGIE COMMISSION AND PUBLIC BROADCASTING (AFTER 1967)

In December of 1964, the National Association of Educational Broadcasters (NAEB), working with the U.S. Office of Education, called a conference to discuss the problems facing educational broadcasting. This conference proposed the establishment of a commission to study the financial needs of ETV and how they should be met. The Carnegie Corporation, a philanthropic organization, was interested in such a study and agreed to fund it. Thus the Carnegie Commission on Educational Television was born, and a chain of events was set in motion that would change the face of educational broadcasting.

The final report of the Carnegie Commission was published in 1967 as *Public Television: A Program for Action*, with twelve specific recommendations for action. The most significant was the proposal that a "Corporation for Public Television" be formed to "receive and disburse governmental and private funds." The commission also recommended that the corporation support two production centers and contract for production with others; support local station production of programs "for more than local use"; support the production of strictly local programming when possible and appropriate; encourage and support research and development leading to improved programming; support technical research to upgrade television technology; and help recruit and train technical and artistic personnel. Federal funding for the corporation was to come from an excise tax on television sets, starting at 2 percent and eventually reaching 5 percent—the tax being dedicated solely to the corporation.

Interconnection was also seen as essential by the Carnegie Commission and it was recommended that funds be provided to allow for full, commercial-grade interconnection to expedite a steady flow of programs for all stations. The number of educational television stations was to be increased to a total of 380 by 1980, with funding for this expansion to come from the Department of Health,

Education and Welfare. Finally, federal, state, and local agencies were encouraged to provide funds to improve facilities and stimulate research on the "use of television in formal and informal education."

Moving with unaccustomed alacrity, both houses of Congress agreed on a bill and sent it to President Johnson in October of 1967. He signed it in November and the Corporation for Public Broadcasting (renamed to allow for support of public radio) was born. The bill set four primary goals for the corporation (CPB): (1) to develop programs of high quality from diverse sources; (2) to help establish a system or systems of national interconnection to distribute programs to radio and television stations; (3) to strengthen and support those stations; and (4) to organize those functions in a manner that assured "the maximum freedom of those stations from interference with or control of program content or other activities."

The bill also authorized $9 million for CPB (only $5 million was appropriated), $10.5 million for grants to aid radio and television stations, and $500,000 for a study of instructional television. Additional funds were forthcoming from a number of organizations, including CBS ($1 million), the Carnegie Corporation ($1 million), and the United Auto Workers ($25,000), giving CPB a little more than $7 million for its first year of operation.

As we will see, CPB has sailed through troubled seas since its launching, but progress has been made on many fronts. Grants have been made to stations and production centers for programming, fellowships, and study centers. Interconnection was extended, at a rate approximately a third of that charged commercial broadcasters, to 148 stations by 1974. Educational, cultural, and informational programs have been produced in ever larger numbers and, in general, the activities of CPB have been highly beneficial to both educational radio and television.

In 1969, the Public Broadcasting Service (PBS) was formed by CPB to manage and allot programming time on the existing public television (PTV) network. At this time, 146 stations were already interconnected and were receiving programming for 2 hours a day, 5 days a week; but these lines were preemptable by AT&T when needed for other services and the arrangement was not completely satisfactory. (In 1969, it was estimated that on 30 percent of the nights the network was in use, one or more stations had been preempted—often throwing them on their own devices with virtually no warning.) This network had been managed for CPB by NET, and the formation of PBS allowed NET to return full-time to a primary role of production.

In 1971, the FCC approved networking with a commercial-grade, full-time interconnection at the two-thirds reduction in cost noted, and ordered AT&T to begin construction of the service now in use. By the 1974–1975 season, PBS was programming 3 to 3½ hours an evening, 7 days a week. The schedule for that year included a thirteen-part series on the history of science, *The Ascent of Man*; a series on the uses of solar power, *Solar Energy*; an anthology of Japanese motion pictures; a series in yoga, *Lilias, Yoga and You*; programs on grass roots crime prevention, *Burglar Proofing;* two cooking programs; *Black Journal* and *Black Perspective on the News;* a six-part jazz series, *At the Top; The Life of Leonardo da Vinci;* and a thirteen-part retrospective on great moments in sports history, *The Way It Was.*

Funding Problems

Financial support for CPB has been a continual problem since the beginning. As noted, the Carnegie Commission had recommended that the corporation be insulated from the problems surrounding annual appropriations from Congress and suggested that the money from an excise tax be placed in a trust fund administered by the U.S. Treasury solely for CPB. The commission explained its position as follows:

> The combination of a private, non-governmental corporate structure and a federally financed trust fund permits the Corporation to be free of governmental procedural and administrative regulations that are incompatible with its purposes, and to avoid the overseeing of its day-to-day operations that would be a natural consequence of annual budgeting and appropriations procedures.

Congress, however, did not agree with the Carnegie Commission on this point and in subsequent years followed a pattern of authorizing one sum, often far less than requested, and appropriating an even smaller amount. Even so, these appropriations had risen from $5 million in 1968 to $35 million in 1972. At this point, CPB ran into turbulent seas. Congress approved an appropriation of $65 million in 1973 and $90 million in 1974. President Nixon, unhappy with some aspects of the CPB programming and direction, had proposed only $45 million for 1973, and he vetoed the congressional action. The corporation operated for another year at the $35 million level amid controversy over centralization (see below), advocacy journalism, the hiring of Nixon administration critics like Sander Vanocur and Robert MacNeil, and fixed-schedule networking.

These were not good years for the idea of long-range financing. Clay Whitehead, director of the Office for Telecommunications Policy (OTP) in the Nixon White House, stated in 1971 that permanent financing would be "bad public policy" because it would remove the element of "accountability"; and the President vetoed 2-year financing, citing fears that "an organization, originally intended to serve only the local stations, is becoming instead the center of control and the focal point of power for the entire public broadcasting system."

Congress tried again in 1973, however, and authorized a 2-year appropriation totalling $120 million for 1974 and 1975. President Nixon approved the authorization this time, but by appropriations time the $55 million authorized for 1974 had shrunk to $50 million (and early in 1974 the administration impounded $2.25 million of those funds) and the $65 million authorized for 1975 had been cut by $5 million.

Long-range funding had not been forgotten entirely, however. Reacting to complaints from many sources about "centralization," public broadcasting modified its structure to meet the criticism. Satisfied, OTP started working on plans for long-range financing that would provide for annual grants but would require public broadcasting to raise $2.50 for every $1.00 of federal money. This plan was submitted to Congress in 1974, but no action was agreed upon until the end of 1976. Late in 1976, the House of Representatives and the Senate agreed on a plan whereby CPB would receive $103 million in 1977; $107.15 million in 1978; and $120.2 million in 1979. CPB was required to raise $2.50 for each federal dollar under this long-range financing plan.

CPB, PBS, and Centralization

Only 4 years after its establishment, the Corporation for Public Broadcasting began hearing the first complaints about what some saw as excessive "centralization" of public broadcasting. Speaking to an audience of ETV representatives in the summer of 1971, Arthur L. Singer, Jr.—who had been instrumental in the establishment of the Carnegie Commission—expressed the view that CPB and PBS were following a path that diverged considerably from that originally envisioned by the commission. According to Singer, the Carnegie Commission report had called for a decentralized system of public broadcasting that would draw upon the resources of public broadcasting stations across the country. Instead of this, Singer saw a system dominated by CPB and PBS and striving to compete with commercial broadcasting on its own terms.

Comments like this from a person who was committed to the concept of educational broadcasting may have been disturbing to some, but they had little immediate effect on the activities of CPB or PBS. Three months later, however, strikingly similar remarks were delivered by a man who made ETV practitioners sit up and take notice. Speaking at the annual convention of the National Association of Educational Broadcasters, OTP Director Clay T. Whitehead flatly stated that there were strong signs that educational broadcasters were "becoming affiliates of a centralized, national network," and indicated that the Nixon administration was not pleased with this trend. As Whitehead saw it, "the concept of dispersing responsibility was essential to the policy chosen in 1967 for public broadcasting. . . . The centralization that *was* planned for the system—in the form of CPB—was intended to *serve the stations,* to help them extend the range of *their* services to *their* communities. The idea was to break the NET monopoly of program production combined with networking and to build an effective counter force to give appropriate weight to local and regional views." Instead of this, according to Whitehead, "CPB seems to have decided to make permanent financing its principal goal and to aim for programming with a national impact on the public and the Congress to achieve it. . . . The local station is asked . . . to sacrifice its autonomy to facilitate funding for the national system."

These strong words were reinforced in July of 1972 when President Nixon vetoed the CPB appropriations bill for 1973. Justifying his veto, the President repeated the charge that CPB was exerting too much control over local stations and stated that he felt this centralization was threatening "to erode substantially public broadcasting's impressive potential for promoting innovative and diverse cultural and educational programming." Significantly, President Nixon's news secretary added that the reason centralization was of such concern to the administration was illustrated by the fact that only 13 percent of CPB money went to local stations in 1972 while 91 percent of prime-time programming was produced by only seven production centers.

There followed a confusing series of events: the first president of CPB, John Macy, was replaced by Henry Loomis, a Nixon appointee who seemed bent on recapturing control of programming, scheduling, and distribution from PBS; a series of "discussions" among CPB, PBS, and NAEB, which *Broadcasting* typified as resembling more "a nose-to-nose confrontation than a friendly forum for the airing of differences"; a reshuffling of the respective chairmanships of CPB and PBS; and, ultimately, a reconciliation and compromise in late 1973. Under the new agreement, CPB would make program-funding decisions, the network would be open to material not financed by the corporation, and PBS would handle scheduling.

Working together again, CPB and PBS developed a rather complicated plan called the National Station Program Cooperative, which both hoped would answer much of the earlier criticism about "centralization." Under this co-op plan, which was put into effect for the 1974–1975 season on a trial basis, local stations were given a voice in the selection of national programs to be made available by PBS—decisions that had been made in the past solely by a PBS committee and CPB. In addition, the local stations were expected to pay for a significant portion of the schedule—approximately 25 percent in 1974–1975—out of their own resources.

Much of this station money, in turn, was to come from direct grants from CPB. Apparently responding to the admonition in President Nixon's veto message of 1972, CPB began increasing the amount of money allocated to what it calls Community Service Grants (CSG). In 1973, CPB allocated $5 million of its $35 million to the CSG program. In 1974 this had jumped to $15 million. This shift in emphasis meant that less CPB money was available for production of national programs and PBS planned to use the increased flow of money from stations as one source of badly needed funds for production. Processing the money through individual stations, of course, does give these stations more of a voice in program selection.

The co-op plan, however, does not provide all the programming needed for the public television schedule. When the dust had settled in the summer of 1974, PBS estimated that the co-op would provide 613 program hours in the 1974–1975 season, with 275 hours in children's programming, 215 in public affairs, and 123 in other cultural programming; in addition, 180 hours of programming had been directly underwritten by CPB and other sources. Public Broadcasting Service scheduled a total of 1,692 hours in 1973–1974, approximately two thirds new and the remainder repeat, and the same ratio of new to repeat programming occurred in 1974–1975.

At this writing, the final word is not in on the co-op plan or on the cooperation between CPB and PBS. Some educational broadcasters complained that the new plan caused a reduction in the number of public affairs programs on public broadcasting and others were concerned because the co-op rejected such long-running programs as *The Advocates, Behind the Lines*, and *Soul*. In addition, there were signs of continuing friction between CPB and PBS over the issue of the percentage of CPB funds that should be distributed to public television stations. On balance, however, the public broadcasting system seems to have found a course that steers between criticisms about excessive centralization and excessive localism. At the same time, the prospects for long-term funding seem brighter than ever before. Only time will tell whether the stormy seas of the first half of the 1970s have been weathered successfully.

EVALUATION OF PUBLIC BROADCASTING

In the late 1960s, during the beginning of CPB functioning, major problems confronted public television (PTV) in three areas: finances, quality, and audiences. These problems have been alleviated somewhat in the subsequent decade, but they still haunt all PTV broadcasters.

The Problem of Finances

As we have seen, the formation of the Corporation for Public Broadcasting and subsequent pressures for "localism" have resulted in an increase in the amount of money available to public broadcasters through the Community Service Grant program, but there still is not enough. Television is expensive. Stations need substantial amounts of money to pay the costs of operation. Commercial stations sell time to advertisers to provide the revenues needed to pay salaries, buy equipment, and produce programs for their listeners. Public broadcasting stations, on the other hand, are by law noncommercial and are barred from selling time. Consequently, they must find other sources of income.

The percentage breakdown for the income of the public broadcasting system in 1973 is shown in Table 10–1. Such sources of income cannot begin to provide the amount of money that commercial broadcasting generates. As a result, public television stations are seriously underfinanced. They simply do not have the money available to provide the type of service in the cultural field that they are expected to offer. Reports to the Federal Communications Commission show that, not including the costs of selling time, the operating expenses of commercial television stations in 1973 averaged about $2.5 million a year. In comparison, the income of the

Table 10–1   Percent of Public Broadcasting Income from Various Sources: 1973

	Percent
Intra-industry	15.9
Federal government	19.6
Local schools and boards of education	7.7
Local government	1.8
State boards of education	7.0
State government	13.1
Institutions of higher education	10.5
Foundations	7.1
Business and industry	2.8
Subscribers	6.3
Auctions	2.6
All other sources	5.6

Source: United States Department of Health, Education and Welfare, *Status Report on Public Broadcasting, 1973* (Washington, D.C.: U.S. Government Printing Office, 1974).

average PTV station in 1972 was approximately $730,000, according to the *Status Report on Public Television, 1973,* of the U.S. Department of Health, Education and Welfare. As a result, the PTV station must limit its hours of operation each week; it is forced to get along with a smaller staff than that of the commercial station in the same community—the average public television station in 1973 had only 34 full-time employees; salaries of employees are usually lower; and the station has far less money to spend in providing programs for listeners. In the words of Wilbur Schramm: "The truth is that ETV from the start has been a shoestring operation, long on imagination but short on cash, high on ideals but low on salaries, strong on program standards but weak in money for talent and equipment."[4]

The same characterization may also be applied to the Corporation for Public Broadcasting and its Public Broadcasting Service. Total income for PBS in 1973 was $216,442,558, a considerable portion of which went into nonprogramming activities; PBS estimates that in 1973 slightly more than $39.8 million was spent in national programming carried on its network. Realistically, $40 million a year will not buy any great number of high-quality programs when the average production cost of evening programs on commercial

---

[4]Wilbur Schramm, Jack Lyle, and Ithiel de Sola Pool, *The People Look at Educational Television* (Stanford, Calif.: Stanford University Press, 1963), p. 13.

networks runs between \$230,000 and \$240,000 for each hour of material broadcast and when the three national commercial networks reported total programming expenses for 1973 at more than \$1 billion.

The public network organization in recent years has found it necessary to supplement its income from foundation grants by arranging for costs of certain program series to be underwritten by various professional groups or industrial concerns. These programs are of course not "sponsored"—the underwriting organization does not pay for time on stations which carry the programs—but credit is given to the underwriting company by inserting in the opening and closing portions of each program the words "produced in cooperation with" or "made possible by a grant from" the agency that paid the program's production costs.

The Problem of Quality

Lack of adequate financing of public television stations creates a problem with respect to the quality of program offerings. Costs of power and equipment and technical operating expenses are just as high on an hour-for-hour basis for PTV as for commercial stations. Consequently the noncommercial station can stay within its limited budget only by holding personnel and program costs to a minimum. The PTV station usually has fewer employees than does its commercial counterpart, although the number of hours of local programming each week may be from twice to three times as great as the number provided by most commercial outlets. Salaries are often lower than those paid for equivalent work by commercial stations, especially for top-level employees. As a result, there is a tendency for producers and writers and on-the-air "personalities" of greater-than-average ability to leave the PTV field for work at higher pay on commercial stations. Simply because of its financial limitations, the public station finds it difficult to compete with commercial outlets in securing or holding the services of competent and experienced program personnel.

Naturally, this weakness in production talent has its effect on the quality of programs developed and presented. Even more serious is the fact that because of the lack of money, most PTV stations cannot even attempt to put on the air the types of locally produced cultural programs their operators would like to provide and that should be provided by stations attempting to offer a real "second television service." Locally produced programs of serious drama are out of the question; they cost far too much both in time and money, even if top-notch scripts could be secured and if the necessary professional quality of dramatic talent were available in the community. The same situation exists with respect to serious musical programs; even in cities that support symphony orchestras, the fees charged for television appearances of such professional organizations are far too great to be within the reach of the average educational station. As a result, public television stations are forced to depend for their cultural programs on those provided by PBS. Some of these programs have been excellent; but, as already noted, the network has been able to supply only a very limited number of really first-rate dramatic or musical programs or programs dealing with literature or the dance or fine arts. Costs of outstanding programs are high, and the public television network organization does not have unlimited funds at its disposal.

Educational broadcasters have succeeded in planning and producing some high-quality programming for television. With funding from private enterprise, foundations, and CPB, the Children's Television Workshop (CTW) has been very successful with such programs as *Sesame Street* and *The Electric Company*. Other program series for children, like *Mister Rogers' Neighborhood, Carriscolendas,* and *Villa Allegre,* have combined with the CTW programs to produce quality programming for children. Such programs may develop a public television "habit" among children, but whether or not this will carry into adulthood will depend on the quality of the adult programs provided.

Although weak in the area of local cultural programs, PTV stations do better in the field of information, providing informative programs ranging over a wide variety of subjects from elementary science to marriage customs in India or to conditions among migratory workers in the southwestern United States. Some of these presentations are in documentary form, usually provided by PBS. Others take the form of round-table discussions. Also, there are libraries of educational television programs that supply programs and series to public television stations. However, most of the programs provided by PTV stations are low-cost "one-man presentations"— lectures by teachers and other authorities or informal "conversations" with invited guests. Such programs can be put together with minimum effort on the part of the station's staff; there are no supporting entertainers, no special settings need to be constructed, little or no rehearsal time is required, and usually no effort is made to employ any special production techniques to make the program more attractive to listeners. All too often, in fact, there is little evidence of the use of much imagination or ingenuity on the part of the producer of the program; the presentation is successful only in the

Figure 10-3 Programs like *Sesame Street* and a special presentation of *Alice through the Looking Glass* illustrate the variety of children's programming offered by PBS. (Courtesy Public Broadcasting Service)

Figure 10–4 PBS has offered drama by established playwrights, like Eugene O'Neill (*Ah, Wilderness,* above), and by those less well-known, like Alexis Deveaux (*The Tapestry,* below). (Courtesy Public Broadcasting Service)

Figure 10-5 Programs from the BBC in Great Britain, like *Upstairs, Downstairs* (above) and some of the Lord Peter Wimsey mysteries (below), have been very successful when aired by PBS. (Courtesy Public Broadcasting Service)

degree to which the speaker who appears is able by sheer force of personality to hold listener attention during the time the program is on the air. As might be expected, not all those who appear on such programs have the vitality and color and the sense of showmanship the situation demands. The "one-man-show" format is not the most effective for television use, but programs using the form can be produced more cheaply than those of other types, and most PTV stations cannot afford to pay the additional costs required for other programs. Limited budgets do not make for high program quality, and until public television is better financed than it has been in the past, a part at least of the programs presented by PTV stations will fail to meet the standards of quality desirable in an effective "second service."

The Problem of Audiences

A third problem that the public television station must face is that of attracting listeners for its programs. A PTV station should reasonably expect to reach enough listeners to justify its costs of operation, just as a commercial station is expected to attract audiences large enough to satisfy its advertisers. Just how many listeners the public station should reach is of course a difficult question to answer. But if public television is to be a significant force in disseminating culture and providing education and organized information for the people living in the community, the number reached and influenced should be substantial; the greater the number who listen to each program, the greater the effectiveness of the station in attaining its educational and cultural objectives.

Unfortunately, with very few exceptions the audiences attracted by public television stations are small, especially as compared with those of commercial outlets. Some of them are assigned to UHF channels in markets served by VHF commercial stations; naturally in such situations the PTV station works at a serious disadvantage. Even the VHF educational stations have comparatively few listeners. In part, the problem lies in the fact that when they turn on their television sets, most people want to be entertained, rather than enlightened or exposed to culture. Possibly, too, the limited number of programs of outstanding quality on public station schedules has something to do with the situation. Lack of station and program promotion is certainly a factor; with a limited budget, the public station does not have the money necessary for elaborate promotional campaigns to make listeners aware of whatever attractive programs the station is able to provide. In addition, these stations schedule few programs intended primarily as "audience-builders," regardless of their instructional or cultural values. Whatever the cause, it is an accepted fact that public television stations are rarely able to attract substantial audiences, even for their most outstanding programs.

Studies by A. C. Nielsen for the Corporation for Public Broadcasting distributed in March of 1975 indicate that during an average week (in late November and early December 1974), approximately 32 percent of the nation's television households tuned to at least one program on a public broadcasting station. Those 21.6 million viewing homes watched an average of 3.15 hours of public broadcasting during that week.

Contrast these figures with the Nielsen Television Index figures for all television viewing in 1973. During that year, the average home in the United States used television for a total of 44 hours and 7 minutes each week, or an average of 6 hours and 52 minutes per day. Obviously, the audiences reached by PTV stations are often discouragingly small. If public stations are serving only a small minority of the listeners in their communities, they are providing to only a very limited degree that "second television service" intended to bring education, information, and culture to the American listening public.

Unfortunately, many operators of public television stations seem relatively unconcerned over the failure of their program offerings to attract substantial audiences. They feel that the function of their stations is to provide instructional materials for use in the classroom and to make available educational and cultural programs to satisfy the needs of a cultured and well-educated minority. If listeners fail to take advantage of the service offered, they maintain that the station is not responsible. A few PTV broadcasters take a different position; they would at least *like* to have their cultural and informative offerings heard by the largest audiences possible; they would also like to reach listeners with only average educational attainments and even the educationally underprivileged, as well as those with a university education. To that end, these station operators schedule some programs with the sole objective of attracting large numbers of listeners—in particular, broadcasts of sports events or even motion picture feature films—in the hope of acquainting more listeners with the availability of service from public stations and of creating some habit of listening to those stations. The policy followed by these station operators is similar to that of the British Broadcasting Corporation, which provides a substantial number of entertainment programs along with the informational materials on the BBC's second or "cultural" television

network, simply to attract a larger audience. Obviously, American
PTV broadcasters are at a considerable disadvantage in this respect; not only does lack of adequate financing make it almost impossible to secure programs of sufficient appeal to attract large
numbers of television viewers, but school administrators and community leaders tend to frown on such efforts to popularize what
they think should be a serious educational effort.

Evaluation of Public Television

America has a "second service" in television, provided by its constantly expanding system of public television stations. Most observers seem to agree that these stations have operated with a reasonably high degree of effectiveness in providing instructional
materials for use in our elementary and secondary schools. However, the stations have been much less successful in their efforts to
provide an educational and cultural service for the adult television
audience. High-quality programs have been offered too infrequently; the number of listeners attracted has been too small. As

". . . Then someone refers to it as the boob tube, and sets us back six months."

Schramm commented on findings of his studies of educational television station audiences, "The loyalty that many ETV viewers feel toward the educational station, the fact that it had a personality for them and an importance, was clearly evident. In the same tone, however, many of the viewers wished that the station had more money to hire needed personnel of high quality, to maintain professional standards of production, to keep on the air longer, to broadcast programs that would be sometimes a little more 'fun,' a little more 'interesting,' a little more 'challenging.'"[5]

A basic problem is money—money to provide better programs, which in turn will attract larger audiences. Some progress is being made; the commitment of the federal government to a "second service" through CPB and PBS has been encouraging and stimulating. Public television has seen its successes with programs like *Upstairs, Downstairs; Jennie; An American Family;* and *The Adams Chronicles.* The agreement between CPB and PBS and the apparent success of the program cooperative are encouraging also and there is every reason to believe that PBS affiliates will have a larger number of outstanding cultural and informative programs available than in the past and that public television will be able to offer a more attractive and more effective "second service" in providing organized information, education, and culture for American television viewers.

Another basic problem with public broadcasting, discussed more fully in Chapter 15, is the lack of a clear sense of purpose in the minds of its leaders. It can be argued that public television has never defined its role in this country. Most agree that it is expected to provide an "alternative broadcasting service" to commercial broadcasting, but the nature of this service remains unclear. Until public broadcasting answers to its own satisfaction the questions of what role to play in our society, what programming to offer, and what audience to appeal to, the availability of more money will do little to upgrade America's "second service."

STUDY AND DISCUSSION QUESTIONS

1. Report on or be prepared to discuss one of the following:

    a. Educational radio before World War II

    b. The designation of specific FM channels for educational use

[5]Schramm, Lyle, and de Sola Pool, *Educational Television*, p. 168.

c. The coordination of educational efforts for the hearings on the designation of educational television channels

d. Educational broadcasting between World War II and the Public Broadcasting Act

e. The influence of the Ford Foundation in the early days of educational television

f. The recommendations of the Carnegie Commission, compared with the realities of the Public Broadcasting Act

g. The financing of the Corporation for Public Broadcasting

h. The growth of National Educational Television (NET)

i. The disputes between CPB and PBS

j. CPB and the Nixon administration

k. The National Station Program Cooperative plan

l. The distinction between public broadcasting, educational broadcasting, and instructional broadcasting

2. Locate an educational radio station in or near your area and analyze its programming as closely as possible. Consider the following:

a. The sources of programming

b. The nature of the music played (format?)

c. The nature of the nonmusical programs aired

d. The balance between local, regional, and national production

e. Target audience for most of the programming on the station

f. Your subjective evaluation of the "success" of the station in serving this audience

3. Prepare a similar analysis of the programming of a public television station in your community or nearby.

4. Report on or be prepared to discuss the sources of income for public radio and television stations.

5. Report on or be prepared to discuss the extent to which financing, program quality, and small audiences continue to affect public broadcasting.

6. Does the public broadcasting service, as it exists at this reading, provide a true "alternative service" to the offerings of commercial broadcasting? Justify your answer.

SUGGESTED READINGS

Robert Blakely. *The People's Instrument: A Philosophy of Programming for Public Television*. Washington, D.C.: Public Affairs Press, 1971.

John E. Burke. *The Public Broadcasting Act of 1967*. Washington, D.C.: National Association of Educational Broadcasters, 1972.

Carnegie Commission on Educational Television. *Public Television: A Program for Action.* New York: Harper & Row, 1967.

Douglass Cater and Michael Nylan, eds. *The Future of Public Broadcasting.* New York: Praeger Publishers, 1976.

S. E. Frost, Jr. *Education's Own Stations.* Chicago: University of Chicago Press, 1937.

John Macy, Jr. *To Irrigate a Wasteland: The Struggle to Shape a Public Television System in the United States.* Berkeley: University of California Press, 1974.

John W. Powell. *Channels of Learning: The Story of Educational Television.* Washington, D.C.: Public Affairs Press, 1962.

Wilbur Schramm, Jack Lyle, and Ithiel de Sola Pool. *The People Look at Educational Television.* Stanford, Calif.: Stanford University Press, 1963.

Wilbur Schramm and Lyle Nelson. *The Financing of Public Televison.* Palo Alto, Calif.: Aspen Institute for Humanistic Studies and the Academy for Educational Development, 1972.

Tracy Tyler. *An Appraisal of Radio Broadcasting in the Land-Grant Colleges and State Universities.* Washington, D.C.: National Committee on Education by Radio, 1933.

Audience Measurement

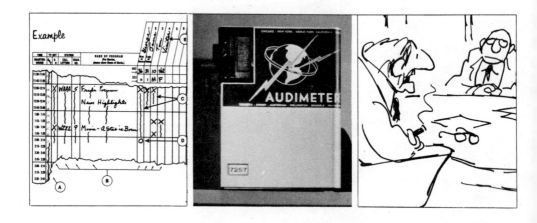

In broadcasting, as in other media that carry advertising, audience measurement is important. When an advertiser pays $25,000 or $30,000 for a full-page advertisement in a national magazine, he knows pretty well what he is getting for his money. The magazine has a guaranteed circulation of, say, 2 million copies each week; consequently, his advertisement will go into 2 million homes and has at least a chance of being seen and possibly read by people living in that number of homes. Similarly, the advertiser who buys space in a local newspaper knows the number of homes in the community in which the newspaper is received and in which the advertisement may perhaps be read. The printed media provide the advertiser with definite figures on circulation.

In the case of broadcasting, "circulation" is not so easily measured. The advertiser who uses radio or television, no less than the newspaper advertiser, is very much interested in the number of homes into which his advertising message is delivered. So the broadcasting industry is forced to provide some system of measurement that will give advertisers an idea of the size of the audience tuned to each program. Networks and stations alike are dependent on audience research—on what some refer to as "the numbers game."

Audience measurement information is provided by several independent research companies not owned or in any way controlled either by broadcasting stations or by networks. The research findings of these companies are published at regular intervals and are made available to those advertisers, advertising agencies, networks, and stations that contract in advance for the service on a regular subscription basis. Some of the major research concerns provide national information on the number of homes tuned to each network program; other companies provide local information concerning program and station audiences in individual cities. For each, national or local, three important measurement figures are reported: (1) a *program rating*, representing the percentage of homes in which, at a given time, sets were tuned into a particular program; (2) a *sets-in-use* figure, indicating for each hour or half-hour period the percentage of area homes in which radio or television sets were being used, regardless of the programs or stations to which they were tuned; and (3) a *share of audience* figure representing, for a given time period, the percentage of sets-in-use homes in which radio or television sets are tuned to a specific program.

Take, for example, a hypothetical community of 100,000 homes. At 9:00 P.M. on a given evening, television sets in 25,000 homes were tuned to Program A. The *rating* of this program would be 25. At that same hour, television sets were being used in a total of 75,000 homes. The *sets-in-use* figure, then, would be 75. Since sets in 25,000 of these 75,000 homes were tuned to Program A, the *share of audience* for this program would be 33.3. If, at the same time, sets in another 10,000 homes were tuned to Program B, the rating of this program would be 10 and its share of audience, 13.3.

Some concerns also provide *time-period ratings*, especially for radio, showing the average percentage of homes in which sets are tuned to each station during each half hour or 15-minute period of an entire week. In some cases, such information is secured over a 4-week span, and results for the period are averaged.

PROGRAM RATINGS

In the commercial system of broadcasting we have in the United States, ratings occupy a position of tremendous importance. Network advertisers buy programs they think will attract large audiences and consequently will receive high ratings; if ratings prove to be low, they withdraw their support, and the program goes off the air. National spot advertisers use local rating figures to select the station in each community on which to place their advertising; the station that falls behind in the ratings race finds itself at a serious disadvantage in its efforts to sell programs or announcement time to advertisers. Program executives of networks are extremely sensitive to ratings; in selecting or developing new programs, they give strong preference to programs of types that have previously attracted large audiences. If the rating of an existing program falls below its earlier level, they either do some frantic "doctoring" to bring the rating up again or begin to look for a replacement to fill the time period. Even in local stations, ratings are widely used as a guide to programming. Television stations buy syndicated programs on the basis of ratings those programs have received in other cities; both television and radio stations plan local program offerings with an eye to their rating potential and drop from their schedules the local presentations that fail to produce satisfactory ratings. Many radio stations have entirely changed their whole pattern and philosophy of programming as a result of consistently low time-ratings that resulted from the programming previously used.

Methods of Securing Rating Information

The companies that provide measurements of the size of listening audiences use a variety of methods in securing the rating informa-

Figure 11-1 The Storage Instantaneous Audimeter (SIA) (left) has replaced the Audimeter (right), used for many years by A. C. Nielsen, which required the viewer to mail the information in. (Courtesy A. C. Nielsen Company)

tion they report. One concern—the A. C. Nielsen Company—has installed *Storage Instantaneous Audimeters* (SIA) in each of some 1,150 television-equipped homes (see Figure 11-1); the homes used have been carefully chosen to provide an accurate cross-section of all families throughout the nation from the standpoint of geographical location, community size, socioeconomic level of the family group, and number of individuals in the household. The SIA unit, attached to the television set or sets in the home, electronically stores information on the exact periods during which the set is in use and the channel to which it is tuned. Each unit is connected by telephone line to a regional Nielsen computer and periodically feeds its stored information to the computer. When this regional information is compiled in a national report, it provides almost a minute-by-minute picture of television program selection and set use throughout the broadcasting day. The Nielsen Company uses its SIAs to provide national television ratings on a weekly basis and to provide overnight rating estimates based on information gathered from the New York, Chicago, and Los Angeles areas. Before 1964, the company also provided national information on radio listening. The American Research Bureau, discussed below, also uses a similar direct-line method of gathering data from a selected sample of television sets for overnight reports from New York, Chicago, and Los Angeles.

A second important method of securing rating information is that of having individuals in a carefully chosen national sample of homes keep *diaries* in which they record all television program listening in which members of the family engage during each day of a selected week—with a separate diary maintained for each set in the house. The diary method is used by a second major program rating

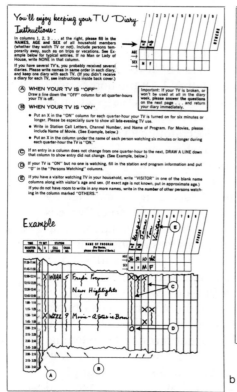
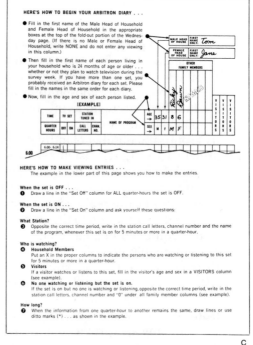

Figure 11–2 Many forms and procedures are used in the gathering and the display of rating information. a. A sample page from the Arbitron viewer diary. (Courtesy American Research Bureau) b. A sample page from the Nielsen diary. (Courtesy A. C. Nielsen Company) c. A sample page from the Arbitron diary. (Courtesy American Research Bureau) d. Arbitron TV audience estimates for the Los Angeles area. (Courtesy American Research Bureau) e. Arbitron radio audience estimates for the Albuquerque area. (Courtesy American Research Bureau)

WEEKLY PROGRAMMING

4 WEEK TIME PERIOD AVERAGES

DAY AND TIME

STATION — PROGRAM

Columns: WEEK-BY-WEEK ADI TV HH RATINGS; ADI TV HH; ADI TV HH SHARE TRENDS; METRO TV HH

TOTAL SURVEY AREA, IN THOUSANDS

TV HOUSE HOLDS | WOMEN | MEN | TEENS | CHILD

SATURDAY

2.00P – 2.30P
- KTLA — RAIN OUT MOV / ANGELS BSBL / MOV SAT AFT T
- KABC — SAT AFTRN MV
- KHJ — FRNTIER FURY
- KTTV — DODGR GAME
- KCOP — SOUL TRAIN
- KCOP — GOMER PYLE
- KMEX — CINE TARDE
- KLXA — N A
- HUT/PVT/TOT

2.30P – 3.00P
- KNXT — SAT EARLY SH
- KNBC — AMBLGN TENNS
- KTLA — PREP SP WRLD / WILDLIFE TH / RAIN OUT MOV / ANGELS BSBL / MOV SAT AFT
- KABC — SAT AFTRN MV / CELEB BOWLNG
- KHJ — FRNTIER FURY
- KTTV — DODGR SCRMBD
- KCOP — OUTER LIMITS / HI CHPRRL SA
- KMEX — CINE TARDE
- KLXA — N A
- HUT/PVT/TOT

3.00P – 3.30P
- KNXT — SAT EARLY SH
- KNBC — WILDLIFE TH / AMBLDN TENNS / NFL ACTION
- KTLA — TWILIGHT ZNE / ANGELS BSBL / MOV SAT AFT
- KABC — SAT AFTRN MV / CELEB TENNIS
- KHJ — BIG WEST MV
- KTTV — SOUL TRAIN / OUTER LIMITS
- KCOP — HI CHPRRL SA
- KMEX — SAL-PIMIENTA
- KLXA — N A
- HUT/PVT/TOT

3.30P – 4.00P
- KNXT — SAT EARLY SH
- KNBC — SATURDAY
- KTLA — WIDE SCRM TH / ANGELS BSBL
- KABC — WATER WORLD
- KHJ — BIG WEST MV
- KTTV — SOUL TRAIN / CREATURE FEA
- KCOP — VIRGINIAN
- KMEX — F FALCON
- KLXA — N A
- KRSC — /MEDI?
- HUT/PVT/TOT

4.00P – 4.30P
- KNXT — SURVIVAL / SPTS SPECTLR
- KNBC — SATURDAY
- KTLA — WIDE SCRM TH / ANGELCRIDE / ANGELS BSBL
- KABC — CELEB TENNIS / HOWL COOKIN
- KHJ — BIG WEST MV
- KTTV — OUTER LIMITS
- KCOP — CREATURE FEA / VIRGINIAN
- KHWY — MATINEE 22
- KMEX — FUTBOL SOCCR
- KLXA — N A
- KRSC — VOICE AGRIC
- HUT/PVT/TOT

4.30P – 5.00P
- KNXT — SPTS SPECTLR
- KNBC — SATURDAY
- KTLA — WIDE SCRM TH / ANGELS BSBL
- KABC — CELEB BOWLNG / BRITISH OPEN
- KHJ — BIG WEST MV
- KTTV — OUTER LIMITS / CREATURE FEA
- KCOP — VIRGINIAN
- KHWY — MATINEE 22
- KMEX — FUTBOL SOCCR

(TECHNICAL DIFFICULTY) / (=B/F PROGRAM AIRED LESS THAN FIVE DAYS) / + PARENT/SATELLITE RELATIONSHIP / *SAMPLE BELOW MINIMUM FOR WEEKLY REPORTING

SATURDAY   JULY   1975   PAGE 64   LOS ANGELES

d

AVERAGE QUARTER-HOUR and CUME Listening Estimates

ALBUQUERQUE
APRIL/MAY 1976

MONDAY-FRIDAY
3.00PM–7.00PM

	WOMEN 18+			WOMEN 18-34			WOMEN 18-49			WOMEN 25-49			WOMEN 25-54			WOMEN 35-64		

Station call letters (left and right): KABG, KAMX, KDEF, KHFM, KKIH, KHYR, KOB, KOB FM, KPAR/KPAR FM·TOTAL, KQEO, KRKE, KRKE FM, KRST, KRZY, KZIA

METRO TOTALS rows shown per demographic group.

MONDAY-FRIDAY 7.00PM–MIDNIGHT

(lower section) — KABG, KDEF, KHFM, KHYR, KOB, KOB FM, KPAR FM·TOTAL, KQEO, KRKE, KRKE FM·TOTAL, KRST, KRZY

METRO TOTALS

FOOTNOTE SYMBOLS (*) means audience estimates adjusted for actual broadcast schedule (-) means AM FM Combination was not simulcast for complete time period.

ARBITRON   PAGE 21

e

NSI AVERAGE WEEK ESTIMATES-4 WEEKS ENDING MAY 26, 1976 — CHICAGO, IL

TUESDAY 5.00PM- 8 00PM

START TIME / STATION / (WEEKS) / PROGRAM	HOUSEHOLDS: DMA% WEEKLY AUDIENCE RATINGS WK 1	WK 2	WK 3	WK 4	MULTI-WEEK AVG RTG	SHR	TREND GUIDE SHARE FEB '76	NOV '75	MAY '75	STATION TOTALS (000) TOTAL HOUSE-HOLDS	PER-SONS 2+	ADULTS	WOMEN 18+	18-34	18-49	25-49	25-54	25-64	50+	WKG WMN TOTAL	FEMALE 15-24
	46	47	48	49	3	4	5	6	7	2	9	10	11	12	13	14	15	16	17	19	20
R.S.E. THRESHOLDS 25-49%	3	3	3	3	1					23	46	33	22	23	23	20	20	19	18	21	24
(1 S.E.) 4 WK AVG 50+%	1	1	1	1	17					6	12	8	6	6	6	5	5	5	4	5	6
5.00 WBBM CH 2 NWS-5	5	5	5	7	5	14	17X			150	202	190	117	15	41	38	51	78	76	24	4
WFLD MONKEES	6	6	3	3	4	12	12X			124	217	42	24	24	24	7	7	7		8	31
WGN I DRM-JEANNIE	8	12	11	8	10	26	25X			287	549	294	176	101	144	79	89	101	32	44	95
WLS DRURY-MURPHY H	10	15	11	12	12	32	31X			327	445	411	256	79	128	90	112	168	128	56	45
WMAQ NWSCENTER 5-5	3	7	2	5	4	11	9X			125	160	152	92	13	25	18	34	54	67	20	8
WSNS LEAVE-TO BEAVR	2	4	2	2	2	6	4X			67	139	65	52	24	42	22	28	29	10	15	29
WTTW SESAME STREET	1	<<	2	1	1	2	5X			26	39	4	2	2	2	2	2	2		1	
HUT & TOTALS *	33	44	35	36	37		48			1106	1751	1158	719	258	406	256	323	439	313	168	212
5.15 WBBM CH 2 NWS-5	4	5	6	6	5	13	15X			146	197	187	115	13	43	40	53	77	72	22	4
WFLD MONKEES	6	5	4	4	5	12	12X			129	216	37	19	19	19	4	4	4		6	31
WGN I DRM-JEANNIE	11	13	11	11	12	29	29X			338	642	336	203	115	162	87	99	114	41	51	113
WLS DRURY-MURPHY H	12	14	11	12	12	31	28X			335	447	420	258	74	125	89	110	169	133	53	40
WMAQ NWSCENTER 5-5	3	6	3	5	4	11	8X			127	163	155	93	15	27	19	35	54	66	22	9
WSNS LEAVE-TO BEAVR	2	3	2	2	2	5	3X			66	132	62	46	21	37	19	24	25	9	14	26
WTTW SESAME STREET	1	2	2	1	1	4	5X			39	54	6	4	4	4	4	4	4		3	
HUT & TOTALS *	35	44	39	39	39		52			1180	1851	1203	738	261	417	262	329	447	321	171	223
5.30 WBBM CBS EVE NWS	5	5	7	8	6	15	12X			174	240	235	134	21	48	43	57	85	86	30	6
WFLD PARTRIDGE FMLY	6	7	6	4	6	14	18X			161	335	74	47	35	43	24	26	28	4	8	44
WGN BEWITCHED	10	14	9	10	11	27	31X			331	584	350	226	126	172	93	109	130	54	65	103
WLS ABC N-REASONER	10	12	10	11	11	27	23X			299	421	392	230	55	102	76	104	151	128	52	30
WMAQ NWSCENTER 5-5	4	4	4	5	4	11	10X			124	168	160	96	18	31	21	34	56	65	20	11
WSNS GOMR PYLE USMC	2	1	2	1	1	4	1X			45	87	51	26	21	22	12	12	13	4	15	14
WTTW SESAME STREET	1	1	2	<<	1	3	6X			31	54	7	5	5	5	5	5	5		2	
HUT & TOTALS *	37	43	40	40	40		53			1165	1889	1269	764	281	423	274	347	468	341	192	208
5.45 WBBM CBS EVE NWS	6	5	7	9	7	16	13X			188	261	255	147	26	54	47	62	93	93	36	8
WFLD PARTRIDGE FMLY	7	8	5	5	6	15	19X			177	372	89	55	40	50	29	32	34	5	8	47
WGN BEWITCHED	11	14	11	11	12	28	32X			352	622	380	243	139	187	99	117	138	56	73	116
WLS ABC N-REASONER	10	12	11	9	10	25	23X			284	387	370	213	51	90	67	95	139	123	50	27
WMAQ NWSCENTER 5-5	4	5	5	5	5	11	10X			131	175	168	99	18	32	22	35	58	67	22	11
WSNS GOMR PYLE USMC	1	1	2	1	1	3	1X			42	82	48	25	20	21	12	12	13	4	14	13
WTTW SESAME STREET	<<	3	2	1	1	3	4X			41	70	10	7	7	7	7	7	7		2	
HUT & TOTALS *	39	45	42	40	42		55			1215	1969	1320	789	301	441	283	360	482	348	205	222
6.00 WBBM CH 2 NWS-6	8	5	8	7	7	16	14X			203	305	282	160	35	62	54	69	106	98	40	9
WFLD BRADY BUNCH	7	9	7	8	8	18	22X			220	504	150	92	62	83	52	56	58	9	26	67
WGN ANDY GRIFFITH	12	13	11	12	12	27	28X			362	644	465	294	159	210	111	131	160	84	99	117
WLS EYEWIT NWS 6	9	13	8	8	9	22	23X			262	406	377	201	44	88	72	99	140	113	58	20
WMAQ NBC NITELY NWS	5	6	5	5	5	12	9X			154	205	203	115	19	33	27	39	68	82	31	6
WSNS REG/BOB ELSON	<<				1	2	3			35	45	41	19	12	18	11	11	12	1	11	8
234 ROOM 222		1	2	2	1	3				47	61	55	33	21	31	19	19	20	2	18	13
WTTW ELECTRIC COMPANY	<<	1	1	1	1	2	3X			25	44	9	7	7	7	6	6	6			1
HUT & TOTALS *	42	47	43	42	43		57			1261	2153	1527	888	338	501	333	411	550	387	265	228
6.15 WBBM CH 2 NWS-6	8	7	8	9	8	17	14X			219	325	299	167	34	67	60	76	115	100	43	8
WFLD BRADY BUNCH	7	10	8	9	9	19	23X			247	554	175	103	70	92	56	60	62	11	30	76
WGN ANDY GRIFFITH	12	10	11	13	11	25	26X			348	614	445	284	153	200	106	125	153	84	96	112
WLS EYEWIT NWS 6	9	13	11	9	11	23	23X			290	435	410	220	49	98	78	109	154	122	67	21
WMAQ NBC NITELY NWS	6	6	5	5	5	12	9X			156	212	210	120	22	37	28	40	71	83	34	9
WSNS REG/ON DECK	<<				1	2	4			34	43	39	20	9	13	8	8	11	7	12	6
234 ROOM 222		1	2	1	1	3				42	53	47	27	17	25	15	15	16	2	15	11
WTTW ELECTR. COMPNY	<<	1	2	1	1	2	3X			25	44	9	7	7	7	5	5	5			2
HUT & TOTALS *	43	49	45	46	46		60			1319	2227	1587	921	344	514	341	423	571	407	282	234
6.30 WBBM CH 2 NWS-6	9	5	8	8	7	16	14X			211	317	296	155	30	61	55	71	111	94	40	8
WFLD ADAM 12	9	11	6	7	8	17	19X			227	474	242	151	83	113	77	83	102	38	43	55
WGN DICK VAN DYKE	9	11	11	10	10	22	22X			308	538	343	197	97	142	90	102	119	55	74	82
WLS EYEWIT NWS 6	8	11	11	8	9	20	21X			258	399	371	196	45	88	69	101	137	108	62	20
WMAQ NAME THAT TUNE	9	10	7	8	9	19	18X			248	418	366	225	73	101	73	93	143	124	57	35
WSNS REG/WHITE SOX BSBL	3				1	2	1			38	55	43	19	5	8	7	10	14	11	6	2
234 TO TELL TRUTH		1	1	1	1	1				22	35	27	18	4	8	7	10	13	16	4	3
WTTW ZOOM	2	2	2	2	2	5	8			60	107	18	11	10	11	10	10	10		1	1
HUT & TOTALS *	47	50	45	43	46		61			1350	2308	1679	954	343	524	381	470	636	430	283	203
7.00 WBBM REG/EAGLE CM HOME		9			12	25	22			346	673	395	225	83	125	95	118	155	100	64	34
134 [illegible]	16		12	13	13	27				371	820	395	213	106	147	109	127	153	66	63	45
WFLD REG/NHL PLAYOFF		3			3	6	5			88	111	104	54	5	15	13	21	31	39	10	2
134 IRONSIDE	3		3	3	3	6				89	107	104	69	3	15	15	25	43	54	11	
WGN STAR TREK	6	6	6	7	6	12	10			188	272	203	82	43	62	43	49	54	20	21	23
WLS HAPPY DAYS	20	26	22	18	21	42	43			591	1321	824	475	231	350	229	261	313	125	172	190
WMAQ REG/W-MAGC/FNNIES		11		4	8	15	16			217	403	306	167	32	64	54	70	107	103	41	15
13 RICH LITTLE	7		8		8	15				208	338	297	166	26	57	45	61	89	109	32	17
WSNS REG/WHITE /CNTRY	4	1			2	3	1			54	72	65	26	5	9	8	12	20	17	11	1
34 NASHVLL MUSIC			1	1	1	2				36	58	56	32	7	12	11	19	23	20	15	2
WTTW REG/IN BEGINNING				3	1	2	5			34	53	45	28	3	11	11	13	19	17	9	1
123 NOVA	1	1	<<		1	1				22	36	29	17	1	6	6	8	11	11	5	1
HUT & TOTALS *	53	54	50	46	51		68														
7.30 WBBM REG/EAGLE CM HOME		11			14	26	18														
134 GOOD TIMES	16		14	15	15	28															
WFLD REG/NHL PLAYOFF		1			2	4	5														
134 IRONSIDE	3		3	2	3	5															
WGN STAR TREK	7	7	4	9	7	12	10														
WLS LAVERNE&SHIRLY	24	23	20	19	22	41	45														
WMAQ REG/W-MAGC/FNNIES		12		5	8	15	21														
13 RICH LITTLE	7		7		7	13															
WSNS REG/WHITE /BOB+ON	4		1		2	3	1														
24 MOV 44		1		1	1	1															
WTTW REG/IN BEGINNING				3	1	2	3														
123 NOVA	2	1	1		1	2															
HUT & TOTALS *	57	54	50	51	53		68														
	46	47	48	49	3	4	5	6	7												

TIME PERIOD

N.B. All data should be used recognizing sampling errors described in Section IV. In addition, 4-week averag standard error in the range of 25-49% or 50+% at the one standard error level. For additional relative sta first page of this section.
NOTE: Relative Error estimates of weekly ratings are based on average weekly sample data. 54

f

g

The Pulse Inc.

CLEVELAND RSA
JAN-FEB, 1975

MEN 18-49
C.Z.= 3970
RSA = 6491

STATION	MONDAY-FRIDAY 7 PM-12 MID R.S.A. AVG. PERS. (00)	R.S.A. CUME PERS. (00)	CENTRAL ZONE AVG. PERS. (00)	CENTRAL ZONE AVG. PERS. RTG.	CENTRAL ZONE CUME PERS. (00)	SATURDAY 6 AM-10 AM CENTRAL ZONE AVG. PERS. (00)	AVG. PERS. RTG.	10 AM-3 PM CENTRAL ZONE AVG. PERS. (00)	AVG. PERS. RTG.	3 PM-7 PM CENTRAL ZONE AVG. PERS. (00)	AVG. PERS. RTG.	7 PM-12 MID CENTRAL ZONE AVG. PERS. (00)	AVG. PERS. RTG.
WABO						15	.4	141	3.6	39	1.0		
WCLV	55	203	55	1.4	180			4	.1	13	.3	2	.1
WDBN	16	80	7	.2	62	9	.2	12	.3	2	.1	35	.9
WDOK	19	303	19	.5	275			21	.5	30	.8	5	.1
WERE	75	395	75	1.9	377	16	.4	52	1.3	87	2.2	23	.6
WGAR	50	423	19	.5	271	17	.4	10	.3	20	.5	3	.1
WGCL	23	383	19	.5	310	29	.7	50	1.3	37	.9	2	.1
WHK	30	231	15	.4	185	44	1.1	99	2.5	82	2.1	16	.4
WIXY	30	201	30	.8	261	42	1.1	21	.5	25	.6		
WJMO	57	448	57	1.4	448	150	3.8	329	8.3	300	7.6	194	4.9
WJW	7	61	7	.2	61	24	.6	18	.5			10	.3
WLYT	21	153	21	.5	153					58	1.5	22	.6
WMMS	226	1168	90	2.3	447	13	.3	142	3.6	177	4.5	66	1.7
WNCR	82	228	20	.5	112	11	.3	15	.4	14	.4	2	.1
WPVL	7	18	7	.2	18								
WQAL	39	211	39	1.0	194	12	.3	34	.9	30	.8	3	.1
WWWE	57	407	45	1.1	361	11	.3	57	1.4	90	2.3	1	
WKEN										4	.1		
CKLW	19	115	19	.5	111	37	.9	68	1.7				
WSLR	13	116			13	5	.1	29	.7	5	.1		
TOTAL			564	14.2	2626	435	11.0	1121	28.2	1047	26.4	384	9.7

STATION	MONDAY-FRIDAY 3 PM-12 MID R.S.A. AVG. PERS. (00)	R.S.A. CUME PERS. (00)	CENTRAL ZONE AVG. PERS. (00)	CENTRAL ZONE AVG. PERS. RTG.	CENTRAL ZONE CUME PERS. (00)	SUNDAY 6 AM-10 AM CENTRAL ZONE AVG. PERS. (00)	AVG. PERS. RTG.	10 AM-3 PM CENTRAL ZONE AVG. PERS. (00)	AVG. PERS. RTG.	3 PM-7 PM CENTRAL ZONE AVG. PERS. (00)	AVG. PERS. RTG.	7 PM-12 MID CENTRAL ZONE AVG. PERS. (00)	AVG. PERS. RTG.
WABO	14	340	14	.4	340	15	.4	189	4.8	68	1.7		
WCLV	50	226	45	1.1	203					11	.3		
WDBN	21	127	12	.3	83	9	.2	3	.1			9	.2
WDOK	31	435	31	.8	367	22	.6	73	1.8	53	1.3		
WERE	70	660	70	1.8	643	33	.8	51	1.3	69	1.7	28	.7
WGAR	74	921	27	.7	528	15	.4	61	1.5	30	.8	19	.5
WGCL	32	587	29	.7	391			17	.4	8	.2	19	.5
WHK	50	714	38	1.0	447	5	.1	72	1.8	82	2.1	35	.9
WIXY	58	482	58	1.5	465	42	1.1	52	1.3	6	.2		
WJMO	83	603	83	2.1	585	38	1.0	89	2.2	264	6.6	141	3.6
WJW	35	335	35	.9	317	38	1.0	35	.9	20	.5	10	.3
WLYT	19	292	13	.3	159					4	.1	6	.2
WMMS	235	1278	86	2.2	487	15	.4	67	1.7	159	4.0	135	3.4
WNCR	75	367	23	.6	168			24	.6	47	1.2	13	.3
WPVL	6	34	6	.2	34								
WQAL	33	259	33	.8	242	11	.3	53	1.3	61	1.5	19	.5
WWWF	50	586	44	1.1	487	15	.4	51	1.3	71	1.8		
WKEN		40			40	4	.1	3	.1			3	.1
CKLW	28	323	28	.7	194	12	.3	19	.5	48	1.2	29	.7
WSLR	40	300	2	.1	69							15	.4
TOTAL			708	17.8	3637	274	6.9	883	22.2	1035	26.1	480	12.1

Page 7

Figure 11–2 *(cont.)*
f. A Nielsen weekly TV audience estimate for the Chicago area. (Courtesy A. C. Nielsen Company) g. A two-month radio audience estimate for the Cleveland area by The Pulse, Inc. (Courtesy The Pulse, Inc.)

service, the American Research Bureau (ARB). The ARB national ratings for network television programs, which it calls its Arbitron Television Reports, are based on diaries kept in approximately 2,400 different homes representing city and rural areas in all sections of the United States—a completely different sample being used for each report. Diaries also provide the data for ARB local television and local radio rating information. Sample sizes for local ratings vary with the size of the market and average between 600 and 700 per market. The Nielsen company uses the diary method as a basis for most of its local television rating reports in major markets.

A third method of securing audience information is the *personal interview* technique with listeners in homes selected on a controlled random basis in communities in which audience measurements are to be supplied. This technique is used by The Pulse, Inc., a firm that specializes in local rating information. Pulse interviewers call at a different group of homes on each day of the week and ask members of the family who are available to indicate, on a roster listing all station call letters and dial positions that the interviewer supplies, those stations tuned in during each quarter hour on the day preceding the interview or during the previous Saturday or Sunday. All interviewing is done after 6:00 P.M. when more members of the family will be home; out-of-home listening as well as that in the home is reported. In a typical market, rating information in each report is based on interviews in 1,000 or more homes in the central area and up to a total of 2,000 in the total listening area. Interviews are usually spread out over a period of from 8 to 10 weeks to insure that results will not be unduly influenced by unusual conditions occurring in any one week.

The diary and personal interview techniques, of course, require considerable time to tabulate the results. Some delay is also inherent in the national Nielsen SIA information, but both Nielsen and ARB offer the so-called overnight services based on data from a few major markets. A fourth research procedure, the *coincidental telephone survey* technique, was once used to secure "quick" ratings. In this method, telephone numbers were chosen at random in some 20 or 25 major cities and interviewers placed calls to the homes so selected during the periods in which network programs were actually being broadcast. When a phone call was completed, the respondent was asked whether the television or radio set was in use at the time the telephone rang and, if so, to name the program to which the set was tuned. By the mid-1970s, this technique was seldom used for national ratings, but one firm, Trendex, Inc., was still using the

"According to *this* survey, the public wants sex and violence in *commercials*."

telephone to gather data for special local reports for radio stations. Such reports provide information on attitudes toward station personalities, station "image" in the community, a profile of the station's audience, and other specialized items of information that could be of use to station management. Individual stations also use this method to secure their own information.

All the major research firms, in both national and local ratings, have always provided gross data on the total number of listeners to radio or television in a given time period. Since the mid-1960s, however, demand has increased for more detailed information about the nature of a given audience. To meet this demand, the rating services now provide such demographic information as the age and sex of the members of this audience. Some reports also include information on income, education, size of family, and occupation of head of family.

The Sampling Principle

Although commercial rating services use a variety of techniques in securing information about listeners, all the methods are alike in one respect: all are based on the principle of *sampling*, or of providing rating figures on the basis of information secured from a sample of the whole population. Since it would obviously be much too expensive to secure data about listening every week or every month from every home in even a single community, the research organizations get information from a relatively small number of homes in the area studied. In most instances, these homes are chosen on a *random* basis—for example, by including in the sample only those householders whose names happen to appear at the tops of columns on pages in a telephone book or city directory. This smaller number of homes is presumably an accurate cross-section of all of the homes in the community. If the sample chosen actually is a good cross-section, then the program selection and listening behavior of families in the sample group should be representative of the program selection and listening engaged in by all the families in the community. If a rating company finds that 15 percent of the sample families tuned their sets to a specified program on a certain date, it is assumed that the program in question was similarly tuned in on that date by 15 percent of all of the families in that community, and a rating of 15.0 is reported for that program.

Of course, the idea of sampling is not used solely by concerns engaged in radio and television research. The same principle is applied in national public opinion polls, the results of which are published in daily newspapers. Manufacturers of automobiles use information secured from a sample of the buying public to check reactions to proposed changes in the design of cars; samples of housewives are used to test new cake mixes or salad dressings. The federal government itself makes extensive use of sampling procedures for its reports on business conditions, total employment, changes in retail prices of consumer goods, the estimated size of the wheat crop for the coming year, and the like.

Interpretation of Ratings

By their use of carefully selected nationwide samples, the major rating organizations are able to provide clients, at specified intervals, with a national rating for each sponsored network program. National ratings are usually released once a week, at least during the "broadcasting season" extending from October through March or April. The Nielsen company issues national television rating reports on a year-round basis. Similarly, the organizations that give local radio or television listening information can, by use of local samples, provide local ratings for radio or television programs broadcast by stations serving each local area. In either instance, as previously noted, the rating is a figure representing the percentage of homes in the rating area in which, on a specified date, television sets or radio sets were tuned to the program for which the rating is given.

At this point, several facts concerning ratings must be remembered. First, with the exception of ratings gathered from diaries, ratings represent *percentages of homes, not of individuals*, since only on rare occasions would all of the members of the family in every household studied be at home and watching the same television program or listening to the same radio station. As a practical matter, the percentage of *individuals* living in the community who would listen to any program would always be considerably less than the percentage figure used as the program's rating; as a general rule, some members of each "listening" household will be away from home while the program is on the air or perhaps in a different part of the house where they are not actually "listeners" to the program. Second, television ratings at least are based only on those *homes that have receiving sets.* Research organizations estimate that at the beginning of 1975 approximately 97 percent of all homes were equipped with television receiving sets—nearly 68.5 million of the nation's more than 70 million homes. In major cities, however, or other communities with local television service, probably 98 or 99 percent of all families had television sets. In view of the somewhat higher incidence of radio set ownership throughout the country, radio ratings are usually based on the total number of homes in the area considered.

A third fact, and one that is highly important, is that *ratings are not completely accurate measurements*. After all, they are based on information provided by only a sample of the whole population, and sometimes by only a rather limited sample. The best assurance that statisticians will give is that 95 times out of 100, a national rating of 10.0 for a network program, based on a national sample of 1,500 homes, will be not more than 1.5 rating points away from the actual percentage of homes from coast to coast that were tuned to the program in question. Similarly, a national rating of 20.0 can be expected to be within 2.0 rating points of the true percentage of homes with sets tuned to the program. Local ratings, based on much smaller samples, are less accurate. Assuming that the sample consists of 300 homes, for example, a reported rating of 10.0 will, in 95 cases out of 100, be within 3.4 rating points of showing the actual percentage of homes tuned to the program. Stated differently, with a rating of 10.0 reported by a sample of only 300 homes, the true percentage will not be less than 6.6 nor more than 13.4. These allowances, according to statisticians, must be made to compensate for errors due to chance in the selection of a sample that accurately represents the entire population.

There is, however, some evidence to indicate that rating figures do represent a reasonably accurate picture of the relative popularity of various programs. An examination of the information obtained from natural surveys made by two different organizations, using different methods and different samples, shows remarkable similarities. Consider, for example, the rankings of the top 20 network television programs for the month of January 1975 as compiled by the A. C. Nielsen Company (using a sample of 1,150 homes) and the rankings compiled by the American Research Bureau (using a sample of 98,000 homes). These rankings are listed in Table 11-1.

Table 11–1 Comparative Ratings of the Top-20 Network Television Programs for January 1975 as Compiled by Two Rating Services

A. C. Nielsen	American Research Bureau
1. All in the Family	1. Sanford and Son
2. Sanford and Son	2. All in the Family
3. Chico and the Man	3. The Waltons
4. M.A.S.H.	4. Rhoda
5. Rhoda	5. Chico and the Man
6. The Waltons	6. M.A.S.H.
7. Maude	7. Little House on the Prairie
8. Good Times	8. Good Times
9. Hawaii Five-O	9. Hawaii Five-O
10. World of Disney	10. Cannon
11. Little House on the Prairie	11. ABC Sunday Night Movie
12. Mary Tyler Moore	12. World of Disney
13. Bob Newhart	13. Maude
14. NBC Sunday Mystery Movie	14. NBC Sunday Mystery Movie
15. Kojak	15. Mary Tyler Moore
16. Rockford Files	16. NBC Monday Night Movie
17. Medical Center	17. Rockford Files
18. Streets of San Francisco	18. Gunsmoke
19. Gunsmoke	19. Bob Newhart
20. The Rookies	20. Streets of San Francisco

Information gathered by the A. C. Nielsen Company and the American Research Bureau and reported in *Hollywood Television Report*, January 28, 1975.

The Values of Ratings

If program ratings are not completely accurate measures of the proportions of homes tuned to broadcast programs, why are they so extensively used? Simply because in a commercial system of broadcasting, some reasonably effective estimate of the size of each program's audience is needed, and ratings do provide what are at worst fairly close approximations. They allow broadcasters and advertisers to make comparisons between programs—to judge whether a given program is more attractive or less attractive to listeners than are other programs broadcast in comparable segments of the broadcasting day. They offer a reasonably accurate index to the relative popularity of various kinds of programs. They allow sponsors and program executives to determine whether programs in which they are interested are gaining in popularity, as compared with the situation a month or a year ago, or whether they are losing their attractiveness to listeners. Similarly, rating reports allow broadcasters to note the changes taking place in the tastes and preferences of the listening public by observing the rise or the decline in average ratings reported for programs of various types.

In addition, ratings give the advertisers a basis for estimating the approximate number of homes the program including his commercial announcement reaches each week, a figure roughly approximating the "circulation" figure of a magazine or newspaper. If, for example, his network television program has an average rating of 20.0, he knows that it has been tuned in by listeners in approximately 20 percent of the nearly 68.5 million homes in this country that have television receiving sets, or in about 14 million homes. A rating of 30.0 for the same program would mean that it was received in approximately 20.5 million homes—and even allowing for possible inaccuracies in the rating figure, the difference is quite a substantial one. Rating companies usually provide such projections of ratings in the form of a total-homes-reached figure for each program, in both their national and their local rating reports.

The major research companies sometimes also offer a special service to advertisers who sponsor five-times-a-week programs—a report on the *unduplicated cumulative audience* reached by the series in its various broadcasts throughout the week. A five-times-a-week news program, for example, might have an average rating of 6.0 for the five days it is broadcast; but, by reaching different homes on different days, the program might in the course of a week be heard at least once in as great a total number of homes as a once-a-week program with a rating of 15.0 or more.

Qualitative Information

Of decided value to advertisers, too, is information made available concerning the *kinds of individuals* included in the audience of each network television program. As early as 1940, the rating companies then in existence reported on the proportions of men, of women, and of children included in the audience of each network radio program. Similar information is now given in the local radio rating reports provided by Pulse, Inc., but with a separate category added for teenage listeners. The American Research Bureau gives considerably more demographic information in both its national and local reports, including for each sponsored program not only a rating figure and an estimate of the number of homes in the survey area tuned to the program but also a fairly detailed analysis of the number and types of listeners included in the program's audience. The same type of information is given in local reports of the A. C. Nielsen Company. One research organization some years ago issued

"Gentlemen, we'll have to rethink our program objectives immediately, it seems that the median age of our daytime audience is 3½."

periodic reports showing, for each network television program, the number of listeners in each 100 homes tuned to the program who were regular users of each of a variety of types of products from prepared cake mixes to filter cigarettes and from safety razors or home permanents to instant coffee. The value of information of this type to advertisers is obvious and is no less valuable than information concerning the age and sex of listeners tuned to specific stations or specific network programs.

Other types of qualitative information about audiences are supplied by a number of research organizations that do not offer a rating service. One such concern, the Home Testing Institute, reports the "TvQ scores" given network television programs by various types of listeners. A TvQ score is an index showing the percentage of listeners in various sex, age, and educational categories who *like* the program—consider it "one of their favorites." For each sponsored program, separate TvQ scores are given for men and for women on each of several age levels and in each educational group, as well as for listeners living in communities of different sizes and in different sections of the country. The Home Testing Institute contends that the TvQ score is not only an index to the degree of liking expressed for the program, but also serves as a fairly reliable measure of the amount of attention listeners are likely to give the program scored.

Variations in Program Ratings

Since ratings show the proportions of homes tuned to various programs, it is generally assumed that they also provide an accurate index to the attractiveness of those programs to listeners generally. On the whole, this is a reasonable assumption; at least, a program that receives an unusually high rating must be one that large numbers of listeners find interesting. However, ratings are also affected by factors in no way related to the basic attractiveness of the programs themselves. For example, a television program broadcast during evening hours usually receives a much higher rating than one presented during the daytime; more people watch television at night than during daytime hours. In January of 1975, for instance, Nielsen estimated that television was watched in approximately 20 percent of all television households between the hours of 9:00 and 10:00 A.M. and that this figure jumped to 66 percent for the 9:00 to 10:00 P.M. hour (see Table 11-2). The season of the year also influences ratings of evening television programs; people simply do not watch television so much in the evening during summer months

Table 11–2   Estimates of Hour-by-Hour Television Usage—January 1977

Hour Beginning[a,b]	Percent of U. S. TV Households[c]	Hour Beginning[a,b]	Percent of U. S. TV Households[c]
7:00 A.M.	7.7	4:00	39.6
8:00	14.8	5:00	48.1
9:00	19.8	6:00	57.9
10:00	23.5	7:00	63.2
11:00	26.8	8:00	67.4
12:00 Noon	30.5	9:00	66.5
1:00 P.M.	32.1	10:00	60.4
2:00	32.3	11:00	41.6
3:00	34.7	12:00 Midnight	24.9

[a] Measured Monday through Friday, 7:00 A.M. to 5:00 P.M.

[b] New York time, except for New York time plus 3 hours in Pacific time zone.

[c] Average percent each minute in hour noted.

Figures compiled by the A. C. Nielsen Company.

as during the winter, partly because they spend less time in the house when the weather is warm, and partly because summer television schedules are largely filled with reruns of programs previously broadcast. Average per-day viewing hours drop from a high of almost 7 in January to a low of below 5.5 in July—a decrease of almost 20 percent (see Table 11-3).

Table 11–3   Estimated Average Hours per Day of In-Home Use of Television Sets During Different Months of the Year

Month	Average hours sets used per day	Month[a]	Average hours sets used per day
January	7.27	July	5.55
February	6.91	August	5.73
March	6.54	September	6.05
April	6.08	October	6.48
May	5.54	November	6.82
June	5.40	December	6.86

[a] Months of July through December were for 1976; of January through June for 1977.

Figures compiled by A. C. Nielsen Company.

A third factor with a decided effect on the rating of any program is its position in the network or station schedule. If the program must compete with an unusually popular program presented at the same hour on a different network or a different station, its rating will naturally be lower than it would be if the competition were weaker. Frequently a program benefits from its position in the schedule; if it precedes or follows an unusually popular program, there may be a substantial lead-in or carryover audience, resulting in a higher rating. Still another factor affecting ratings is the amount of promotion and publicity given each program by its sponsor or by the network. Sometimes a relatively weak program receives a fairly high rating simply as a result of the advance publicity it has received. However, publicity alone will not bring a continuation of high ratings to a program series lacking in basic listener attractiveness; after one or two experiences with the program, the listener will turn to the offerings of other stations or simply turn off the set.

Factors Affecting Local Ratings   Local television ratings are affected by the same factors, as well as by at least three others of considerable importance. First of these is the number of stations that serve the community. Sets-in-use figures do not vary too greatly from one community to the next, at the same hour and the same time of the year. If between eight and nine o'clock in the evening, the sets-in-use figure is 60.0 in a market with only two stations, that 60.0 figure will be divided between the two programs available; if the market is one with four stations, however, there are four programs among which to divide the 60 rating points the sets-in-use figure represents.

A second important factor is the degree of "prestige" enjoyed by the station that carries the program in the local area. If the program is broadcast by a very popular station, one to which listeners tune in more frequently than to other local stations, the program's rating will probably be much higher than it would be if the same program were broadcast over a less popular station in the community.

A third factor is the degree to which stations in the market change or improve their programming during those periods in which data for ratings are being gathered. Rating "sweeps" are made only periodically in local markets and their times are known by the station management. During these periods television stations tend to air their best feature films and otherwise upgrade their programming in an effort to obtain the best possible rating figures.

Some radio stations have gone so far as to schedule contests with large prizes and extensive promotion in an effort to "buy" a large audience during the rating period. However, this practice, known as "hypoing," has been forbidden by the FCC, and stations attempting to "hypo" their ratings in this way can be assessed stiff fines.

Radio Program and Time-Block Ratings   With radio networks carrying few sponsored programs more than 5 minutes in length, it is difficult to draw conclusions about the ratings of radio network programs. However, at least on the local level, the same factors operating in television affect both total radio listening and the ratings received by programs or by time-blocks on radio stations. Hour of the day is important, just as it is in television; in the case of radio, however, the greatest amount of in-home listening in practically every community comes between the hours of seven and eleven o'clock in the *morning*, when it generally exceeds television viewing over the same period. Afternoon radio listening is substantially lower; and, as a result of the competition from television, the amount of in-home listening to radio after 7:00 p.m. is less than a third as great as that reported for morning hours.

Figures for in-home radio listening are misleading, however, because radio has become such a portable medium. Morning and afternoon audiences are inflated considerably by in-car listenership during drive-time hours and total late afternoon radio audiences are estimated to be almost as high as those in the morning. Portable radios also add significant numbers to radio audiences, especially in the afternoons when teenagers are released from school.

Seasonal variations in radio listening are less important than in television; although in-home use of radio sets is somewhat less during summer months than in the winter, the decrease is probably offset by a greater amount of out-of-the-home listening during warmer weather. The average time-block ratings of any radio station are naturally affected by the number of stations that serve the community; if the total amount of listening done is divided among eight or ten stations, the proportion of homes tuned to any one of that number is necessarily much smaller than if signals of only three or four stations are available. Relative popularity of individual stations seems to be a much more important factor in radio than in television ; a listener who tunes in a well-liked radio station tends to stay tuned to that one station as long as his set is in use, especially in view of the fact that distinct changes in program materials at 15- or 30-minute intervals have all but disappeared from radio.

RATINGS AND PROGRAMMING

As has already been noted, ratings provide much-needed information for advertisers who use radio or television; they are also of great value to program executives of networks or stations and to those who plan and develop new programs. Philip von Ladau's excellent analysis of how ratings can be used as an aid to programming was published in 1976 in the official publication of the Institute of Broadcasting Financial Management.[1] The author has granted permission to include significant portions of his analysis in this section. Although his comments were directed toward the programming of local television stations, many of the principles he outlined apply to network programming as well.

Use of Ratings in the Selection and Scheduling of New Programs

Von Ladau begins by pointing out that it is generally necessary to take into account in programming a television station the following five basic considerations:

1. *Program selection*—what programs shall be used
2. *Time-period placement*—where the programs shall be placed in the schedule
3. *Sequencing*—which programs go next to which
4. *Competition*—what is most likely to oppose each program
5. *Cost of each property*—how much a program costs and how much advertising must be secured to make it profitable

He goes on to discuss ten basic programming principles to be followed in preparing the schedule for a local television station.

1. *Attack when shares of audience are equally divided.* It is assumed that most programs can increase audiences primarily at the expense of other programs on the air at the same time. Few programs, in other words, can be relied upon to attract many new listeners from among those not regularly using television at a particular hour. Given this assumption, it is easier to take a little audience from each of several stations than a lot of audience from a dominant program.

---

[1]Philip von Ladau, "Ratings: An Aid to Programming and Purchase of TV Properties," *Broadcast Financial Journal*, Vol. 5, No. 1 (March 1976), p. 36.

2. *Build both ways from a strong program*. The advantages of following a strong program are fairly obvious. The new program can capitalize on the tendency of listeners to keep sets tuned to the same station unless strongly motivated to change channels. The new program is sampled, then, by fans of the previous show and is judged by its ability to hold the lead-in audience. A new program placed before a strong existing show can benefit from sampling that comes from early tune-ins, although this influence is probably somewhat less significant than the benefit from following a strong program.

3. *Sequence programs demographically*. When putting together a sequence of programs, the programmer should take care to be sure the potential audience for one program is not too different from that of the preceding or following programs. This helps avoid unnecessary audience turnover from program to program.

4. *When a change in appeal is called for, accomplish it in easy stages*. At a time in which audience composition is changing, such as late afternoon on weekdays when schoolchildren are entering the audience, or when stiff competition from another program dictates a change, make the change with a program that will hold as large a share of the preceding audience as possible. Do not try to change completely the demographic appeal.

5. *Place "new" programs at time periods of greatest tune-in*. It is easier to introduce a program during periods when the sets-in-use figure is high than when it is low because the new programs benefit from free advertising through happenstance sampling. Because people generally leave sets tuned to the station last used, at times of increasing set usage a significant number of people may inadvertently be exposed to the new show.

6. *Keep a "winning" program in its current position*. It is tempting to consider shoring up a weak position on the schedule by moving in an already successful series and this has, at times, been tried successfully by the networks. It is wiser, however, as a general principle, to avoid tinkering with success. Unless changing competition forces a move, it is best to leave a successful program in the time period at which people are in the habit of finding it. An audience loss is risked by moving the program.

7. *Counterprogram to present viewers with a reasonable alternative to other fare*. The term *counterprogramming* refers to the practice of scheduling in a given time slot a program which is differ-

ent from and attracts a different kind of audience than the competing programs at that time. Offering a program that appeals to different tastes than those attracted by existing programming is usually more successful than offering a different version of the types of programming being aired by the competition.

8. *Program to those people who are available.* In counterprogramming against a dominant program in a given time period, many executives err, when selecting the counterprogram, by looking at the demographic makeup of the total audience using television at the time. The audience available for the new program, however, is that portion of the audience that remains after the dominant program has taken its share. Counterprogram for this audience.

9. *In buying, always consider how it would be to have the offered program opposite you.* In many instances, primarily on the local station level, the programming executive considering purchase of a specific show must assume that, if he turns it down, it will be offered to the competition. Thus he must consider both the value of the program to his station and the effect on his programming if it should appear on a competitor's schedule. With this in mind, an executive might purchase and schedule a program that has marginal potential in his schedule in order to avoid a significant loss that could be created if the same show were scheduled opposite his existing properties.

10. *Do not place an expensive program in a time period that has insufficient audience or revenue potential.* As has already been pointed out, total audiences are greater in some hours than in others. The amount advertisers will pay for a program or a commercial spot within a program depends on both the size and the composition of the audience for the program. If a station is to recapture the money spent for a program and make a profit, it must charge more for spots in an expensive program than in one of moderate price. It follows, then, that expensive programs should be scheduled in high sets-in-use periods and should not be purchased if such time periods are not available (subject, of course, to the considerations raised in point 9).

Scheduling Patterns

Application of the above principles frequently results in the appearance of some fundamental scheduling patterns, one of which has already been noted and one implied. These are counterprogramming, block programming and strip programming. In *counter-programming*, of course, the station counters a competing program by scheduling a program of a completely different type that will attract a different kind of listener—for instance, an action-adventure to compete with a variety show. Application of points 2 and 3 above results in *block programming*, that is, a block of two, three, or even four programs in sequence all aimed at the same general type of listener. The programs mutually interact to help each other by attracting and holding some particular kind of listener. In the 1970s, the CBS television network successfully used this technique by scheduling its popular situation comedies in groups of four—going into the 1976–1977 season with blocks of four situation comedies beginning the prime-time period on Monday, Wednesday, and Saturday nights. *Strip programming* refers to the presentation of programs in the same series at exactly the same hour, five days a week, so that those listeners who like the series can remember its broadcast time without difficulty. Virtually all network daytime programming is stripped, as is the network evening news. Local stations also strip many of their nonnetwork offerings.

Television Network Ratings

Some illustrations of the effects of ratings on television prime-time schedules can be seen by examining the 1975–1976 schedule. Seven of the Top-10 programs in the September 8 to January 18 period were situation comedies with a 26.3 average rating. Thus it is not surprising to see that slightly more than 30 percent of all programs on the 1975–1976 schedules were situation comedies with an average rating of almost 20.

That success seems to breed success in the ratings is illustrated by the 1975–1976 track record of so-called "spin-offs"—program series that are based on characters originally appearing in an already established series. (In the following discussion figures in parentheses represent average ratings for the September 8 to January 18 period.) The top-rated *All in the Family* (32.4), for instance, introduced *Maude* (27.3), which, in turn, introduced the characters in *Good Times* (21.9). Later, characters also in *All in the Family* moved to Manhattan and became *The Jeffersons* (21.7). Similarly, The *Mary Tyler Moore Show* (22.0) provided the lead characters for both *Rhoda* (25.4) and *Phyllis* (26.3). While such spin-offs are not always successful—*Sanford and Son* (26.1) was not able to transfer its popularity to *Grady* (13.9)—the advantage of trying new characters and situations in an already established program plus that of an occasional "visit" by one of the stars of the "parent" program provides a measure of rating insurance that is attractive to many producers.

Following closely behind situation comedies in popularity is a category of action-adventure-mystery programs—including both police and detective drama. While only two such programs were in the 1975–1976 Top 10 (*The Six Million Dollar Man* and its spin-off, *The Bionic Woman*), the network schedules included 24 such programs with an average rating of 18.2. That success in the ratings breeds imitation is illustrated by the fact that the two program categories noted above—situation comedies and action-adventure-mystery—represented almost 63 percent of the entire 1975–1976 network prime-time schedule.

Ratings are also a factor in the scheduling of theatrical features. Because of the variation in quality of a motion picture "package" offered over a full season, regularly scheduled "movie" periods receive only fair average ratings. Seven such time periods received an average rating of only 17.3 during the first half of 1975–1976. Ratings of some individual features are quite high, however. In the 1974–1975 season, for instance, the first part of *The Godfather* received a rating of 39.4; the second part of *The Godfather* got a 37; and a repeat of *Airport* earned a 30. Indeed, the Top-10 theatrical films for that year averaged a 29.0 rating. These numbers are balanced, of course, by an average rating of 6.7 for the bottom ten features—all repeats, with two exceptions, and all shown in the summer months. Nevertheless, the lure of a "blockbuster" feature capable of capturing almost 40 percent of all television homes in the United States (and, for part II of *The Godfather*, a 57 percent share of audience) keeps regular motion picture slots a durable portion of the prime-time schedule.

Average ratings for a motion picture time period on a network schedule, of course, are also affected by the ratings of what have come to be known as made-for-television features. Made necessary by the diminishing backlog of first-run theatrical features suitable for television, this category of motion picture has come to include virtually all dramatic programming that runs 90 minutes or more—with the exception of some dramatic specials. In 1974–1975, 227 theatrical features were shown on network schedules—125 first run and 102 reruns—and 251 made-for-television features—121 first run and 130 reruns. Of the made-for-television features, 26 represented pilots for new series, 8 were informative in nature, 7 were expanded episodes of existing series, and the remainder were the kind of film one could reasonably expect to see in a motion picture theater.

While made-for-television features rarely receive the ratings of a popular theatrical feature, the best get respectable numbers. The top-rated made-for-television film in 1974–1975, for example, received a rating of 31.1; and the average rating of the Top-10 such features was 26—only 3 points below the average for the Top-10 theatrical films.

As pointed out in earlier chapters, the networks regularly carry special programs in both news and educational categories, but most such programming does not receive the ratings expected for entertainment programming. For the 1974–1975 season, the ten specials with the top ratings for the year (an average of 32.7) included only one program that could be placed in either category—the Smithsonian production of *Monsters—Mysteries or Myths?* (32.6). On the other end of the scale, the ten episodes at the bottom of the 1974–1975 list (with an average rating of 4.6) included four news specials, three sports specials, and three dramatic efforts. Analysis of the 381 1974–1975 specials listed in *Variety* shows 64 in the informative-educational-cultural category with an average rating of 15.7. In the same season, the networks aired 49 news-public affairs specials, which received an average rating of 10.7. Given a choice between programs in these categories and entertainment, it seems the great majority of the citizens of the United States will choose the latter.

Criticisms of Ratings

Although advertisers and program executives are thoroughly convinced of their values, ratings are often criticized by others interested in broadcasting. Entertainers whose programs receive unsatisfactory ratings protest that "you can't really measure popularity" by getting the "opinions of a few hundred listeners." Owners of radio stations also challenge the accuracy of rating figures that indicate a drop in radio listening to levels far below those of pretelevision days. They charge too, and with some justice, that radio is discriminated against in some rating reports that fail to include out-of-home listening. More serious are the criticisms of nonindustry people who can hardly be accused of personal bias. Congressional committees have conducted hearings questioning the accuracy of the figures reported by some of the rating concerns, especially in local areas; the Federal Communications Commission has made its own investigation of the methods used by the rating companies; the Federal Trade Commission has warned against unwarranted claims that ratings provide accurate measurement of audiences of programs or stations.

Although these nonindustry critics usually base their opposition to ratings on the contention that rating figures are not completely accurate, their real objection is that, because of their low rating potential, programs of types they would like to see broadcast are kept off the air. An often cited example is a program of concert music that was carried on television network schedules over a period of 10 years but which, in its last five seasons on the air, had January ratings ranging from 10.0 to as low as 6.0—in spite of being scheduled at the very desirable hour of 8:30 P.M. The sponsor was satisfied, in spite of the low rating. The network, however, found it impossible to build up large enough audiences for programs that followed; and when the sponsor refused to move the program to a period later at night, the network dropped the program from its schedules. In other instances, equally desirable programs have been dropped by their sponsors when ratings fell below expected levels.

Admittedly, low ratings do keep many programs off the air, including some programs with above-average cultural values. A program with a rating of only 10.0 costs its sponsor twice as much for each home reached as does a program with equal time and production costs that can show a 20.0 rating. In the circumstances, advertisers can hardly be expected to continue their support for low-rated programs, regardless of the cultural advantages such programs may offer. Nor can a network company afford to retain a low-rated program when its presence seriously weakens the audience-attracting abilities of adjacent programs and prevents those programs from finding sponsors. The fault in such situations, if any fault exists, does not lie in the system of ratings, as such; ratings are merely a measurement of the approximate size of the audiences reached by programs. If the situation produced by low ratings is in any way an undesirable one, the fault lies not in the system of measurement, but in other existing conditions—perhaps in the prevailing level of culture of the American people, which makes them unwilling to tune in those programs that the critics of ratings believe should be broadcast.

In any event, ratings for programs will continue to be reported, and the rating companies will continue to "count the vote" that the listening public casts for each network or local program. In the future, more attention will be given by advertisers to the *kinds* of listeners reached; it may be quite possible that a relatively small audience of the "right kind" of people may be more valuable to certain sponsors than a much larger total audience that includes only a small proportion of listeners of the special type that the advertiser wants to reach. With more qualitative information available concerning audiences of programs, network executives and representatives of advertisers may be able to select more intelligently than in the past those programs that will be tuned in by listeners of types most needed by the advertiser.

STUDY AND DISCUSSION QUESTIONS

1. Try to secure from a local radio or television station, advertising agency, or other source a copy of a rating report from a national rating service (for example, ARB, A. C. Nielsen, or Pulse). Analyze the data presented and report on or be prepared to discuss the following:

   a. Stations included in the survey
   b. Area included in the survey and the period of the survey
   c. Information about the sample provided by the service
   d. The method of collecting data for the report
   e. Varieties of information provided concerning audience size and times of day
   f. Demographic breakdowns provided
   g. Additional information provided
   h. Margin of error specified

2. Report on or be prepared to discuss the uses to which rating information is put in sales and promotion efforts by local stations. Include your evaluation of the soundness of the judgment of the station in the use of rating numbers.

3. If possible, locate a station in your area that does not purchase the services of a rating firm. Interview the manager to determine why the service is not purchased and what alternative sources of information are used.

4. Report on or be prepared to discuss the meaning of the following terms used in rating jargon:

   a. Program rating
   b. Sets-in-use
   c. Share of audience
   d. Time-period ratings
   e. Area of Dominant Influence (ADI)
   f. Stratified and random sampling
   g. Sampling error
   h. Standard Metropolitan Statistical Areas (SMSA)
   i. Demographics
   j. Cumulative figures ("cumes")

5. Report on or be prepared to discuss the strengths and weaknesses of the major methods of collecting rating information (audimeters, diaries, coincidental telephone calls, personal interviews, and the like).

6. Select a recently completed television season and locate reviews of as many as possible of the programs introduced at the beginning of the season (try *Variety* and *Broadcasting*, for a start). Check the ratings received by these programs as the season progressed and see if you can draw any conclusions as to the relationship between critical acceptance and audience acceptance as measured by rating figures.

SUGGESTED READINGS

How Good Are Television Ratings? (Continued). New York: Television Information Office, 1969.

Lawrence W. Lichty. *Broadcast Program and Audience Analysis*. Madison, Wisc.: American Printing and Publishing, Inc., 1973.

William G. Madow, Herbert H. Hyman, Raymond J. Jessep, Paul B. Sheatsley, and Charles R. Wright. *Evaluation of Statistical Methods Used in Obtaining Broadcast Ratings*. House Report 193, 87th Congress, 1st Sess. Washington, D.C.: U.S. Government Printing Office, 1961.

Television Ratings Revisited: A Further Look at Television Audiences. New York: Television Information Office, 1971.

United States Congress, House of Representatives, Committee on Interstate and Foreign Commerce. *Broadcast Ratings: A Progress Report on Industry and Programs Involving Broadcast Ratings*. House Report 1212, 89th Cong., 2d Sess. Washington, D.C.: U.S. Government Printing Office, 1964.

What the Ratings Really Mean. Chicago: A. C. Nielsen Co., 1964.

Broadcasting and the Federal Communications Commission

The system of broadcasting used in the United States is based on private ownership and operation of radio and television stations and on the licensing and regulation of such stations by an agency of the federal government. The first radio law, enacted by Congress in 1910,[1] required American passenger ships to install wireless equipment as a safety measure; both transmitters and the operators who used them were licensed by the Department of Commerce. The Radio Act of 1912[2] covered wireless installations on land and made it illegal to operate "any apparatus for radio communication" without a license issued by the Secretary of Commerce and Labor. Both laws, of course, dealt with radio as a device used for point-to-point wireless communication; broadcasting, or the dissemination of radio signals to be picked up by the public at large, had not yet come into being.

When more or less formal broadcasting operations did begin about 1920, the early stations were licensed by the Department of Commerce (The Department of Commerce and Labor having been separated into two Cabinet-level departments); as the number of broadcasting stations increased, the department specified the wavelength on which each station could operate and the hours during which it would be allowed to broadcast. In 1926, as noted in Chapter 3, a ruling by a federal court held that the Department of Commerce had no legal right to impose such restrictions on radio stations. The result was a state of chaotic interference between signals of various stations—and the enactment by Congress of the Radio Act of 1927.[3]

CONGRESSIONAL AUTHORIZATION

The act of 1927 created a five-member Federal Radio Commission (FRC); it gave the commission power to "classify stations"—partly at least to differentiate between broadcasting stations and those engaging in point-to-point communication—and to issue and renew licenses if the granting of such authorizations would serve "the public interest, convenience, or necessity." Specific authority was given to assign each broadcasting station to a particular fre-

---

[1]"The Wireless Ship Act of 1910," *in* Frank J. Kahn (ed)., *Documents of American Broadcasting* (New York: Appleton-Century-Crofts, 1973), p. 3.

[2]"The Radio Act of 1912," *in* Kahn, *Documents*, p. 7.

[3]"The Radio Act of 1927," *in* Kahn, *Documents*, p. 36.

quency, to designate the power it might use, and to specify the hours during which it could operate. Through regulations it issued and through policies it applied in the relicensing of stations, the new commission was able to put broadcasting on a much more orderly basis and to deal with the problem of interference, eliminating in the process a number of stations that failed to meet the regulatory body's minimum engineering requirements.

The Federal Radio Commission, however, was never considered by Congress to be a permanent regulatory commission. It was created in 1927 as a licensing authority for a period of 1 year only. At the end of that time all such authority was to revert to the Secretary of Commerce, and the FRC was to become a body to consider appeals to rulings by the Secretary. The authority of the FRC was renewed annually until the end of 1929, at which time Congress extended its life "until otherwise provided by law."

By 1934, it was evident to many that a permanent regulatory body was needed to supervise all forms of communication relying on wires, cable, or radio. In February of that year President Franklin D. Roosevelt asked Congress to create such an agency, to be known as the Federal Communications Commission. Congress responded with the Communications Act of 1934[4] which, among other things, created the new commission.

The FCC has seven members, appointed for 7-year terms by the President of the United States with the consent of the Senate; the President also designates the member who is to act as chairman of the commission. Those appointed to the regulatory agency may have no financial interest in any broadcasting operation, including the manufacture of equipment; not more than four commissioners serving at any one time may be members of the same political party. The act of 1934 gives the FCC jurisdiction both over broadcasting stations and over those engaging in point-to-point wireless communication—amateur stations; airplane, ship, taxicab and other industrial radio installations; police radio; and the like. The commission also regulates interstate telephone and telegraph communications, whether by wire or by microwave relay systems. However, the act of 1934 gives the agency no authority to regulate network operations, at least directly, or to deal with telephone or telegraph wire systems entirely within the borders of a single state. Similarly, the FCC has no jurisdiction over closed-circuit television installations, since such installations do not engage in broadcasting

---

[4]"The Communications Act of 1934," in Kahn, *Documents*, p. 54.

or wireless transmission of signals and, being intrastate in character, are not covered by the congressional authority to "regulate interstate commerce."[5]

The Communications Act of 1934 includes practically all the provisions of the earlier Radio Act of 1927; licensing of stations in "the public interest, convenience, or necessity" is continued as the basis of regulation. Also included in Section 326 of the act of 1934 is the "no-censorship" provision of the earlier law: "Nothing in this Act shall be understood or construed to give the Commission the power of censorship over the radio communications or signals transmitted by any radio station." However, in view of court decisions that limit the interpretation of censorship to some form of prior restraint, any questions as to the power of the Federal Communications Commission to consider the past or proposed programming of a station in passing on applications for licenses has become almost entirely academic, although the situation is one that many broadcasters resent.

COMMISSION ORGANIZATION

The Federal Communications Commission, of course, consists of more than seven commissioners. A large staff carries a substantial part of the workload of the FCC, gathering data and formulating options for the commissioners, administering policies set down by these commissioners, and exercising a degree of discretionary power delegated to it.

Because the FCC has jurisdiction over all forms of electric communication, from telegraph to satellite transmission, some portions of its activities have no bearing on broadcasting. What follows, then, is a description of the major offices and bureaus concerned with broadcasting. In this discussion, the word *commission* will refer to the seven commissioners alone. The terms *FCC* and *Federal Communications Commission* will include both commission and staff.

The Office of the Executive Director   The executive director plans and directs all administrative affairs of the FCC and coordinates all staff

---

[5]FCC jurisdiction over cable television (see Chapter 6), of course, represents a major exception to this principle. The Federal Communications Commission assumed such jurisdiction in 1965 without requesting congressional authorization, arguing that it had the right to protect the existing broadcast service from unfair competitive use of its own programming. Federal courts subsequently upheld this commission action.

activity. It is his responsibility constantly to review and attempt to improve administrative procedures. Under the direction of the defense commissioner (one of the seven commissioners carries this title and supervises FCC activities related to national defense), he coordinates all FCC defense activities. He reports directly to the commission and works under the supervision of the chairman.

The Office of the General Counsel As that title implies, the general counsel represents the FCC in all legal matters before the courts. This office advises the commission about proposed communications legislation; assists in the preparation of reports to Congress about such legislation; and interprets agency rules, laws, and international agreements on communications matters. The office gives advice concerning rulemakings and proceedings concerning more than one bureau of the FCC.

The Office of Chief Engineer This office is responsible for long-range planning toward the more effective use of communication in the public interest. It advises the commission and staff on technical matters, and it collaborates on the preparation of the technical requirements of FCC Rules and Regulations.

The Office of the Secretary The name of the secretary of the FCC appears on all official documents issued by the agency because he is charged with the responsibility of signing everything. With few exceptions, all correspondence directed to the FCC is addressed to this office. The office is simply an entry and exit point, however, and has virtually no voice in the formulation of decisions. It also maintains all dockets (records) of hearings and rulemaking proceedings and a comprehensive library and reference facility.

The Office of Information This is an important source of information for the public since this office is responsible for distributing information on FCC actions. Among other services, it issues Public Notices regularly on the work of the FCC.

The Hearings and Review Office As a part of its activities, the FCC must frequently hold comparative hearings to gather the data necessary to make decisions on initial grants of licenses, renewals, revocations, and the like. Such hearings are conducted by *administrative law judges*, who function very much like judges in a court of law, ruling on the admissability of evidence, the competency of witnesses, and other legal points. At the conclusion of a hearing, the examiner issues an initial decision which becomes effective in 50 days unless reversed or modified by appeal or direct action by the commission.

Initial decisions, except those involving license renewal or revocation, and rulings by administrative law judges may be appealed to a *review board*, which is composed of three or more senior FCC employees (presently five). Parties not satisfied with a review board decision may then appeal directly to the commission itself. Any further appeal must be taken to the courts.

In some instances, initial decisions are reviewed directly by the commission, without passing through the review board. In such cases, the *office of opinion and review* assists and makes recommendations in both the review and the draft decision.

The Broadcast Bureau   This bureau is charged with major responsibility for the broadcast service. Its functions include processing of license applications, participation in rulemaking and application hearings, the study of frequency allocations and planning for their broadcast use, establishing technical requirements for broadcasting equipment, and preparing recommendations concerning standards. Among its operating divisions are the *renewal and transfer division*, responsible for all license-renewal applications and for action on any transfers of ownership; the *hearings division*, responsible for applications designated for hearings or other proceedings; the *license division*, responsible for receipt, initial examination, and routing of all broadcast license applications; the *office of network study*, which conducts studies relating to radio and television network operations; the *complaints and compliance division*, responsible for handling all complaints about the conduct of radio and television stations and assuring compliance with FCC Rules and Regulations.

The Field Operations Bureau   A substantial portion of FCC activity is conducted in the field. Broadcast-related functions include monitoring stations to ensire compliance with frequency standards, directional patterns, and the like; inspection of antenna towers; and inspection of stations themselves to insure compliance with Rules and Regulations. These activities are supervised by the field operations bureau, which maintains field offices and monitoring stations throughout the United States.

The Cable Television Bureau   As you would expect, this arm of the FCC is responsible for the planning, development, and execution of regulatory programs for community antenna television systems. It also reviews and evaluates the operation of cable systems to insure compliance with Rules and Regulations.

COMMISSION PROCEDURES

The Federal Communications Act of 1934 authorized the FCC to grant applications for station licenses if "public interest, convenience, or necessity will be served by such grants." It may also revoke licenses, in certain situations. However, the act gave the commission no other powers with respect to the operation of broadcasting stations, aside from requiring licensees to file such reports as the regulatory agency finds necessary. Consequently, for years the commission's only direct means of requiring stations to operate "in the public interest" was that provided by the agency's power to grant or to refuse applications for station authorizations—or, perhaps even more important, applications for renewal of station licenses. In the 1950s and early 1960s, the FCC was given the right to issue cease-and-desist orders and to levy fines in cases in which violations were not sufficient to warrant a short-term license or outright revocation.

When a would-be owner wishes to construct a new radio or television station, he files with the Federal Communications Commission a detailed written application, indicating the community in which the proposed station will be located, the frequency or channel on which the station will operate, the power to be used by the station transmitter, and the proposed hours of operation. The application also includes information about the applicant's legal, technical, and financial qualifications; a detailed description of the type of technical equipment to be used; and information with respect to the type of programming to be provided by the station and general program policies to be followed. If an examination by the commission's staff shows that the proposed station can operate without creating harmful interference with signals of other stations, that the equipment proposed conforms to commission requirements, and that the applicant is fully "qualified"—and if no other applicant has filed for the same facility—a construction permit is usually issued without further formality. Later, after the station has been built and the equipment tested, its owner may apply for and receive a regular license to broadcast.

The licensee of an operating station is required to make certain reports to the FCC—an annual financial report and special reports, including copies of contracts with network organizations, other agreements that might in any way affect ownership or control of the station or supervision over the station's financial or programming operations, and the reports on programming and employment discussed in Chapter 5. In addition, licensees are required to keep operating logs and other records, which are open to inspection from time to time by commission representatives. The most important element in commission regulation of broadcasting stations is the requirement that at the expiration of each 3-year license period, the owner of every broadcasting station must file an application for renewal of the station's license. Applications for license renewal call for substantially the same information as that required from applicants for new station facilities, but with one major addition: The applicant for license renewal must describe the type of programming his station has provided during the period the existing license has been in effect, as well as outlining plans for future programming operations. This gives the FCC staff an opportunity to compare actual programming performance with the promises made in earlier applications—and to evaluate the reasons the licensee offers if he has failed to live up to those earlier promises. In most actions on license renewal the FCC staff finds no serious ground for objection to the licensee's programming or other activities or to the program proposals outlined in the application, and license renewal is granted without question. However, when the application shows serious discrepancies between promise and performance in programming or when the FCC staff is not satisfied with proposals for future programming or when questions have arisen concerning the licensee's character qualifications or when serious complaints have been made by listeners about the operation of his station, the application may be held up to give the licensee an opportunity to explain the apparent shortcomings. In many instances, the application is set for a public hearing.

Hearings

When two or more applicants contest for the same new broadcasting facility, a public hearing is held to determine which applicant is to receive the grant. Sometimes a hearing is ordered when only one applicant is involved, if questions are raised with respect to his financial or character qualifications, if the owner of an existing station protests on grounds that operation of the new station would create serious interference, or if an existing licensee claims the presence of a new station would cause him financial problems serious enough to adversely affect the public interest. As already noted, hearings are occasionally held on applications for license renewal; a license for a broadcasting station is never revoked or license renewal permanently refused without a hearing to determine whether the licensee's conduct warrants such an action.

Whether on applications for new facilities or for license renewal by existing stations, hearings are open to the public. Each hearing is presided over by an administrative law judge from the Federal Communications Commission's staff; procedures followed are generally similar to those in a court of law, with witnesses appearing and with applicants represented by attorneys. Following the hearing—in most cases, several months later—the administrative law judge issues his decision, either granting or refusing the application for license renewal or, in situations involving a number of applicants for a new station facility, indicating the applicant to whom the facility is to be granted. The examiner's opinion summarizes the evidence presented and states the basis for the decision rendered. An adverse decision may be appealed to a staff review board or, in some instances, to the Federal Communications Commission itself; occasionally, without an appeal the commission may itself elect to review and possibly overturn the examiner's decision. If no appeal is filed or if no review is ordered, however, the examiner's decision becomes final in 50 days—at least as far as the commission is concerned. The Communications Act provides, however, that any commission or administrative law judge's decision on the grant of a station license may be appealed to the United States Court of Appeals in the District of Columbia, and the court may order the commission to reconsider its original action. Appeals from commission decisions are fairly frequent, but only in a small proportion of cases are such appeals successful.

Issues in Hearings

In every hearing, the decision of the hearing examiner is based on evidence presented on a number of issues, announced before the hearing begins. In a hearing on license renewal, issues may concern the question of whether control over the station has been transferred illegally to a person other than the licensee or whether the licensee has made false statements in reports filed with the commission or whether the licensee has been guilty of serious shortcomings in programs put on the air. In hearings on grants of new facilities, issues may range from the financial qualifications of applicants to the types of programming the various applicants expect to provide.

Sometimes a dozen or more such issues will be considered in a hearing.

For many years, hearings examiners and broadcasters faced these hearings with no clear statement from the Federal Communications Commission as to which issues it felt were the most important. As a result, the examiners' decisions were usually based on two or three key issues, and the emphasis laid upon each of the issues varied greatly from one hearing to the next. In 1965, however, the FCC moved to clear up this confusion in hearings to choose among applicants for the same broadcast facilities. It did so in its Policy Statement on Comparative Broadcast Hearings,[6] which listed the following significant factors to be given a major significance in future hearings.

1. Diversification of Control of the Media of Mass Communications   This has always been a concern of the FCC. Specifically, the statement pointed out, "we will consider interests in existing media of mass communications to be more significant in the degree that they: (a) are larger, i.e., go towards complete ownership and control; and to the degree that the existing media: (b) are in, or close to, the community being applied for; (c) are significant in terms of numbers and size, i.e., the area covered, circulation, size of audience, etc; (d) are significant in terms of regional or national coverage; and (e) are significant with respect to other media in their respective localities."

2. Full-Time Participation in Station Ownership by Owners   From the earliest days of radio, the regulatory body supervising broadcasting has adhered to a "local-institution policy" for broadcast media in which all stations are seen as outlets for community expression and sources of news, information, and other services to the community in which they operate. From this policy naturally flows a desire to have as many stations as possible owned and operated by citizens of their communities because, among other things, "there is a likelihood of greater sensitivity to an area's changing needs, and of programming designed to serve these needs" under such circumstances.

3. Proposed Program Service   Citing a court decision that stated "comparative service to the listening public is a vital element [in comparative hearings], and programs are the essence of that service,"

---

[6]"Policy Statement on Comparative Broadcast Hearings," *in* Kahn, *Documents*, p. 543.

the Policy Statement makes it clear that the FCC will consider the quality of proposed programming in comparative hearings.

4. Past Broadcast Record   When one of the competing applicants for a broadcast facility is the owner of the other stations, his past record with the other station or stations can also become a factor in the hearings. The FCC, however, expects "average performance" from any applicant and "will not give a preference because one applicant has owned stations in the past and another has not." The agency is instead interested in "records which, because either unusually good or unusually poor, give some indication of unusual performance in the future."

5. Efficient Use of Frequency   The possible variations of "efficiency" in comparative hearings are so numerous that the FCC avoided virtually any discussion of this factor. It simply pointed out that the frequency question could become an issue if there were sound engineering reasons for preferring one frequency over another.

6. Character   According to the provisions of the Communications Act of 1934, the FCC must consider the character of any applicant for a broadcast facility. The commission is concerned with the past history of all applicants to be sure none have any criminal record or have engaged in any activities that would not reflect with favor on the owner of a radio or television station. Because virtually everyone knows this, the character issue is not so common as many others, although it does come up from time to time.

7. Other Factors   Having listed six significant factors, the FCC left the door open to "the full examination of any relevant and substantial factor" that might come up in a given hearing. It did so simply to avoid painting itself into a corner that would preclude it from considering significant factors that could arise in the years following the issuance of its Policy Statement.

This 1965 Policy Statement attempted to limit the application of the above factors to competitive hearings "to choose among qualified new applicants for the same broadcast facilities," as distinct from hearings "where an applicant is contesting with a licensee seeking renewal of license." In subsequent years, however, the FCC referred to these factors in several decisions in license renewal cases and, in 1971, a decision by the U.S. Court of Appeals in the District of Columbia instructed the FCC that, before the law, there should be no real difference in the procedures for the two types of hearing (initial application and renewal). As a result, the factors discussed above are the major issues considered in virtually all hearings relating to broadcast licenses.

The commission is represented at all hearings by one or more attorneys from its own legal staff; in hearings on license renewal, attorneys for the commission serve, in effect, as prosecuting attorneys, presenting evidence compiled by commission staff members concerning the alleged misdeeds of those licensees whose right to license renewal has been questioned.

Sale of Broadcasting Stations

Securing an authorization for the construction of a new station is often a difficult matter, especially if a number of competing applicants are involved. In comparison, purchase of a station already on the air usually offers few problems, at least as far as the commission is concerned. As a rule, no hearing is required on an application to transfer the ownership of station facilities. The only questions usually considered by the commission are whether the person seeking to buy the station is "legally, technically, and financially qualified," whether he meets the necessary character requirements, and whether he is not already the owner of the maximum number of stations allowed by the commission. If the applicant is found to be qualified in all these respects, he is allowed to purchase the station.

In recent years, however, the FCC has been forced, by actions of concerned citizens supported by the courts, to consider the question of "format change" if it is an issue in a transfer. The question arises in situations in which the new owner is proposing a change in programming format for the station—usually a radio station—he wishes to purchase. This situation can arise when a station is being sold because it had not been able to compete successfully in its market. Under these circumstances, the new owner will often wish to change the format to one which is more likely to garner a larger audience.

The first inclination of the Federal Communications Commission has been to leave format questions to the marketplace and not to enter into such programming decisions. In some instances, however, relatively small groups of people who preferred the original format have persuaded the courts that a format change would deny a significant portion of the public the unique service that the station had provided. Seeing that as a public interest question that should take precedence over economic issues, the courts have told the FCC that format changes must be reviewed very carefully and that the economic question should not necessarily take precedence. The FCC remains reluctant to move with the vigor encouraged by the courts and, in the summer of 1976, issued a Policy Statement in which it restated its belief that the question of format should remain in the hands of the licensee. This statement, however, has been appealed and the issue has yet to be resolved.

Enforcement of Commission Requirements

As already stated, the Federal Communications Commission exerts its regulatory control over broadcasting primarily by the granting or the withholding of station licenses. A regular license is issued for a 3-year period; at the end of that time, an application must be made for license renewal, and the station's past record is taken into account in actions on license renewal. Before 1952, the only method provided in the communications act for punishment of licensees who failed to live up to commission requirements was the outright revocation of the station's license or refusal to grant license renewal. However, a 1952 amendment to the act gives the commission the right to issue cease-and-desist orders, requiring a station or another offender to discontinue an objectionable practice, and another amendment passed 8 years later allows the commission to impose fines for noncompliance with regulations.

Only a relatively small number of stations have been actually taken off the air by the commission since the regulatory agency was created in 1934. Most of those that have failed to receive license renewal were guilty either of making false statements in applications or reports to the commission or of transferring control over station facilities to unauthorized persons. A few stations have lost their licenses to broadcast for other offenses, as noted earlier. The commission's power to issue cease-and-desist orders has been used almost as infrequently—sometimes against owners of diathermy equipment or other electronic devices that interfered with reception of signals of radio or television stations. The power to assess fines on station operators has been used much more often; a number of stations have been forced to pay penalties for using more power than the amount specified in the license or for failure to have a licensed engineer on duty or for similar violations of regulations.

In addition to the methods provided specifically in the communications act, the Federal Communications Commission has developed a number of informal but highly effective devices for applying pressure on station licensees who fail to conform to its standards of operation, particularly in the area of programming. One such method, of course, is the issuing of public notices outlining the commission's ideas of the obligations of station operators—sometimes in formal publications and Policy Statements, sometimes in informal press releases, sometimes in speeches delivered by members of the regulatory body. These notices outline the commission's view on program requirements, on practices to be taken into account in consideration of license renewal, on use of advertising, or on other subjects concerning which no formal regulations have been adopted.

Another and more direct form of pressure consists merely of sending a letter to the owner of a station, inquiring about some alleged failure to live up to the station's obligations. In a number of situations, the commission has simply failed to take any action whatever on renewal of a station's license—often with no reason given—so that the station automatically is placed on a temporary license basis. In still other situations, a letter may be sent to a station licensee asking him to show cause why a hearing should not be ordered on the renewal of his license; if the licensee could not report that the alleged shortcoming has been corrected, an actual hearing might be ordered. All these devices, of course, are either indirect or very direct *threats* of commission action—not actual punishment for offenses.

The requiring of a hearing on license renewal is a much different matter; even if the outcome is favorable to the station and a license renewal is granted, station prestige with advertisers and listeners is seriously damaged by the fact that a hearing is held; and, in addition, the station is subjected to the not inconsiderable expense of defending its record in the hearing. One 1950 hearing on renewal of the license of a high-power Los Angeles radio station accused of serious news bias is estimated to have cost the licensee nearly $2 million; in this case, hearings were continued at intervals over a period of more than a year. Less protracted hearings have frequently cost the licensees involved from $75,000 to as much as $200,000 for attorneys' fees, the photostating of records, and the preparation of exhibits. Of course, although actual refusals of license renewals are rather infrequent, a hearing *can* result in the imposition of the "death penalty" on the station involved.

By use of fines for violations of regulations, by use of its variety of pressures and threats, by its ordering of hearings on license renewal, the Federal Communications Commission has been generally successful in inducing broadcasters to "go along," willingly or otherwise, with the policies and standards the commission has adopted for the regulation of broadcasting stations.

COMMISSION ACTIONS

The Communications Act of 1934 states that its purpose is to "make available . . . [an] efficient, nationwide . . . radio communication service," and by implication, to maintain competition in broadcasting, since "all laws of the United States relating to . . . monopolies and to combinations in restraint of trade are declared to be applicable to . . . radio communications." The act offers no further guides to the commission's activities in regulating radio or regulating television, since television is considered technically as a form of radio broadcasting. The act gives the commission authority to make such rules and regulations and to require such reports and other infor-

"The FCC says 'yes', the FTC says 'maybe', and the SEC says 'no'."

mation from licensees or applicants "as may be necessary in the execution of its functions." However, it leaves to the commission the decision on what constitutes the public interest in broadcasting and what principles should be applied to achieve its basic objectives.

As interpreted by the Federal Communications Commission, the responsibility of serving the public interest in the licensing of radio and television stations has several aspects. The commission is concerned with the formulation and execution of policies that will provide an efficient broadcasting service throughout the nation, that will place the operation of stations in the hands of well-qualified persons, and that will maintain a high degree of competition in broadcasting.

Efficient Broadcasting Service

The commission's first objective, of course, is to insure the creation of a nationwide, efficient broadcasting service. In this area, the regulatory body has been guided by four basic principles. (1) As far as possible, service should be made available to listeners in all sections of the United States—in remote rural areas as well as in areas of dense population. (2) Listeners in each area or each community should have access to signals of as many different stations as possible to permit a wide choice in the selection of programs. (3) A *local* broadcasting service should be available in as many different communities as possible, to serve distinctly local needs. (4) Interference between stations should be held to a minimum; the communications act specifically directs the commission to adopt regulations "to prevent interference between stations."

Certainly, no one would question the desirability of any of these objectives. In putting the principles into practice, however, the commission has encountered serious problems. All too frequently, steps taken to attain one objective have resulted in serious injury to others.

The Clear-Channel Problem

Take for example, the matter of clear-channel stations. In 1928, the Federal Radio Commission set aside as clear channels 40 of the 86 channels or frequencies then available for use by standard radio stations in the United States. Each such channel or frequency was to be used by a single, high-power AM station; no other station was to be permitted to use the same frequency at night, and daytime operation of a secondary, low-power station on that frequency was to be authorized only in rare instances. The purpose obviously was to insure a dependable, interference-free service, day and night, to listeners in every part of the United States. However, the exclusive use of these frequencies by a few high-power stations conflicted with other basic commission objectives: the availability of service from as many different AM stations as possible for listeners in each area and the providing of local station service in large numbers of individual communities. So although the commission still supports the clear-channel idea in theory, in practice the concept has been greatly weakened by the authorization of a constantly increasing number of secondary stations operating on the theoretically clear channels. By the end of 1974, a total of 106 high-power, 50,000-watt AM stations had been assigned to the 43 channels then designated as clear, as well as nearly 500 secondary stations, with 82 of these operating at 10,000 watts and 72 at 5,000 watts. Approximately 40 percent of these secondary stations also remained on the air at night as well as in the daytime.[7] As a result, the areas over which the 50,000-watt clear-channel stations are able to provide interference-free service have been greatly reduced.

The Increasing Number of Stations

The Federal Communications Commission's objectives of providing local service in as many communities as possible and of giving listeners a choice of signals of a large number of different stations have also resulted in serious interference between radio stations assigned to local and regional channels. During the 1930s, the commission's rules required that there be a substantial mileage separation between any two stations operating on the same frequency—the distance of course was greater when the stations involved used power of more than 250 watts. Since the end of World War II, these standards had been so much relaxed that four or five times as many stations are now assigned to each frequency as the number that could have been allowed to use that frequency in 1940 and earlier years. Each of the 41 regional channels in the standard band of frequencies now accommodates from 19 to 73 stations with power of from 1,000 to 5,000 watts, with approximately 45 percent of them broadcasting

---

[7]In addition, by 1974 a total of 26 high-power 50,000-watt American stations and more than 500 stations with lower power had been assigned by the FCC to 16 channels reserved by treaty for primary use by high-power stations in Canada, Mexico, and Cuba.

at night as well as during the daytime. In addition, each of the six local channels is used by an average of 165 full-time stations, all using
no more than 250 watts of power at night; but most are allowed to
increase power to 1,000 watts during the daytime. The result is that
even though nearly all the full-time regional stations are required to
use directional antennas, interference between stations on the same
frequencies has become a serious problem. The Federal Communications Commission has recognized the seriousness of this problem
and has, since 1962, struggled with it through a series of freezes and
slow-downs in AM applications. Even in the face of this, however,
the number of AM stations and the power they are permitted to use
have steadily increased.

It might be noted in passing, too, that station overpopulation
has probably been one factor contributing to the economic problems faced by many of the stations in the AM band, referred to in
Chapter 7.

For television, interference between stations using the same
channel has not become a problem, largely because the FCC made
plans for assignment of stations before issuing authorizations for
any considerable number of television facilities. At the end of the
television freeze in 1952, the Federal Communications Commission
issued a table of allocations specifying the exact channels that
might be used in each of about 1,300 large and small cities; mileage
separations between stations using the same channel were made
great enough to prevent possible serious interference. Of the nearly
2,000 commercial television stations provided for in the table, only
about 550 were to be VHF (very high frequency) stations; the remainder would be assigned to UHF (ultra-high frequency) channels.
In 1965, the commission made a major revision of its allocations
table that reduced the possible number of UHF stations that might
be constructed; no major change was made, however, in allocations
for VHF stations.[8]

Although the commission's original allocations table made provision for a possible total of nearly 2,000 commercial television
stations, many of the cities to which assignments were made were
far too small to support a television operation—some specified
communities had no more than 4,000 inhabitants. In addition,
nearly three-fourths of the stations provided for in the original table
were to be assigned to UHF channels; and, collectively at least, the

---

[8]In 1963, the FCC issued a table of allocations for FM radio stations, to minimize the
possibility of interference between stations in the FM band.

UHF stations that have come on the air since 1952 have not been financially successful. Adding to the problem, the allocations table created nearly 250 "mixed markets" in which any UHF stations constructed would be forced to compete with stations on VHF channels in the same community. Partially to deal with this problem, the commission has since "de-intermixed" a few cities, shifting channel assignments to require all stations in some markets to operate on UHF channels and in other communities on VHF channels. This sort of action has been feasible only in a small number of situations; in most of the "mixed markets" created by the allocations table, the problem still remains. Of course, difficulties of UHF stations have been somewhat lessened by the requirement of all-channel tuning equipment on television sets. With few unused VHF channels still remaining, except in extremely small markets, it is doubtful whether the number of commercial television stations will increase beyond the 750 mark in the predictable future; even with all-channel tuning, UHF stations are still at a competitive disadvantage in markets also served by VHF television outlets.

Qualifications of Licensees

A second aspect of public interest in the granting of licenses relates to the type of individuals to whom the commission grants the privilege of operating broadcasting stations. The Communications Act of 1934 provides only that applicants for licenses must be citizens of the United States and that an authorization for a station may not be granted to a person who has had a previous license revoked for violation of federal antitrust laws. Beyond this, standards are left to the discretion of the Federal Communications Commission; the act merely provides that written applications for licenses must set forth "such facts as the commission may prescribe" as to the citizenship, character, and "financial and other qualifications" of the applicant.

Legal, Technical, and Financial Qualifications

The commission's requirements with respect to the personal qualifications of an applicant are reasonably clear. As provided in the communications act, an individual licensed as the owner of a station must be an American citizen. If the applicant is a corporation, it must be incorporated under the laws of one of the states of the Union; no officer or director of the company may be an alien; and not more than one fifth of the capital stock of the corporation may be owned by aliens or their representatives. The charter of the corporation must also authorize it to engage in broadcasting activities, either specifically or in general terms.

A licensee must also be technically qualified. As interpreted by the commission, technical qualifications relate to the special technical knowledge and skills required to construct and operate a broadcasting station. Either the applicant must himself possess these technical skills or he must show that he has or will engage a staff of employees with the competence to carry on the actual operations of the station, including engineers with the necessary technical qualifications. The commission also considers the applicant's plans for construction of studios and for the equipment to be used, as set forth in the written application, to determine whether they are such as to make possible an effective operation.

For an applicant to be financially qualified means simply that he has enough money in hand—or assurances of its availability from loans or from sale of stock in a corporation—to cover costs of construction of the station and to pay for its initial costs of operation. Although requirements vary from one situation to another, the commission usually expects the applicant to have the financial resources needed to operate the station for at least 2 or 3 months without having to depend during that period on revenues derived from the sale of advertising time.

Character Qualifications

In addition, the commission considers the character qualifications of the applicant, whether the application is for the construction of a new station or for renewal of license of an existing station. Licenses for broadcasting facilities have consistently been denied to individuals who have been convicted of violations of federal laws, especially of laws relating to monopolistic practices. However, license renewals have in a few instances been granted to corporations wholly owned by larger nonbroadcasting concerns, after officers of the parent corporation have been found guilty in federal courts of violating antitrust laws. Licenses and license renewals have also been denied in a number of cases to individuals found to have made false statements in applications or in reports to the commission; the commission holds that the making of such false statements is prima facie evidence that the applicant "lacks the character qualifications necessary for the licensee of a broadcasting station."

In several instances the commission has refused to grant licenses or license renewals to applicants who have broadcast misleading medical advertising or have used station facilities to launch attacks on racial or religious groups. In one or two instances, license renewals have been refused to stations whose owners conducted fraudulent promotional contests; in at least one case a station was ordered off the air because an employee was allowed, over a period of several months, to make frequent use of "smutty" or suggestive language in programs of recorded music. In all these situations, the commission held that the objectionable activities reflected on the character of

"Please don't say anything that will offend anyone—our license is up for renewal."

the applicant or licensee and made him unfit to be the licensee of a broadcasting station.

Preventing Network Monopoly in Broadcasting

The Federal Communications Act of 1934 provides that all federal laws relating to illegal monopolies are to apply to broadcasting. The Federal Communications Commission interprets the act as requiring it to take such steps as may be necessary to preserve competition in broadcasting and, to some degree at least, competition in the control of the various media of communication in any given community. Many of the commission's policies in this are set forth in formal Rules and Regulations. One set of regulations is intended to prevent a network from exercising too great a degree of control over the programming or other activities of affiliated stations. Since the communications act gives the FCC no direct authority over network companies, the regulations in each case relate to stations; usually the regulation starts with the language, "No license shall be granted to any station which has a contract with a network organization which," followed by the type of network activity at which the regulation is aimed. As noted in an earlier chapter, a station may not enter into an exclusive contract with a network that prohibits it from carrying programs offered by another network or preventing the network company from offering programs to other stations in the same community. A station may not give a network company an option on the use of any specified hours of its broadcasting time; it must retain for itself the right to reject any program offered by the network with which it is affiliated. One commission regulation, prohibiting affiliation of any station with a network company operating more than one national network system, forced the National Broadcasting Company in 1943 to dispose of one of its two national radio networks. When NBC challenged the legality of this regulation in federal courts, the commission's action was upheld by the Supreme Court of the United States.

Concentration of Control over Media of Communications

Both by regulations it has adopted and by its actions in the licensing of stations, the Federal Communications Commission has indicated its concern over the possibility of any one individual or corporation exercising too great a degree of control over agencies of mass communication. Regulations referred to in Chapter 6 limit the number of stations that may be licensed to any one owner or owning group.

In addition, the FCC refused to allow one licensee to operate two stations of the same type in the same community or two stations of the same type in different communities when the primary service area of one "substantially overlaps" the primary service area of the second. In one case, an applicant for a new television station was refused the grant at least partly on the grounds that the applicant company owned several other television stations in the same general part of the country; the commission's position was that while no overlapping of station service areas would be created, the addition of the proposed new station would result in an "undue concentration of ownership of the agencies of mass communication" in the area. In four or five cases in which several applicants were competing for the same facility, the commission has rejected the application of a local newspaper publisher to prevent a "concentration of control over media of communications" in the community. In a number of other cases, station authorizations have been refused because applicants were charged with "unfair competition" in nonbroadcasting business activities related to mass communications.

This "concentration of media control" issue will be discussed in greater detail in Chapter 13.

Maintaining Competition in Broadcasting Business Interests

The desire of the Federal Communications Commission to maintain competition in broadcasting was a major cause of the prime-time access rules discussed in Chapter 5. These rules, freeing some prime-time hours from network productions and encouraging certain kinds of programming, are seen as an effort by the FCC to encourage independent producers and increase the number of programming sources available to television. The same rules forced the networks to remove themselves from the syndication of off-network programming to stations in the United States (foreign syndication was not affected), thus increasing competition further. The rules were directly in line with a number of earlier actions taken by the commission to restrict the activities of network companies in areas not related directly to network operation. Objections from the commission as early as 1941 forced the national network companies to dispose of their company-owned talent agencies, which represented—and collected talent-management fees from—the announcers, actors, vocalists, and other entertainers who appeared on network programs. The commission has also expressed its strong disapproval of network-owned spot-sales agencies—NBC Spot Sales, CBS Radio Spot Sales, and the like—acting as station representatives for radio and television stations not owned by the networks themselves. Members of the regulatory body have been consistent in their belief that network companies should not be allowed to exert too great a power over the business activities of other facets of the broadcasting industry.

Few Americans would disagree with the commission's basic purpose of maintaining competition and preventing monopoly control in broadcasting. Nor would any question the fact that, at least partially as a result of the commission's activities in this field, a high degree of competition actually does exist in the broadcasting industry in the United States.

THE COMMISSION'S PROBLEMS

Many of the policies of the Federal Communications Commission have been vigorously opposed by broadcasters. No one really wants to be regulated—and those in the broadcasting industry are no exception. Most broadcasters feel that the commission's exercise of control over programming operations, commercial practices, and the relations between networks and stations has gone far beyond the kind of regulation of broadcasting that members of Congress had in mind when they created the regulatory body. Although, as intelligent citizens, they may deplore the existence of conditions that have led to commission action, most broadcasters feel that any corrective measures should be left to the industry itself, at least in the areas of programming and business affairs.

At the same time, broadcasters recognize the fact that numerous problems involved in broadcasting can be dealt with only by the commission, and that many of those problems are not of a type easily solved. What, for example, should be the commission's policies with respect to the number of radio stations? What methods can be found to deal with the financial problems encountered by UHF television stations and to allow listeners to receive television service from a greater number of stations? What about fraudulent or deceptive advertising practices or about unfair competition between stations in the same community or about unauthorized use of television programs by community antenna systems? These are problems with which the broadcasting industry itself cannot deal—and problems typical of those with which the commission *must* deal if a more effective broadcasting service is to be provided for American listeners. In many fields, the formulation of intelligent policies concerning broadcasting becomes a very complex and difficult matter.

The problems of the Federal Communications Commission are made all the more acute by the very volume of the licensing and regulatory activities in which the commission and its staff are engaged. Not only does the government agency regulate broadcasting and determine policies affecting broadcasting, as well as handling the day-to-day activities of licensing radio and television stations, but also the commission is required by the federal communications act to regulate and to pass on rates charged by interstate telephone and telegraph systems. In addition it issues licenses for radio transmitters used in point-to-point communications—those on fishing and pleasure boats, passenger vessels, airplanes, and taxicabs and those used by railroads, police authorities, large industrial companies, and even private individuals who have radio telephones in their automobiles. The recent popularity of Citizen's Band (CB) radio has resulted in an additional work load of up to 600,000 license applications per week. Each of these licenses must be periodically renewed, of course, as well as the licenses for broadcasting stations. In view of the work load involved, it is surprising that even with the assistance of a large staff of employees the Federal Communications Commission ever finds time to deal with the vital problems of the American broadcasting industry.

The commission's difficulties have not been lessened by the fact that, with very few exceptions, the persons appointed as members of the Federal Communications Commission have had, at the time when they were appointed, no previous contact with broadcasting or the broadcasting industry and almost no knowledge of the complex problems with which they have been expected to deal. Commissioners have usually been political appointees, very often selected because of outstanding services rendered to the party in power rather than because of any technical training or experience relating to broadcasting. Even after their appointment, they have had little opportunity to become acquainted with the day-to-day problems of operating a radio or television station; their regulatory activities necessarily have had something of an "ivory tower" limitation. The situation naturally has been disturbing to station operators who are subject to regulation. However, nearly all broadcasters would concede that most of the individuals appointed to the commission have conscientiously tried to "serve the public interest" in their efforts to regulate broadcasting and have made every effort to be fair and impartial in their decisions. Despite the fact that commission members are frequently political appointees, charges of partisanship or political bias in decisions have been exceedingly rare. Mistakes undoubtedly have been made; policies adopted by the commission have sometimes failed to work out in practice in the way they were intended. However, most leaders of the broadcasting industry feel that the mistakes made have been honest ones, resulting in most cases from the complexity of the problems to be solved and the difficulties of finding solutions that are equally applicable in every situation.

CRITICISMS BY BROADCASTERS

However, no matter how great may be their respect for the integrity and good intentions of the individual commissioners, broadcasters generally have two serious complaints with respect to the commission's regulatory activities—complaints other than those related to specific commission policies or to the regulatory agency's apparent desire to extend its jurisdiction into new areas. First, they complain, and with a good deal of justice, that in making decisions the commission is often much too slow. The television freeze, which lasted for 3½ years while the commissioners pondered the problems of station allocations, of television color systems, and of providing for educational television, illustrates the extremely deliberate nature of many commission actions. More recently, consideration of proposed revision of application forms for new and renewed licenses dragged on for more than 4 years before new forms were finally approved. An even more striking example has been the agency's inability to arrive at any final decisions concerning the future status of high-power, clear-channel radio stations. These, of course, are matters involving major policy decisions; perhaps deliberate action is justified. Even in the licensing of individual stations, however, the commission has at times been almost painfully slow; in some instances, applicants for new station facilities have waited for as long as 3 or 4 years before final action was taken, and occasionally license renewal applications have been held up for as long as 15 or 18 months, with the stations involved not even told the reason for delay.

A second complaint of broadcasters is that commission policies are constantly changing. Things accepted a week ago by the commission as right and proper may today be held to be objectionable; practices frowned upon a year ago are now permitted—and in some cases even approved. Take for example the commission's varying rulings on the requirement of "balanced" programming. Regulatory policies do change; often the changes are of major importance.

In part, modified policies of the commission are a result of changing conditions in the broadcasting industry; but probably to a greater degree the changes in major policies reflect the constantly changing membership of the commission. New members often have different ideas from those of their predecessors about the obligations of station licensees or the extent of regulation desirable. Similarly, appointees of any administration tend to reflect administration attitudes as to the desirability of regulation in general. Many of the commissioners appointed by President John F. Kennedy, for example, were much more "regulation minded" than those who served during the Nixon administration, and commission attitudes changed correspondingly.

Whether or not this is the major cause of changes in policies applied by the Federal Communications Commission, it is an unquestionable fact that policy changes have been frequent from the time the commission was first organized in 1934. The result is that broadcasters find themselves threatened by a sort of regulatory "sword of Damocles," not knowing from one year to the next or sometimes even from one day to the next just what is required of them as licensees of stations. The frequent changes in commission policies have created serious problems for station operators and undoubtedly have been one cause behind the opposition of many broadcasters to regulation of any type.

STUDY AND DISCUSSION QUESTIONS

1. Report on or be prepared to discuss one of the following:

    a. The Wireless Ship Act of 1910
    b. The Radio Act of 1912
    c. The breakdown of the Radio Act of 1912
    d. The Radio Act of 1927
    e. The Communications Act of 1934
    f. Recent hearings on the revision of the Communications Act of 1934
    g. Regulation of broadcasting by the Department of Commerce
    h. Regulation of broadcasting by the Federal Radio Commission
    i. Regulation of broadcasting by the Federal Communications Commision

2. Report on or be prepared to discuss the responsibilities of the major divisions of the Federal Communications Commission dealing with broadcasting. Consider the following:

    a. The office of the executive director
    b. The office of the general counsel

    c. The office of the chief engineer
    d. The office of the secretary
    e. The office of information
    f. The hearings and review office
    g. The broadcast bureau
    h. The field operations bureau
    i. The cable television bureau

3. Report on or be prepared to discuss the levels of sanction available to the Federal Communications Commission in its regulation of broadcasting.

4. Secure from the Federal Communications Commission a copy of the forms and instructions for one of the major reports required of commercial broadcasters and report on or be prepared to discuss the amount and kinds of data required of the licensee to successfully complete the form. Consider items such as the following:

    a. Initial applications for a license
    b. Applications for license renewal
    c. Annual program reports
    d. Equal employment opportunity reports

5. Report on or be prepared to discuss the actions of the Federal Communications Commission—and the results of these actions—in areas such as the following:

    a. Clear-channel authorizations
    b. Public service responsibilities of broadcast licensees
    c. The development of FM
    d. The introduction of television
    e. The development of color television
    f. The allocation of commercial television channels (UHF and VHF)
    g. The growth of AM after World War II
    h. The relationship between network affiliates and networks
    i. The development of CATV and pay-television

6. Review the backgrounds of current FCC commissioners and assess the knowledge of broadcasting (economics, programming, management, engineering, law) that each brought to the commission.

SUGGESTED READINGS

Walter B. Emery. *Broadcasting and Government: Responsibilities and Regulations.* East Lansing: Michigan State University Press, 1961.
Henry Geller. *A Modest Proposal to Reform the Federal Communications Commission.* Santa Monica, Calif.: RAND Corporation, 1974.

Ralph M. Jennings and Pamela Richard. *How To Protect Your Rights in Radio and Television.* New York: United Church of Christ, 1974.

Daniel W. Toohey, Richard D. Marks, and Arnold P. Leitzker. *Legal Problems in Broadcasting: Identification and Analysis of Selected Issues.* Lincoln, Neb.: Great Plains National Instructional Television Library, 1974.

United States Congress, House of Representatives, Committee on Interstate and Foreign Commerce. *Regulation of Broadcasting: Half a Century of Government Regulation of Broadcasting and the Need for Further Legislative Action.* 85th Cong., 1st. Sess. Washington, D.C.: U.S. Government Printing Office, 1958.

13

Regulation of
the Broadcasting Industry

As we have seen in Chapter 12, broadcasting in the United States is regulated by the Federal Communications Commission, as are all other electronic communications media. Regulation of the electronic media is justified by the finite nature of the electromagnetic spectrum and the need to choose between conflicting applications for the right to use frequencies in this spectrum. Regulation is implemented, in the public portions of the spectrum, at least, by the issuance of short-term licenses to be awarded and renewed only if the public interest, convenience, and necessity are served thereby.

This "textbook approach" to broadcast regulation is accurate to a degree and, indeed, was followed in Chapter 12. A major weakness in the approach, however, lies in the fact that it can leave the student of broadcasting with the impression that the Federal Communications Commission is an independant regulatory agency operating in splendid isolation as it shapes and guides the broadcast industry in policies and procedures that will serve the public interest in ever-greater measure. Appealing as this image may be, however, it severely distorts the realities of the regulatory process. Commissioners are appointed by the President and confirmed by the Senate. Congress approves the budget of the FCC, and committees of Congress exercise a supervisory oversight function relative to its actions. All FCC decisions can be, and often are, appealed to the United States Court of Appeals in the District of Columbia. The regulated broadcasting industry is a powerful social force in its own right, and in recent years the citizens being served have been given and have learned to exercise a greater voice in the formulation of the policies of the Federal Communications Commission. In other words, the FCC often finds itself at the focus of pressures exerted by other agencies in our society; and, as a result, its decisions often reflect a consideration of these pressures and cannot be understood simply as the rational decisions of seven persons who regulate broadcasting.

THE POLITICS OF BROADCAST REGULATION

Take, for example, the forces at play in the evolution of the Fairness Doctrine. As early as 1929, the Federal Radio Commission, predecessor of the Federal Communications Commission, stated in its *Great Lakes* opinion that, according to its interpretation of the congressional "public interest, convenience, and necessity" mandate, "it would not be good service to the public to allow a one-sided presentation of the political issues of a campaign." This policy statement went beyond the statutory provision that all *candidates* must be given "equal opportunity" and blocked any station manager from doing what his competitor down the street at the newspaper had been doing for years—editorializing in favor of particular candidates during an election campaign.

Twelve years later, the Federal Communications Commission found a station that had been doing just that and, in its 1941 *Mayflower* decision, it effectively discouraged all editorializing by radio stations. The Commission stated forcefully:

> Radio can serve as an instrument of democracy only when devoted to the communication of information and the exchange of ideas fairly and objectively presented. A truly free radio cannot be used to advocate the causes of the licensee. It cannot be used to support the candidacies of his friends. It cannot be devoted to the support of principles he happens to regard most favorably. In brief, the broadcaster cannot be an advocate.[1]

This decision was not well received by a broadcasting industry that was rapidly becoming a primary source of news and information to an American public concerned about the approach, and later the progress, of World War II. By 1947, segments of the industry had put enough pressure on the Federal Communications Commission to justify public hearings on the matter of editorializing by broadcast licensees. These hearings were held in the spring of 1948 and a Policy Statement was issued in mid-1949.[2] The 1949 statement, in effect, reversed the *Mayflower* decision and permitted broadcasters to express editorial opinions. With this right, however, came an obligation—"an affirmative duty generally to encourage and implement the broadcast of all sides of controversial issues over their facilities, over and beyond their obligation to make available on demand opportunities for the expression of opposing views." This policy of an "affirmative duty" quickly came to be known as the commission's Fairness Doctrine.

The doctrine became a part of the Communications Act of 1934 when, in 1959, the Congress amended the act to provide for some exceptions to the equal-time provisions of Section 315. Following the exemptions, the amended act now reads, "Nothing in the foregoing sentence shall be construed as relieving broadcasters . . . from the obligation imposed upon them . . . to afford reasonable oppor-

---

[1]"The *Mayflower* Decision," *in* Frank J. Kahn (ed.), *Documents of American Broadcasting* (New York: Appleton-Century-Crofts, 1973), p. 367.

[2]"The Fairness Doctrine," *in* Kahn, *Documents*, p. 380.

tunity for the discussion of conflicting views on issues of public importance."

To this point, then, we have the Federal Radio Commission and the Federal Communications Commission attempting to interpret the statutory public interest guideline; the broadcast industry persuading the FCC to change its policy; and the Congress giving the doctrine more stature by referring to it in the communications act itself. The nature of the Fairness Doctrine, its range and its application, was defined in subsequent years as a result of pressures from other forces.

In the 1960s and 1970s, both major political parties, usually when out of power, worked hard to force application of the Fairness Doctrine to all speeches by an incumbent President. Although the FCC has refused to rule that an address by an incumbent President automatically triggers the Fairness Doctrine, it has ruled that in some cases specific subject matters raised by a President can raise Fairness Doctrine questions (for instance, President Nixon's discussions of Vietnam issues). The party in control of the White House generally wishes to limit these applications, while the party out of power usually has the opposite attitude, so, in this area, Fairness Doctrine interpretations are often the product of a balance of political pressures on the FCC.

The Fairness Doctrine has also been shaped by actions of citizens and citizens' groups. The most obvious example of this influence, of course, is the 1967 application of the Fairness Doctrine to cigarette advertising. This use of the doctrine, which some say hastened the day that advertising for cigarettes was banned from broadcast media, was initiated by a single individual in New York City who complained to the FCC that a local television station had refused him time "to present contrasting views on the issue of the benefits and advisability of smoking." The commission responded by ruling that the Fairness Doctrine would be applicable to that single product—cigarettes. This action stimulated a series of "antismoking spots" that continued until all advertising for cigarettes was removed from the air.[3]

Since the cigarette ruling, several groups have attempted to persuade the Federal Communications Commission to apply the Fair-

---

[3]At the time of the ban on cigarette advertising some broadcasters proposed a continuation of "antismoking" spots that would, by reversing the original commission logic, justify the airing of "prosmoking" spots. The FCC sidestepped this possibility simply by stating that the removal from the air of an annual $200 million in tobacco advertising effectively removed the issue from Fairness Doctrine considerations.

ness Doctrine to specific products, and the Federal Trade Commission has suggested its application to a broad range of product categories. In 1976, however, the commission adopted a Policy Statement that denied such requests and flatly stated that the original 1967 policy was mistaken. Such commission actions are subject to appeal, of course; and the courts may add still another dimension to the ever-changing Fairness Doctrine.

This brief summary of the pressures the FCC faces while trying to shape and apply its Fairness Doctrine demonstrates how many forces are involved. The Congress, of course, makes the basic law and provides the guidelines; the Federal Communications Commission tries to interpret these guidelines; the broadcast industry "assists" the commission in its deliberations; and the Congress can, when it wishes, expand or modify the basic law. The White House, the major political parties, citizens, and the Federal Trade Commission all provide input for FCC decisions; and the courts always have the ultimate power to review and reverse commission decisions.

"As far as I can see, we *have* no policy on counter-counter-commercials to counter-commercials."

THE DETERMINERS OF REGULATORY POLICY

Erwin G. Krasnow, a Washington attorney, and Lawrence D. Longley, a political scientist, have examined this balance of forces that has great influence on the Federal Communications Commission and on the regulation of broadcasting. They conclude that "the FCC does play a central role in the regulation of broadcasting, but often the crucial decisions in policy making come about through the action, interaction, or indeed, the inaction of persons or institutions other than the FCC."[4]

Krasnow and Longley go on to identify six "major participants in the regulatory policy making process"—the Federal Communications Commission, the Congress, the White House, the courts, citizens' groups, and the broadcast industry. Each of these "determiners of regulatory power" will be discussed in following sections.

The Federal Communications Commission

The organization, powers, and procedures of the Federal Communications Commission were considered in Chapter 12, which, however, did not explore the nature of the regulatory body with the statutory power to regulate broadcasting. Over the years, many studies of the FCC, scholarly and otherwise, have revealed certain characteristics of the commission.

Congressional Domination   One of the most frequent criticisms of the Federal Communications Commission is the contention that the agency is not sufficiently independent of Congress. From the days of the Federal Radio Commission, whose functions had to be renewed by Congress at the end of each year of its existence, the Congress has demonstrated interest in and concern for the agency regulating broadcasting. Congress, of course, controls the budget, the Senate confirms the appointment of all commissioners, and congressional committees exercise supervision over FCC activities. These powers are the source of much of the congressional pressure on the Federal Communications Commission.

In addition to these influences, the FCC is faced with more than its share of unofficial contacts from members of Congress. Congressmen and senators think nothing of calling a commissioner to

---

[4]Erwin G. Krasnow and Lawrence D. Longley, *The Politics of Broadcast Regulation* (New York: St. Martin's Press, 1973), p. 23.

discuss matters relating to communications policy. This is true of any regulatory agency, but some authorities feel that no others are more subject to individual contacts than the Federal Communications Commission. This has been explained as the result of the fact that the FCC has the power to grant individuals extremely valuable broadcast licenses or as a result of the fact that members of Congress depend on broadcast media to stay in touch with their constituencies. Whatever the reason, the fact remains that the FCC faces almost daily pressures of some sort from Congress.

Absence of Long-Range Goals Anyone studying the history of the Federal Communications Commission is soon struck by the fact that the commission has consistently failed to formulate the broad policies needed to guide its decisions. Indeed, it has been argued that commission failure to establish clear-cut policy guidelines that go beyond the "public interest, convenience, and necessity" is the primary reason Congress has continued to exert so much pressure on the FCC.

When Congress created the FCC, according to this argument, it did so with the expectation that the agency, through its accumulated expertise, would formulate the standards and policies needed to guide its actions in specific cases. Unfortunately, the commission has failed to do so and has produced instead an often bewildering series of case-by-case decisions in which few clear-cut patterns can be detected. This failure to establish policy resulted in confusion and delay and encouraged both Congress and the courts to participate in FCC activities with increasing vigor in an effort to impose some order on the chaos created by the commission.

In a more contemporary restatement of this position, former commissioner Nicholas Johnson had this to say in his early days as a commissioner:

> The FCC has a plan for our Nation's communication systems of the 1980s. It doesn't know it. It has never thought about it or expressed it. Where is the plan? It lies within thousands of decisions that, taken together and projected twenty years hence, spell the kind of America we are building if we "do nothing." . . . What does that kind of America look like? . . . I don't know. But I do know we are closer to it today than we were yesterday, and that the task of reversing course next week will be harder still.[5]

---

[5]Nicholas Johnson, "Reevaluating the Regulatory Role" (a speech delivered May 13, 1967, to the Iowa Association of Broadcasters convention, Waterloo, Iowa), *in* John H. Pennybacker and Waldo W. Braden, *Broadcasting and the Public Interest* (New York: Random House, 1969), p. 34.

Inadequacy of the "Public Interest" Standard Unfortunately, the Federal Communications Commission has not been given much help by Congress to aid it in the formulation of long-range goals. For one thing, Congress has consistently failed to give the commission sufficient funds to make long-range studies. An even more important factor, however, is the inadequacy of the "public interest, convenience, and necessity" standard.

The vagueness of this term, usually shortened to "the public interest" for convenience, has been a major source of controversy in the field of broadcasting. For almost 50 years, both the FRC and the FCC have been forced to make such decisions as who shall or shall not operate a broadcast station, what kinds of proposed programming are appropriate and how new technology shall be introduced with nothing from Congress but the statement that "the public interest" must be served. With no more guidance than this, different commissions, with different commissioners facing different pressures, have come up with different interpretations of what "the public interest" is. This, of course, is a source of great frustration to broadcasters, who often find it very difficult to read the tea leaves of past commission decisions in the search for guidance for future actions.

The FCC as a Bureaucracy In addition to being a regulatory agency, the Federal Communications Commission is a bureaucracy, with all the conservatism and self-interest that the title implies. Whereas the commissioners themselves are appointed for 7-year terms by the President (with Senate confirmation), the staff of the FCC is made up largely of Civil Service appointees who stay on, in most cases, no matter what changes are made in the composition of the commission itself.

Predictably, the result is a certain policy momentum with concomitant reluctance to change—a situation that is very difficult for individual commissioners to alter. Since bureaucracies fear failure—as a threat to individual jobs—and, as a result, are often reluctant to make hard decisions, "the commission often substitutes the act of evaluating and studying a problem or policy for the act of actually dealing with a problem or making policy."[6]

We will see later in this chapter, for example, that for more than 7 years the FCC had before it various aspects of the question of undue concentration of control of mass media. The decisions to be made on this question were extremely difficult—dealing, as they

---

[6]Krasnow and Longley, *Politics of Broadcast Regulation*, p. 26.

did, with conflicting views of "the public interest" and the future of large and powerful media interests—and the FCC took final action in 1975 only as a result of pressures from both the Justice Department and the courts.

The Background of the Commissioners   The commissioners who struggle to control this bureaucracy do, of course, have considerable impact on the activities of this regulatory body. A study of the backgrounds of those commissioners who have served on the FRC and the FCC since 1927 shows that more than half were either lawyers or had studied law, and that virtually all had held other governmental positions before joining the FCC.

One result of this common administrative and legal background has been a "tendency to see regulatory activities in legal and administrative terms rather than in political or even broad social terms."[7]

The picture that emerges from this brief study of the Federal Communications Commission is one of an agency, with vague charge from Congress and few long-range goals to guide its actions, that suffers from bureaucratic lethargy and a legalistic point of view while under the thumb of Congress. This view of the FCC, perhaps, helps explain its susceptibility to outside pressures.

The Congress

As noted above, the Congress can be a very important factor in the regulatory process. Krasnow and Longley identify seven forms of congressional influence: statute, the purse, oversight responsibilities of standing committees, supervision by other committees, investigations, approval of appointments, and pressures from individual congressmen and their staffs.

Control by Statute   The Communications Act of 1934 represents, of course, the basic law governing broadcasting. Where this act is specific, as in Section 315 governing political broadcasts, the Federal Communications Commission can act with resonable dispatch and predictability. Other statutes forbid the broadcasting of obscene, indecent, or profane language, fradulent information, or material concerning a lottery.

In clearly defined statutory areas, then, the FCC has little

---

[7]Krasnow and Longley, *Politics of Broadcast Regulation*, p. 27.

latitude for decision making. The agency cannot change the equal-time provisions of Section 315, nor can it unilaterally extend the term of a license to 5 years. When changes are to be made, Congress must make them—as it did in 1959 to exclude certain types of news and information programs from equal-time requirements and as it may do in the future to extend the license period.

As we have already seen, however, in most areas of FCC jurisdiction the only guidance provided by Congress is the "public interest" standard. The absence of clearer guidelines makes the FCC susceptible to second-guessing from many sources and especially vulnerable to other forms of congressional influence.

Budgetary Controls As it must for most federal agencies, Congress approves and appropriates the money for the annual budget of the Federal Communications Commission. Thus the House and Senate appropriations subcommittees each year have the power to examine commission activities and "suggest" changes and modifications in policies or procedures. While without the force of law, these "suggestions" are generally regarded just as seriously by the FCC since, understandably, any federal agency is reluctant to offend those who control the purse strings.

The appropriations subcommittees also have direct control over specific items in the commission budget and can stimulate a program or policy by generosity or kill it by neglect. Thus, as we have already seen, Congress has consistently made long-range planning unfeasible by withholding necessary funds. Congressional direction was responsible for FCC adoption of a fee schedule designed to recoup a part of its budget each year. Also implicit in this control is the power to affect the introduction of new technology (such as community antenna television and satellite transmission) by restricting funds to commission agencies attempting to study and supervise them.

Oversight Responsibilities of Standing Committees The Communications Act of 1934 established the Federal Communications Commission as an agency to administer the details of the act—a policy followed by Congress in many other instances. The result was an ever-growing number of such administrative agencies receiving various degrees of attention from Congress. In an attempt to gain a greater measure of control over these agencies, Congress has set up a system whereby each standing committee in the Senate and the House is charged with the responsibility of supervising the agencies administering laws that fall under its jurisdiction. Thus the House Committee on

Interstate and Foreign Commerce and the Senate Committee on Commerce, and their respective subcommittees on communication, have major responsibility for studying the communications industry and considering legislation affecting the FCC.

Because of these oversight responsibilities of Congress, the FCC and its staff have frequent contact with the congressional committees and *their* staffs, during which an exchange of views on matters before the commission inevitably takes place. Frequent hearings are also held, forcing both commission and staff to justify policies (or an absence of policies) and procedures before the committees. Obviously, a forceful committee with the power to recommend and initiate legislation relating to any aspect of the job of the FCC, including its very existence, can have considerable impact on commission judgments and decisions.

Supervision by Other Committees   While the Senate and House Commerce Committees have primary responsibility for overseeing the activities of the Federal Communications Commission, other committees have also paid close attention to the commission when their areas of interest overlapped some FCC activity. Krasnow and Longley point out that in recent Congresses, commission activities have been reviewed by the Senate and House Government Operations Committees, the Science and Astronautics Committees, the

Figure 13–1   The subcommittee on communications of the House Interstate and Foreign Commerce Committee holds frequent hearings on matters of interest to broadcasters. (Courtesy Library of Congress)

Judiciary Committees, the Senate Foreign Relations Committee, the Select Committee on Small Businesses, and the Joint Economic Committee. Such multiple supervision, of course, simply adds to congressional pressures on the FCC.

Congressional Investigations The Federal Communications Commission has the responsibility for regulating an industry that has become an important force in our society. Politicians, for example, depend on broadcasting for a substantial portion of their contact with their constituencies during campaign periods and also while they serve in office. Broadcasting is also a major source of news for most people, and many feel the electronic media have the power to create public issues by choosing to focus on them and to shape attitudes toward these issues by the nature of the coverage given them.

Because of this importance and power, Congress has always paid close attention to the activities of the FCC. As a matter of fact, few other federal agencies have experienced the number of investigations the commission has been exposed to. In the period between 1938 and 1952, for example, Congress always had before it some legislation looking toward a reorganization of the FCC. Such legislation almost inevitably included hearings in which the commission was required to explain or justify its actions and comment on the proposed changes. Since 1952, legislative efforts to reorganize the FCC have slackened, but the Congress has continued its periodic hearings on a variety of topics related to broadcasting and the commission.

Some will argue that such investigations are salutary because they force the FCC to move with caution and help it focus its attention on new problems. Others maintain that hearings take large amounts of time away from an understaffed commission and reinforce a reluctance to make decisions that can be second-guessed by Congress and are thus harmful. Most will agree, however, that continual investigations do help keep a regulatory body in tune with the wishes of the legislature.

The Approval of Appointments The seven commissioners at the top of the organization chart of the Federal Communications Commission are appointed by the President, but must be approved by the Senate. Custom further decrees that the President will consult with a senator who is from his party and from the home state of a potential nominee before announcing nomination. This combination of law and custom is another source of control by Congress, for the nature of the commissioners determines, in great measure, the nature of the FCC. The more stable staff, of course, does exert a moderating effect and is given a measure of independent discretionary power; but it is the commissioners who establish priorities, have the power to reverse staff actions, and finally say "yea" or "nay" to an issue. The Kennedy appointees to the FCC, for instance—Newton Minnow, E. William Henry, and Kenneth Cox—were seen as much more activist and critical in their attitudes toward broadcasting than were such Nixon appointees as Robert Wells, H. Rex Lee, and Charlotte Reid; and FCC actions during the tenure of the former group often reflected this difference in attitude.

The Senate, then, can use its approval power to shape the commission and its actions, to a degree. In addition, confirmation hearings also provide a forum in which senators express their views on communications policy and these views are given close attention by commissioners and potential commissioners.

Individual Pressures Noted earlier was the fact that individual legislators and their staffs think nothing of calling the FCC to express opinions on issues facing the agency. It is difficult to assess the impact of such contacts, but they cannot be overlooked. Some authorities believe that, in the unique atmosphere of Washington, such individual contacts can have at least as much influence on FCC activities as do congressional hearings. Whatever their influence, they must be considered as another source of congressional pressure on the Federal Communications Commission.

The White House

The White House, of course, is the official residence of the President of the United States and, as a building, can exert no power at all. What has come to be known as "The White House," on the other hand, consists of a large group of individuals organized in an executive department of considerable size, and this White House does indeed exert power.

The President himself appoints all commissioners, subject to Senate confirmation, and names the chairman. He is restricted somewhat by the provisions that no more than four commissioners may be of the same political party, but most Presidents have had little difficulty finding individuals in tune with their regulatory and administrative views, no matter what their party. As already noted, the nature of the seven commissioners has considerable effect on the nature of the Federal Communications Commission, so the appointment power alone is an important influence on broadcasting regulation.

Within the structure of the larger White House concept exist many other sources of influence on the FCC and on broadcasting. The Office of Management and Budget, for instance, must review and approve all FCC budget requests and legislative proposals before they are submitted to Congress; it approves all report forms, applications—including the license renewal form—and questionnaires before they can be adopted or revised; and it has the power to authorize the high-salaried staff positions needed to attract and keep talented and dedicated workers.

The Justice Department serves as the legal arm of the President, and it has not hesitated to enter the regulatory picture. The Justice Department, for instance, objected strenuously to the proposed merger between the American Broadcasting Company and International Telephone and Telegraph Corporation and caused the long delay that finally persuaded ITT to withdraw the merger proposal. The Antitrust Division of the Justice Department has shown continued concern over what it sees as excessive concentration of media control and has consistently pressured the FCC to adopt tougher rules to break up powerful media combinations. Justice has also shown an interest in the growth of pay-television as a competitive medium and has attempted to persuade the FCC that commercial broadcasters are showing excessive concern about a new competitor.

In 1970, President Nixon established in the Office of the President the Office of Telecommunications Policy (OTP) to be the advisor to the President on telecommunications matters. From the beginning, the relationship between OTP and the FCC was unclear, and many feared the White House would come to dominate the supposedly independent regulatory agency. Such domination never occurred, however, but the Office of the President has been influential in several areas of communications policy. In 1971, the OTP played a significant role in bringing together representatives of the broadcasting and cable television industries and helping them arrive at a compromise that led to the CATV rules issued by the FCC in 1972 (a compromise that, unfortunately, broke down after a few years). The efforts of the FCC toward simplifying its Rules and Regulations for radio ("re-regulation") came at the initiative of the Office of Telecommunications Policy, and statements by the OTP, combined with speeches by its director, have had a significant impact on the development of the Corporation for Public Broadcasting and the Public Broadcasting Service.

The Courts

Every action by the Federal Communications Commission—be it a decision in a hearing, a license renewal, a policy statement, or a clarification—is subject to review by one court—the U.S. Court of Appeals in the District of Columbia—with ultimate appeal to the U.S. Supreme Court. The appeals court can reverse a decision, strike down a policy statement, or remand a decision back to the FCC for further study. Although only a small percentage of FCC actions are considered by the court, the threat of such review is always a factor in commission deliberations and decisions.

The District of Columbia Court of Appeals is made up of nine judges, who are appointed by the President with the advice and consent of the Senate and who have life terms on the court. Most decisions are made by a three-judge panel, to divide the work load, but parties may request a hearing by the full court.

The power of the appeals court over the FCC seems, at first glance, to be absolute, but it is limited by one significant factor. The court can rule only on cases that are brought before it; it cannot move independently to review FCC actions it may question. If the Office of Communications of the United Church of Christ, for instance, had not appealed a 1964 short-term renewal of the license of WLBT (TV), in Jackson, Mississippi, the court could not have stepped in and opened the door to citizen participation in hearings.

In spite of this limitation, the court exerts a powerful influence on the regulatory process and provides a unique point of access into this process. Whereas the Federal Communications Commission, the Congress, and the White House are most likely to listen to and be influenced by groups and individuals with money and political power and the broadcasting industry is devoted, in large measure, to the protection of its own interests, the appeals court will listen to an individual or small groups almost as readily as it will to powerful vested interests. Indeed, it was the Court of Appeals that encouraged citizen participation in the first place, and it is through this court that much citizen pressure continued to be applied.

Examples of the activities of the U.S. Court of Appeals in the District of Columbia can be found throughout this book. In recent years it has issued rulings on citizen participation in renewal procedures, FCC license renewal policies, the constitutional basis of the Fairness Doctrine, and FCC intervention in radio license transfers that include a format change. Clearly, the court is an important factor in the dynamics of broadcast regulation.

Citizens' Groups

Broadcast licensees are, of course, expected to serve "the public interest" of their communities. For more than 30 years, however, the citizens of a community were not permitted to intervene as parties in radio and television licensing proceedings. As late as the mid-1960s, only parties claiming electrical interference or possible economic injury could so intervene. The interests of the public, supposedly, were represented by the Federal Communications Commission.

The WLBT(TV) decisions in 1966 and 1969 referred to in Chapter 5 changed all this. The case grew from the contention that WLBT(TV) in Jackson, Mississippi, had been discriminating against the black citizens of Jackson in its programming. The owners of WLBT ultimately lost their license, but of greater long-range importance was the grant of standing before the FCC to significant community organizations and groups of citizens having a legitimate interest in programming. The significance of the case was summarized in *Broadcasting* magazine:

> The case did more than establish the right of the public to participate in a station's license renewal hearing. It did even more than encourage minority groups around the country to assert themselves in broadcast matters at a time when unrest was growing and blacks were becoming more activist. It provided practical lessons in how pressure could be brought, in how the broadcast establishment could be challenged.[8]

These lessons were learned well and the "broadcast establishment" was indeed challenged. The activities of these citizens' groups in the late 1960s and early 1970s have been summarized in Chapter 5. Among the results of this activity have been changes in employment practices and programming by many licensees, a

---

[8]"The Pool of Experts on Access," *Broadcasting* (September 20,1971), p. 36, cited in Krasnow and Longley, *Politics of Broadcast Regulation*, p. 37.

greater emphasis on and attention to the Fairness Doctrine, and the ascertainment provisions of license renewal that have forced a continuing dialogue between station management and the community served.

The Broadcasting Industry

It is difficult, if not impossible, for any regulatory agency to function without a reasonably close relationship quickly developing between the regulators and the industry regulated—a general development that is especially true of the interplay between the Federal Communications Commission and the complex and rapidly changing broadcasting industry. In this relationship, power and influence generally flow in both directions with, it is hoped, the regulatory agency avoiding domination by the industry.

This two-way flow is not necessarily something to deplore, considering the nature of any regulatory agency, and the FCC provides a good example of why this is so. Through the years, a great majority of the commissioners appointed came to the FCC with little or no background in broadcasting, primarily because no one is permitted to serve on the FCC and retain any interest in any property or business connected with broadcasting. As a result, few broadcasters are in a position to take the steps necessary to qualify for the position. Also, there is a strong feeling both in Congress and in the public that no regulatory body should be dominated by appointees from the industry regulated. These factors produce a situation in which most new commissioners are expected to participate in the regulation of a complicated and dynamic industry with precious little background information to guide them in their deliberations.

It is true that the FCC does have a staff to assist its commissioners and that this staff has less turnover and is better able to build for itself a generally sound body of knowledge about the industry. Noted earlier, however, was the fact that this staff exhibits many of the characteristics of any bureaucracy and is often slow and conservative in its actions. Broadcasters also argue that, while the staff can, over the years, compile a body of information, the fact that none of them are participating in the day-to-day operation of a broadcast property makes all this information theoretical and often irrelevant and outdated.

The argument can be made, then, that the broadcasting industry is needed to help fill this partial information vacuum, and many opportunities to do so do present themselves. The FCC often openly asks for information in oral hearings that focus on specific issues. In recent years, for instance, the FCC has held such hearings on the Fairness Doctrine, its ascertainment policies, and the growth of community antenna television. Many interests testify in such hearings, of course, for the commission is interested both in facts and in a broad range of interpretations of these facts, but representatives of the industry are almost always on hand in an effort to protect its interests. Even when oral hearings are not held, the FCC asks for written comments and reply comments on virtually every proposed policy statement or change.

In addition to these formal channels, the FCC operates in a network of informal contacts that allows for a great deal of input from the industry. Many broadcasters visiting Washington for business or pleasure drop by the FCC offices and talk with commissioners or staff members about general problems facing the industry—although no broadcaster who is a party in a docket before the commission may make such contacts. The commissioners and the staff attend national trade conventions and are often invited to the meetings of state associations of broadcasters, and these meetings often provide a forum for a lively exchange of ideas and opinions between the regulators and the regulated. Individual broadcasters with questions about the interpretation or application of a rule or regulation may phone the FCC in Washington for direction and advice from staff members, and these contacts often include a flow of information and opinion from the industry to the FCC. In recent years, groups of commissioners and staff have visited small-market radio stations in an effort to gain a better understanding of the special problems of this segment of the industry.

Another type of informal contact also deserves special attention here. Virtually every television station and many radio stations retain the services of communications attorneys or firms in Washington. The task of these communications attorneys, in theory, is simply to interpret FCC policies for their clients and to assist them in satisfying commission Rules and Regulations. In reality, however, the relationship between these attorneys and the Federal Communications Commission is often so close that they can exert a significant influence on commission decisions. Joseph Goulden describes the relationship between Washington attorneys and regulatory agencies in general terms:

> Relations between some Washington lawyers and officials of the regulatory agencies can be so intimate they embarrass an onlooker. The lawyers and the regulators work together in a tight, impenetrable community where an outsider can't understand the language, much less why things are done the way they are. The lawyers and the regulators

play together, at trade association meetings, over lunch, on the golf courses around Washington. They frequently swap jobs, the regulator moving to the private bar, the Washington lawyer moving into the Commission on a "public service" leave of absence from his firm.[9]

Finally, one cannot overlook the work of the National Association of Broadcasters (NAB) in providing information for and trying to put pressure on both the Congress and the FCC on behalf of broadcasting interests. Speaking for the entire industry, the NAB has more than 4,000 member radio and television stations and is headquartered in a building only a few blocks from the FCC. As a leading spokesman for the industry, the NAB works to maintain its contacts in both Congress and the commission and is ready to file comments to give oral testimony on virtually any issue facing the industry. Members of the commission and its staff regularly attend and participate in NAB annual conventions and regional meetings and, despite an uneven pattern of success in recent years, the National Association of Broadcasters must be considered as a major channel of influence and pressure from the industry to both the FCC and the Congress.

THE DYNAMICS OF BROADCAST REGULATION

From the above, it must be evident that broadcast regulation is the result of a combination of interacting forces as various elements of the regulation complex work to meet their responsibilities, protect their rights, and advance their interests. A few illustrations will demonstrate how these forces combine to regulate the broadcasting industry.

Diversification of Control of Mass Media

The threat of excessive concentration of media control in the hands of one person or corporation has always loomed large in the minds of those concerned with the media and our democratic system. A society depending on a free and balanced flow of information and opinion can ill afford, it is said, to allow a small group of powerful

---

[9]Joseph C. Goulden, *The Superlawyers: The Small and Powerful World of the Great Washington Law Firms* (New York: Weybright and Talley, 1972), p. 6, cited in Krasnow and Longley, *Politics of Broadcast Regulation*, p. 33.

interests to control the nation's major channels of communication. Because of the importance of the issue during the past 50 years, all six of the "determiners of regulatory policy" discussed above have entered the debate and have affected national policy.

Congress has been concerned about the issue since the early days of radio. According to a congressional study:

> During the period of the middle and late thirties, Congress was more concerned with the problems of monopoly than of any other aspect of the radio industry. Congressional concern reached a new high in 1937, when there were pending at the same time no less than four resolutions for investigation of monopolistic practices. None of these resolutions passed; but in 1938, under congressional pressure, the Commission itself appointed a committee of three of its members to determine what regulations should be effected concerning chain broadcasting.[10]

As a result of this congressional pressure, the committee appointed by the FCC recommended that NBC be forced to sell one of its two radio networks, and the full commission concurred. NBC fought the decision through the Court of Appeals and the Supreme Court but lost; and its Blue Network was sold, to become the American Broadcasting Company.

Concern about monopoly also lay behind the FCC rules prohibiting a licensee from owning more than one AM station, one FM station, and one television station in the same market or owning more than a total of seven AM stations, seven FM stations, and seven television stations throughout the country. Since 1965, however, the FCC, the Congress, the courts, and the Justice Department have expressed doubts that these rules were strong enough.

The Federal Communications Commission moved first; and, in June 1965, it proposed a rule that would limit television ownership in the Top 50 markets to three, with no more than two to be VHF channels. It justified this proposal as a step to open up major markets to a larger number of licensees. At the time of the action, nineteen licensees owned more than the proposed limit, but the FCC backed away from the idea of forcing them to sell stations in order to conform to the limit (a concept that was to be known as forced divestiture). The rule, as proposed, would apply only to transfers negotiated after its adoption, although the FCC did indicate that it

---

[10]United States Congress, House of Representatives, Committee on Interstate and Foreign Commerce, *Regulation of Broadcasting: Half a Century of Government Regulation of Broadcasting and the Need for Further Legislative Action.* 85th Cong., 1st Sess. (Washington, D.C.: U.S. Government Printing Office, 1958), p. vi.

would consider the proposal as a general policy in considering any request for transfer that arose before its final adoption as a rule.

The so-called Top-50 rule never emerged, however, and as a policy, it began to erode almost immediately. By early 1968, it was evident that the FCC was ready to discard it entirely. In the 2½ years of its existence, the policy was waived eight times and was never applied to a transfer application. In February 1968, by a 4 to 3 vote, the FCC quietly buried its Top-50 experiment.

Soon thereafter, however, the FCC moved with more conviction and consistency on a related front. In March of 1968, it proposed a rule that would prohibit the licensee of an AM, FM, or television station from acquiring a license for any other class of broadcast service in the same community. Thus, the owner of an AM station could not purchase an FM or television outlet in his market; and the owner of an AM-FM-TV combination wishing to sell the package would be forced to find three buyers instead of one. This proposal was adopted (and promptly labeled the "one-to-a-customer rule") in 1970. It was amended in 1971 to permit the transfer of AM-FM packages and stands today as an example of the commission's interest in a measure of diversification.

As in the Top-50 situation, the FCC did not propose forced divestiture of holdings in markets in which a licensee already operated more than one service. The one-to-a-customer rule applied only to transfers occurring after its adoption in 1970. Pressure from Congress, the courts, and the Justice Department, however, did force the FCC to consider such divestiture in a special category of case—multiple ownership that also included newspaper ownership in the market.

In the early 1940s, Congress and the FCC had investigated the possible dangers of cross-ownership of newspapers and radio stations in the same market but had decided that the danger was more apparent than real. The introduction of FM and television as viable services tripled the number of media available to a single owner, however, and the concentration-of-control issue was raised from time to time in the Congress in the early and middle 1960s. The issue was always raised in connection with other problems, however, and little was done until 1968 when the Senate announced that one of its committees would hold hearings to probe cross-ownership. That same year the Justice Department stepped in with a letter to the commission proposing a hearing on a station sale in Texas to the owners of two newspapers in the same market. This action by the Antitrust Division of Justice prompted the newspapers to withdraw their offer, but the division increased its pressure on the FCC by forcing the owner of an Illinois newspaper to sell his television station because of the threat of antitrust questions raised. At the same time, the Justice Department urged the commission to consider a rule that would break up all existing cross-ownership situations.

The decision by the FCC not to renew the license of WHDH (TV), Boston, based in part on the concentration-of-control issue, indicated that the commission was beginning to respond to these pressures; and it took further tentative steps by setting two renewals for hearing on the same issue in March of 1969. The Court of Appeals in the District of Columbia entered the picture in 1970 by encouraging the FCC to consider the concentration-of-control issue in a broad rulemaking and not on a case-by-case basis.

Under pressure from all three branches of government, the commission announced in March 1970 a proposed rulemaking aimed at the break-up of all multimedia combinations that included newspapers in the same market. The proposal would have given such owners 5 years in which to reduce their holdings to an AM-FM combination, a television station, or a newspaper.

This proposal was vigorously opposed by both newspaper and

broadcast interests, and for 3 years the commission showed little inclination to pursue the matter. Neither the Justice Department nor the citizens' groups that had become interested in the issue as a possible basis for a petition to deny were content to allow the FCC to assign a low priority to this issue. In 1972, a large coalition of Mexican-American and black organizations, aided by the United Church of Christ and others, blocked the transfer of five television stations from Time-Life, Inc. to McGraw-Hill on the grounds of racial discrimination and concentration of control (three of the stations were located in Top 50 markets). The FCC had approved the sale, but the Chicanos and blacks appealed the decision to the Court of Appeals. Before the suit was heard, however, a compromise was reached in which McGraw-Hill agreed to acquire only two of the three stations in the Top 50 markets and met certain minority demands. With this agreement, the appeal was withdrawn.

In 1973 and 1974, both citizens' groups and the Justice Department pressured the FCC further to reach a decision on the concentration-of-control issue. The citizens filed a petition to deny renewal of a southern television station owned by interests controlling an AM-FM outlet and two newspapers in the community; and, in 1974, the Justice Department filed petitions to deny three midwestern license renewals, using the same concentration-of-control issue.

Faced with such pressures, the FCC tried to resolve the matter in 1975 by banning any further newspaper acquisitions of a broadcast license in the same community and by forcing the break-up of media concentrations only in those markets in which the only newspaper also owned the only radio or television station (or both). On appeal, the District of Columbia Court of Appeals stepped in again, however, and told the FCC that it had erred in formulating its divestiture policy. The court stated that the public interest had not adequately been taken into account and directed the FCC to formulate a new policy to include divestiture unless it could be proved that such a policy would not be in the public interest in a given market.

Reviewing the above, we see the Federal Communications Commission, as usual, in the center of the issue from the beginning. Congress was active in the 1930s, forcing the FCC to study the network problem, and again in the late 1960s, when the threat of a Senate investigation encouraged the FCC to continue its study of cross-ownership. The White House was represented here by the Anti-trust Division of the Justice Department, which pressured the FCC to reach a decision by filing petitions to deny and was displeased with the decision reached. The Court of Appeals upheld the FCC decision on NBC, persuaded the commission to adopt a policy and not consider concentration-of-control issues on a case-by-case basis, and struck down the policy when it was issued. Citizens' groups, through petitions to deny and court appeals, put even more pressure on the FCC to resolve the issue. The influence of the industry is somewhat more difficult to pinpoint, but commission waivers of the Top-50 ruling came as a result of successful industry arguments in favor of such waivers. Industry spokesmen worked also to persuade the FCC that, in many cases, concentrations of control could work for the public interest by providing a large pool of news and information expertise and financial buffers for less successful portions of the concentration.

License Renewal Problems

To a broadcaster, of course, the most important thing the Federal Communications Commission can do is to renew his license every 3 years. Without the right to use a portion of the electromagnetic spectrum, even the best-supplied broadcasting plant is worthless. It is not surprising, then, that any threat to the "stability" of licenses (the probability that they will be renewed at the end of each license period) produces an immediate and violent reaction from the industry. Nor is it surprising that groups or individuals trying to affect the communications industry in any way will focus on the license procedure.

All of which helps explain the reaction of the broadcasting industry to the decision of the FCC in 1969 not to renew the license of WHDH. This commission decision ended a long and complex case that began in 1947, when several applicants filed for the same television channel in Boston. The decision not to renew was based on many factors, one of which was the concentration-of-control issue, and the FCC took the position that, because of the peculiar nature of the case, it should not be looked upon as a precedent for future commission actions.

Nevertheless, the broadcasting industry expressed shock and alarm over the decision and was not reluctant to make its feelings known. In an editorial, *Broadcasting* magazine, often a spokesman for the entire industry, concluded that

> Congress has become the broadcaster's only real hope for a restoration of order in an F.C.C. that has clearly gone out of control. At a minimum, the broadcasters must seek amendments to the Communications Act to prohibit the F.C.C. from taking ad hoc actions that can lead

to wholesale divestitures. Perhaps even larger measures of legislative action may be obtainable, including a remedy that looks more desirable every day—the re-organization of the commission.[11]

The industry received another shock in 1969 when the Court of Appeals reversed the renewal of WLBT's license by the FCC and called for hearings to select a new licensee for the station in Jackson, Mississippi. By this time, however, actions toward legislative relief were already under way, and the industry had persuaded Senator John O. Pastore to introduce a bill that would have required the FCC to find that a licensee had not been operating in the public interest before any competing applications could be considered. If a licensee was found to have been operating in the public interest, his license would be renewed on the basis of satisfactory past performance.

This bill was quickly tagged as racist and was attacked as a bill guaranteeing broadcasters "licenses in perpetuity" by such groups as Black Efforts for Soul on Television (BEST) and Action on Smoking and Health (ASH), which saw a more fluid renewal situation as an opportunity for greater minority participation in broadcasting. After a year of turmoil in the industry and in the Senate, the FCC, under pressure to rescue Senator Pastore and the bill's sponsors from legislative defeat, in January of 1970 issued a Policy Statement that stated that the incumbent licensee would be favored at renewal if he could show that his programming had been "substantially" in tune with the needs and interests of his community. The industry found this statement reassuring and Senator Pastore withdrew his bill.

Five elements had interacted to achieve this development—the Federal Communications Commission, the Court of Appeals, the industry, the Congress, and citizens' groups—but the issue was far from being resolved. Having been forewarned by press accounts of the impending FCC Policy Statement on License Renewal, several groups, including the Citizens Communication Center (CCC), almost immediately united to file an appeal to the decision. The court thereupon delivered another jolt to the rattled broadcasting industry by overturning the Policy Statement in mid-1971. This *CCC* decision further instructed the commission to hold license-renewal hearings in all situations in which there are competing applications, outlined several criteria that were to be followed in these hearings, and directed the FCC to define what it might mean by

---

[11]"Boston Stake: $3 Billion" (Editorial), *Broadcasting* (February 3, 1969), p. 84.

"superior service" (a term the court preferred to "substantial service").

This decision by the Court of Appeals was not met with enthusiasm by the industry, now under what it saw as a state of siege by citizens' groups already encouraged by the *WHDH* and *WLBT* decisions. They turned to Congress, as they had in 1969, but Senator Pastore was not interested in being tagged a racist again on behalf of the broadcasters. Nevertheless, the NAB did find congressmen and senators willing to introduce and support acceptable bills—many lengthening the license terms to 5 years—and mounted a massive lobbying effort to get a license-renewal bill through Congress before the end of the 1974 session. This effort fell just short, however, when the two houses passed bills differing in some particulars and no conference committee was called in the confusion of the year-end rush. The industry has not slackened its efforts to seek relief, and in the late 1970s is focusing its attention on including a longer license term in the revision of the Communications Act now under consideration.

It is interesting to note that in the controversy surrounding license stability the Court of Appeals and the Congress have been the major forums for debate, with the Federal Communications Commission often appearing as one of the parties in a dispute. The *WLBT* and *CCC* decisions by the court were central to the issue, and the lack of success by the industry in Congress has kept it alive. Indeed, with the exception of the *WHDH* decision and some early opposition to the Pastore bill, the FCC, more often than not, has seemed to side with the industry in license-renewal matters.

Restrictions on Commercial Time

All the above is not meant to imply that the Federal Communications Commission is powerless to act when it wishes to do so. Even in the face of congressional opposition, the FCC can, on occasion, find ways to accomplish its goals. A good example of this is found in a review of FCC actions to limit the amount of commercial time on radio and television.

Broadcasters must sell commercial time if they are to pay the bills and stay on the air. They must also serve the public interest if they are to keep their license to use the public's airwaves. The FCC has always been concerned lest broadcasters allow this balance of responsibilities to tilt too far toward the financial side, and, in 1963, the commission announced it was considering policies to restrict commercial volume on radio and television stations. Following an internal debate as to whether this should be accomplished on a case-by-case basis (making examples of those stations that "overcommercialized") or by adopting a policy, the commission, by a narrow 4 to 3 vote, chose the latter and proposed rules that would force compliance with the commercial limits in the NAB Radio and Television Codes.

These codes of good practices had always been voluntary, however; and the NAB quickly voiced its opposition. Broadcasters in every state were mobilized to line up congressional support and the Subcommittee on Communications and Power of the House Committee on Interstate and Foreign Commerce was persuaded to hold hearings on a bill that would prohibit the FCC from adopting such a rule (the Rogers bill). Hearings on the bill were held, in which the FCC found few friends, and the bill was unanimously approved by the full commerce committee. At about the same time, further heat was put on the FCC when a Senate appropriations subcommittee cut $400,000 from its 1964 budget, criticizing the commission for entering policy areas not intended by Congress.

The House ultimately passed the Rogers bill; but a shift in commission membership had already resulted in a 4 to 3 line-up *against* the adoption of the NAB code restrictions, and no action was taken by the Senate. The newly composed commission did not look with great favor on a case-by-case approach either; and, for the moment, it appeared that broadcasters had succeeded in working through Congress to restrain the Federal Communications Commission.

In 1966, however, the composition of the commission changed again and the appointment of Nicholas Johnson resulted in a swing back to approval of some sort of commercial limitation policy. Having learned a lesson in 1963, the FCC approached the problem this time in an administrative manner and issued a questionnaire to all licensees asking them to report the maximum amount of time they intended to devote to commercial matter in any hour and to state how often and under what circumstances they might expect to exceed these limits. Significantly, licensees who proposed carrying more than the NAB code limit were asked further to explain how their proposals served the needs and interests of their audiences.

Although the commission chairman, Rosel Hyde, assured broadcasters that the questionnaires were for informational purposes only—to help in the formulation of a clear and practical policy everyone could live with—the policy that emerged in March of 1967 had a familiar ring. At that time the FCC announced that the 18-minute radio and 16-minute television limitations would be a standard for all license-renewal applications to observe. Stations proposing more than these limits without sufficient justification would be asked to report again on their commercial practices midway through the 3-year license term. Thus what had been forbidden as a rule in 1964 emerged as a policy—somewhat more flexibly applied, perhaps, in 1967.

This policy was soon embedded in the license-renewal procedure. License-renewal forms now include questions concerning both past and proposed commercial practices and the licensee who has exceeded, or proposes to exceed, the NAB code limits, as modified slightly to allow for special considerations, can expect a letter from the FCC asking him to demonstrate how he can justify this "excess" in the light of his public interest responsibilities. Such actions by the Federal Communications Commission are generally sufficient to persuade broadcasters to avoid inquiries by restricting commercial matter.

We have seen that the regulation of broadcasting is a complex matter, involving a mix of many forces brought to bear on specific problems. Despite the statutory proscription against censorship, many of these problems are related to programming—the most visible portion of a broadcaster's activity. The effects of broadcast regulation on programming, then, will be the subject of the next chapter.

STUDY AND DISCUSSION QUESTIONS

1. Report on or be prepared to discuss some of the ways Congress can influence the actions of the Federal Communications Commission. Consider such things as the following:

   a. The approval of appointments
   b. Determination of the annual budget
   c. Committees of Congress influencing the commission
   d. Congressional hearings (other than oversight)
   e. Congressional resolutions
   f. Informal contacts between Congress and the commission

2. Report on or be prepared to discuss some of the ways the administration in power in Washington can influence the actions of the Federal Communications Commission. Consider such things as the following:

   a. The appointment power
   b. The Office of Management and Budget
   c. The Office of Telecommunications Policy
   d. The Justice Department
   e. The Department of Defense

3. Report on or be prepared to discuss the origin and evolution of the "public interest, convenience and necessity" standard of the Communications Act of 1934.

4. Report on or be prepared to discuss the impact of a recent court decision on the policies of the Federal Communications Commission. Consider such cases as:

  a. The Network case
  b. The Brinkley and Schuler cases
  c. Red Lion
  d. United Church of Christ I and II (WLBT)
  e. The Citizens Communication Center case (CCC)
  f. The NBC "Pensions" case
  g. The Family Viewing decision.

5. Report on or be prepared to discuss the growth of citizens' groups concerned with broadcasting. Include in your discussion some of the successes and failures of these groups.

6. Report more fully on one of the issues used in this chapter to illustrate the complex nature of broadcast regulation. Your instructor may wish to add other, more recent topics to this list:

  a. Diversification of control of mass media
  b. License renewal
  c. Restrictions on commercial time

SUGGESTED READINGS

Walter S. Baer et al. *Concentration of Mass Media Ownership: Assessing the State of Current Knowledge.* Santa Monica, Calif.: RAND Corporation, 1974.

Walter S. Baer, Henry Geller, and Joseph A. Grundfest. *Newspaper-Television Station Cross-Ownership: Options for Federal Action.* Santa Monica, Calif.: RAND Corporation, 1974.

William T. Gormley, Jr. *The Effects of Newspaper-Television Cross-Ownership on News Homogeneity.* Chapel Hill: Institute for Research in Social Science, Manning Hall, University of North Carolina, 1976.

Erwin G. Krasnow and Laurence D. Longley. *The Politics of Broadcast Regulation.* New York: St. Martin's, 1973.

Philip B. Kurland, ed. *Free Speech and Association: The Supreme Court and the First Amendment.* Chicago: University of Chicago Press, 1976.

Don R. LeDuc. *Cable Television and the FCC: A Crisis in Media Control.* Philadelphia: Temple University Press, 1973.

14

Programming and the Public Interest

In the preceding chapter it was noted that regulation of the broadcasting industry is often the result of a combination of social forces working toward goals that may or may not be directly related to broadcasting. In the concentration-of-media-control issue, for instance, the concern of both Congress and the Justice Department grew as much from fear of monopoly in general as it did from concern over the power of multiple owners. In another case, citizens' groups, in their drive for greater access to the media, saw broadcasting simply as a means toward the greater end of drawing public attention to perceived injustices and inequities. Broadcast regulation, in other words, is often not the result of the deliberations of a rational group of individuals moving under constitutional restraints to accomplish a task set out by Congress. The Federal Communications Commission (FCC) must react, as we have seen, to multiple pressures from many quarters, and the result has often been confusing and distressing to the regulated broadcasters.

THE FRC, THE FCC, AND PROGRAMMING

One consequence of this regulatory pattern has been relatively frequent incursions into programming by the FCC and, before it, the Federal Radio Commission (FRC). When the Federal Radio Commission was created, most broadcasters believed that its authority was to extend only to technical matters so that problems of interference between stations could be dealt with effectively; and the Radio Act of 1927 included a provision stating specifically that the FRC was to have no power of censorship over programs. However, members of the new commission took a broader view of their responsibilities. They were instructed by the radio act to issue licenses in "the public interest, convenience, or necessity"; this at least implied that they were to take into account the *kind of material* a licensee put on the air, no less than his technical engineering record, before granting license renewal to his station.

During the first 2 or 3 years of its existence, the FRC refused to grant license renewals to several radio stations whose owners had persistently broadcast materials that commission members felt were contrary to "the public interest." One licensee had used his station to advertise a cancer cure; another gave wide publicity over his station to a "goat-gland" rejuvenation operation performed regularly in the hospital he owned; two others had broadcast what the FRC held to be vicious attacks on religious and civic groups. When the stations involved were denied license renewals and their owners appealed to federal courts, the courts held that the commission was required by law to determine the elements involved in broadcasting "in the public interest." Consequently, in the courts' opinion, the FRC had not exceeded its legal authority by refusing license renewal to stations that broadcast materials that, in the judgment of members of the regulatory agency, were not in that "public interest." With the FRC's authority so upheld by the courts, the offending stations were taken off the air.

The reasoning used by the FRC in justifying its actions in spite of the "no censorship" provision of the act of 1927 is interesting. Censorship, argued the commission, refers only to the use of *prior restraint*. For example, refusal by the federal regulatory body to allow a station to broadcast some specific program would constitute censorship as prohibited in the act; however, consideration of a station's previous programming operations, taken as a whole, to determine whether or not the station has operated "in the public interest" during the period of its license, is not censorship. No *prior restraint* is involved, even when the commission considers the applicant's past record as indicating the type of programming he will likely provide in future years. This interpretation of the "no censorship" provision of the law has been held consistently by federal courts whenever the issue has been raised.

The *Great Lakes* Opinion

Almost immediately after its creation, the Federal Radio Commission outlined its ideas on the requirements of providing programs in "the public interest." In the *Great Lakes* opinion in 1929, it held that broadcasters were expected to provide a balanced or "well-rounded" program structure, including programs of such types as agricultural information, religion, education, and discussions of public issues. In addition, the FRC held that the broadcasting of programs or materials that tended to injure the listening public—attacks on civic or religious groups, for example, or fraudulent medical advertising—raised serious questions as to the desirability of granting license renewals to owners of offending stations. As has already been noted, several stations were taken off the air by the Federal Radio Commission because of the objectionable character of materials they broadcast.

Following its creation in 1934, the Federal Communications Commission gave relatively little attention to the requirement of balanced or well-rounded program service, possibly because at that time practically all radio stations *did* offer programs of a wide variety of types, including the kinds of program offerings that had been recommended in the *Great Lakes* opinion in 1929. However, in the years before World War II, the FCC did follow the policies of the FRC with respect to the broadcasting of objectionable or harmful materials. Stations were taken to task for carrying questionable medical advertising; hearings were ordered on license renewals of stations that had broadcast astrology programs or other materials tending to "create superstition." Similar action was taken against stations advertising lottery schemes, and in one or two cases the commission threatened punitive action against any stations carrying network programs that included profanity or "materials bordering on obscenity." In 1939, the FCC released an informal memorandum warning stations against practices that "would be taken into consideration when licenses came up for renewal"—among them hard-liquor advertising, overcommercialization, the broadcasting of programs creating excessive suspense, the overuse of phonograph records, and failure to provide "balance" in discussions of controversial public issues.

In the years immediately preceding and during our nation's participation in World War II, the commission seemed most concerned with problems relating to controversy and with the need to make time available for the views of minority groups. In any event, no actions were taken against stations for program shortcomings of other types until after the release in 1946 of a commission memorandum popularly known as the Blue Book.

The Blue Book of 1946

The official title of the FCC's 1946 memorandum was *The Public Service Responsibility of Broadcast Licensees;* it has been more widely known as the Blue Book[1] because of the color of its paper cover. In it, the commission laid down two major criteria for determining whether or not a radio station was "serving the public interest" in its programming. The first criterion was an elaboration of the standards outlined in the Federal Radio Commission's *Great Lakes* Opinion. To meet its responsibilities, a broadcasting station was expected to provide "balance" in programming. This involved the carrying of "a sufficient number" of local, live programs—as opposed to recorded materials or programs provided by networks. In addition, to insure that it provided "balance" in the programs it

---

[1] "The Blue Book," in Frank J. Kahn (ed.), *Documents of American Broadcasting* (New York: Appleton-Century-Crofts, 1973), p. 151.

offered, a station was expected to include in its weekly schedule a "reasonable number" of educational programs, news programs, programs providing agricultural information, programs devoted to the discussion of important public issues, programs serving the interests of local nonprofit civic and religious groups and labor organizations, and programs intended to appeal to minority interests and tastes, such as broadcasts of classical music.

The second Blue Book criterion of "public interest" in programming related to the number of commercially sponsored programs and the number of spot announcements included in the station's weekly schedule. For the first time, the regulatory body took a strong stand against "the evils" of overcommercialization. Although intentionally vague as to the amount of advertising a station might properly carry, the Blue Book made it very clear that stations were expected to schedule a "sufficiently large" number of sustaining programs each week to insure balance in its overall program structure. Also branded as objectionable was the carrying of an excessive number of commercial spot announcements—the memorandum noted that in some instances, stations had scheduled as many as 1,000 spots each week—and the "piling up" of commercials, or presenting two or more announcements in succession, without intervening entertainment materials.

To give effect to its new programming requirements, the Federal Communications Commission adopted new forms to be used in applications for new station authorizations and for renewal of licenses of stations already on the air. The new forms required applicants to indicate the proportions of time to be devoted each week to programs of each of the types called for in the Blue Book and the maximum number of spot announcements that would be carried. In addition, applicants for license renewal were asked to state the number of hours and minutes actually devoted to each of the types of programs and the number of commercial announcements broadcast during a week chosen by the commission. Applicants were warned that promises made in applications would be compared with actual performance when applications for license renewal came up for consideration.

Broadcasters were understandably concerned over the Blue Book's assertion of the commission's right to *require* stations to provide certain specific types of programming—even though such programs were already included in the schedules of nearly all stations. They were equally disturbed at the imposition of even vague limits on the amount of station time that could be sponsored and on the number of commercial announcements broadcast each week. However, in several cases in which applicants appealed commission decisions to federal courts, the courts ruled that consideration of future program plans was not censorship, as prohibited by the Communications Act of 1934, and that the commission was not exceeding the powers given it by Congress in laying down its Blue Book standards of programming.

Application of Blue Book Standards   For several years following the release of the 1946 memorandum, the programming and commercial standards laid down in the Blue Book were rigidly applied by the commission in acting on license renewals and applications for new facilities. In a number of instances, stations already on the air were allowed to operate for months on a temporary license basis, until the program plans outlined in renewal applications were changed to meet commission requirements. In other instances, stations were called to account by the FCC staff for carrying an excessive number of commercial announcements. The rapidly increasing number of radio stations, combined with economic problems created by the growing importance of television, forced the commission after 1950 to make some modifications in its requirements.

In a number of major markets, the regulatory agency allowed certain stations to develop highly specialized types of programming aimed at limited segments of the total audience; for such stations, the Blue Book requirement of a "balanced" program structure was waived on the ground that other stations in the community were providing other kinds of programs. Radio stations using a news-and-music format are now generally allowed to offer noncommercial spot announcements in support of community undertakings in place of presenting complete programs serving the interests of local groups; stations in large cities are not required to provide programs of farm information; and only a small proportion of radio stations schedule programs that could technically be called educational or offer broadcasts of classical music or other programs of types described in the Blue Book as serving "minority interests and tastes."

Changing conditions in broadcasting have also resulted in a relaxing of the commission's standards with respect to commercial schedules. The Blue Book called for broadcasting stations to carry "a sufficient number" of programs on a sustaining basis; it also implied, at least, that a station broadcasting as many as 1,000 commercial spot announcements in any one week was guilty of "commercial excesses." However, with sponsorship of programs largely replaced by spot-announcement advertising, the commission's views have been materially modified. Since the middle 1950s, few radio or television stations have devoted more than 3 or 4 hours a week to sustaining programs; at the same time, the number of spot announcements has increased steadily, with no formal objection from the FCC. To be sure, members of the regulatory body still evidence a concern over "commercial excesses," but their ideas have changed considerably—perhaps as a result of the fact that so many radio and television stations are operating at a loss.

In any event, the radio commercial time limitations encouraged by the nature of the present license renewal form allow a station to establish a policy limit of no more than 18 commercial minutes per hour. Stations are further permitted to increase this maximum to 20 or even 22 minutes for some hours under special circumstances (seasonal merchandising emphases, a large number of political advertisements, or the like). A station carrying 18 commercial minutes per hour for only five 12-hour days per week will air 1,080 minutes of commercial material. Depending on the number of 30-second spots included, such a station could easily double the "1,000-spots-per-week" that so concerned the FCC in the Blue Book.

The Public Interest Standard   As has been noted, the commission has consistently been supported by the courts in its actions in the programming area, in large part because the regulatory agency has moved very cautiously every time it has dealt with programming. The FCC realizes that it must walk a very fine line. The following statement from its 1960 Programming Policy Statement illustrates the nature of this line:

> The regulatory responsibility of the Commission in the broadcasting field essentially involves the maintenance of a balance between the preservation of a free competitive broadcast system, on the one hand, and the reasonable restriction of that freedom inherent in the public interest standard provided by the Communications Act, on the other.[2]

Over the years, the Federal Communications Commission has developed a very careful justification of its programming decisions which it feels maintains this "balance." In essence, the FCC maintains that every broadcaster's First Amendment rights are limited by the facts that a license is required to broadcast and that fewer channels are available than people wishing to use these channels. By law, the FCC was established to determine who shall receive broadcast licenses and who shall keep them. The standard established by Congress was "the public interest, convenience, and necessity." In effect, a broadcaster's right to freedom of speech on the air is not absolute; he must use this freedom to advance the

---

[2]Kahn, *Documents*, p. 234.

public interest or his *license to broadcast* will be taken away. (His personal freedom of expression, then, is not really really restricted; he is only denied the right to use the public's airwaves to distribute his message.)

The commission argues further that, since it does have the responsibility of enforcing the public interest standard through the licensing procedure, it also has the responsibility of giving the broadcasters some guidelines to the kinds of program that are considered to be in the public interest. Such guidelines are seen to be aids to broadcasters, not restrictions; and, since they do not refer to specific programs and are not a form of prior restraint, they cannot be considered censorship. The FCC sees itself as merely helping the broadcaster meet his responsibility to program in the public interest. The 1960 Programming Policy Statement was the most recent comprehensive commission effort to provide this assistance by calling for attention to community needs and interests in program planning and by establishing fourteen broad categories of programs "necessary to meet the public interest."[3]

The Federal Communications Commission, then, does move with caution when considering questions of programming. Congress, on the other hand, has been less reluctant to regulate programming and has legislated fairly often. With the exception of criminal code restrictions on the broadcast of lottery information, fraud, and obscene, indecent, and profane language, this legislation is found in the communications act as follows:

Section 312 establishes situations in which the commission can revoke a license and includes a provision for revocation "for . . . failure to allow reasonable access to . . . the use of a broadcasting station by a . . . candidate for Federal elective office."

Section 315 sets out the "equal opportunity" provisions for political candidates and waivers for specific kinds of program.

Section 317 requires that an announcement be made identifying the name of any person or organization that pays "any money, service, or other valuable consideration" for the broadcast of any material. This has come to be known as the "sponsor identification" provision of the communications act.

---

[3]These elements are (1) opportunity for local self-expression, (2) the development and use of local talent, (3) programs for children, (4) religious programs, (5) educational programs, (6) public affairs programs, (7) editorialization by licensees, (8) political broadcasts, (9) agricultural programs, (10) news programs, (11) weather and market reports, (12) sports programs, (13) service to minority groups, and (14) entertainment programming. Kahn, *Documents*, p. 246.

Section 325 prohibits the broadcast of false distress signals and the rebroadcast of any signal from another station without the permission of that station.

Section 399 restricts educational radio and television stations from carrying editorials in favor of candidates for public office.

Section 508 is aimed specifically at what has come to be known as "payola" and requires any station employee who accepts payment or the promise of payment for the broadcast of any matter (other than normal payment from the station itself) to disclose such payment to the station.[4]

Section 509 was added in response to the "quiz-rigging" scandals of the late 1950s and makes it unlawful to assist any contestant in a quiz program with the intent of deceiving the listening public.[5]

Section 606 establishes certain emergency war powers available to the President of the United States.

REGULATION AND PROGRAM BALANCE

The other elements of the regulatory mix discussed in Chapter 13 have felt few inhibitions about trying to influence programming, and the pressures on the Federal Communications Commission and Congress to "do something" about programming have often been intense. As a result, the influence of the regulator can be seen in many aspects of programming. Some of these programming influences have grown from a general concern for programming balance in the public interest. Others came as a result of reaction to specific programs or types of program.

---

[4]In the 1950s, it was discovered that some radio disc jockeys were accepting money and other considerations in exchange for the play and promotion of records they otherwise would not have considered favorably. Widespread air play was seen by the record industry as essential to the success of a record and "payola" came to be the term applied to the bribes paid to insure this air play.

[5]In the 1950s, producers of several prime-time network quiz programs, chief among them being the *$64,000 Question*, sought to maintain audience interest by making sure that some attractive contestants did not make mistakes that would eliminate them prematurely. The producers attempted to justify this practice, when it was discovered, by arguing that they were producing entertainment programs, not genuine intellectual contests, but they found few supporters when the deceptions were made public. Big-money quiz shows quickly disappeared from network prime-time schedules and Section 509 was added to the communications act.

Program Balance and Ascertainment

In its 1960 Statement on Programming Policy, the Federal Communications Commission put great emphasis on what has come to be known as "ascertainment of community needs." No fewer than six times in the relatively brief statement there are variations of the following statement: "The principal ingredient of the licensee's obligation to operate his station in the public interest is the diligent, positive, and continuing effort by the licensee to discover and fulfill the tastes, needs, and desires of his community or service area, for broadcast service."

As the ground rules for ascertainment evolved throughout the 1960s and 1970s, the process came to include four elements: (1) a survey of community leaders; (2) a survey of the general public; (3) an evaluation of the results of these surveys; and (4) programming. In the two surveys, the licensee is expected to determine the problems, needs, and interests of his listening audience—not the programming preferences of this audience, but those issues and interests that are seen by the public as being important to the community.[6] In his evaluation, the licensee must examine the community problems uncovered by his survey, determine the relative importance of each, and decide which can best be treated by his station.

With the first three steps completed, the licensee must then broadcast matter designed to treat the selected problems, needs, and interests. This treatment can take the form of programs, news items, and public service announcements, although it should not be restricted to the latter two forms. The programs need not *solve* community problems. They need only *treat* the problems by identifying, analyzing, or discussing them so as to bring them to the attention of the listening audience.

Programming, then, is the ultimate goal of all the ascertainment rules. Through these rules the Federal Communications Commission is forcing all licensees to become involved in their communities and to serve their public with their programming. Thus commission concern about the public service responsibilities of licensees has led it to force balance in programming by requiring certain kinds of program be aired—no matter how specialized the station

---

[6]As first perceived by the FCC, these surveys were to be conducted in a reasonably scientific manner during the 6-month period before license renewal. In 1976, however, these rules were changed to call for "continuous ascertainment" throughout the license period and to allow the licensee to maintain a running record of all contacts made with community leaders in which community problems were discussed. The survey of the general public was retained, but its scheduling was left to the licensee's discretion.

format—and to a later requirement that a list of no more than ten of the most significant problems ascertained, with a companion list of illustrative programs dealing with these problems, be placed annually in a "public inspection file" that is always open to public scrutiny. Working from a clear-cut "public interest" position, then, the FCC has moved with authority to establish special programming responsibilities for all broadcast licensees.

Program Balance and the License-Renewal Form

The ascertainment procedures do force attention on programming aimed at community problems, and this often leads to greater programming for minority groups; but the FCC does not depend entirely on ascertainment in its effort to insure an "overall program balance." The commission is well aware that many of its fourteen categories result in programs that attract small audiences and are difficult to sell to advertisers. Since commercial broadcasters show a natural tendency to maximize the number of programs that are easy to sell and to minimize those that are less attractive to advertisers, the FCC finds it necessary to counter this tendency with pressures of its own.

Arguing that it is simply keeping track of licensees' adherence to their public interest responsibility, the Federal Communications Commission includes in the license-renewal forms questions that have the effect of giving strong encouragement to the scheduling of certain types of program. Radio and television renewal applicants now use different forms and slightly different emphases are evident in these two forms.

The radio form, for instance, requires for the composite week[7] a listing of the amounts of time (rounded to the nearest minute) devoted to news, public affairs, and "all other programs, exclusive of entertainment and sports," as well as percentage figures for each category. From time to time, both Congress and the FCC have considered establishing minimum acceptable percentages in these categories for license renewal. There has been no action yet, but the question is still open.

The radio renewal form also asks for typical and illustrative

---

[7]For convenience in reporting programming and commercial information in the renewal form, the FCC establishes each year a "composite week" made up of 1 day from each of 7 different weeks during the previous 12 months. It selects the days at random, 3 from the first and 3 from the last part of the year and one from the summer months. Weeks with holidays are eliminated.

programs or series (exclusive of entertainment) that have served the needs of the public. The same question instructs the applicant to indicate which programs were designed to inform the public on local, national, or international problems of greatest public importance. Another question asks for details of the station's news-gathering facilities and the percentage of its news time devoted to local and regional news. The applicant's public affairs programming is explored by asking for a statement of the station's policy with respect to making time available for the discussion of public issues. Each radio applicant is asked to identify its programming format and to state how this format contributes to the overall diversity of program service in his community. Finally, the applicant must state the number of public service announcements (PSAs) carried during the composite week.

The television renewal form asks for even more details. In addition to stating the number of public service announcements in the composite week, the television applicant must designate the number of such announcements broadcast for local organizations, for those outside the community, and for organizations serving both. The number of PSAs broadcast between 8:00 A.M. and 11:00 P.M. must also be shown. In the news and public affairs area, applicants with network affiliations must indicate whether or not they carried more than 50 percent of the news and public affairs programs offered by the network during the entire license period. Stress is put on another area of programming by a question asking for a brief description of programs or program series broadcast during the license period that were primarily directed toward children aged 12 and under. Both the radio and television forms also include the commercial time limitations discussed in Chapter 13.

The Federal Communications Commission, then, uses the renewal form to influence programming in a manner that seems to avoid congressional or judicial intervention. Broadcasters working with the renewal forms quickly learn the range of acceptable answers to the various programming questions and tailor their offerings to fit FCC expectations, and program balance is enhanced.

Program Balance and Politics: Sections 315 and 312

The provision for balance in political programs that include the actual candidate for public office has been a part of the law governing broadcasting since the Radio Act of 1927. Section 18 of that act reads:

If any licensee shall permit any person who is a legally qualified candidate for any public office to use a broadcasting station, he shall afford equal opportunities to all other such candidates for that office in the use of such broadcasting station.[8]

When the Communications Act of 1934 was passed, that portion of the act dealing with radio incorporated most of the old radio act and the "equal opportunity" provisions cited above became Section 315. Several additions have been made to this section since 1934, as we will see, but the application of even the fundamental requirement noted raises some difficult questions. In order to schedule political programming properly, a licensee must know the answers to questions like the following, drawn from a publication of the National Association of Broadcasters published to assist broadcasters:[9]

Who is a legally qualified candidate for public office?

Need a candidate be on the ballot to be legally qualified?

When a name is on the ballot must it be presumed that the individual is a legally qualified candidate for public office?

What constitutes "use" of broadcast facilities?

Must a broadcaster give equal opportunity to a candidate whose opponent has broadcast in some other capacity than as a candidate?

When are candidates opposing candidates?

What constitutes equal opportunities?

If a station sells time to candidate A, must the station give free time to opposing candidates who request it?

May a station delete material in a broadcast by a candidate because it believes the material contained therein is, or may be, libelous?

When must a candidate make a request of the station for opportunities equal to those offered his opponent?

As these and other questions arose, of course, they were ultimately answered by the Federal Communications Commission,

---

[8]Kahn, *Documents*, p. 36.

[9]*Political Broadcast Catechism* (Washington D.C.: National Association of Broadcasters, 1976).

which, as a result, often found itself closely involved in political programming decisions of individual licensees. Additions to Section 315 since 1960 have complicated matters even further.

One particularly troublesome aspect of Section 315 was the matter of nonpolitical "use" by a candidate. For more than 25 years, the commission was rigid in its interpretation of the law and any appearance by a candidate on a radio or television station was interpreted as "use" requiring "equal opportunity." As a result, opponents of an incumbent running for reelection could carefully monitor all local news coverage, clock the number of minutes and seconds in which the incumbent appeared on the news—whether he was greeting a visiting dignitary, announcing a new appointment or discussing the budget—and demand and get "equal opportunity" for use of the facilities of all stations carrying the news item that included the incumbent.

The 1960 presidential campaign saw this rigid application of "equal opportunity" stretched to ridiculous extremes. The result was a 1960 amendment to the act that exempted the following categories of program from the provisions of Section 315: (1) bona fide newscasts; (2) bona fide news interviews; (3) bona fide news documentaries, if the appearance of the candidate is incidental to the subject; and (4) on-the-spot coverage of bona fide news events.

Such exemptions seem reasonable enough; but they immediately involved the FCC in still more programming decisions because the nature of each of the above program categories had to be carefully defined—and, indeed, is still being defined. In the fall of 1975, for example, the commission reversed an earlier ruling and declared that debates and news conferences including candidates could be considered exempt as "bona fide news events" if they were covered live and in their entirety. This ruling opened the door for the debates of 1976 between presidential candidates Jimmy Carter and Gerald R. Ford.

Section 312, which provides the commission with administrative sanctions to help it enforce its rulings, became entangled in politics in 1971 when the Campaign Communications Reform Act was passed. This act was designed primarily to control campaign expenditures, but included the provision, added to Section 312, that any license could be revoked for "willful or repeated failure to allow reasonable access to or to permit purchase of reasonable amounts of time for the use of a broadcasting station by a legally qualified candidate for federal elective office on behalf of his candidacy."

Needless to say, this provision embroiled the FCC even further in political programming decisions (the 1976 NAB *Political Broadcast Catechism* includes fifteen questions in this area alone). "Reasonable access" can be a slippery term, but, of necessity, some guidelines have evolved as the result of commission decisions since 1972. These include some relaxation of the requirement in situations in which there are a "multiplicity" of candidates (but then, just how many is a "multiplicity"?); a statement that a licensee cannot adopt a policy of restricting candidates from prime time; and a refusal to permit a licensee to reject all political spots of 60 seconds or shorter on the grounds that the time is not sufficient for the discussion of political issues. Clearly, then, both Sections 312 and 315 force the FCC to involve itself closely in political programming decisions.

Program Balance within the Market: Format Change

In developing its ascertainment policies, the Federal Communications Commission has moved to implement principles outlined in its own 1960 Programming Policy statement. In political situations, the regulatory body has been required to interpret congressional mandates. In the 1970s, the FCC also faced from federal courts pressures that forced it into still another programming area.

As radio struggled to adapt to the competition of television and as the number of radio stations grew, the commission came to accept the premise that, in multistation markets, radio licensees would be permitted to aim the bulk of their programming toward specialized audiences. Given this freedom, radio has evolved a number of formats—contemporary, middle-of-the-road, country-and-western, classical, all-talk, all-news, and so forth—each designed to appeal to a specific target audience selected by the management of the station. Some balance in terms of news, public affairs, and the like is still required of these stations, but most of their programming time is devoted to the chosen format.

The commission has accepted this multiplicity of formats as an economic necessity and has consistently held that the nature of a station's format should be determined by the licensee as a result of his analysis of the needs of his market. Since 1970, however, the Court of Appeals in the District of Columbia has been urging the commission to become more closely involved in the format-selection process.

In 1970, the FCC approved, without a hearing, the sale of a radio station in Atlanta; the new owner had stated that he planned to change the format from classical music. The Court of Appeals reversed this commission action on the grounds that loss of the only classical music format in Atlanta would deny a unique service to a significant audience. Similar cases came before the court in the following years, and the decisions in these cases seemed to imply that the court, on appeal, would approve only those format changes, resulting from a change in ownership, in which it had been demonstrated that the previous format was not economically viable and that the format change would not remove a unique service from the market.

A court decision in a 1973 transfer case in Chicago, however, demonstrated that these criteria were not as firm as had been believed. In this *WEFM(FM)* case, the commission had approved a transfer that included a format change from classical to rock music on the grounds that there were two other classical music stations in the Chicago area and that WEFM(FM) was losing money. The Court of Appeals reversed this FCC action in a decision that directed the agency to involve itself more closely in the format-change issue.

Basing its decision on the public interest standard and the belief that this interest is best served by the maintenance of as wide as possible a diversity of formats in a market, the Court of Appeals told the FCC that it could no longer rely solely on licensee judgment in the determination of formats. If free competition and the forces within a market lead to an increasing number of stations utilizing a decreasing number of formats it is the responsibility of the Federal Communications Commission, according to the court, to protect the public interest by moving to protect formats with a significant number of listeners, without considering whether or not stations with such formats were making money.

The commission has not been happy with the implications of the *WEFM(FM)* decision, and various commissioners have expressed concern about the constitutionality of such intervention in programming decisions. As a result of this concern, the agency, in early 1976, issued a notice of inquiry "to examine whether the Commission should play any role in dictating the selection of entertainment formats," and, in the summer of 1976, it issued a Policy Statement expressing an unwillingness to interfere with programming judgments of this sort. In spite of its reluctance, however, the FCC continues to be faced with a court mandate that seems to require the agency to involve itself in still another aspect of programming.

Program Balance and the Prime-Time Access Rule

The evolution of the prime-time access rules has already been traced in Chapter 5. These rules were designed to reduce network control of prime-time evening hours by limiting them, in the Top 50 markets, to 3 hours of programming between 7:00 and 11:00 P.M. (between 6:00 and 10:00 P.M. Central Time). Their basic thrust was toward greater diversity in programming sources, and they had only a secondary effect on programming decisions by licensees. In a 1975 modification, however, the commission seemed to be trying to use the rules to encourage the networks to program certain specific types of program—even to the point of singling out *The Wonderful World of Disney* as a good program example.

The third version of the access rules, issued in January of 1975, indicated that three kinds of program—children's programming, documentaries, and public affairs programs—would be permitted in the access hour (that prime-time hour the networks chose not to program—usually 7:00 to 8:00 P.M. Eastern Time). By exempting these programs from the access rules, the FCC was virtually telling the networks and local television stations what programs it prefers and will make exceptions for. Such guidelines are seen by some as another example of FCC intrusion into programming.

PROGRAMMING AND CONTROVERSY: THE FAIRNESS DOCTRINE

Many critics of the Federal Communications Commission and of broadcast regulation feel that the deepest and most persistent commission intrusion into programming has been in its application of the Fairness Doctrine. The evolution of this doctrine from the *Great Lakes* statement of 1929, through the *Mayflower* decision of 1941 and the statement on editorializing of 1949, to the 1960 amendments to the Communications Act of 1934 that embedded the fairness concept in the basic law governing broadcasting, has been discussed in Chapter 13. It remains for us here to examine some of the applications of the Fairness Doctrine to programming situations.

In its 1974 statement on the Fairness Doctrine, the FCC made clear its interpretation of the doctrine to mean that a licensee must devote a reasonable percentage of his programming time to the coverage of public issues and that this coverage must be fair in providing opportunity for the presentation of contrasting points of view. The Fairness Doctrine, then, is not seen as a passive document requiring fairness only after a licensee chooses to take the first step of allowing the presentation of one side of a controversial issue. Nor is the interpretation of "fairness" passive, requiring the licensee to make his facilities available for other sides of an issue only when requested to do so. Instead, the licensee must make a positive effort to encourage the presentation of contrasting viewpoints. By thus rejecting a passive interpretation of the Fairness Doctrine, the FCC has placed itself in a position in which it must make some hard programming decisions.

The Red Lion Case

Some of these decisions led to the *Red Lion* case[10]—a U.S. Supreme Court ruling that supported and strengthened the Fairness Doctrine. The case that came to be known as *Red Lion* came before the FCC in 1965 when Fred J. Cook, an author, charged a Pennsylvania radio station, operated by the Red Lion Broadcasting Company (WGCB), with a violation of the Fairness Doctrine. Cook claimed that his character and good name had been attacked in a program broadcast by WGCB and that the station had denied him free time to reply. The station did not dispute the attack but argued that the program that had carried the attack had been a paid program and that it was meeting its Fairness Doctrine obligations by offering to sell reply time to the author. Cook, on the other hand, insisted that he should not be forced to pay for the right to defend his name.

The primary issue, then, was whether or not a station could be forced to provide free reply time to an individual who had been attacked over its facilities. The FCC ruled in favor of Cook and told the Red Lion Company to give him free time in which to reply. Red Lion thereupon appealed the decision, saw the position of the FCC upheld by the Court of Appeals in the District of Columbia, and took the case on to the U.S. Supreme Court.

Before we discuss the ultimate disposition of this case, however, we must pick up another thread. Not long after the initial *Red Lion* decision was appealed, the FCC attempted to clarify the personal-attack aspect of the Fairness Doctrine by issuing its personal-attack rules. These rules impose certain obligations on a licensee who permits his facilities to be used, during the presentation of a controversial issue of public importance, to attack the honesty, integrity, or the like of a group or person. The licensee must, within a week of the attack, notify the person or group of the attack; send a recording, script, or accurate summary of the attack; and offer a reasonable opportunity to respond.

These personal-attack rules were appealed as unconstitutional by the Radio and Television News Directors Association (RTDNA)

---

[10]"The *Red Lion* Case," in Kahn, *Documents*, p. 412.

and the Court of Appeals agreed with this contention. The FCC then took this adverse decision to the U.S. Supreme Court, which combined the *Red Lion* and *RTDNA* cases into one consideration, known simply as *Red Lion*.

In June of 1969, the Supreme Court handed down a *Red Lion* decision that supported the Fairness Doctrine in no uncertain terms, saying that it would "enhance rather than abridge the freedoms of speech and the press." Portions of this decision relate directly to the programming function.

In both the *Red Lion* and the *RTDNA* cases, the Fairness Doctrine was attacked on First Amendment grounds, with claims that the rules restricted freedoms of speech and press. The court rejected this contention, saying that "differences in the characteristics of new media justify differences in the First Amendment standards applied to them." With this statement, the Supreme Court dismissed the argument of the electronic media that they should be granted all the First Amendment rights accorded the print media.

The Supreme Court did not stop there in its analysis of the First Amendment rights of broadcast licensees. Turning the broadcaster's argument around, the court stated that "it is the right of the viewers and listeners, not the right of broadcasters, which is paramount"; and further, "the First Amendment confers no right on licensees to prevent others from broadcasting on 'their' frequencies and no right to an unconditional monopoly of a scarce resource which the Government has denied others the right to use."

The *Red Lion* decision also supported the FCC in its aggressive interpretation of the Fairness Doctrine. In opposing the doctrine, broadcasters had argued that it could "inhibit" journalism by leading broadcasters to avoid or reduce controversy out of fear of their reply responsibilities. The court rejected this argument, saying, "If present licensees should suddenly prove timorous, the Commission is not powerless to insist that they give adequate and fair attention to public issues."

The *Red Lion Case* then, supports interpretation and application of the Fairness Doctrine in a manner that can involve the FCC in many programming judgments. The personal-attack rules, with their specific statements as to what programming time must be offered in certain situations, stood, and still stand, intact. First Amendment rights of broadcasters were clearly qualified by the public interest responsibilities that grow from the administration of a scarce natural resource. Finally, the First Amendment rights of the public were seen as more important than those of licensees. The *Red Lion* decision had begun as an affirmation and defense of one portion of the Fairness Doctrine—the personal-attack rules—and had developed into a statement that supported the entire doctrine and reaffirmed the right of the Federal Communications Commission to supervise programming in specific situations.

Public Access to the Media

The *Red Lion* statement that "it is the right of the viewers and listeners . . . which is paramount" spoke to the spirit of a time in which many groups were clamoring to be heard. Two such groups, the Business Executives' Move for Vietnam Peace (BEM) and the Democratic National Committee (DNC), set in motion another series of decisions and counterdecisions that again involved the FCC in programming issues.

In 1970, BEM asked WTOP, an all-news radio station in Washington, D.C. to sell the group time for spots opposing the war in Vietnam. The station refused to do so, maintaining that the anti-war position had been adequately covered in its regular programming. The BEM group appealed this decision to the FCC, citing *Red Lion*; the commission supported WTOP; and BEM appealed further to the Court of Appeals in the District of Columbia.

At about the same time, the Democratic National Committee came to the conclusion that it was not being given sufficient broadcast time to reply to statements from the Nixon administration on controversial issues. They sought relief by asking the FCC to issue a ruling that broadcasters could not adopt a general policy of refusing to sell time for the discussion of controversial issues to "responsible entities," like the DNC. The FCC refused to issue such a ruling, and the DNC also turned to the Court of Appeals.

In August 1971, this court ruled in favor of BEM and the DNC and asserted that commercial broadcasters violated the First Amendment when they imposed a flat ban on the sale of time for the discussion of controversial issues of public importance. The FCC, joined by the Justice Department, ABC, CBS, NBC, and WTOP, thereupon appealed the decision of the Court of Appeals to the U.S. Supreme Court.

Among the issues before the Supreme Court was whether or not individuals and groups were to have limited First Amendment rights of access to the media to speak directly on the issues of the day, rather than through reporters and commentators of broadcast stations. The FCC and the broadcasters maintained that the Fairness Doctrine, properly applied, worked to keep the public informed about all sides of controversial issues and that broadcast journalists had the right to exercise certain discretion as to how the issues should be presented. The DNC and BEM argued that such discretion denied citizens the basic First Amendment rights referred to in the *Red Lion* decision.

In June 1973, the U.S. Supreme Court ruled in favor of the FCC and the broadcasters and rejected the contention that the public had certain rights of access to the media. The ruling was viewed with relief by the FCC, which had felt that the decision of the Court of Appeals, if upheld, would have forced the agency into day- to-day supervision of programming judgments by individual licensees to insure that they were being reasonable in their decisions concerning citizen access.

In the *BEM–DNC* case, then, the Supreme Court ultimately relieved the FCC of a measure of programming responsibility. The history of the case, however, demonstrates how interpretations of the Fairness Doctrine could be used to force the FCC into increased supervision of programming decisions.

We have touched on only few of the controversies that have been stirred up by the Fairness Doctrine. Elsewhere we have noted the application of the doctrine to cigarette advertising, the FCC refusal to apply it to the advertising of other products, attempts by the major political parties to obtain automatic reply time to addresses by the President of the United States, and other controversial interpretations. The Fairness Doctrine may often seem troublesome to the FCC—indeed, in 1976 Chairman Wiley suggested that, as an experiment, it might be suspended for radio in some small markets. Its application often seems cautious and inadequate to a general public that does not really understand the doctrine. However, it seems certain that the Fairness Doctrine will be a fact of life to broadcasters for many years, for neither the FCC nor Congress has found a better way to insure that the broadcast media continue to program a measure of discussion and controversy in the public interest.

DIRECT PRESSURES ON PROGRAM CONTENT

In the preceding discussion, we considered pressures on programming resulting from concern over larger issues. In large measure, ascertainment was the result of FCC efforts to be sure licensees were aware of and attempting to deal with the major concerns of their community. Section 315 restrictions grew from a concern lest some licensees misuse the advantages provided by access to a broadcast facility in a political campaign. The license-renewal form has been used to encourage balanced programming, but little effort is made to use the form to influence the content of specific types of program. The format-change issue seems to have developed from concern in the Court of Appeals in the District of Columbia and among groups of citizens, that as wide as possible a range of radio formats be available in a given community. The prime-time access rules grew from a fear of monopolistic control of programs by the television networks. Finally, the Fairness Doctrine seems to have developed from the same worries that stimulated Section 315—a fear that broadcasters would use the facilities granted them to the public detriment by choking debate or concealing issues.

Network and local programming, both radio and television, has also been affected by pressures that arise from reactions to specific programs or program types. Except for the statutory restrictions noted earlier in this chapter, the FCC does not have the right to step in and declare that a specific program or type of program shall not be broadcast. Over the years, however, the commission has been subjected to extreme pressures from Congress and the public to "do something" about specific programs. Caught between these pressures and the "no censorship" provisions of the communications act, the commission has developed some relatively subtle techniques for influencing program judgments by broadcasters. Among these techniques are the "lifted eyebrow" and "jawboning"—labels that have been applied to commission actions in some specific cases.

"Topless Radio" and "The Lifted Eyebrow"

One of the most recent examples of the "lifted eyebrow" technique is found in the reaction to a radio format that developed in the early 1970s. During the latter part of 1972 and into 1973, a few radio stations across the country discovered that talk programs that permitted explicit sexual discussions ("What does your man do to turn you on?") would attract large and enthusiastic audiences. A few of the more successful such programs went into syndication—one in at least 26 markets—and other stations tried to imitate the format, which came to be known as "topless radio."

Local successes notwithstanding, such sex-oriented programming was viewed with dismay by both Congress and the FCC—and by a significant portion of the listening audience exposed to such programs. Senator John O. Pastore, chairman of the Communications Subcommittee of the Senate Commerce Committee, expressed great concern over the programs and urged the FCC, in no uncertain terms, to get them off the air. The commission, however, did not believe it had the authority to cancel specific programs and at-

"The barriers are falling. A double entendre, and it's only 8:15."

tacked the problem from another angle, announcing a closed inquiry into allegations of obscene and indecent broadcasts.

The FCC chairman at the time, Dean Burch, chose to put additional pressure on the industry in a speech delivered in 1973 to the annual meeting of the National Association of Broadcasters. In his speech, Chairman Burch specifically attacked the "prurient trash that is the stock-in-trade of the sex-oriented radio talk show." He reminded the industry further that it was, at the time, working very hard to push through Congress a license-renewal bill that would offer some protection from citizen challenges and extend the license period from 3 to 4 or 5 years. The chairman followed this reminder with the suggestion that the broadcasting of "smut" and "electronic voyeurism" did little to support the claim of "maturity," which was being advanced to support the longer license term.

These remarks represented only a relatively brief portion of the complete address, but their meaning was clear. The chairman of the Federal Communications Commission was warning the industry that some of its members might be endangering a larger goal. Further, he was making it clear to the assembled broadcast executives, through his use of such words as "prurient trash," "smut," and "electronic voyeurism," that he and, by implication, the entire commission were offended by the programming. The NAB understood the message clearly and, at the same meeting, adopted a resolution condemning "tasteless and vulgar" programming.

The speech by Chairman Burch and the reaction by the NAB were well covered by the press. The "guilty" stations reacted quickly and "topless radio" vanished. No official action had been taken; but Congress had spoken, the FCC had "lifted an eyebrow," and a specific program format had disappeared.

Few would argue that the American public was denied an important service when such sex-oriented talk programs were removed from the air. The events leading to this removal, however, were disturbing to some. Among those so disturbed was Justice David Bazelon of the U.S. Court of Appeals in the District of Columbia. He expressed his discomfort in a 1975 decision against one of the original "topless radio" stations for violating the obscenity statute.

In a statement accompanying the decision, summarized in *Broadcasting* magazine,[11] Judge Bazelon specifically criticized the "raised eyebrow" technique in broadcast regulation and looked with concern upon the actions of the FCC and NAB in 1973. He charged that the FCC "effectively terminated sex-oriented talk shows without any due process for the licensees, without any consideration of the individual merits of different shows, and without any participation by the courts which are given the primary burden of defining obscenity." Speaking directly to censorship, he accused the FCC of working toward this end while trying to give the appearance of not doing so: "The F.C.C. is as aware as the licensees of the relationship between licensees and the commission and knows exactly how the raised eyebrow technique works. That technique was used with precision and success to achieve the goal of eliminating the sex-oriented talk shows."

Many lessons can be drawn from the relatively brief "topless radio" incident. Among these is the fact that when pressured by Congress, the public, and elements of the broadcasting industry itself, the Federal Communications Commission can find ways to alter or eliminate specific program types, in spite of the provisions of the communications act.

Violence on Television and "Jawboning"

The term *jawboning* seems to have come into common usage during the administration of Lyndon B. Johnson. At that time it usually referred to President Johnson's ability to extract a compromise or concessions from hostile groups or individuals by simply talking to them at great length and with great persuasiveness.

In the context of FCC actions relating to programming, "jawboning" has come to refer to efforts by the commission chairman to

---

[11]"Bazelon Blasts FCC's Tactics in Squelching Sex-Talk Shows," *Broadcasting* (May 24, 1975), p. 21.

persuade broadcasters to take steps that he is legally restricted from ordering. "Jawboning," then, goes beyond the pressures of a single speech and the harsh language of Chairman Burch. It relates to more persuasive efforts over a longer period of time and, in the mid-1970s, was used with some effectiveness by Chairman Richard Wiley.

Take, for example, the linked issues of televised violence and its effect on children. As discussed in Chapter 5, the question of the effect of television violence on children has been studied several times in the 1960s and 1970s and the results, while not completely conclusive, have been sufficient to lead many influential people to the conclusion that such violence must be reduced. This belief has led to pressure on Congress, which has turned to the FCC and asked for "action." Faced with congressional urging to take steps that could prove to be unconstitutional, the commission has again "found a way."

Dealing first with the question of programming specifically

"Having someone get hit 73 times is unnecessary violence. Have him get hit, say, 49 times."

aimed at children, the commission broadened the issue beyond the single question of violence and encouraged an overall upgrading of the quality of such programs.

Since 1970, the FCC had been considering the overall question of children's programming as a result of a petition filed by a group known as Action for Children's Television (ACT). This group had asked the commission to ban all advertising on children's television and to require all stations to carry a minimum of 14 hours of such programming each week as a part of their public service responsibility.

Over the next 4 years, the FCC held occasional hearings and pondered what action it should take. By 1974, pressures were building on the agency to do something about the ACT proposals, with both the Senate and the House making it clear that they wanted some action.

A policy statement was issued in late 1974, but even before this action Chairman Wiley turned to "jawboning." In a series of speeches, he made it clear that the FCC was concerned about the amount and content of commercials in children's programming. In June 1974, the NAB responded by changing its television code restrictions to reduce the amount of "nonprogram material" in these shows. The code changes also required a clear separation of program and commercial material and the disclosure of such facts as the absence of batteries in advertised products. Further "jawboning" by the chairman persuaded the Association of Independent Television Stations also to accept the commercial time limitations.

In October 1974, the FCC concluded its consideration of children's television by issuing a Policy Statement designed to encourage broadcast stations to improve such programs. The statement called for "reasonable" amounts of children's programming, with a "significant" portion to be educational or informative; provision for the needs of preschool children; a reduced level of advertising; more children's programming during the week; the avoidance of "host selling"; and a clear separation between programming and advertising. The commission did not issue any rules on children's programming, but it indicated clearly that such rules would follow if broadcasters did not voluntarily respond satisfactorily to the Policy Statement.

None of this action by the commission, however, was directly related to the specific question of violence on television, and Congress remained unsatisfied. The House and the Senate continued to pressure the agency about television violence, a House committee going so far as to threaten a reduction in the FCC budget if some steps to reduce violence were not taken.

Figure 14–1 Children of Puerto Rico (above) and a boy of Louisiana bayou country (below) shown on *Rebop*, one of several excellent PBS programs that have encouraged some to push for better children's programming on commercial networks. (Courtesy Public Broadcasting Service)

Details of the specific commission reactions to these congressional pressures are not completely clear and the degree of "jawboning" actually employed is still at issue, but some facts are not in dispute. In November of 1974, Chairman Wiley met in his office with the programming vice presidents of the three major television networks and later with the presidents of the three networks. The subject of both meetings was violence in network television programming. In early January 1975, CBS proposed that the NAB Television Code be modified to restrict the first hour of network prime-time schedules to programs suitable for "family viewing." Chairman Wiley followed this proposal with another invitation to the network presidents to meet in his office on January 9.

The Television Code Review Board first postponed action on the CBS proposal until April; but the three television networks refused to wait and, in mid-January, issued a statement that they would adopt the "family-hour concept." By early February, the code board has reconsidered its postponement and proposed a "family-hour restriction" that actually ran for 2 hours, from 7:00 to 9:00 P.M. Eastern Time. The NAB Television Board adopted the proposal and the 1975–1976 season was the first to feel the impact of "the family hour."

Predictably, perhaps, the major television producers objected to the concept, branded it censorship, and took the issue to court. One of the issues in the case was the degree to which the discussions between Chairman Wiley and the network executives hastened the imposition of "family-hour restrictions." To some, the circumstances surrounding the birth of the concept represent a clear example of "jawboning" and improper FCC interference in programming. To others, they indicate a network and industry acceptance of an idea whose time had come and an FCC role that was simply advisory. In 1976 a federal court in Los Angeles agreed with the former view and struck the rules down in a decision that criticized the chairman of the FCC for his actions. The networks, however, continued voluntarily to adhere to the "family-hour" concept in the belief that such a position would protect them from some criticism about violence.

The FCC and "Drug Lyrics"

One danger of the "lifted eyebrow" technique, of course, is the chance that some actions of the FCC will be perceived as efforts along these lines when the agency actually had no such goal in mind. A brief flurry of activity in 1971 is a good example of this possibility—although some will insist that the FCC had censorship in mind all along.

In the late 1960s and early 1970s, as the use of and concern over such illegal drugs as marijuana, hashish, cocaine, and heroin reached new peaks, mention of these drugs—both favorable and unfavorable—began to creep into the lyrics of the "contemporary" music of the time. Many radio licensees were of another generation, not fully aware of what was happening and not really interested in the details of the lyrics in the records they were playing. The result was that songs in which the use of drugs was glamorized were heard on the air—because management had not listened closely to the lyrics or because they didn't recognize the "hip" references.

Aware of this phenomenon and concerned about it, the FCC, in early 1971, issued a reminder to licensees that they were responsible for everything aired over their facilities and were expected "to ascertain, before broadcast, the words or lyrics of recorded musical or spoken selections played on their stations."[12]

One of the commissioners at the time, Nicholas Johnson, vigorously dissented to this action in a strongly worded opinion issued with the commission statement. Commissioner Johnson called the action an attempt "to censor song lyrics that the majority disapproves of," and an effort "by a group of establishmentarians to determine what youth can say and hear." He claimed the FCC statement ignored the problems posed by alcohol and over-the-counter drugs and intimated it was a "thinly veiled" move by the Nixon administration to divert attention from the real problems of the day and to attack the "youth culture" opposing its policies.

Apparently taking its lead from the Johnson dissent, the press generally covered this story as a directive from the FCC ordering radio stations not to play certain kinds of record. Petitions for reconsideration were filed by many groups, including the Federal Communications Bar Association, the Recording Association of America, and several large broadcasting companies.

The FCC responded with a clarifying statement in April 1971 in which it denied intent to ban any type of record. The purpose of the original notice, according to the commission, was simply to remind licensees of their responsibility for everything aired on their stations. Since statements promoting or glorifying the use of illegal drugs are clearly not in the public interest and since such statements were being aired, the agency felt such a reminder was in order.

---

[12]"Brouhaha over Drug Lyrics," in Kahn, *Documents*, p. 282.

The second statement quieted the turmoil, and the issue faded from public consciousness as quickly as it had risen. Early in 1973, the Court of Appeals upheld the position of the FCC and the event stands as an example of overreaction to an "eyebrow" that may have moved slightly but apparently was never "lifted" with intent to censor.

Network Reruns and a Reluctant Commission

While the federal courts and the Congress at times can move an unwilling Federal Communications Commission to consider programming, citizen pressure alone is often less successful. The commission, for example, lingered over the ACT-inspired hearings on children's programming for 4 years and concluded them only under pressure from Congress. Action by the agency on the rerun issue is another case in point.

As we saw in an earlier chapter, economic pressures have resulted in a change from the 39-to-13 ratio of new to rerun programming, common in the days of radio network dominance, to the 26-to-26 ratio typical in television today. As this has happened, many of the individuals involved in producing television programs have argued that their ability to make a living has been affected. In 1972, a Hollywood film editor asked the commission to adopt a rule that would force the networks to return to the 39-to-13 pattern.

President Nixon expressed his sympathy for the affected workers—and television viewers—and directed his Office of Telecommunications Policy (OTP) to find a solution to the problem. Efforts were made by OTP to persuade the networks to restrict reruns on a voluntary basis, but no progress was made. The White House office thereupon turned to the FCC and asked the agency to study the matter.

Moving with obvious reluctance, the commission issued, in 1974, a notice of inquiry into the matter of network television reruns in prime time. While concurring with the move, three commissioners expressed their reservations at the time of the notice. The chairman remained unconvinced that the rerun issue was one that should be considered by the FCC at all. A second commissioner questioned the wisdom of the agency involving itself so closely in matters of program content. A third simply said he did not believe the public interest standard could be used to solve every problem facing the industry.

The networks continue to insist that economic realities simply prohibit the production of 39 episodes of each series a year and that less expensive quiz shows and the like would be substituted if such a pattern were imposed on them. Since the FCC is still moving slowly and reluctantly, it seems unlikely that much will come of these hearings in the absence of other outside pressures.

It has not been the intention of this chapter to cover all the situations in which broadcast regulation has affected programming. The commission's 1946 Blue Book was a strong statement of its programming policy at the time and its influence was felt until the 1960 Programming Policy Statement. Actions by the agency during the 1970s to define and deal with the slippery term *indecent* certainly have had an effect on programming. The efforts of the Nixon administration to decentralize the Public Broadcasting Service and to force it to deemphasize news and public affairs have had long-range effects on the composition of the system and the nature of its program offerings. The situations discussed in this chapter are offered only as relatively clear-cut examples of the effects of broadcast regulation on programming—the face the broadcasting industry turns to the public. The interested student is encouraged to seek other examples.

STUDY AND DISCUSSION QUESTIONS

1. Report on or be prepared to discuss the explanation used by the Federal Communications Commission to justify its actions that influence the programming of radio and television stations in the United States.

2. Report on one of the statements issued by the Federal Radio Commission or Federal Communications Commission over the years concerning programming. Choose one of the following:

   a. The FRC statement of 1928
   b. The *Great Lakes* statement
   c. The Blue Book
   d. The 1960 Programming Policy Statement
   e. Portions of ascertainment statements relating to programming
   f. Portions of Fairness Doctrine statements relating to programming

3. Report on or be prepared to discuss the influence of broadcast regulation on a specific area of programming. Consider topics such as the following:

   a. Ascertainment of community needs
   b. Programming influences in the license-renewal form
   c. Section 315 and political advertising
   d. Radio station formats
   e. The prime-time access rules
   f. The Fairness Doctrine
   g. Regulation by "lifted eyebrow"

h. The family-hour concept
i. Network reruns

4. Report on or be prepared to discuss the relative balance between the rights of broadcasters under the First Amendment to the Constitution and their responsibilities to the public under the "public interest, convenience, and necessity" standard of the Communications Act of 1934. Consider questions such as the following:

   a. Are the First Amendment rights of individual broadcasters seriously restricted by existing law and regulation?
   b. Can the First Amendment be interpreted to sanction access to broadcast media by all who wish to use them to disseminate a message?
   c. Who shall define what activities of broadcasters are in the public interest? The broadcasters? The public? The government?
   d. Should differences in the characteristics of media justify differences in the First Amendment rights granted them?

SUGGESTED READINGS

Harry S. Ashmore. *Fear in the Air: Broadcasting and the First Amendment—The Anatomy of a Constitutional Crisis*. New York: Norton, 1973.

Jerome A. Barron. *Freedom of the Press for Whom? The Right of Access to Mass Media*. Bloomington: Indiana University Press, 1973.

Broadcast Political Catechism. Washington, D.C.: National Association of Broadcasters, 1976.

Douglass Cater and Stephan Strickland. *TV Violence and the Child: The Evolution and Fate of the Surgeon General's Report*. New York: Russell Sage Foundation, 1975.

Fred Friendly. *The Good Guys, The Bad Guys and the First Amendment: Free Speech vs. Fairness in Broadcasting*. New York: Random House, 1976.

Henry Geller, *The Fairness Doctrine in Broadcasting: Problems and Suggested Courses of Action*. Santa Monica, Calif: RAND Corporation, 1973.

Evelyn Kaye. *The Family Guide to Children's Television*. New York: Pantheon, 1974.

Gerald F. Kline and Peter Clarke, eds. *Mass Communications and Youth: Some Current Perspectives*. Beverly Hills, Calif.: Sage Publications, 1971.

Robert M. Liebert, John M. Neale, and Emily S. Davidson. *The Early Window: The Effects of Television on Children and Youth*. Elmsford, N.Y.: Pergammon, 1973.

Robert Lowe. *The Fairness Doctrine*. Staff Report for the Senate Committee on Commerce, 90th Congress, 2d Session. Washington, D.C.: U.S. Government Printing Office, 1968.

William Melody. *Children's Television: The Economics of Exploitation*. New Haven, Conn.: Yale University Press, 1973.

15

Broadcasting and the Future

The preceding chapters have been devoted to a summary of the history and organization of the broadcasting industry in the United States (with one chapter devoted to foreign systems). We will conclude with a more speculative chapter that considers some of the questions that will face the industry in the last quarter of this century.

We do not attempt to make any predictions on the course that broadcasting may take in the next decade or so because there are simply too many variables. Broadcasting, as we have seen, has not evolved in this country as a result of a series of well-thought-out, consciously stated principles or policies set out by a regulatory agency. The status and nature of the industry at any given time have virtually always been determined by the relative balance among those forces that combine to regulate the industry—the FCC, the

"For one thing, I don't expect to see programs like this much longer."

industry, the public, the courts, the White House, and the Congress. The future of broadcasting in the United States will also be shaped by the interaction of these forces as they face the impact of population growth and shifts, new technologies, and a rapidly shrinking globe.

It is possible, however, to pose some questions that must be considered and resolved in the coming years. Some of these questions have been with us for half a century while others are more contemporary. We do not pretend to include herein all the major problems that will face the industry in the 1970s, 1980s and 1990s—to do so would take another book. We do hope, however, to raise a few questions and stimulate some thought on the future of the American system of broadcasting.

LOCAL SERVICE VERSUS CENTRALIZATION

The point has been made repeatedly, in this text and elsewhere, that the Federal Radio Commission and the Federal Communications Commission have never elaborated a set of long-range policies to guide the growth and development of broadcasting. When such statements are made, however, the key term *policies* generally refers to a set of explicitly stated objectives set down to provide guidance and long-term goals. Such objectives are rare in the regulatory history of broadcasting. This is not to say, though, that a study of a series of related decisions by the commissions will not reveal a pattern that helps explain the actions but is not really binding on future actions. These patterns can be considered "policies" of a sort, and one in particular can be seen running through many decisions since 1927. This policy has been one of favoring local broadcast service over centralization.[1]

The FRC and FCC Choose Localism

An emphasis on local service in as many different communities as possible, so as to meet purely local needs, is evident from the very first days of the Federal Radio Commission and has been carried forward by the Federal Communications Commission. The em-

---

[1]This discussion of FRC and FCC devotion to the "local-service concept" is drawn largely from an analysis by Don R. LeDuc, *Cable Television and the FCC: A Crisis in Media Control* (Philadelphia: Temple University Press, 1973), pp. 43–59.

phasis stands, as a matter of fact, as a basic premise behind the ascertainment requirements of the FCC.

A pattern of localism means simply that local broadcasting services will be encouraged and approved in as many different communities as possible. Both regulatory bodies supervising the development of broadcasting have followed this pattern, "consistently evincing greater concern for creating new opportunities for broadcasters than for broadening the number of alternative program sources available to various audiences."[2]

Local service, however, is not the only course the two commissions could have followed, and it is not necessarily the best course in the light of the evolution of the broadcasting industry. An alternative to a proliferation of local stations serving local needs would have been, in the 1920s, a series of clear-channel and regional stations strategically placed so as to provide as many broadcasting signals as possible to audiences in all parts of the United States. To a large extent, however, the two alternatives were mutually exclusive. An emphasis on local service in the context of a scarcity of frequencies meant that most interference problems were decided to the detriment of clear or regional channels in order to protect the precious local service. In AM radio, the result was a steady erosion of both the clear and regional concepts and the conversion of most of the radio industry into local broadcasters. Similar interference problems in television were minimized by the allocation of frequencies and the lack of a nighttime "sky-wave," but the spirit of localism resulted in channel allocations to communities much too small to support a television service and in commission policies that, for many years, stunted the growth of cable television systems, which were challenging the local service concept by bringing in signals from distant markets.

Even in the face of such regulatory devotion to a pattern of action, however, since 1927 the broadcasting industry has evolved away from the local-institution concept to the point that the concept simply does not fit the realities of today's industry. In 1927, when the Radio Act was passed, broadcasting was essentially a local institution, but when the FRC brought order to the industry and solved the interference problem a flood of advertising dollars and public demand for better programming brought fundamental changes to the industry.

One result of these changes was the development of networking. The sheer novelty of radio sustained audience interest in the early

[2]LeDuc, *Cable Television*, p. 42.

1920s, but, as listeners became more sophisticated and as interference declined, the American people came to look for better programs than those provided by local stations. Network programming was the obvious answer, and by the 1930s national networks dominated radio programming. In the 1950s, this network dominance shifted to television, and radio was forced to localize, but the result has hardly been the diversity of services envisioned by the Federal Radio Commission in 1927. Networking may have run contrary to the local-institution concept but "the economic advantages of network affiliation simply outweighed the risk of regulatory displeasure."[3]

Another trend working against the local service concept from the very beginning of broadcasting was the transition of the United States from a rural to an urban society. As our people moved from the farms to the cities they tended to concentrate along the eastern and western coasts and in the east north central states. Radio broadcasters were naturally attracted to these populous areas while rural communities found themselves unable to support even one station. In April 1927, for example, New York City had 61 stations while the combined areas of Montana, Idaho, and Nevada were served by only three stations.

From an engineering point of view, the solution to the problem of underserved areas was obvious—provide high-power, interference-free clear-channel service to those areas. Clear channels were indeed created, but from the very beginning their service was limited by the commission's continuing willingness to restrict clears by allowing other stations to operate on the same frequency. By the end of World War II, "two decades of the radio regulatory policy of constantly sacrificing program coverage for local service had resulted in a broadcast system in which one family in six still remained without nighttime entertainment or news while urban dwellers received multiple channels of music, covering areas, not communities, with homogeneous, nationally distributed recorded programming."[4]

The Local-Service Concept in the 1970s and Beyond

In the mid-1970s, the Federal Communications Commission continued to place emphasis on the local-institution concept of broad-

---

[3]LeDuc, *Cable Television*, p. 48.

[4]LeDuc, *Cable Television*, p. 53.

casting stations.[5] This continuing inclination of a regulatory body to cling to a vision of its regulated industry that is a half-century out of date is more than an interesting footnote to history. Broadcasting is a powerful and influential medium, and its regulation is an important part of our national policy. It seems important that a regulatory agency have a reasonably accurate image of its regulatee, and the vision held by the FCC of broadcasting as an industry made up of a large group of independent stations in control of virtually all their programming was inaccurate in 1928 and will be completely obsolete in the late 1970s. Consider some of the contemporary trends working against this image.

In the first place, the trend toward urbanization was greatly accelerated by World War II; and, in spite of a recent halt in the growth of most cities and an apparent drift back to less populated areas, the vast majority of the population of this country is clustered on the eastern and western coasts, across the south Great Lakes area and in scattered cities in the south. Climate aside, the fundamental conditions of urban life do not differ that much between Boston and Atlanta or between Cleveland and Houston, and the regional and local differences that were to be encouraged and drawn upon by local broadcast stations are eroding rapidly. Other factors are also combining to emphasize national similarities and to minimize local and regional differences.

The national television networks, including the Public Broadcasting Service, do have a leveling effect, providing the same entertainment and news, the same cultural and fashion cues, to all sections of the United States. Networks aside, the dependence of television stations on syndicated programs for nonnetwork time means that the same, or very similar, local programs are watched by audiences in Maine and Arizona. Even in the area of local television news, which still gives all stations an opportunity for localism, the influence of news consultants has produced a narrow range of news formats, which can be found, with virtually interchangeable young and sincere—or mature and steady—faces delivering local news stories, on almost every station in the United States.

Not even radio, relatively free of network domination since the early 1950s, has resisted this trend toward sameness. With some

[5]A 1976 Policy Statement on ascertainment of community needs reaffirmed the following statement from the 1960 Programming Policy Statement: "The principle ingredient of the licensee's obligation to operate his station in the public interest is the diligent, positive, and continuing effort by the licensee to discover and fulfill the tastes, needs, and desires of his community or service area, for broadcast service." Frank J. Kahn (ed.), *Documents of American Broadcasting* (New York: Appleton-Century-Crofts, 1973), p. 246.

exceptions in the scattered truly local radio stations that have hung on, stations across the country have turned to all-news, all-talk, and all-music formats and each has busily tried to sound like the most successful example of its chosen course.

There is some variety in radio music formats, of course; but, within such subgroups as contemporary (or Top 40), middle-of-the-road, good-music, country and western, and so forth, the restricted play lists and tendency to imitate success creates a monotonous similarity in markets across the country. Indeed, radio-station subscribers to one of the recorded music services that provide taped material for almost the entire broadcast day are identical in sound to the many other stations using the same service.

Within our system, there are sound economic reasons for the continuation of this strong trend away from localism and regionalism and toward national homogeneity. As long as advertising continues as the financial base for our system of broadcasting, advertisers will look for those programs that attract the largest audiences and these numbers are most easily reached through national networks and national spot campaigns carried in successful syndicated programs. Even if pay-television becomes a viable national alternative to advertiser support, it is hard to imagine its investors being content with audiences of 2 million or 3 million if audiences ten times that size can be captured by general interest national programming. Local advertisers are also more likely to invest their money in programming or formats that have a proven track record—either at home or in other markets—and this tendency will continue to encourage national similarities in local broadcasting.

Finally, we must consider the impact of new communication technologies on a philosophy of local service. All the new devices in use or on the horizon will, it seems, continue the trend away from this philosophy. Cable television systems, as they become dominated by multiple-system owners and interconnect to import those distant signals allowed by the Federal Communications Commission, must contribute to the erosion of local differences. Satellite interconnection for pay services—like the Home Box Office concept—will accelerate the trend toward national uniformity, as will satellite-to-home transmission, if this concept ever comes to pass. The technology for consumer video recording and playback seems to be concentrating on the phonograph-record concept of playback only—except for the record-playback units that Sony is offering in the $1,000 to $2,000 range—and the successful video systems will naturally distribute products on a national basis.

In the last quarter of the twentieth century, then, most trends seem to be working against the fond FRC–FCC dream of a series of relatively independent local broadcasting stations serving local audiences with local programming. Affection for this dream has, among other things, led the Federal Communications Commission to place severe restrictions on the growth of cable television and pay-television and has produced a radio system that continues to underserve audiences in sparsely populated areas—especially at night. Significantly, one of the topics being considered in the debates surrounding the revision of the 1934 Communications Act is the basic concept of "localism."

PUBLIC BROADCASTING AS AN ALTERNATIVE SERVICE

As we saw in Chapter 10, an alternative system to commercial broadcasting has been developing slowly in this country since the early 1950s. This development has been haphazard and some very real questions continue to face public broadcasting.

The Nature of Public Broadcasting

The term *public broadcasting* is widely used to refer to that class of noncommercial radio and television stations created by the Federal Communications Commission to serve educational and cultural needs presumably not being served by commercial broadcasters. However, the fundamental question "What does 'public broadcasting' mean?" has never really been answered satisfactorily. Indeed, as many commercial broadcasters are quick to point out, all broadcast licensees are required to operate their stations "in the public interest."

Until 1967, these noncommercial stations were generally referred to as educational stations, and the Rules and Regulations of the FCC continue to use this designation.[6] Education, however, was never seen as their only goal, and they came to be looked upon also as a source of both cultural and minority programming.

The term *public broadcasting* came into being in 1967 in the

---

[6]Section 73.503 of the FCC Rules and Regulations states that FM educational stations "shall furnish a non-profit and non-commercial broadcast service." Section 73.621, referring to television channels, states that "the proposed stations will be used primarily to serve the educational needs of the community; for the advancement of educational programs; and to furnish a non-profit and non-commercial television broadcast service"; and further: "stations may transmit . . . cultural and entertainment programs."

Public Broadcasting Act that followed the report of the Carnegie Commission on Educational Television.

While the report discusses some of the objectives of the proposed system, it does not have the force of law or the influence of legislative history, and the act is not really very helpful. The report advanced the following opportunities for public television:

> Public Television programming can deepen a sense of community in local life. It should show our community as it really is. . . .
>
> Public Television programs can help us see America whole, in all its diversity. . . . Public television should be a mirror of the American style. . . .
>
> Public Television can increase our understanding of the world, of other nations and cultures, of the whole commonwealth of man. . . .
>
> Public Television can open a wide door to greater expression and cultural richness for creative individuals and important audiences. . . .
>
> Public Television should . . . bring to us new knowledge and skills, lifting our sights, providing us with relaxation and recreation, and bringing before us glimpses of greatness.[7]

None of these expansive goals found its way into the Public Broadcasting Act, however. The declaration of policy concerning the Corporation for Public Broadcasting that was inserted in the communications act provided the most general of guidelines, saying:

> It is in the public interest to encourage the growth and development of non-commercial educational radio and television broadcasting, including the use of such media for instructional purposes. . . .
>
> It furthers the general welfare to encourage non-commercial educational radio and television broadcast programming which will be responsive to the interests of people both in particular localities and throughout the United States, and which will constitute an expression of diversity and excellence.[8]

What, then, is the role of public broadcasting to be? "The general understanding seems to be that the alternative broadcast service is to be complementary to commercial programming,"[9] but the na-

---

[7]Carnegie Commission on Educational Television, *Public Television: A Program For Action* (New York: Harper & Row, 1967), pp. 92–93.

[8]Kahn, *Documents*, p. 90.

[9]Anne W. Branscomb, "A Crisis of Identity: Reflections on the Future of Public Broadcasting," *in* Douglass Cater and Michael J. Nylan (eds.), *The Future of Public Broadcasting* (New York: Praeger Publishers, 1976), p. 11.

ture of this programming remains unclear. Most who work in the medium would agree that it should include several elements. It should provide educational opportunities for its audience—formal and sequential for both in-school and in-home use as well as continuing education for adults and "cultural enrichment." It should provide programming otherwise unavailable for racial, religious, and cultural minorities. It should develop new sources of talent and programming—and new program forms—and present varied offerings of a type not available on commercial stations. It should program some material with a broad appeal in order to attract new audiences and, it is hoped, hold some of them for its more specialized presentations.

Given these elements, however, there is little agreement about priorities or relative balance among them. In addition, there is some very real uncertainty about the last element. Many public broadcasters are uncomfortable about programming designed primarily to gather a large audience and offer little such material. Commercial broadcasters, generally rather supportive of the alternative system, can be very vocal when they perceive public broadcasters to be setting out to compete for the mass audience.

> As public broadcasters continue to make tentative moves in the direction of attracting a mass audience, they are incurring the wrath not only of the commercial broadcasters but also of another significant political force in the community—the minority groups whose taste for special-interest programming is not being satisfied by commercial broadcasting. As a result, the FCC finds both groups knocking at its door for the kind of decision making which the commission has assiduously avoided in the past with its tradition of leaving the "educators" alone. . . . Pressure is certain to increase for a clear definition of the concept of alternative programming and for answers to two fundamental questions: Is the alternative programming requirement enforceable? If so, by whom?[10]

When these questions are answered, public broadcasting will be closer to a definition of its role.

Localism versus Centralism

Unlike its commercial counterpart, public broadcasting has never developed a strong, centralized system of program production and

---

[10]Branscomb, "Crisis of Identity," p. 12.

distribution. From the days of educational radio and television, most programming has been produced locally and exchanged between stations or purchased from outside suppliers, with the British Broadcasting Corporation being a prime source.

> The Public Broadcasting Act continued this emphasis on decentralization when it created the Corporation for Public Broadcasting [CPB] to: facilitate the full development of educational broadcasting in which programs of high quality, *obtained from diverse sources*, will be made available to noncommercial educational television or radio stations[11] (emphasis supplied).

Since 1967, any drift toward centralization by CPB has met with strong political resistance, some of which was noted in Chapter 10.

The result has been a system of independent public broadcasting stations, scattered production centers, and an often inefficient system of selecting the programs that are to be aired. In this context, it is interesting to note that the British Broadcasting Corporation—a favorite outside source of such programs as *The Forsyte Saga* and *Upstairs, Downstairs*—is a highly centralized organization.

This decentralization of public broadcasting facilities has created some problems, especially for television. The Public Broadcasting Service (PBS) was created by CPB primarily to assist in the planning and operation of an interconnected public television network. While it is often perceived as a network which is very similar to the commercial networks, the contrary is true, in many respects.

Programming executives of ABC, CBS, and NBC each year plan their network schedules with very little input from their affiliated stations. The main concerns at the commercial networks are past ratings, the "track records" of various program suppliers and producers, competition from the other networks, and whether or not the programs will attract advertisers. PBS, on the other hand, turns to its affiliated stations both for much of its programming and for decisions as to which programs will be carried.

Working through the Station Program Cooperative (SPC), PBS distributes to its stations each year a catalogue of proposed programs—most produced by local stations—and thus begins a process of several rounds of voting and elimination that ultimately result in the selection of the bulk of the network offerings for the coming year. Station executives read brief descriptions—and, in later rounds, view taped "pilots" of proposed series—and vote directly on what will and will not be offered.

---

[11]Kahn, *Documents*, p. 93.

Such a plan is certainly an interesting expression of cultural democracy, but it has one unfortunate result. The SPC procedures force station executives first to vote on a short, written summary of a series idea and later to make decisions in some haste on the basis of a limited sample of the series. Since money is involved—the stations will have to pay for the selected programs—and since trustees and ultimately audiences must be satisfied, such procedures result in a tendency toward conservatism and a resistance to anything new. As Nathan Katzman has noted:

> It is difficult to imagine a scenario in which the SPC voting procedure can ever support much innovative programming. In fact, it is difficult to imagine how this procedure can do much more than sort through old programs and proposals to repackage material produced elsewhere and to determine which stations want which. A single decision-making entity, or a deliberative body meeting face-to-face, might ponder questions of balance, diversity, innovation and quality. But the accumulated decisions of 150 entities create a statistical force toward the known, the safe, and the cheap. It is a case of the sum of the parts adding up to less than the whole.[12]

The question of the balance between centralism and localism in public broadcasting, then, is more than a regulatory and philosophical one. It goes directly to the heart of the question of programming. Until it is resolved to the satisfaction of public broadcasters, the public, and the government, it seems likely that our alternative system will find it impossible to find a programming policy that retains the advantages of both local originality and centralized efficiency.

Public Broadcasting Funding

The financial problems that have faced educational broadcasters from the beginning have already been discussed in Chapter 10. The Carnegie Commission tried to solve this by recommending that support come from a dedicated tax—actually, an excise tax on the sale of television sets—which would provide a steady source of funds and insulate public broadcasting from the problem of annual appropriations.

---

[12]Nathan Katzman with Ken Wirt, "Program Funding in Public Television and the SPC," *in* Cater and Nylan, *Future of Public Broadcasting*, pp. 259–260.

Congress, however, has never been willing to permit a public broadcasting system to function without accountability. For most of the first decade of the Corporation for Public Broadcasting only annual appropriations were provided. In the mid-1970s multiyear appropriations were approved, but accountability to the public was emphasized by requiring CPB to raise up to $3 from outside sources for each federal dollar.

This congressional decision has not closed the overall funding question, however. Some critics are still unhappy with even short-term financing; others continue to feel that congressional appropriations will never be the answer. Some other sources are available, each with its strengths and weaknesses.

The Dedicated Tax This proposal by the Carnegie Commission still has its supporters, and it does have the advantage of providing a dependable source of income over the long haul while insulating programming from second-guessing by Congress and the White House. It seems unlikely, however, that congressional resistance to such a plan will diminish.

In addition, the concept of a dedicated tax fund raises some real questions. In the first place, it is not completely clear that a public broadcasting system that is not called to account periodically would be in the public interest. Second, it seems probable that any dedicated tax suggested would be broad-based, touching a wide segment of the American public. Would Congress be justified in asking this public to pay for a broadcast service that has not defined its nature and purpose and that seems, in its programming, to be leaning toward a sort of elitism?

Nonprofit Operation Educational FM and television stations are required by Congress to be "noncommercial." When the issue was being discussed in the early 1950s, some educators urged that educational stations be designated instead as "nonprofit"—permitted to raise money through the sale of time but required to invest all revenues in the operation of the station. "Noncommercial" became the operative phrase, but the "nonprofit" option still remains. If the experience of commercial broadcasters is any example, this option could ease the financial burden of public broadcasting a great deal.

Commercial opposition to nonprofit operation would be swift, well-organized, and vocal, of course. In addition, it seems inevitable that stations operating in this manner, even with the profit motive absent, would rapidly be forced into a competition with commercial broadcasters for large audiences. Such competition would, in turn, lead to an increasing sameness in the program offerings of the two systems. An alternative system would be difficult to maintain under nonprofit operation.

Membership Subscriptions   Another manner of funding public broadcasting would be to provide that it be supported by its own audiences through membership subscriptions and donations. Some public radio stations now gain most of their support through such subscriptions and many other stations—both radio and television— supplement their incomes through such devices as the sale of monthly program guides, membership dues, and auctions.

There is a certain logic to this idea, but its practicality is questionable. Such a source of income would be especially susceptible to downturns in the nation's economy and it seems unlikely that enough money could be collected even in the best of times. In addition, the search for audiences to increase subcriptions could easily become as important to public broadcasting as is the search for audiences to attract advertisers for commercial broadcasting, with the same consequences, and this would lead public broadcasting away from the alternative programming concept.

Other sources of income for public broadcasting may be possible—indeed, in the 1960s the recommendation was made that satellite interconnection for commercial networks should replace the AT&T system of wires, cables and microwave relays and that a portion of the savings be given to support educational broadcasters. Whatever funding method or combination of methods emerges, however, it seems inevitable that the financing procedures will influence the structure and programming of the alternative system as dramatically as commercial funding has influenced commercial broadcasting.

THE NEW TECHNOLOGIES

For almost a decade, communications experts have promised a communications revolution soon to be unleashed. Led by the possibilities of satellite transmission across the world and cables in every home, this revolution, it is promised, will completely transform our societies and our lives. The satellites, of course, will allow real-time contact with any portion of the world, turning our globe into the "global village" of Marshall McLuhan. The real revolution, however, would be in everyone's home in the form of a Home Information Center (HIC).

Figure 15–1 Videodiscs, home recording, and "Lounge Modules" are among the technological advances already on the horizon. (Videodiscs courtesy of Philips; other units courtesy RCA)

Through the magic of cable interconnection, the HIC, it is said, will provide us with a total information service. We will have direct contact with computers and libraries across the country—and around the world. Two-way, talk-back capability in HIC will allow us to do our banking, pay our bills, shop, and conduct business without leaving our homes. News and information will be available at any time, in summary form, on special channels devoted to this service. If we prefer the permanence and depth of print, HIC will print out our daily newspaper. Entertainment will also be available in abundance—both mass and minority—possibly with the illusion of three dimensions on wall-sized screens. Video recording systems will free us from the tyranny of broadcast schedules and permit us to record our favorite programs for viewing at a convenient time. The wonders to be wrought by HIC, it seems, will be endless.

When one considers the nature and scope of the communications revolution that took place in the first half of this century, such predictions seem conservative; and the chances are good that advances

"Dear, will you please play your wall a little softer?"

not even imagined by our prophets will make them seem almost quaint by 2025—a time that most readers of this book could easily live to see. From the perspective of the last quarter of the twentieth century, however, these wonders seem slow in arriving, and a serious consideration of them reveals some questions that must be answered before HIC enters our homes in any form.

Broad-Band Cable

From the point of view of the user, the key to HIC is a broad-band cable connection to each home. Most homes today are in fairly regular contact with three communication channels. Two of these—radio and television—are one-way channels, delivering signals to the home but carrying no information back to the source of the signals. The third channel—the telephone—does allow for two-way communication, but carries only voice. Approximately 15 percent of the nation's households are also connected to a community antenna television (CATV) system by cable but, to the communications prophets, these are primitive systems, for the cables are not truly broad-band.

When applied to channels of communication, the term *broadband* refers to the amount of information the channel can carry at a given time. A narrow-band channel can carry little information; a broad-band channel carries more. Telephone lines into the homes are limited to one voice, with rather poor fidelity at that. Radio represents a communication channel with somewhat greater capacity.

Considering each station as a separate channel (a properly tuned set can only pass one station at a time), radio can only carry one message at a time, but there is more room in the channel than in telephone and this is used to carry additional audio information for higher fidelity. Operating on the same principle, a single television channel carries only one message at a time, but this message includes the picture information and thus the television channel must carry much more information.

Each of these channels of communication, then, is limited in its ability to carry information. Telephone lines and radio and television channels are used, primarily, to carry one message at a time and the available channel space is used to pack in as much information as possible about that message. The capacity of radio and television to carry information is further restricted by the finite nature of the electromagnetic spectrum, which limits the number of channels available.

The cable system of the future, however, will be truly broad-band, with a much greater information-carrying capacity than is available in today's media. Technology seems to promise cable, connecting each home, that could carry (using fiber optics) hundreds, or even thousands, of television channels. The channels needed to provide entertainment and information would hardly make a dent in this capacity. The additional channels could be used, singly or in combination, to carry all of the other services promised for HIC.

Before the Home Information Center becomes a reality, however, a few practical questions must be answered. In the first place, even if thousand-channel cables were available today, a substantial portion of the nation would have to be interconnected to make HIC worthwhile. It is true that the United States has already wired itself twice—for telephones and electricity—but in each case the process was long, drawn-out, and full of conflict and confusion. It could be argued further that the economic incentives behind the push for nationwide telephone and electrical service were greater than those that would be behind the drive for a nationwide cable system—that telephone and electric services were seen as more important than would be the case with HIC. The growth of a nationwide cable system, then, would not necessarily be the natural consequence of the emergence of techniques to make it possible. Under our system, such growth could be accomplished only by private enterprise. Without sufficient promise of a reasonable return, it would be difficult to find investors willing to lead the way into the brave new world of HIC.

Interconnection aside, it is difficult to conceive of the scope of the switching requirements necessary to route the cable services to the proper homes and handle, at the same time, all of the information and requests coming from the homes. It would be necessary to devise switching centers to handle audio and video information— with audio connected to the proper video, data to and from computer terminals, facsimile information for newspaper printouts and many other kinds of data; to route this information with privacy to and from the proper points; and to build these centers in every part of the nation as cable expanded. To some engineers, the switching problems of HIC seem much more formidable than those posed by simple interconnection by cable.

What of the social implications of HIC? What are the questions we should ask ourselves while there is still time for questions? Some come quickly to mind and are easily understood: "How many channels of entertainment, information, and news will the American public support?" "Where will we find the talent to prepare the material for and perform on all these channels?" "What will be the fate of the existing over-the-air broadcasting service?" "What is the best economic base for HIC?"

Two additional questions deserve a bit more thought. The first revolves around the question of privacy. Most of us take for granted certain minor invasions of our privacy when we read and discard "junk mail," when telephone salespersons call us at home to read their sales pitches or when kitchenware salesmen knock on our doors and attempt to sell their product in our living rooms. These and similar commercial invasions of our homes are fueled by information about us—name, address, phone number, age, and the like—which is purchased from legitimate compilers of such information. Often mailing lists with such information are purchased from state and local governments, schools, and business organizations. In all probability, each of us is already on many such lists, and some companies are always eager to purchase new collections of potential customers.

These practices are a fact of life today with which many of us have learned to live, but consider the kinds of information that HIC could generate. Assume that problems of wiring and switching have been solved. Assume further that part of this solution is a computer that receives the information coming from the HIC in your home and routes it to the proper receiver. Assume finally that, for the past year, you have been using HIC for your banking transactions, for most of your shopping, and for newspaper and magazine orders. In a year's time, a computer capable of storing this information would be able to compile a profile of you that would include the size and disposition of your monthly paycheck, the nature of some of your debts, your preferences in food and clothing, and your reading habits. Such information would be invaluable to many commercial entities, but its release would represent a monumental invasion of your privacy. Does the American public want to take the chance that effective safeguards against such incursions would be devised and effectively maintained?

Still another implication of HIC should be considered. As it is usually described, the Home Information Center would allow us to conduct much of our day-to-day business without leaving our homes. Its possibilities, it seems, would also permit many businessmen to function almost entirely at home. With HIC, our homes could really become our castles, sanctuaries of a surface privacy to be broken only for a select few.

The natural question, of course, is whether or not we really want to stop going to stores, libraries, theaters, and places of business.

Many people still find pleasure in the social contacts that accompany such activities and one wonders if, after the novelty wore off, we would really use these services enough to justify their existence.

Nationwide Pay-Cable

Technology that exists today can be used to put together an entertainment service that is considerably less revolutionary than the Home Information Center but seems to be more commercially feasible. The service combines two familiar concepts—CATV and pay-television—with communications satellites to create a pay-cable system with considerable potential.

The basic concept is relatively simple. A company already engaged in purchasing or producing program material (or both) for sale to pay-cable systems leases communications-satellite channels needed to distribute its signal to potential customers. Cable systems within reach of these satellite retransmissions build earth stations to pick up the signals and contract with the originating company to carry its programming on pay-channels. As the number of subscribing cable systems grows, potential income from customers increases and the producing company is in a position to bid for exclusive rights to more and more desirable programming.

Home Box Office, Inc. was the first to enter this field, in September of 1975; and it has distributed sports events, movies, and some special comedy and variety performances incorporating material that would not have been permitted on broadcast television. Customer interest in, and potential financial returns from, the Home Box Office operation were sufficient to persuade another company, Optical Systems Corporation, to start a similar service in 1976.

The implications of a successful nationwide pay-cable system are, to say the least, disturbing to commercial broadcasters. The reasons for this nervousness are not difficult to understand. In 1976, the publishers of the *Broadcasting Cable Sourcebook* estimated that operating cable systems reached 10 million subscribers with a potential of 30 million viewers. If only a third of these viewers had access to interconnected pay-cable and another third of these actually paid for a program on the cable, the potential audience for this program would be 3.3 million. If these viewers were willing to pay $5 for the program, it would generate $16.5 million. When one considers that the National Broadcasting Company paid $3 million for rights to broadcast the 1975 Super Bowl game, the economic potential of interconnected pay-cable begins to come into focus. Even figures generated at a time when cable reached only 15 percent of the nation's homes demonstrate that a successful national pay-cable system would easily be able to outbid the commercial networks for programs of outstanding audience appeal.

In arguing for regulation to prevent the unrestrained growth of pay-cable, commercial broadcasters make the point that a pay system that was able to outbid them for such programs would force audiences to pay for programming they now receive free. Such "siphoning," it is argued, would drain from broadcast television its most attractive product, drive advertisers away, and ultimately destroy our present system of "free broadcasting."

These appeals by broadcasters may be overstated, and it is not our purpose to discuss their merits. It does seem reasonable to assume, though, that even a moderately successful interconnected national pay-television service would outbid commercial television for *some* programs and would force payment for these programs. Given these assumptions, it would be prudent for anyone interested in the future of broadcasting to consider some questions raised by the pay-television specter, among them: "Would pay-television provide programming not available on commercial television— cultural happenings, sports events not broadcast, mature drama and variety, and the like—or would it draw most of its programming from the same sources tapped by commercial broadcasters?" "If our present, commercially supported broadcast system is in the public interest, would that same interest be served by permitting the unrestrained growth of a parallel pay system?" "How far should government regulation go in protecting broadcasting from competition in a time of changing technology and public tastes?" "Do we want a program distribution system that reaches only those population concentrations served by cable and that delivers programs only to those willing and able to pay for them?" "Is *any* form of pay-television desirable?" "If so, how shall it be regulated so as to allow for commercial success while protecting the public interest?"

Other Technologies

The long-range implications of the Home Information Center and interconnected pay-television seem to be the major problems posed by technology visible in the last quarter of this century, but this is not to say that they raise the only questions. Satellites are central to each of the above, of course, but another satellite possibility should be considered also—satellite-to-home transmission. Such in-home reception of satellite signals without the help of an intervening broadcast station or cable system is impractical today—it requires too large a "dish" to receive the signal and too much amplification to be commercially feasible. Engineers assure us, however, that miniaturization will continue and that the possibility of practical home reception is not many years away.

These electronic developments would present us with the possibility of still another alternative to our existing broadcast system. A few production centers could provide programming that could be beamed to satellites and then directly to our homes. Presumably, regional centers could also be established to provide more local services. Thousands of miles of interconnection facilities and thousands of stations would be made obsolete, ultimately saving millions of dollars.

The objections to such a complete conversion to satellite transmission should be obvious. The idea flies directly in the face of the devotion of the Federal Communications Commission to the local-institution concept and would make any truly local service virtually impossible. In addition, dependence on a few production centers and satellites would produce a very vulnerable system. It would be virtually impossible to seize control of or incapacitate our present, decentralized system, but the centers and the satellites would be easy targets.

Complete conversion, however, is not the only possibility and, when the technique becomes feasible, it seems likely that some satellite-to-home transmissions will be planned and attempted. If successful, the problems of controlling this new technique and blending it into the system in existence at the time will be difficult and challenging.

What about video recording? At this writing, both RCA and Phillips/MCA have developed videodisc playback systems that are not compatible with each other (discs made by one system cannot be played back on players of the other), and both are optimistic. The companies planned to put their systems on the market by 1977, with players to be priced in the neighborhood of $500. The willingness of two such giant companies to make large investments and prepare for head-to-head competition for the entertainment market speaks well for the possibility of success for one system.

This willingness to go ahead with videodiscs is a gigantic gamble fueled by the belief that there will be a close parallel with the success of audio recording. This belief has never been tested, however, and it is quite possible that the entertainment consumer will not embrace video with the enthusiasm given audio. Video playbacks, like television programs, require considerable attention—much more than that required by phonograph records. The consumer who buys and plays such records for mood and background purposes is not likely to switch to videodiscs. Neither is the lover of classical music likely to discard his quadraphonic system simply because videodiscs will allow him to see the Philadelphia Orchestra play his favorite selections.

Also unanswered is the question of whether video recordings will wear as well as audio. Buyers of phonograph records make their purchases with the expectation that they will be played and enjoyed again and again. No one yet knows if the more expensive videodiscs will be so received. If not, will consumers pay more for a product they will use less?

The video-recording "revolution" has already seen one failure on the consumer market. Videotape record-playback systems attached to television sets were not accepted in the early 1970s, and only Sony continued to try to develop this market. Perhaps the less expensive discs that promise playback only will succeed where tape failed—and perhaps not.

PROGRAMMING ON COMMERCIAL NETWORKS AND STATIONS

Few critics of the programming of commercial broadcasters in the United States would deny that these broadcasters do some things very well. Radio, at least in the medium and large markets that support several stations, provides music for a fairly wide range of tastes, while offering news summaries and maintaining a low-cost communication service that keeps a large portion of our population in touch with its world.

Television, of course, is the great provider of mass entertainment, but it does other things well also. It is unsurpassed in its ability to take us to the scene of happenings of importance to the nation—to the surface of the moon, to Peking, to congressional hearing rooms, and to the resignation of a President. Television has become a major journalistic force, providing most of the news to a majority of the people in our country. Television has also demonstrated it can do an excellent job with the documentary and documentary drama, as illustrated by *The Autobiography of Miss Jane Pittman, The Selling of the Pentagon,* and *Alistair Cooke's America.*

Minority Programming for Minority Tastes

The critics argue, however, that this is not enough because the tastes of significant minority groups in this country are virtually ignored by a broadcasting system that concentrates on the mass audience. Defenders of our system, on the other hand, maintain that this argument really overstates the case:

> Television is a combination mostly of lowbrow and middle-brow, but there is more highbrow offered than highbrows will admit—or even seek to know about. They will make plans, go to trouble and expense, when they buy a book or reserve a seat in the theater. They will not study the week's offerings of music or drama or serious documentation in the radio and TV program pages of their newspaper and then schedule themselves to be present. They want to come home, eat dinner, twist the dial, and find something agreeable ready, accommodating to *their* schedule.[13]

Whatever the merits of the two positions, no one maintains that commercial broadcasters offer too much highbrow. More could be provided, certainly, and it could be more widely distributed. Few lovers of classical music are served as well as virtually every fan of radio's "contemporary" music. Seekers of cultural television programming have more success in New York or Los Angeles than they do in Baton Rouge, Louisiana, or Columbus, Ohio.

It is unlikely that commercial broadcasting will ever accommodate itself any more fully to minority tastes. Economic forces will continue to force a focus on the mass audience. Other tastes, by and large, will be satisfied by other media, and a few possibilities will be discussed below.

Before turning to this, however, we should point out that some scholars maintain that the physical characteristics of television make the success of some such programming—specifically, cultural programming—unlikely. They argue that the location of the television set in the home and the size of the picture impose serious limitations on the amount of attention that can be given to any specific broadcast. Martin Mayer states this position as follows:

> Watching television is an activity that excludes doing anything else than eating and knitting. The requisite minimum level of attention is

---

[13]From Eric Sevareid's remarks made before the Washington Journalism Center, Washington, D.C., June 3, 1976.

fairly high. At the same time, unlike films or plays in a properly designed theatre, television pictures do not absorb the peripheral vision; and it may be that the attainable maximum level of attention is fairly low. At best, the spread between minimum and maximum is much reduced from that experienced in the use of other media.[14]

This maximum level of attention possible for television may be enough for *All in the Family*, but would it be sufficient for *Hamlet* or a performance of the Metropolitan Opera Company?

These considerations aside, what hope is there for minority programming in the electronic media? The prospects may seem dim on commercial stations and networks, but the new technologies do offer some promise.

The economics of cable, for instance, are quite different from those of commercial broadcasting and at first glance these differences would seem to work to the advantage of minority programming. In commercial broadcasting, of course, the advertiser pays the bills in return for large audiences. In a cable system, the viewer pays the cost directly, paying a monthly fee for access to cable programming. The significant point here is the fact that the cable customer pays for the entire package—his monthly fee buys access to *all* the channels on the system. If the programming on half of twelve channels that are available is sufficient to capture and hold subscribers, cable operators need not worry about pleasing everyone on the remaining channels; and programming for minority tastes is possible.

Thus cable can provide the channels for minority programming, at least on successful systems. Cable economics, however, do not provide much incentive for an investment in the production or purchase of such programming. The primary incentive for such expenditures would be an increase in the number of subscribers attracted by the programming, and this forces the cable operator to take most of the risks. The establishment of a cultural channel, for instance, would require purchase of a substantial amount of appropriate programming and a large investment. It would be necessary to continue such programming over 2 or 3 months, at the least, to establish whether or not it was attracting and holding new subscribers. If no such increase in subscriptions occurred or if it proved insufficient to cover costs, the initial investment would simply be lost.

The more common approach is to program additional channels

---

[14]Martin Mayer, *About Television* (New York: Harper & Row, 1972), p. 394.

with the tried-and-true—movies, sports, news, and information— and let others experiment. Minority programming has yet to prove itself to be a good investment for television or cable and few CATV systems are willing to take such a chance.

It is possible, however, that increased programming for minority tastes will be assisted by pay-cable. The operator of a pay-channel could take a smaller risk and see the results of his experiment more quickly. Single cultural programs could be placed on the channel, reducing the size of the needed investment. Information as to success or failure of the program would be quickly available, since viewers of the program would have to pay for 'it. A large number of programs and a delay of months simply would not be necessary.

Pay-cable, in other words, may be the medium in which programming for minority tastes finds its place. If it is to do so, however, it will only be after pay-cable has expanded to a nationwide system—and, as we have seen, such expansion is far from certain.

Commercial, Mass-Appeal Programming

What about the future of the bulk of broadcast programming on the air today? Will its nature remain the same over the next two or three decades or will it change to accommodate changes in mass tastes?

It is not difficult to conclude that some changes will take place. Change seems to be built into our society, and few areas are as mercurial as mass taste and mass culture. The nature of these changes, however, is another matter, and we intend to stick to our resolve to avoid prophecy. Instead, we will look at the nature of programming in the mid-1970s and point out some straws in the wind that could indicate changes in emphasis in television programming.

First, consider the fact that the most popular television programs seem to be dramatic in form. This applies to action-adventure, theatrical features, general drama, and situation comedies—the bulk of our programming. One characteristic of the dramatic form is the fact that it requires careful preplanning of even the smallest details. Each program must be completely scripted and requires a story line, characterization, dialogue, action, dramatic climaxes, and the like—often tailored to fit within the basic outlines of a series situation. Before production, virtually every detail of every program must be planned, written, reviewed and revised, all of which requires an enormous pool of creative talent.

This pool, however, is faced with the facts of a finite number of plot lines and variations, a huge demand for suitable material, and severe time limitations. Too often, the result is a minor variation of a plot used last month, stock characters, and stilted dialogue. Considering the amount of dramatic material of this sort that is run, and rerun, on network television today, it is surprising that the popularity of dramatic forms has remained as high as it has.

This dramatic, highly structured, and carefully planned programming is not the only form available, however. Another possibility is a format in which a basic situation, or framework, is established and the performers ad-lib within certain carefully defined limits. Panel and audience-participation programs are common examples of this format, as are sports events; interview-talk programs; and, to a degree, awards programs, like the Academy Awards.

Interestingly enough, dramatic forms may be the most common programs on television, but the looser formats attract the really large audiences. As shown in Table 15–1, when the A.C. Nielsen Company, in 1977, compiled a list of the 25 programs on television with the all-time largest audiences, 10 programs on the list were sports events and 3 were Academy Awards programs. Another 4 were motion picture features and one was an NBC 50-year retrospective. The remaining 7 were episodes of *Roots*. Not one of these programs was an episode of an ongoing series.

The 21 nondramatic programs on the list were similar in that they were relatively unstructured in form. All 25 programs shared another characteristic. They were special events—Super Bowl games, World Series games, college football bowl games, awards ceremonies and "blockbuster" movies. Given television's ability to devour material and a practical limit on the demands that can be placed on creative talent, these facts could point to a direction that the television networks could take in coming years. Indeed, NBC moved in this direction in 1976–1977 with its *Big Event* concept on Sunday nights—a regularly scheduled series of nonrecurring events of varying types and lengths.

Our purpose here is not to imply that scripted dramatic programs will ever be completely replaced by less structured forms. Situation comedies are a durable breed; it seems likely that action-adventure will always be with us; and there will always be an audience for drama of the sort popular today. If television should reduce its dependence on the dramatic form, however, perhaps more time and care could be devoted to the remaining dramas as other forms occupied larger portions of the prime-time schedule. Both drama and television would certainly benefit from such a trend.

Table 15-1   Nielsen All-Time Top-25 Programs (through April, 1977)

Total Audience Estimates (Projected Households)

Rank[a]	Program Name	Telecast Date	Total Audience (thousands)
1	Big Event Pt. 1 (Gone With The Wind-Pt. 1)	Nov. 7, 1976	41,940
2	Super Bowl XI	Jan. 9, 1977	41,720
3.	Roots	Jan. 30, 1977	40,940
4	World Series	Oct. 22, 1975	40,580
5	NBC Monday Movie (Gone with the Wind-Pt. 2)	Nov. 8, 1976	39,520
6	Roots	Jan. 28, 1977	37,590
7	Big Event Pt. 1 (The First Fifty Years)	Nov. 21, 1976	37,450
8	Super Bowl X	Jan. 18, 1976	37,380
9	World Series	Oct. 21, 1975	37,030
10	Super Bowl IX	Jan. 12, 1975	36,920
11	Roots	Jan. 24, 1977	36,530
12	Academy Awards	Mar. 29, 1976	36,190
13	Academy Awards	Mar. 28, 1977	36,030
14	Roots	Jan. 27, 1977	35,600
15	CBS NFL Championship	Jan. 4, 1976	35,220
16	Super Bowl VII	Jan. 14, 1973	35,060
17	Roots	Jan. 23, 1977	34,960
18	Academy Awards	Apr. 2, 1974	34,890
19	ABC Sunday Movie (Patton)	Nov. 19, 1972	34,730
20	Airport (Movie Special)	Nov. 11, 1973	34,490
21	Roots	Jan. 25, 1977	34,460
22	Super Bowl VIII	Jan. 13, 1974	34,360
23	World Series	Oct. 16, 1973	34,230
24	Super Bowl VI	Jan. 16, 1972	34,160
25	Roots	Jan. 26, 1977	34,100

[a] Rankings based on reports through April 17, 1977 for sponsored programs telecast on individual networks. No unsponsored or joint telecasts are included.

Adapted from: A. C. Nielsen Company, "Nielsen All-Time Top-25 Programs," *Nielsen Newscast*, Number 1 (Chicago: A. C. Nielsen Company, 1977), p. 6.

We have attempted in this chapter to raise some questions about the nature and the future of broadcasting in the United States. In a broad sense, the direction to be taken by broadcast media will be determined by the forces shaping our mass culture. One of these forces, of course, will be the questions asked and the goals determined by a generation just entering the media. It is hoped that some of the issues raised herein will be considered and resolved by members of this generation.

STUDY AND DISCUSSION QUESTIONS

1. Explore further the emphasis on localism in our broadcast system versus centralization. Assess the impact of the preference of the Federal Communications Commission for localism in such matters as the following:

    a. AM clear-channel allocations
    b. Frequency assignments for FM and television
    c. The development of networks
    d. The development of cable and pay-television
    e. Service to sparsely populated areas
    f. The use of communications satellites

2. Report on or be prepared to discuss the role of public broadcasting in our country. Consider such points as the following:

    a. The definition of *public broadcasting*
    b. Desirable goals for a public broadcasting system
    c. The relationship of public to commercial broadcasting
    d. The nature of the programming to be provided by a public broadcasting service
    e. The most desirable structure for a public broadcasting system
    f. Sources of funding and desirable levels of support for a public broadcasting system

3. Assess the potential impact of one or more of the means of communication being made possible by expanding technology. Consider such possibilities as the following:

    a. The Home Information Center
    b. Nationwide pay-cable television
    c. Satellite-to-home transmission
    d. Home videotape and videodisc recording systems
    e. Holographic (3-D) television
    f. Large-screen projection systems
    g. Video games

4. The following questions were posed in various sections of this chapter. Report on or be prepared to discuss one of them.

    a. How many channels of information and entertainment will the American public support?
    b. Where will we find the talent to prepare the material for and perform on all these channels?
    c. What will be the fate of the existing over-the-air broadcasting service?
    d. What is the best economic base for the Home Information Center?
    e. How shall we protect the privacy rights of the American people in the face of the possibilities of the Home Information Center?

f. Would pay-television provide programming not available on commercial television?

g. If pay-television is to develop, what should be its relationship to existing commercial broadcasting?

h. How far should government regulation go in protecting broadcasting from competition from new technologies?

i. Is any form of pay-television desirable?

j. Are minority programming tastes adequately met by the existing system of broadcasting? If so, how would you answer critics claiming the contrary? If not, should these tastes be better served and (if so) how?

k. What changes should we expect in commercial programming in the next decade?

SUGGESTED READINGS

Richard Adler and Walter S. Baer, eds. *The Electronic Box Office: Humanities and Arts on the Cable.* Palo Alto, Calif: Aspen Institute Program on Communications and Society, 1974.

Ben H. Bagdikian. *The Information Machines: Their Impact on Men and the Media.* New York: Harper & Row, 1971.

Douglass Cater and Michael J. Nylan. *The Future of Public Broadcasting.* New York: Praeger Publishers, 1976.

Ithiel de Sola Pool, ed. *Talking Back: Citizen Feedback and Cable Technology.* Cambridge, Mass.: MIT Press, 1973.

Martin Mayer. *About Television.* New York: Harper & Row, 1972.

Harold Sackman and Barry Bohlen, eds. *Planning Community Information Utilities.* Montvale, N.J.: AFIPS Press, 1972.

Harold Sackman and Norman Nie, eds. *The Information Utility and Social Choice.* Montvale, N.J.: AFIPS Press, 1971.

Robert R. Smith. *Beyond the Wasteland: The Criticism of Broadcasting.* Falls Church, Va.: Speech Communication Association, 1976.

Index

INVENTORY 1983